ONCE WE WERE SLAVES

ONCE WE WERE SLAVES

THE EXTRAORDINARY JOURNEY OF A MULTIRACIAL JEWISH FAMILY

LAURA ARNOLD LEIBMAN

OXFORD
UNIVERSITY PRESS

OXFORD
UNIVERSITY PRESS

Oxford University Press is a department of the University of Oxford. It furthers
the University's objective of excellence in research, scholarship, and education
by publishing worldwide. Oxford is a registered trade mark of Oxford University
Press in the UK and certain other countries.

Published in the United States of America by Oxford University Press
198 Madison Avenue, New York, NY 10016, United States of America.

© Oxford University Press 2021

Library of Congress Cataloging-in-Publication Data
Names: Leibman, Laura Arnold, author.
Title: Once we were slaves : the extraordinary journey of a multiracial
Jewish family / Laura Arnold Leibman.
Other titles: Extraordinary journey of a multiracial Jewish family
Description: New York, NY : Oxford University Press, 2021. |
Includes bibliographical references and index.
Identifiers: LCCN 2021016423 (print) | LCCN 2021016424 (ebook) |
ISBN 9780197530474 (hardback) | ISBN 9780197530498 (epub) |
ISBN 9780197530627
Subjects: LCSH: Jews—New York (State)—New York—History—19th century. |
Moses, Sarah Brandon, 1798–1828. | Brandon, Isaac Lopez, 1793–1855. |
Brandon family. | Moses family. | Jews—Barbados—Bridgetown—History—19th century. |
Racially mixed people—New York (State)—New York—History—19th century. |
Racially mixed people—Barbados—History—19th century. |
Bridgetown (Barbados)—Biography. | New York (N.Y.)—Biography.
Classification: LCC F128.9.J5 L45 2021 (print) | LCC F128.9.J5 (ebook) |
DDC 974.7/10040592409697298—dc23
LC record available at https://lccn.loc.gov/2021016423
LC ebook record available at https://lccn.loc.gov/2021016424

DOI: 10.1093/oso/9780197530474.001.0001

1 3 5 7 9 8 6 4 2

Printed by LSC communications, United States of America

Once we were slaves to Pharaoh in Egypt, and now we are free.

—Avadim Hayinu, Passover Hagaddah

CONTENTS

Preface   ix

PREFACE

———◦◦◦———

ON JANUARY 4, 1942, BLANCHE MOSES was sitting in her "high quarters" at 415 West 118th Street in New York City, writing yet another letter to Rabbi Meyer, the librarian at the American Jewish Historical Society. At eighty-two, the reclusive heiress was losing her patience. Her collection of daguerreotypes—"one of my precious possessions"—had been lost while on loan, and she was unable to get into the library to look for the family keepsakes. She begged Rabbi Meyer for assistance. As she noted, she hoped to have his help, as she preferred "not to court *personal publicity.*" This was something of an understatement. As Moses explained when she gave the rabbi the number for her newly installed phone, she could be "reached at any hour—day or evening, as *I do not go out.*"[1]

Blanche Moses's letter came three weeks after Pearl Harbor, and despite her obsession with the objects of her ancestors, Moses was not immune to the impending war. Her building was in the process of being fitted for possible alert. Her upper-story apartment with its exposed walls was conventionally more desirable, but now was "being considered quite unsafe" in event of airstrikes. Hence, she and her collection were moving down to a lower floor.[2]

Rabbi Meyer was apparently able to help Moses, because today the daguerreotypes are safe as part of the collection of the Moses and Seixas Family Papers at the American Jewish Historical Society. The daguerreotypes

Blanche Moses's uncle, Lieutenant-Colonel Israel Moses. Daguerreotype. AJHS.

include stiff portraits of Moses's uncles in Civil War uniforms and her beautiful young mother Selina Seixas in lacy fingerless gloves (all the rage in 1854), her braided hair wound in heavy loops on the sides of her head like a Victorian Princess Leia. Today the daguerreotypes are reunited with other family portraits, including photos from Moses's own childhood, such as several of her beloved sister Edith in blond ringlets and Blanche herself, characteristically pouting with her dolls. They are portraits of a lost era, a time when the Moses family prospered in the young nation. When Blanche Moses died in 1949, the war was over. The photos, along with her family's other memorabilia, became part of the collection of the oldest ethnic historical society in the United States.

Moses would be pleased with the collection's treatment. The descendant of some of the earliest Jewish families to settle in the country, she wanted to leave her priceless collection to a Jewish archive, but her letters suggest she equally wanted to ensure that the objects would receive the love she herself afforded them. The American Jewish Historical Society of the twenty-first century bears little resemblance to the library that temporarily misplaced her collection of daguerreotypes. Once run by volunteers, today AJHS is a flagship for preservation standards. The Moses and Seixas collections are cherished and well maintained.

In an elegant, climate-controlled building on West 16th Street, the Moses collection nestles among the donations of other families who have been eager

Blanche Moses's mother *Selina Seixas [Moses]* (1854). Daguerreotype. AJHS.

to preserve the past. After all, Blanche Moses was not the only American Jew on the eve of the Holocaust who felt desperate to look back in solace on days gone by. Today, genealogy is the second most popular hobby in the United States after gardening. Few of us are as lucky, however, as Moses in having such an illustrious family to study. Among her possessions were items relating to two of her great-grandfathers. The first, the Reverend Gershom Mendes Seixas, oversaw New York's and Philadelphia's earliest synagogues for nearly fifty years and was one of Shearith Israel's most beloved spiritual leaders. The second, Isaac Moses, was a Revolutionary War hero and real estate tycoon who balanced religious devotion with administering a vast mercantile empire.[3]

Yet even Moses would be surprised by recent interest in two of the artifacts she donated. Amid the memorabilia of eminent men are two ivory miniatures, painted in watercolor, depicting relatives Blanche Moses never met and knew almost nothing about: her great-uncle Isaac Lopez Brandon (1793–1855), and her grandmother Sarah Brandon Moses (1798–1829), a woman who died thirty years before Blanche was born, and a mere ten days after Blanche's father's third birthday.

Moses certainly knew scraps about Sarah and Isaac's past. Their father was a given: all available records pointed to Abraham Rodrigues Brandon of Barbados, the island's wealthiest Jew. Yet despite being a meticulous family historian who regularly corrected articles appearing

Charles D. Fredricks & Co., *Blanche and Edith Moses*
(1862). Photograph. AJHS.

in the *New York Times* and American Jewish Historical Society's scholarly journal, Moses drew an uncharacteristic blank when it came to her
grandmother and great-uncle's maternal line. Who was their mother?
Moreover, why was so little known about her, when she had married a
man so famous?[4]

When it came to Sarah and Isaac's early life, the documents that typically cluttered Blanche Moses's apartment were absent. This was bad news.
Moses was Sarah's only grandchild who was still alive, and all of the family
papers had slowly funneled down to Moses's apartment on the Upper West
Side. Moses was left to guess about Sarah and Isaac's background. "Abraham
Rodrigues Brandon Barbados," Moses scribbled on the margin of one paper,
"*married Sarah Esther*?"[5] Even Malcolm Stern, the premier genealogist of

Blanche Moses's grandmother. Anonymous, *Portrait of Sarah Brandon Moses* (ca. 1815–16). Watercolor on ivory, 2 3/4 x 2 1/4 in. AJHS.

early American Jews, could do no better. Using information from New York's Shearith Israel synagogue about Moses's great-grandmother's death in 1823 in New York, he too could only conjecture about Sarah Brandon Moses and Isaac Lopez Brandon's mother, speculating she was part of the Lopez clan of Barbados.[6]

They were both wrong.

Moses and Stern were right about one small thing, though. Moses's great-grandmother *had* been raised in the Lopez household and she sometimes used their last name. She gained the surname Lopez, however, not as a child born into the family, but because she was enslaved by them. Moses's grand-mother Sarah and her great-uncle Isaac had also begun their lives poor, Christian, and enslaved in the late eighteenth-century Lopez household in Bridgetown, Barbados. Within thirty years, Sarah and Isaac had reached

Blanche Moses's great-uncle. Anonymous, *Portrait of Isaac Lopez Brandon* (early nineteenth century). Watercolor on ivory, 3 1/8 x 2 1/2 in. AJHS.

the pinnacle of New York's wealthy Jewish elite. Once labeled "mulatto" by their own kin and by the Anglican church in Barbados, by 1820 Sarah and her children had been recategorized as white by New York's census. Likewise, Isaac was accepted as white by the New York Jewish community, who helped him gain citizenship. What makes this change all the more surprising is that it was not a secret. Although it was a mystery to Sarah's granddaughter, Sarah and Isaac's partial African ancestry was known by numerous people everywhere they lived. Sarah and Isaac's ability to change their lives and their designated race—despite this knowledge—tells us as much about the early history of race in the Atlantic world as it does about the lives of early American Jews.[7]

Blanche Moses's great-grandfather. John Wesley Jarvis, *Portrait of Abraham Rodrigues Brandon* (ca. 1824). Oil on canvas, MCNY.

Today the small portraits of Sarah Brandon Moses and her brother Isaac Lopez Brandon are understood to be among the rarest items owned by the historical society, as they are the earliest known portraits of multiracial Jews. For over two centuries, the remarkable story of Sarah and Isaac lay buried in archives across three continents. Were it not for a small, random footnote about Isaac's ancestry in the records of Barbados's Nidhe Israel synagogue, the cocoon of assumptions obscuring their past might have remained intact. They would have forever been the lesser-known members of an illustrious family.

But sometimes the people we know the least about turn out to be the most interesting. This book traces the extraordinary journey of Sarah and Isaac as they traveled around the Atlantic world. In the process, they changed their lives, becoming free, wealthy, Jewish, and—at times—white. They were not alone. While their wealth made them unusual, Sarah and Isaac were not the only people in this era who had both African and Jewish ancestry. The siblings' story reveals the little-known history of other early multiracial Jews, which in some of the places the Brandons lived may have made up as much as 50 percent of early Jewish communities. Until now, that story was largely hidden from history, wrapped in the tissue of the past, like the delicate portraits of Sarah and Isaac, swaddled in acid-free paper in a box in the depths of an archive. This book is their unveiling.[8]

I

Origins

Bridgetown, 1793–1798

YEARS LATER, ABRAHAM RODRIGUES BRANDON would claim that his daughter Sarah had always "professed our holy religion."[1] Technically that was not true. Sarah Brandon was baptized as an Anglican at Saint Michael's Church in Bridgetown, Barbados, on June 28, 1798. The faded ink of the record book would become the first documentation of either her or her brother Isaac's life. It was also the start of a series of distortions that would harrow the siblings' ascent through the ranks of wealthy Jewish society.[2]

Brandon's white lie was typical of his relationship with Sarah and Isaac. Brandon was nothing if not ambitious. When Sarah was born, he was just over thirty and a minor player in the island's economy and synagogue. His earliest portrait is a fashionable ivory miniature, showing him in a velvet frock coat and the hedgehog hairstyle popular in the mid-1780s. The bright blue of the velvet, along with the large golden buttons, signaled an aristocratic dignity. Yet the portrait is amateurish compared to the later miniatures of his children. The portrait's wishful thinking is reflected in what else we know of Brandon from the era. In the 1780s and early 1790s, Brandon rarely appears in synagogue records or in the Levy books of St. Michael's parish, suggesting he neither owned property in town nor was the primary renter of an establishment. Taken as a whole, Brandon's early self-presentation is more aspiration than arrival.[3]

Yet by the time of his daughter's death in 1828, Brandon had become the most influential Jew in Barbados. When Brandon had a second portrait made around 1824, he had more than realized his earlier dreams. The

Sarah Rodrigues Brandon's father around the time of her birth.
Anonymous, *Portrait of Abraham Rodrigues Brandon* (late eighteenth
century). Watercolor on ivory. Courtesy of Ann Gegan.

portrait was larger (nearly three feet tall rather than a few inches) and painted
by New York's premier portrait artist, John Wesley Jarvis. Behind Brandon
stands a rich pastoral scene (albeit one of New England) that called to mind
that he was now not merely a successful merchant but also the owner of
three prosperous labor camps: Hopeland, Dear's, and Reed's Bay, where at
least 168 enslaved people had worked in 1817. Brandon also now ruled the
island's synagogue, first becoming a member of the *Mahamad*—the governance board—in 1796 and then the synagogue's *Presidente* in 1810.[4]

Whatever longing had driven Brandon to success, at least one eye was
on his future line. His support helped his oldest children rise up through
the social ranks alongside him. In this way he was probably the best of
parents: even at his death he left a note explaining to Isaac that the hefty

sum Isaac inherited would have even been more if the recent depreciations of West Indian property had not diminished Brandon's wealth. The inheritance was still twice what Sarah and Isaac's much younger half-siblings would receive.[5] Brandon likewise asked Barbadian Jews to see his son as an equal, and when some of his fellow Jews refused, the president of the synagogue reported that they "inflicted a wound that stings Mr. Brandon to the quick."[6] Words against Isaac became an "envenomed dart which rankles in the bosom of Mr. Brandon . . . lacerat[ing] his feelings."[7] No wonder, synagogue president Benjamin Elkin explained, Brandon had decided to absent himself from the synagogue in their wake.

Yet while Abraham Rodrigues Brandon's relationship with the siblings' mother would last more than thirty-five years, he used the white man's prerogative not to marry (Sarah) Esther, who like her children had been born enslaved. Brandon would persist in this decision, even when the family moved off island to places where an interracial marriage was technically possible if not completely accepted. Brandon's resolution would continue to haunt Sarah and Isaac's lives, affecting their racial and social status as they moved about the Atlantic world.

Just as Brandon later hedged about his daughter's religious history, so too was something off in the original church records. Although the record keeper listed Sarah as a "free Mulatto," that was a dodge.[8] Like her brother Isaac, Sarah was born enslaved, and she would not become free until the nineteenth century dawned, her manumission detailed in the record books of the same church where she had been baptized. Although Isaac's own accounting suggests he was born five years earlier, in 1793, his birth went unrecorded. This was not unusual: before 1800, people of African ancestry were rarely baptized on the island, and slave records were spotty at best.[9]

Equally strange as being listed as a "free Mulatto" is the fact that Sarah carried her father's rather than her owner's last name. Back when Sarah was born, Brandon's willingness to admit paternity at all was unusual: most white fathers in Barbados failed to recognize their children with women of color, refusing to give their children their last name, let alone emotional or monetary support. Yet despite the open suggestion of paternity in the church records, early on Sarah and Isaac did not share their father's home. They resided instead with the Lopezes, who enslaved many of the siblings' kin. Like the Brandons, the Lopezes were Jewish refugees of the Inquisition.[10]

Despite their differences, persecution had brought both sides of Sarah and Isaac's clan—as well as that of their owners—to the tropical island. The promise of riches had drawn or forced immigrants westward toward the island's central crop: sugar. Today the average American consumes roughly 152 pounds of sugar a year, or three pounds a week. In contrast, in the medieval era, sugar cost as much per ounce as silver. Sugar was still a luxury reserved for nobles in the sixteenth century, and was sometimes molded into large, elaborate sculptures that conspicuously displayed their owner's wealth. By the seventeenth century, widespread production in places like Barbados made sugar available to the middle class. By the middle of the nineteenth century, sugar prices would drop further so that even the poor could put the white gold in their tea. This is only one way of measuring the cost of sugar, however. As a Surinamese slave explained in Voltaire's *Candide*, "When we work in the sugar mills and we catch our finger in the millstone, they cut off our hand; when we try to run away, they cut off a leg; both things have happened to me. It is at this price that you eat sugar in Europe."[11]

Born enslaved, Sarah and Isaac would have been keenly aware of the cost of sugar. In the 1790s, enormous mahogany trees still grew on some of Barbados's highest hills, but sugar cane fields filled most of the island's 166 square miles. The vast majority of residents were enslaved, outnumbering white Barbadians by four to one. Most worked in the cane fields. It was terrible work. As early as the 1650s, the Irish indentured servants brought to work the fields complained of being "used like dogs . . . grinding at the mills and attending the furnaces, or digging in this scorching island."[12] Even after arriving in Barbados, neither enslaved nor indentured servants had a guarantee of family life. In a petition to the English Parliament, indentured servants in Barbados complained about how they had been "bought and sold still from one planter to another, or attached as horses and beasts for the debts of their masters, being whipt (as rogues) for their masters' pleasure, and sleeping in sties worse than hogs in England."[13]

Plantation owners eventually ameliorated the working conditions of Irish servants, but only by replacing their labor with that of enslaved West Africans. DNA evidence from one of Isaac's descendants suggests the siblings' ancestors came from the region of Africa known today as Nigeria, the homeland of the Hausa, Yoruba, Igbo, and 350 to 450 other ethnic groups. Those ancestors also had genetic connections to people living today in Eastern and Southern Africa. This spread suggests that either the siblings had ancestors from multiple regions of Africa or (more likely) their ancestors belonged to the Bantu peoples originally from what is now Nigeria, as the Bantu would later spread across the continent.[14]

If those ancestors were Bantu, they were not alone in experiencing slavery. At the time when Sarah and Isaac's ancestors were captured, Europeans referred to the Bantu homeland as the Bight of Biafra. Eventually more than 1.6 million people were forced to endure the terror of the transatlantic slave trade from this region alone. They made up about 13 percent of all enslaved Africans in the Americas. Many were sold in Barbados: by the end of the seventeenth century, nearly half of all enslaved people arriving in Barbados had been captured in the Bight of Biafra, with many others coming from the nearby Bight of Benin. The flags dotting the coastline in maps of the era speak to Europeans' horrific rush to profit from the slave trade and the decimation of the area.[15]

Unlike the Irish, who had to serve out only a limited number of years before being freed, Africans transported to Barbados served for life. Work like cane holing—the readying of the soil for planting cane tops—took such a toll on enslaved people's bodies that some planters rented other people's slaves to do the brutal work rather than destroy the bodies of their own slaves, which, after all, were a form of investment for the owners.

Even being an investment, however, did not save enslaved people from having to feed cane into the enormous rollers that pressed out the sugar juice. If a slave pushed her hand in too far, she—like the slave in *Candide*—would get caught in the press, rolled inward to her excruciating death. Sometimes heads were severed from bodies. Overseers kept a hatchet next to the press to cut off trapped limbs. It was not uncommon to see enslaved people in Barbados—many of them women—missing fingers, hands, or arms. From the 1810s to the 1830s, this was the kind of work enslaved people performed in the labor camps Abraham Rodrigues Brandon owned.[16]

Sarah and Isaac's African ancestors who had been forcibly transported across the Atlantic were most likely originally brought to Barbados to work in the cane fields. But by the middle of the eighteenth century, the family found itself living in the main port of Bridgetown as part of the urban enslaved. Being an urban slave exempted one from the painful labor of the cane fields, but it brought its own hardships. Half of the enslaved people in town were domestics who undertook the arduous work of washing, cleaning, cooking, and child care in the tropical heat. Many others were jobbed out by their owners, working in the shipyards, or as fishermen, laborers, transport workers, or hucksters who wandered between town and countryside selling goods.[17]

Enslavers also unabashedly hired out enslaved women for sexual purposes. Some were forced to work in the city's brothels, including hotels run by free women of color. Others were hired out by owners on a less formal basis to sailors and townsmen. According to a British naval officer stationed on the island, even respectable women who hired out enslaved women for jobs such as washing clothes assumed that the inflated price they charged would include sexual benefits for the men doing the hiring. The officer noted that one enslaver "lets out her negro girls to anyone who will pay her for their persons, under the denomination of washerwoman, and becomes very angry if they don't come home in a family way."[18]

Women like Sarah and Isaac's mother and grandmother often sought refuge in longer-term sexual relationships with whites who might discourage owners from selling their bodies to random men. These relationships, however, were also not always voluntary, nor were they equal partnerships. Just as the siblings' mother (Sarah) Esther Lopez-Gill had a long relationship with the Sephardic Jew Abraham Rodrigues Brandon, so too their grandmother Jemima Lopez was the mistress of a British man named George Gill.

Like his father before him, Gill was a schoolmaster and a devout Anglican. Although the Europeans on the island obsessed over how enslaved people were "addicted" to polygamy, adultery, and sex, white men like Gill typically had multiple extramarital relationships with women of color without any fear of being censured by the Anglican church.[19] Certainly, there was no expectation that Gill would marry Jemima Lopez, despite having four children with her. Although interracial marriage was technically not illegal, there is only one known instance of a church marriage between a white person and a person with African ancestry in Barbados during the era of slavery. That marriage took place in the seventeenth century, more than a hundred years before the Brandon siblings were born. The imbalance between Gill and Jemima Lopez was further underscored by the fact that Jemima Lopez was one of several Afro-Barbadian women who bore Gill's children.[20]

Sarah and Isaac's family was matriarchal, like that of most urban enslaved families. Female and urban enslavers tended to buy women, both because they were cheaper to purchase than men and because they gave a high return on one's investment. As a case in point, the siblings' great-grandmother Deborah Lopez was the matriarch of at least ten descendants born in bondage to the Lopez family. Born in 1798, Sarah Brandon, daughter of (Sarah) Esther Lopez-Gill, daughter of Jemima Lopez-Gill, daughter of Deborah Lopez, was the youngest of this enslaved family.[21]

Unlike Sarah's father, neither Sarah's mother nor her grandmother nor her great-grandmother had their portraits painted. Everything we know about these women is biased by the violent way the archives erase certain lives and privilege others. (Sarah) Esther Lopez-Gill's story is similar to those of so many enslaved women in the Caribbean in that her experiences were written down at the time by flawed witnesses, who transcribed nothing she said and didn't wonder about what she thought. Like many enslaved women in Barbados, most of what we know about the matriarchs of Sarah Brandon's family is through the lens of whites, men such as London-based painter Agostino Brunias, who traveled and lived in the West Indies in the 1760s–1790s, painting sensual portraits of multiracial women, typically for wealthy plantation owners. Portraits of women like (Sarah) Esther Lopez-Gill almost always failed to record the names of the women depicted. They were works like Brunias's 1779 *The Barbadoes Mulatto Girl*, which depicted types, not specific people.[22]

In *The Barbadoes Mulatto Girl*, the category of woman presented is a radiant Venus. The woman is painted for the viewer's pleasure, in a classic contrapposto pose with her weight placed on one leg, the S of her torso calling attention to her womb. One hand lifts her apron, as if she desires to expose herself, even as her skirt hides her legs. Although labeled a "girl," she is all woman, pregnant, with a star drawing our attention to her bustline. Like the mango she is offered, the woman symbolizes fertility. Brunias parallels her production and that of the island's labor camps by positioning her finger to draw our attention to the nearby cane fields and plantation house. The darker-skinned women on either side of her are reduced to props, who center our gaze on the lighter-skinned woman's face and body. And like Abraham Rodrigues Brandon's early miniature, the painting reeks of aspiration, though here the aspiration is all Brunias's, namely, his desire to present women of mixed ancestry as safe and beneficial to the colonial economy.

Yet everything we know about (Sarah) Esther Lopez-Gill suggests that her life was anything but safe. Although born enslaved, she gained her freedom and rejected attempts to pin her down to one thing. One name could not hold her. As her white father remarked, sometimes her first name was Sarah, sometimes Esther, sometimes Sarah Esther. Who decided when and what to call her? Did she have the ability to object? We do not even know what the versions of her name meant to her: was Esther—the Jewish bride of Persian King Ahasuerus—a hope for her future as a savior of her people? Was Sarah for the Jewish matriarch, who married Brandon and spawned a dynasty? I refer to her as (Sarah) Esther, in part so readers will not confuse her with her daughter, but mainly to emphasize the hubris of thinking we will ever truly *know* her. (Sarah) Esther's last name was just as unstable as her first, shifting from Lopez to Gill to Brandon depending on who told her story in

The Barbadoes Mulatto Girl

No portraits remain of Sarah and Isaac's mother. Paintings
of multiracial women from Barbados during this era tend to
be types, not individuals. Agostino Brunias, *The Barbadoes
Mulatto Girl*, after painting (ca. 1764), published in London
in 1779. BMHS.

the colonial records and who claimed her as kin. (Sarah) Esther Lopez-Gill's
fluidity and that of her close kin network among free and enslaved people
would be crucial, as the siblings made their way in the world.[23]

For when Sarah and Isaac were born, they did not live alone with the
Lopez-Gill matriarch. Their family also included (Sarah) Esther Lopez-
Gill's three brothers—Jonathan, William, and Alexander George Gill—and
Sarah and Isaac's sisters, Rachel and Rebecca Brandon, both of whom died
young. Although most of the family would eventually receive their freedom,
Deborah Lopez was never freed. At her owner's death in 1815, she was willed
to her great-grandchildren to care for her in her dotage, the cost of manu-
mission beyond their reach.[24]

If abduction brought the siblings' African ancestors to Barbados, persecution combined with economic opportunities explained how their Jewish ancestors and enslavers had ended up on the island. Sarah and Isaac's ancestors were Portuguese Jews, also known as Sephardim, from the Hebrew word for Iberia, *Sepharad*. After centuries of living under Muslim rule, the Jews of Spain were forced out by Isabella and Ferdinand, the new Catholic rulers. The Alhambra Decree of 1492 gave Spanish Jews four months to convert or leave and abandon any gold, silver, or minted money. While some fled to North Africa and the Ottoman Empire, many went to nearby Portugal. It was here that the Lopezes and Brandons settled.[25]

But their respite proved only temporary. In 1496, a marriage alliance with Spain led King Manuel I of Portugal to demand that all Jews in his realm convert. Those who chose exile were required to leave behind their children, a price few would pay. As time passed, some forced converts and their descendants became faithful Catholics. Others continued to practice what Judaism they could in secret, even as they publicly attended Mass, ever fearful of the Inquisition's flames. Even those New Christians who practiced Catholicism faithfully were not safe. Throughout the seventeenth and eighteenth centuries, whenever natural disasters or the economy caused unrest, the Inquisition blamed the *conversos*—forced converts and their descendants. New Christians were rounded up, thrown in jail, and tortured into confessions. The motive to finger a converso as a heretic was high: half of the estate of anyone convicted would go to the church, the other half to the informant. Convicted conversos who refused to reconcile themselves to the church were ritually paraded in yellow sackcloths and large conical hats, then burned at the stake in public *autos-da-fé*. Scholars have suggested that the Inquisition made more Jews than it killed: according to the autobiographies of some of the interned, they first learned about Jewish rituals from the Inquisitors' questions. For others, the punishments sparked a flame of defiance: if they were going to be punished anyway, why not commit the crime?[26]

Both the Lopez and Brandon families were swept up in purges by the Inquisition. The records in the Arquivo Nacional da Torre do Tombo in Lisbon contain extensive accounts of their imprisonment, torture, and trials. When released, the families fled to Amsterdam, Hamburg, London, and France. These were men like João Rodrigues Brandão, a young merchant, who was imprisoned in the 1720s, forced to complete a public penance, then released. After gaining freedom, he married his brother's stepdaughter Luisa Mendes Seixas. Conversos who maintained Jewish practices in secret often married close relatives in order to ensure that their offspring would have Jewish bloodlines. Marrying relatives also allowed conversos to better predict whether a spouse would be sympathetic to Crypto-Judaism, sympathies which if revealed to the Inquisition could result in death. At various points João Rodrigues Brandão and Luisa Mendes Seixas's parents, siblings, and children were imprisoned, tortured, and punished. They were lucky to survive: the Inquisition's court in Coimbra sentenced 9,547 heretics between 1541 and 1781, more than 330 of whom were burned at the stake. By the 1760s, João Rodrigues Brandão and Luisa Mendes Seixas gave up on Portugal. They made their way to London, where they took Hebrew names and remarried according to the Jewish rite. João, now Joshua, and the other male members of the family underwent painful adult circumcisions. When Joshua's brother, Abraham Rodrigues Brandão, died in 1769, his will mentioned relatives still living in Portugal as well as others in London and Bayonne, France.[27]

Other branches of the family fled Iberia to Protestant-run Amsterdam and Hamburg, where—like in London—they could practice Judaism openly. Economic opportunities then pushed the refugees farther west. By the late 1600s, branches of both the Lopez and Brandon families had made their escape to the British West Indies, hoping to make their fortune in the white gold.[28]

They were not the only Sephardic Jews to take the journey. Sephardim were key to Barbados's sugar trade. Sugar was a tricky crop, and successful transformation of the cane into granulated sugar was no easy feat. Prior to planting sugar in the Americas, the Portuguese planted cane on São Tomé. Conversos exiled to the island off the African coast played a role in developing this industry. Conversos likewise helped transport Portuguese knowledge to early plantations in Brazil, where they sought refuge from the Inquisition. Early settlers included members of the extended Brandon clan. By 1590, nearly a third of all sugar mills in the Bahia region of Brazil were owned by New Christian families. When the Dutch invaded in 1624, they offered these families the chance to worship openly. The Jews stayed until 1654, when the Portuguese recaptured the Brazilian port of Recife. The refugees then spread across the Caribbean and up the North American coast to New Amsterdam. Those who settled in Barbados founded the Nidhe Israel synagogue and helped set up the island's sugar plantations and refineries.[29]

Jewish involvement in the sugar production business proved to be short-lived. British planters became wary of the Jews' success and used the Anglican-controlled legislature to limit the number of slaves Jews could own, making it impossible for Jews to run their own plantations. By the time Sarah and Isaac's father Abraham was a boy, most Jews made their livelihood as merchants and shopkeepers in ports like Bridgetown. Both Abraham Rodrigues Brandon and the siblings' owners were merchants. Familial ties in Europe's great cities were a tremendous boon for traders like Abraham Rodrigues Brandon, as kin in other ports helped provide reliable trading partners for the sugar he exported. Even smaller shopkeepers like the Lopezes, who mainly sold goods in town, benefited from transatlantic coreligionists who served as creditors or trustworthy suppliers for the goods they sold. Eventually Abraham Rodrigues Brandon would break this mold, but during the children's early years he was still a small-time trader.[30]

Bridgetown was a superb place to be a merchant. Today Bridgetown may seem small to continental visitors, but in the seventeenth and eighteenth centuries, it was the flagship city of the British colonies. According to one late eighteenth-century visitor, Carlisle Bay—the main harbor for the city— was the Thames of the West Indies. The port held a dizzying array of ships. In one hour alone, another astonished visitor noted more than a dozen varieties of vessels: "English ships of war, merchantmen, and transports; slave ships from the coast of Africa; packets; prizes; American traders; island vessels, privateers, fishing smacks, and different kinds of boats, cutters, and luggers."[31] By the 1770s, the population of Bridgetown was larger than its rival Kingston to the north in Jamaica, and almost as large as Boston, dwarfed only by Philadelphia and New York. The vast wealth to be made through sugar also made Bridgetown phenomenally resilient. Although the city was nearly destroyed in the fire of 1766 and then in the hurricane of 1780, it was quickly rebuilt using enslaved labor. The fortune to be made in the island's main port would dramatically shape the siblings' lives.[32]

Most Bridgetown residents were Anglican, but Methodists and one of the largest Jewish American communities also called the port home. By the middle of the eighteenth century, 400 to 500 Jews lived in Barbados, almost all in Bridgetown. Two things brought Jews to that port: trade and the synagogue. At the town's center, just north of the wharves, lay Swan Street, sometimes called Jew Street because of the number of Sephardic merchants living on it. Swan Street became one of the main shopping streets in the port, but it was also in easy walking distance of the Nidhe Israel synagogue—the Scattered or Exiles of Israel.[33]

Jews are commanded to pray with a minyan (quorum) of ten men; thus in the 1650s, the refugees from Dutch Brazil began construction on a house of worship, though later hurricanes and fires would require the synagogue to be rebuilt. Like most early Sephardic congregations in the Atlantic world, the synagogue was part of a complex of structures that also included four houses: one for the rabbi or *hazan* (Torah reader), one for the ritual slaughterer, one for the beadle, and one for the female attendant who ran the ritual bath or *mikveh*. In addition, the complex housed the mikveh, the Jewish school, and—rather uniquely—the community cemetery. The synagogue itself was small but delightful, modeled on the much larger synagogues in Amsterdam and London. As in those buildings, women sat upstairs in the balcony, in a section that echoed the women's court in Solomon's Temple. Rich hardwoods from tropical rainforests were the material for the seats, Torah ark, and reader's platform. On the four corners of the reader's platform were carved pineapples, the universal symbol of hospitality. It was a place Brandon called home.[34]

It was also their enslaver family's spiritual haven. The Lopezes had been central members of both Congregation Nidhe Israel and Tzemah David in nearby Speightstown, whose synagogue had been destroyed in 1739 in an antisemitic riot that began after a Christian claimed he had been maliciously slandered at a Jewish wedding. By the time Sarah and Isaac were

Nidhe Israel Synagogue, Bridgetown, Barbados. Photo by author.

born, their owner, Hannah Esther Lopez, was a widow. Like many widows, she struggled financially. Most of her husband's estate went to her sons, and by 1792, she was no longer able to pay even minimal taxes to the synagogue. She must have known from watching her friends that being taken off the synagogue's tax list was often the first step for elderly women before having to rely on the synagogue for financial handouts. Her financial decline also most likely explains why, slowly over the next two decades, Lopez became willing to sell members of the siblings' family to their fathers or lovers. Even then, Lopez often put conditions on the sales, holding out the promise of eventual freedom while forcing the Lopez-Gills to eke out the present caring for the lonely widow.[35]

These financial challenges were common for women of her class, and Hannah Esther Lopez was lucky that she had some extended family to help her. The Lopezes were related to nearly every Jew on the island, including those who ruled the Nidhe Israel governance board. As a woman, Lopez had less to do with the synagogue's day-to-day activities, even before she stopped paying taxes. But back in the family's heyday, Lopez's husband Mathias Lopez had been a close associate of Raphael Hayyim Isaac Karigal, the island's most notable rabbi. Hannah Esther Lopez's son Moses Lopez carried on that tradition.[36]

Since women typically inherited only a minor portion of their husband's property, after Mathias Lopez's death, the couple's younger son, Moses Lopez, took over the family store. Hannah Esther Lopez no longer had a home of her own, instead living in a house in Bridgetown owned by her older son, Isaac Lopez, a local silversmith. Moses Lopez also owned a house in town, and in 1787 he bought a small country estate where he raised sheep, milk cows, geese, yams, corn, and plums. He, too, was a slave owner. He had inherited three enslaved people from his father, but he also bought five new people—Malchiezedeck, Daphny, Izabel, Cudjoe, and Sammy—to run the country property. He kept his other enslaved people in town, and hired them out when he did not need them to help at home or the store. When Isaac Lopez Brandon was born in the early 1790s, it was the Lopezes not the Brandons who were the synagogue elite. Like his father, Moses Lopez was involved in synagogue life: he was alternately the *Gabay* (treasurer) and Presidente of the Nidhe Israel synagogue until 1794, when he, like many other Barbadian Jews, sought to escape the island's lagging economy by heading north for the United States.[37]

By the time Moses Lopez left, both of Hannah Esther Lopez's daughters-in-law, Rachel and Devora Lopez, had been laid to rest in the synagogue cemetery. One of Hannah Esther Lopez's young grandsons was nestled in the ground beside his aunt. When Sarah Brandon was born, Hannah Esther Lopez's other two grandsons—sons of Moses Lopez—were farther away, alive but distant in the cold northern cities of the United States. The years that follow reveal an increasingly lonely Hannah Esther Lopez, her closest blood relations dead or miles away. As her kinfolk abandoned her, she tightened her emotional grasp on the people she enslaved, bribing them with the potential freedom of other relatives and gifts to be received after her death. Yet unlike their father, Lopez would never see the siblings or their family members beyond a racial lens. Every time she mentioned their names, it was quickly followed by the explanation of their racial category. To her, the family members were always either a "Mulatto Woman Slave," "a mulatto Girl Slave," a "free Mulatto," or "a free Mulatto Boy," rather than ever just themselves.[38]

Although (Sarah) Esther Lopez-Gill's own father was Anglican, the home Hannah Esther Lopez offered Sarah and Isaac was decidedly Jewish. Even after she lost her position in the synagogue and many of her immediate kin through death or migration, Lopez's home on Swan Street placed her—and her slaves—at the center of the island's Jewish community. Of the fifty-five houses on Swan Street in 1793, forty-four were owned by Jews. Owning property on Swan Street placed the Lopez clan among the better half of the island's Jewish community. Like white Anglicans and free people of color, over half of the island's Jews were poor. Some had come to the island as impoverished refugees and never managed to get a leg up. Others had lost what wealth their family had accumulated in the economic downturn that followed the American Revolutionary War. The greatest portion of Jews on the poor lists, however, were women—often widows like Lopez. These poor Jews were also extremely visible, a warning to Lopez in her final years. One traveler complained that no English eye visiting Bridgetown could look on the wretched appearance of those poor Jews without feeling disgust.[39]

Despite her financial advantages, Lopez worked in her old age. Like most residents of Swan Street, Lopez lived upstairs from the family store. Records from her son Moses Lopez's store reveal Hannah Esther Lopez and her widowed sister-in-law bought large quantities of fiddle strings and Dilworth's Spelling books, one of the most popular books for teaching reading. The quantity of their purchases suggests that they may have run a private children's school and offered fiddle lessons. The two widows most

Charles W. Blackburn, *Swan Street Barbados* (ca. 1897–1912). Photo negative, glass plate. International Center of Photography, No. 2013.81.33.

likely were trying to gain some semblance of independence. If so, it does not seem to have worked very well: the women's store purchases do not suggest an increase in their spending allowance in the years that followed.[40]

Although many Jews lived along Swan Street, it was not a ghetto. Jews also favored the other streets near the synagogue: Tudor Street, Back Church Street, and Church Street. The same streets were popular with the island's growing community of free people of color, who also lived on nearby James, Marl Hill, High, and Roebuck Streets, and the area along the Bay. As the financial help of white relatives allowed the Lopez-Gill family slowly to gain their freedom, the children, grandchildren, and great-grandchildren of Deborah Lopez would live alongside their former enslavers and other members of the Jewish community.

The Lopez-Gills were not the only free people of color in Bridgetown with Jewish ties. Hannah Esther Lopez's son Isaac Lopez fathered several children outside of wedlock with women of color who lived nearby, including a daughter named Christian Lopez who lived with her mother Martha Blackman on nearby Tudor Street. Other people of color with Jewish connections, like Hester Lindo, lived on White Street. Ruby Ulloa,

Princess Castello, and William Nunes all lived on James Street, just above Swan. Finella Abarbanell had a house on Reed Street. Esther Massiah and Sarah de Castro lived on Tudor. And those were just the few free people of color with Jewish ties who were wealthy enough to own a house. All bore the last names of Sephardic Jews who were either former enslavers or their kin, or both.[41]

Jews did not enslave more people than their Protestant neighbors nor were they more likely to bear offspring by women of color. Both Jews and free people of color did, however, settle disproportionately in Bridgetown. The large number of formerly enslaved people in the city with Jewish last names reflects this convergence.[42]

Given all the family's ties to the Jewish community, why did Sarah Brandon's mother take her to St. Michael's Church to be baptized? The act speaks to (Sarah) Esther Lopez-Gill's ambitions for her children. Despite living amid the Jewish community, the siblings technically were not part of it. In order to have one's birth recorded in the Jewish synagogue, a person either had to be born of a Jewish mother or convert to Judaism. Sarah and Isaac's mother's maternal line went back to Africa, with no known Jewish foremother. Since the Middle Ages, Arab travelers had suggested there were Jews in Africa, including the Bilad al-Sudan whose homeland was near the part of western Africa where the siblings' ancestor(s) had first been enslaved. But even if there had been such an ancestress who was part of the Jews of the Bilad al-Sudan, any knowledge of her not lost in the middle passage would have been passed down through an oral tradition that would not have satisfied synagogue officials. Moreover, conversions were almost unheard of in Barbados. By baptizing her, Sarah's mother had done the best she could.[43]

And Sarah's baptism was no small thing. The early church in Barbados had tended to reserve both marriages and baptisms for whites, but about the time Sarah Brandon was born, the church had just begun to loosen its policy. Without a baptism, a woman could not marry in the Anglican church. Unless she converted, Sarah could not marry in the synagogue. Marriage mattered. In addition to being a public celebration of commitment and family, marriage provided legal protection. While not everyone might have wanted to marry, those who were denied the right could find themselves at an economic and social disadvantage. By baptizing Sarah, her mother laid the groundwork that one day Sarah might be able to control her own body. (Sarah) Esther Lopez-Gill gave her daughter a gift neither she, nor Jemima Lopez-Gill, nor Deborah Lopez had: the possibility to marry if she were ever freed. Although Sarah would not choose a church marriage, it was a gift she held on to. But before she could cash in on that gift, an unanticipated death changed her life along with that of her mother and brother forever.[44]

2

From Slave to Free

Bridgetown, 1801

IN EARLY SEPTEMBER 1801, SARAH and Isaac's British grandfather, George Gill, lay dying amid feather pillows in his mahogany bed in Bridgetown, Barbados. In the weeks following the end of the rainy season, he had time to consider his life and the households he would leave behind. He described himself as "Sick & Weak of body but of Sound & Disposing mind," as he struggled to put his worldly affairs in order while he still had "strength & Capacity so to do."[1] His affairs were surprisingly complicated in the ways that actual people's lives tend to be. The way he wrapped up those affairs would change the fortunes of his children and grandchildren. The quick whisk of a quill-tipped pen would set generations in motion in unforeseen directions.

For enslaved people, the death of owners and white kin was an anxious business. One cross word, and lives could be ruined. Whites were often unpredictable in their affections. The 1804 will of Hannah Esther Lopez's son Isaac Lopez is a case in point. The first version of his will, written on the ninth day of November 1803, was entirely generous. Debts were to be paid, a plain marble stone requested for his grave, and charity given, both to the island's synagogue and to the Jewish communities of Hebron, Jerusalem, and Safet. His mother, brother, and nephews were to receive large bequests and his multiracial daughter a small one. Most crucially for Loretta and King, two enslaved people whose lives depended on the dying man's goodwill, there was a bequest specifying that they be freed by proxy in England, a legal loophole that allowed for their manumission without anyone having to pay the island's exorbitant fees. King, whom Lopez described as "my faithful man Slave," was also to receive "all my wearing apparel for his proper use and benefit."[2]

By the sixteenth of January, however, Lopez had had a change of heart with regard to King. Some unrevealed slight prompted the dying man to lash out against King's "late ungrateful and misproper conduct."[3] In a codicil to his will, Lopez withdrew the bequest of both freedom and clothes. Instead, the will's executor—Abraham Rodrigues Brandon—was to sell King. The money from the sale would go to Lopez's surviving white relatives. King was ruined, his years of faithfulness discarded in a flash of white anger.

Surely when Sarah, Isaac, their mother (Sarah) Esther Lopez-Gill, their grandmother Jemima Lopez-Gill, and their aunts and uncles sat around George Gill's deathbed in 1801, they felt anxiety for their insecure future, much as other Barbadian enslaved people suffered when a white benefactor's death neared. Of all the relatives, only Jemima Lopez-Gill was owned by George Gill, purchased a mere month before his will was written. Would she be freed? Passed along to white kin? Or, worst of all, sold?

George Gill's largess could also change the lives of his mixed-race kin owned by other people, as he had the means to leave his children and grandchildren enough money to buy their freedom. Gill had never legally married and had no legitimate children. Who would inherit the bulk of Gill's estate, including his houses, furniture, small country parcel, and the people he had enslaved? In addition to Jemima Lopez-Gill, George Gill owned eight other women, men, and children: Sally, Mary Grace, Christine, Jenny, Sally Celia, Jack James, George, and William Edward. What would their fates be?

Gill had fathered several children out of wedlock with different women of color, but the custom in Barbados was that when whites died, they left the majority (and often the whole) of their estate to their white relations. In Gill's case this meant his brothers and sisters or their children, of which there were many. If the white Gills inherited Jemima Lopez-Gill along with the other people George Gill had enslaved, Jemima Lopez-Gill's fate would be anyone's guess. Sometimes white relations treated their deceased relatives' paramours with affection or respect. More often, though, the women and their offspring were punished for their former status. At least one Jewish man in Jamaica was concerned enough about tensions between his white and multiracial relations that his will specifically stipulated that any white relatives who challenged his multiracial son's bequest would automatically forfeit their own inheritance.[4]

On the plus side for those who waited anxiously to hear their fate, Gill, a schoolmaster and devout Anglican, was known for his benevolence. While other teachers on the island sought out the patronage of the planter elite, Gill taught at the parish's Free School—a place dedicated to trying to change the lives of the lower classes that made up over half of white Barbadian society. There is no indication, however, that prior to 1801 Gill felt charitable toward anyone with African ancestry. On the island, charity often meant helping only people one felt were most like oneself. Moreover, as the codicil to Lopez's 1804 will demonstrates, giving charity did not preclude harsh treatment of the enslaved.

Further complicating the fates of Jemima Lopez-Gill and her descendants was the fact that they were most likely not the only people surrounding Gill's deathbed. Jemima Lopez-Gill was only one of three Afro-Barbadian women with whom Gill had an ongoing relationship: there was also Celia Lovell, "a free Mulatto Woman," and Joanna Gill, a "free Black Woman" with whom Gill had had two children, Christian(a) Gill and John Gill.[5] Like Jemima Lopez-Gill, Joanna Gill had once been enslaved by the siblings' grandfather, George Gill. Unlike Jemima Lopez-Gill, however, Joanna Gill and her children had been freed and baptized by George Gill. Jemima Lopez-Gill might be "my mulatto Woman" to Gill, but as his slave and concubine, Jemima Lopez-Gill had no legal right to expect monogamy from the Anglican teacher. Prior to his death, Gill had been *less* generous toward Jemima Lopez-Gill and her children than toward Joanna, Christian(a), and John Gill. Why expect that in death he would act differently?[6]

Amid all these attendant anxieties, George Gill died and was buried in the churchyard's sandy earth on November 19, 1801. He was fifty-six. His will surely spawned a tangle of emotions: it set no one free, but his largess would be one of several monumental flights of fate that changed Sarah and Isaac's lives and helped the children's progress from enslaved to free people of color with property of their own.[7]

The will that was read into the public record less than a week after Gill's burial opened with good news for the siblings' family. The first person mentioned was "my beloved Daughter Sarah Gill otherwise called Esther"— that is, Sarah and Isaac Brandon's mother.[8] Although still herself enslaved, (Sarah) Esther Lopez-Gill became an heiress. Along with George Gill's other multiracial kin, she received the bulk of his estate.

She also became enmeshed in the tangle of slavery's ironies. (Sarah) Esther Lopez-Gill inherited two of the nine people her father had enslaved: a "Negro Woman" named Sally and a "Negro Girl" named Mary Grace, along with any children they might bear.[9] (Sarah) Esther Lopez-Gill was suddenly complicit in the oppressive system that had strangled her own options for so long. Each of her full brothers, Jonathan, Alexander George, and William Gill, along with her half-brother and half-sister, John and Christian(a) Gill, also received an enslaved person. The final person Gill had enslaved, eponymously named George, was to be sold by the will's executors in order to fund the other bequests.[10]

To make people who had endured slavery the enslavers of others seems cruel, but George Gill probably hoped to position his multiracial relations alongside the ranks of the top quarter of the free Afro-Barbadian community, who like wealthy whites tended to be enslavers. While some free people of color inherited relatives in wills or bought children or spouses with the short-term goal of keeping them safe and the long-term goal of earning the money to pay for their manumission, most people enslaved by people of color were not relations but workers.[11]

Indeed, elite free people of color fought hard to maintain their rights as enslavers. In 1803, more than 300 free men of color petitioned the island's Assembly to reject a bill that would have limited their ability to own land and people. The bill, the men explained, would bring great hardship since "we have all our lives been accustomed to the assistance of slaves."[12] The petitioners shuddered at the idea that their children would have no one to help with manual labor: "Surely death would be preferable to such a situation!"[13] Such were the views of a small, privileged elite. Although none of the Lopez-Gills was used to the assistance of any enslaved people other than themselves, their transformation from property to propertied was crucial to the remaking of the status of George Gill's multiracial children and, in turn, grandchildren.

The only person enslaved by George Gill who escaped being transferred to a new owner was Jemima Lopez-Gill. Gill may have loved Jemima Lopez-Gill, but he did not spend the extra £50 to make her legally free during his lifetime. Maybe he wanted power over her devotion. Or perhaps he was still angry at having paid the somewhat inflated sum of £35 to the Sephardic widow Hannah Esther Lopez to purchase Jemima Lopez only a month earlier. Possibly he thought the legal change was unnecessary. Jemima Lopez-Gill was no longer of child-bearing age and George Gill made sure to stipulate that "my mulatto Woman Jemima Gill, should have her time

& free Liberty as long as she liveth, & that she should not be molested nor hindered by any person or persons whatsoever."[14] He also left Jemima Lopez-Gill fifty pounds, the exact sum needed to buy her freedom. If she wished to spend her inheritance on manumission fees, it was her business. Apparently, Jemima Lopez-Gill decided it was worth the expense. By the time she was baptized in 1805, she was listed as a "free mulatto woman."[15]

Gill also ensured Jemima Lopez-Gill's comfort in her dotage. This attention was important because Jemima Lopez-Gill had many years ahead of her. Although ten years older than George Gill, Jemima Lopez-Gill went on to live another twenty-four years after George Gill's death, dying at ninety in 1825. George Gill specified that one of the girls he had given to his daughter (Sarah) Esther Lopez Gill—Mary Grace—was to "wait and attend on Jemima Gill mother of the above said Sarah Gill otherwise called Esther as long as she [Jemima] liveth." Gill also specifically left Jemima Lopez-Gill the "large mahogany Bedstead, a Feather Bed, Bolster & two Pillows."[16] He cared about how well Jemima Lopez-Gill slept.

Perhaps most crucially, Gill left Jemima Lopez-Gill and her children his house on Hartles [Hartley's] Alley and "the furniture belonging to the House for their use."[17] Gill's other paramours, Joanna Gill and Celia Lovell, also inherited houses. For Jemima Lopez-Gill's children, the house on Hartley's Alley signaled a sea change in the family's ability to control their everyday lives and changed the quality of their dwelling. Enslaved Barbadians typically lived in wattle and daub houses. These were handmade from the cheapest of materials: wicker-like branches woven between posts then cemented over with a sticky mixture of straw, clay, sand, and dung.[18]

The urban enslaved built wattle and daub structures in the yards on their enslavers' property or lived in tenement houses they rented elsewhere in the city, often from Jews or free people of color. Some of this small tenement housing was extraordinarily dense: one woman of color had twenty-four rental houses on two small urban plots of land. Another freedman, William Knight had twenty-one rental houses on his plot in Bridgetown.[19]

By inheriting Gill's house on Hartley's Alley, the family no longer had to live at the margins of their owner's property or in second-class rentals, but had control of their domestic arrangements. Referred to in the stock language of probate records as a "mansion or Dwelling House," the building on Hartley's Alley was most likely a typical townhouse similar to those inhabited by Jews like Hannah Esther Lopez on Swan Street, just a few blocks away.[20] The Hartley's Alley house would become Sarah and Isaac Brandon's first real home, a place where they lived rather than served.

Early photograph of a wattle and daub house in Jamaica that
is similar to ones depicted in drawings of Barbadian houses
from the 1820s. Frances G. Carpenter, *Blacks on a Tobacco
Plantation, Jamaica* (ca. 1890–1924). Library of Congress.

Like most residences in this part of town, the Hartley's Alley house
was probably a two-story building with a cantilevered balcony on the
second floor and a shop entrance below. Balconies and levered windows
allowed crosswinds that were key to comfort. As Bridgetown resident
Elizabeth Fenwick explained, in a good Barbadian house there would
be such a "current of wind blowing through the rooms that without
weights we could not keep anything on the Tables."[21] Balconies likewise
allowed one to enjoy the cooling evening breezes. Townhouses echoed
Georgian austerity, but reshaped the British style to meet island needs.
Roofs tended to fly off during hurricanes. To prevent this, islanders
often slanted roofs sharply upward with a small wall around the bottom.

Copper gutters diverted the deluge of summer rains. By the middle of the nineteenth century, elaborate gingerbread balconies would be all the rage in Bridgetown, but in 1801 the Lopez-Gill house's balcony was more likely simple wrought iron or wood. Behind the house would be a small yard with outbuildings, an outhouse, and possibly tenements. It was not the most expensive house on the street, nor the least, but, suddenly, in November 1801, it was theirs.[22]

By the time George Gill died, Sarah and Isaac Brandon were free to live in the new house. Although their own father was not mentioned in Gill's will, the siblings had already benefited from Abraham Rodrigues Brandon's affection in 1801. The timing of Brandon's attention was superb. That same year, panicked by the growing number of free people of color—or freedmen, as they were then known—the island's Assembly decided to raise manumission fees from £50 per person to £300 for females and £200 for males, a cost that often far exceeded the purchase price of the enslaved. To manumit someone, an enslaver had to pay fees to the local Anglican church, which in turn provided the newly freed person a small yearly stipend and further financial support if they fell on hard times. The exorbitant rise in costs, set to take effect in 1802, meant that those who had been close to gathering enough money to pay for their freedom through years of jobbing themselves out would now most likely face a life of enslavement.[23]

Any enslaved person who could afford to do so, or could convince white or free relatives to free them, rushed to pay the manumission fees before they skyrocketed. The Lopezes, Gills, and Brandons were among those who scrambled to gain their freedom. The status of nearly every member of the Protestant Lopez-Gill clan, including Sarah and Isaac, changed radically in 1801.

The process of freeing the siblings took nearly a year, and it was not finalized until a few months before George Gill died. Brandon supplied both financial and legal help to free his children. As a woman, Hannah Esther Lopez legally could not manumit someone without the help of a man, but she entered into a tripartite indenture on August 8, 1800, that conveyed Sarah, Isaac, and Rebecca to Abraham Rodrigues Brandon and a kinsman who was leaving for England, where manumission fees did not apply. While in England, the kinsman could legally free the children. Meanwhile the indenture ensured the children's future. Should Hannah Esther Lopez die, the children would belong to their father. During Lopez's lifetime, however, they would continue to serve her until word of their release came back across the seas.

For the privilege of someday owning his own children, Brandon paid Lopez £40 and 10 shillings on a hot August day. Twelve days later Lopez's sixteen-year-old grandson Matthias Lopez conveyed the indenture to the warden of St. Michael's Church, who entered it into the record. Although Matthias Lopez had moved to the United States a few years earlier, he appears to have traveled back for visits.[24]

The plan to free the children only after Hannah Esther Lopez's demise became problematic when the legislature announced the manumission fee hike. Instead of merely owing the church £100, Brandon would have to pay £500 to free his two children. As 1801 marched forward, the children were no closer to being freed. So Lopez, Brandon, and the errant kinsman entered into a new indenture. Rebecca Brandon was not included nor ever mentioned again. Infant and child mortality was rampant on the island, and she most likely fell prey to tropical disease, though no records confirm this.

The new indenture, dated May 1801, reshaped the surviving Brandon children's future. Isaac and Sarah were immediately to be "freed and discharged of and from all and all manner of Slavery labour servitude and duty whatsoever."[25] For Sarah—as for all girls and women being freed—an extra phrase was added to free "her issue and her increase hereafter to be born." In other words, her future children and their descendants were also guaranteed their freedom. To complete the contract, the siblings each ritually handed their father ten shillings, and £50 currency each were collected by Jarratt Hamden for Thomas Hordle Esquire, Church Warden "to be placed in the Parish funds for . . . [their] future benefit according to the laws."[26] Given Lopez's limited finances, it is highly doubtful that she paid the combined £100 fee. More likely the fee was paid by Brandon himself, who was on his way to becoming the island's wealthiest Jew.

On August 5, 1801, the siblings' manumission was recorded by John Ince, and the children were officially free. Henceforth, they would be known on the island as "free mulattos." Less than four months later, their mother's inheritance from George Gill conferred on them a home, servants, and a place in the world. Through their mother, Sarah and Isaac would also be connected to what would become one of the most important free colored families on the island: they were the niece and nephew of the island's only female official national hero, Ann Jordan Gill. A wealthy, free woman of color, Jordan Gill would go on to become one of the leaders of the Methodist Church and an ardent supporter of the rights of the enslaved to worship, a position she maintained despite numerous threats of violence against her. Although not as prosperous as other multiracial families in Bridgetown, the

Gills were deeply religious and had ties to the Anglican and later Methodist church. Like Ann Jordan Gill, other family members put their own lives at risk to ensure everyone had a place to pray. The siblings shared their mother's family's deep spirituality, but with a Jewish twist. Like his much-celebrated aunt, Isaac's spiritual beliefs would eventually lead him to agitate for civil rights.

Sarah and Isaac's manumission did not end their struggles. Although free, they remained bound in many ways. As free people of color in early nineteenth-century Barbados, Sarah and Isaac could not participate in the island's legislature. They could not vote nor hold office. For many years they could not even testify in court. Moreover, despite their Sephardic lineage, they could not be married in the island's synagogue, take part in any of its services, or be buried in its cemetery. The next crucial step in gaining the right to live and pray as they pleased came in 1811, when they boarded a small ship and left behind the only home they had ever known. Their destination was the nearby colony of Suriname, home to the second-largest Jewish community in the Americas, and the largest Afro-Jewish community in the world, outside of Africa.

3

From Christian to Jew

Suriname, 1811–1812

IT WOULD HAVE TAKEN SARAH and Isaac four to eight days by schooner to reach Paramaribo, Suriname's main port, but in many ways the former Dutch colony was a world away. The quickly covered distance made Paramaribo a popular destination for Bridgetown's Jews, and the cost of the journey was relatively small: £7.10 to £12.10 per person each way, roughly the same cost as a floor cloth, miscellaneous kitchen furniture, or—more poignantly—a young enslaved boy in Bridgetown. The Brandons were also young, particularly to make the journey alone. Isaac was only nineteen, Sarah thirteen. According to synagogue records, religion pushed them forward toward the only Jewish community in the Americas that regularly accepted people with African ancestry into its fold. So, in November of 1812 in the strange new town, the siblings celebrated their last Chanukah as non-Jews. Less than a month later, in the heart of this vibrant South American colony, the Brandons become *nação*, Jews of the Portuguese nation. That identity was hard earned, and would shape how they and their children would be received for the rest of their lives.[1]

The ritual itself was deceptively simple. Once Isaac provided the *Mahamad* with an official declaration that he wanted "to be circumcised and considered as a Portuguese Jew professing the Judaic religion," the synagogue board gave a local *mohel* permission to circumcise Isaac "according to the rites of our Holy Law."[2] Following his *brit milah*, Isaac was immersed in the cool waters of the congregation's ritual bath, still housed today under a trap door in the small wooden structure behind the Sephardic synagogue. It was the same building where—above ground—the congregation met after services to eat and celebrate. When the siblings finalized their conversions, though, almost everyone would have gone home, the trap door hidden in the floor raised to reveal the secret pool. Once filled with water bubbling up from the slate floor, today the pool lies empty beneath the wooden panel.

Stripped bare, Isaac would have descended carefully down the slate steps until he stood waist-high in the water. Three men of the *beth din*— the Jewish law court—would quiz him briefly on points of law to assure themselves of Isaac's willing acceptance of the covenant. Then they blessed him, and asked him to repeat the *Shema* and the prayer for immersion. Finally, Isaac lowered his body fully beneath the surface of the pool, lifting his feet off the floor until he floated like unborn child in his mother's womb. When he walked back up the steps, he looked the same but was changed. For female converts like Sarah, there was no circumcision, just the ritual at the bath house. A female attendant rather than the beth din witnessed her naked submersion. Once the siblings' ablutions were finished, the Brandons were born again: pure Jews with the biblical figures Abraham *avinu* (our father) and Sarah *imeinu* (our mother) as their new parents.[3]

Tzedek ve-Shalom bath house with *Mikveh* inset where Isaac Lopez Brandon and Sarah Rodrigues Brandon completed their conversions. Photo by author, 2007.

The simplicity of the process belied the enormity of the change. First there was the danger of being circumcised as an adult before the trip to the bath house. For eight-day-old male infants, a *brit milah* was not particularly dangerous, but for adult converts in an era before either microbes or anesthesia were well understood, having one's foreskin removed was a true test of one's faith. Fortunately for Isaac, Suriname contained an astonishing number of experienced ritual circumcisers. Even in 1767, seven men made their living this way in the colony. Yet Suriname's *mohelim* typically initiated the very young. Depictions of circumcisions and circumcision tools can be found on the gravestones of men honored for their craft, but they always feature a man holding a baby to be circumcised, never an adult.[4]

Though it is hard to believe Isaac would not have had some concerns about his manhood coming under the knife, at least the local mohel and Mahamad would not have flinched at Isaac's heritage as they might have in Barbados. Suriname's Jewish community was more diverse than that of Barbados or the Jewish communities of the early United States. During the brief British occupation of the Dutch colony (1805–16), Governor Pinson Bonham reported to London that Suriname's Portuguese Jewish community

Most male Jews were circumcised as infants. Detail of gravestone of Ribi David de Leon (1793) in the Old Sephardi Cemetery, Paramaribo, Suriname. Photo by author, 2007.

consisted of 745 whites and seventy-nine "coloureds." The High German (Ashkenazi) congregation contributed an additional 547 whites and sixteen "coloureds" to the mix. Initially, some of Suriname's diversity came from converting slaves or children born to Jewish men by women with African ancestry. Guidebooks for mohelim in Suriname even included prayers for circumcising and immersing slaves.[5]

By the time the siblings arrived in Paramaribo, however, many people with African ancestry had been Jewish there for generations, inheriting the covenant through their mothers and grandmothers. Yet even in Suriname, the community's inclusiveness had limits. Isaac would quickly have discovered that he did not conform to Paramaribo's ideal of the best Jewish male. According to Jewish law, after circumcision he was the same as any other man born into Judaism. Yet like the nearby meeting of the tea-stained waters of the Rio Negro and pale sandy water of the Rio Solimões in Brazil, traditional Jewish law and colonial prejudices ran alongside each other in an uneasy mix, touching but always refusing to recognize the other.

Behind this uneasy confluence stood the dream of equality. In November 1812, as Sarah and Isaac prepared for Chanukah, their destiny must have seemed as bright as the stars. The warm air was festive. Oil lamps with a reservoir for each night of the holiday lit the windows, and Jews filled the colony's streets. Unlike Bridgetown, where Jews made up only a small portion of the population, in Suriname roughly two-thirds of the white population was Jewish. Moreover, as Bonham's survey made clear, most Jews were Portuguese, like the siblings' father Abraham Rodrigues Brandon. Although Jews lived on streets spread across the town, many lived on the gorgeous, wide, tree-lined streets next to the synagogues.[6]

Yet lurking under the starlit sky were signs of trouble. It was not just the financial disparities that muddled the ideal of equality in the Jewish community, though that too was a problem. Paramaribo's Jewish community ranged from outrageously rich to unspeakably poor. When Dutch Jews became overwhelmed with refugees flooding into Amsterdam from Iberia and Eastern Europe, they gave migrants a one-way ticket to the colonies. Some Surinamese Jews, including the De Leons, Robles de Medinas, and Ledesmas, had prospered, building beautiful mansions along the *Waterkant* (waterfront). They also helped out their co-religionists in need: wealthy Jews had donated six dwellings to house the Jewish poor. It was not enough. Many of the poor continued to wait for their dreams of prosperity to be realized. Poverty and racism would mar the opportunities the colony offered.[7]

As the Sabbath ended on November 28, 1812, the first night of Chanukah began. Jews—rich and poor, white and not—left their wooden houses and walked along the shell-lined streets to the Jewish houses of worship. Disparity dogged their heels and followed them as they moved toward the city's two synagogues. Wealthy men dressed in dark suits, their necks wound tight and high with yard upon yard of heavily starched, fine Irish muslin. The neckcloths held their chins so upright that they could not have looked down to see their high polished boots even if they had wanted to. Their wives and daughters were dressed more colorfully, wearing deep blues or pearly white empire-waisted gowns, their hair piled aloft on their heads. Their throats were decorated with coral, ribbons, and delicate lace. Their feet whispered along the paths in beaded silk slippers. The poor dressed as best they could, almost certainly wishing for more.[8]

The interior of the synagogue would have been similarly magical on the first night of Chanukah. Like the candles, promises were held up high, just out of reach. The small, curved oil Chanukah lamp that hung on the wall was the least of the sights awaiting the siblings. Hundreds of candles filled the multi-tiered lamps that hung above the synagogue's floor, making the radiant brass globes glow from within. The mahogany altar would have

Mansions along the *Waterkant* (waterfront). Jacob Eduard van Heemskerck van Beest, *View of the Government House in Paramaribo* (ca. 1860–1862). JCBL. Original in the John Carter Brown Library at Brown University.

been open, revealing the velvet-wrapped Torah scrolls. In front of the altar, ten candlesticks stood with impossibly tall tapers. Shorter candles rested above the dark wooden benches, sparkling like small stars, the polish of each bench reflecting the light back up as if the benches were covered in white silk. Light also bounced off the high, white, wood-domed ceiling and the rounded purple glass arches above the windows, giving the interior a transcendent, regal air.

The holiday marked the rededication of the Temple and of Jews to God. On the first Chanukah, ancient heroes had thrown out an enemy, buried the idolatrous past, and built a new future. Yet while the holiday of Chanukah was intended to mark the banishing of non-Jewish ways, prejudices nurtured by the British and Dutch governments were not so easily eradicated. Instead of throwing out non-Jewish ideas, the Jewish leadership had allowed them to play a role in determining who got to sit on which synagogue bench, who was honored in the congregation, and even who got buried where. All might be Jews, but colonial law and even the nação's own history dictated that not all Jews were the same.

Sarah and Isaac had leapt gracefully over the first stumbling block placed before them in the path toward social success. The siblings had chosen to become nação, and throughout the Atlantic world, and particularly in Suriname, being nação meant being better. This sense of self was in some ways a defense against years of denigration. For generations, descendants of forced converts in Iberia had been blamed for natural disasters, economic downturns, and disease. They were also told they were physically and spiritually inferior to other Iberians due to their supposedly impure blood. Spanish Franciscans had prohibited people with Jewish ancestry even four generations back from being part of their elite order. Their excuse was that New Christians inherited Jewish qualities such as arrogance and greed that made them spiritually impure and dangerous. When the nação complained within the hearing of Old Christians, or just made themselves anything but invisible, they were hauled before the Inquisition and tortured, judged, paraded for general amusement, and even burned at the stake. Now that the shackles were gone, the nação sometimes bolstered their pride by separating themselves from others. Once people had judged them, but now the nação would sit in judgment.[9]

In Amsterdam and London—the main feeder communities for Suriname—being nação meant being better than gentiles *and* other Jews. Back in Amsterdam, the Portuguese called Ashkenazi Jews *tudescos* (Germans), but they also used the very same word to mean beggar or servant. This was not all prejudice: the Ashkenazi refugees escaping pogroms *were* often indigent, and sometimes turned to begging or even crime to feed themselves. When not pleading for help, Ashkenazi Jews were at times patronizing about their Talmudic knowledge, which they valued far more than courtly manners and Iberian languages. Overwhelmed by the Ashkenazi poor, members of the Portuguese synagogue of London decided they would allow tudesco foreigners to stay in the community for only four days, after which they would be sent to Rotterdam or Amsterdam on the first available ship. In Amsterdam, the nação created further distinctions by forbidding Ashkenazi women from entering the Portuguese synagogue altogether. When alliances did occur, the resulting marriages were stigmatized.[10]

In Suriname, things were not much different. Although the Portuguese had initially allowed Ashkenazi Jews to pray with them, in 1735 they drew a line. The nação sold their majestic synagogue on Keizerstraat to the High German Jews and built Tzedek ve-Shalom for themselves alone a few blocks away. Apparently even this was not enough of a distance. In the 1750s, the Portuguese congregation instituted regulations similar to those in Amsterdam and London that restricted the participation of High German Jews in the Portuguese synagogue and demoted anyone who married tudescos to a secondary status of *congregante* (congregant) rather than *yahid* (full member). Just as *limpieza de sangre* (purity of blood) had disadvantaged people with Jewish ancestry in Iberia, now the same sort of logic was turned against other Jews who were not nação.[11]

In coming to Paramaribo, then, the Brandons sought to enter not just any synagogue, but the elite inner sanctum of the nação. They did so by virtue of their father's Portuguese roots. Yet while ancestry was important, by the time the Brandons arrived in Paramaribo, people also proved they were truly nação by being sophisticated, genteel, and erudite. This was harder for people born enslaved, as it involved learning not one, but several, languages. Despite their past sufferings, the nação were proud of their Iberian heritage. Spanish was used in the prayer books and taught in school. Portuguese was often the language used for sermons and synagogue records. Even the Jews of Bridgetown wanted a *hazan* who would be able to teach the synagogue's young to *ladinar*, that is, to read the Pentateuch in the ornate, Baroque, elegant Spanish used in the nação's prayer books.[12]

More so than in Barbados, the elite families of Paramaribo's Portuguese Tzedek ve-Shalom synagogue were aggressively cosmopolitan and Francophilic in ways that must have been exciting, if not intimidating, for the Barbadian Brandons. Whether at the dinner table or gathering at the theater, the nação of Paramaribo prided themselves on their refinement. While the Brandons were in town, The Risen Phoenix, a Jewish literary society, put on productions of *Artaxerxes, or Innocence Defamed* (a tragedy) and *Nymph of the Spree* (a farce). The plays sponsored by The Risen Phoenix complemented the Portuguese literary salon Docendo Docemur ("we are taught by teaching"). There the nação studied the classics, as well as scientific writings.[13]

The nação's cosmopolitan culture intertwined the generations. In 1785, leaders of the Portuguese community argued vociferously for the need for a college specifically for Jewish students that promoted an extensive education in liberal arts and the sciences, including Jewish and Dutch history, agriculture, navigation, commerce, philosophy, medicine, and politics, with lectures alternating between French and Dutch. It is unclear whether Isaac availed himself of these learning opportunities while in Paramaribo, but other Jews of color certainly did. Members of the nação who were too old to be educated in such an institution were often self-taught bibliophiles, with private libraries that included hundreds of books on subjects ranging from literature, philosophy, and medicine to Jewish theology. Their libraries demonstrated their polyglot culture by including works in French, Dutch, Spanish, Portuguese, Latin, Hebrew, and English.[14]

As Sarah would quickly learn, being worldly was not just for men. The domestic sphere was similarly cosmopolitan. One late eighteenth-century Dutch Sephardic cookbook reveals that the nação's food was a sophisticated, multicultural blend. Although Portuguese Jews cooked *stokvispastei* from dried whitefish, as the Dutch did, they used oil instead of butter, making it easier to serve with a meat meal. They also had recipes that recalled Iberia with chickpeas and spinach, and tarts with almond paste. Even today the popular Surinamese drink *Orgeade*, made from a syrup of almonds, sugar, and either orange blossom or rose water, is thought to be a Portuguese Jewish contribution to local culture.[15]

In sum, to be nação was to belong to something important. But it was also a community divided among themselves, often along racial lines. When the Brandons stepped off the boat at the *Waterkant*, they nestled in, taking their place among the ranks of other Brandons, some of whom were white families like the Pereira Brandons and Hoeb Brandons. During the 1790s, male members of this part of the family numbered among the regents of the Sephardic congregation. Yet nearby also lived the "colored" families of Annatje Brandon, Susanna Brandon, and M. S. Brandon, and the Black family of Adjuba van Brandon. We do not know if Sarah and Isaac sought out any of these extended kin, but if they had, they would have heard some stories that would have disheartened them.[16]

When the siblings arrived in the city, Susanna Brandon lived on Zwartenhovenbrugstraat, just a half a block west of the High German synagogue on Keizerstraat. Zwartenhovenbrugstraat was a middling sort of street where houses ranged from some of the town's poorest to almost respectable. Susanna Brandon could have told her Barbadian kin that being multiracial nação in Paramaribo was a mixed blessing at best. Like Sarah and Isaac, Susanna and her three children were listed as "colored" rather than Black in the city's 1811 census. Terminology mattered. In Paramaribo, as in Bridgetown, racism oppressed even free, lighter-skinned people with African ancestry, even as it encouraged those same people to wield the color line against people with darker skin or the enslaved. White Jews might refer to all multiracial congregants as "mulatto Jews" (*mulatten joden*), but among themselves, multiracial Jews clung to the small gradations in status that the color line provided, insisting they be called *couleurlingen* (coloreds) rather than mulatten, as couleurlingen was a more indefinite term that included lighter-skinned people. Intraracial prejudice thrived in early Suriname.[17]

One impact of this intragroup prejudice was that Susanna Brandon owned slaves, just as (Sarah) Esther Lopez-Gill did. Enslaved people outnumbered the free in Susanna Brandon's household. Five people enslaved were "colored" (four woman, one boy, one girl), and six Black (one woman, one boy, one girl). Of the Blacks, four were creoles—that is, they were born in Suriname—while the other two had begun their lives in Africa. Susanna Brandon used European names for the "colored" people she enslaved— names like Johannis and Frederica—but called enslaved Blacks names that tended to call attention to their Africanness or enslaved status, such as Coba. Black people in her house also did harder, more heat-exhaustive labor such as cooking and washing.[18]

The much more limited household of Adjuba van Brandon (a Black woman) reflected the disadvantages of the color line. "Van" before a last name may sound fancy to people in the United States, but in colonial Suriname the van in Adjuba van Brandon's name indicates she had not been born free but was once enslaved to the Brandon family. Unlike Susanna Brandon, who signed her census form, Adjuba van Brandon did not, strongly suggesting she had not had the same access to education as people like Susanna Brandon who were born free. Moreover, Adjuba van Brandon and her son Johann Brandon (also listed as Black) were on their own. No enslaved people washed their floors, cleaned their clothes, cooked them food, or helped them earn money for a brighter future.[19]

Whereas Adjuba van Brandon was most likely related to the nação through labor rather genealogy, Susanna Brandon's family had strong kin ties to the Portuguese community. Yet they still seemed stuck outside of it. In this way, Susanna Brandon's position was similar to that of Sarah and Isaac when they had lived in Barbados. Although each of Susanna Brandon's children appears to have had a different father, two of her children bore explicitly Sephardic names: Joshua Henriques Brandon and I. D. de Lyon. Moreover, Susanna Brandon's signature suggests she too had Sephardic influence and education, as it contains the *rubrica* (flourish) typically found under signatures in Iberia and cultivated by members of the nação in Western Europe and the colonies. Unlike Sarah and Isaac, though, Susanna Brandon never crossed over to Judaism: when she died in 1822 at about fifty-six years of age, her son Joshua Henriques Brandon buried her in the Nieuwe Kerkhof—the New Cemetery of the Dutch Reformed Church.[20]

Other Surinamese Brandons with Portuguese and African ties, including Sipora van Brandon, would have told Sarah and Isaac that white bias kept multiracial children of nação at bay. Sipora van Brandon, a free woman of color, was named for Moses's wife in the Hebrew Bible. The name itself predicted her marginal status: Tzippora was married to Moses but was born to a Kenite priest. Indeed, when van Brandon's son was born she gave him the very non-Jewish name of Christian Matatias Brandon. Born around 1799, Christian Brandon was almost exactly the same age as Sarah. Like Sarah and Isaac, Christian Brandon's father was white. The border between whites and people of color was more fluid in Suriname, though. Dutch colonial records marked down Christian Brandon's race as "mustee"—that is, one-eighth African—and specified his mother was a "mulatto," meaning she had one African and one European parent.[21] These nuances had not mattered

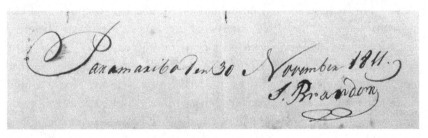

Signature of Susanna Brandon with a Sephardic-style *rubrica*. 1811 Census, Paramaribo. 278/24, No. 576.

as much in Barbados. As the daughter and granddaughter of two white men and two multiracial women, Sarah was technically also a "mustee," but St. Michael's Church did not bother with such distinctions.

Like the siblings, Christian Brandon had clear Jewish ties. Despite his non-Jewish first name, when he died at the age of ten in 1809 he was buried by Jacob León Aron, a Jew, to whom his mother bore at least three other children. Christian Brandon's marginal status was not just about his name but about structures that kept his parents apart.[22]

For despite her Hebrew name and free status, Sipora van Brandon never married Jacob León Aron. The lack of marriage limited her son's prospects. According to the nuances of Surinamese racial law, if Jacob *had* married van Brandon in the synagogue, their son would have been categorized as white instead of "mustee" or "colored." Even if Jacob married van Brandon after their sons were born, Christian Brandon's race would have changed retroactively from "colored" to white. Whitening was such a normal part of Surinamese society that one scholar has estimated that while only about 10 percent of Suriname's Jewish community was officially designated "colored," the majority of Jews in Suriname during this era had at least one African ancestor.[23]

Nevertheless, no offer of marriage was in the wings for Sipora van Brandon. Jacob León Aron married a different woman, Abigail Salomons, whose father was extremely wealthy. Like Jacob, Abigail Salomons was deemed white. Salomons went on to bear Jacob a brood of legitimate, white children. As Sipora van Brandon knew all too well, even when white paramours were unmarried, they often refused to marry non-white lovers.[24]

After arriving in Suriname, Sarah and Isaac would discover that the very synagogue they hoped to join was partially to blame for white men like Jacob being reluctant to marry their multiracial partners. Moreover, despite having suffered in-group hostilities themselves, the High German congregation was not any better. This meant that even after conversion, Sarah could not hope for much better treatment in Suriname than either Susanna Brandon or Sipora van Brandon had endured. If the siblings' paths had crossed with fellow Jewess Mariana Levij, she too could have told them of how the white Jews' restrictions had marred her life before and after marriage.

Although born Jewish, Levij had lived out of wedlock for years with David de Vries, a High German Jew of European descent. She bore him three children before he finally agreed to marry her in the synagogue. De Vries had not refused to wed Levij because he was anti-marriage. When he was only nineteen, de Vries had been married briefly to fellow Ashkenazi (and European) Jew Rachel Polak, who had died tragically in childbirth within a year of their wedding. Nor was de Vries unconcerned about sin. On his first wife's gravestone, de Vries himself is called a *Hakham*, that is, a man with extensive religious training. The inscription made sure people knew de Vries was the minister of the High German congregation as well as the son of "the late prominent and eminent, our honored teacher . . . Abraham de Vries."[25] Yet despite his religiosity, local prejudice had kept him from marrying Levij until a few months before his death.

A color line divided de Vries's treatment of Levij from his behavior toward his first wife. Like de Vries's parents, Rachel Polak's family had come to the South American colony from Amsterdam. The same year Polak was born in that bustling Dutch port, half a world away her future husband was born near the muddy waters of the Suriname River. Their marriage represented the merging of two families at the center of the Jewish community: like de Vries, Polak was the daughter of an Ashkenazi leader, judge, and teacher. It was an even match.[26]

De Vries's alliance with Levij was not. Although Levij's grandfather Jacob Levy had been born in Amsterdam, some of her maternal relatives were descendants of slaves, forcibly transported to Suriname from Africa. Born to Jewish fathers in the colony, the mixed-race children had converted, and they and their descendants co-existed—sometimes uneasily—with the rest of the Jewish community. Like other mixed-race Jews who were considered non-white, they were *congreganten,* second-class members with limited rights, not *yahidim,* full, voting members.

Some of Levij's kin married other openly multiracial Jews. This was the path taken, for example, by Levij's sister Lea Levy. Yet women like Mariana Levij, who chose (or were forced into) sexual relationships with European Jewish men, usually faced the discrimination encountered by mixed-race people in the colony more generally. Only rarely did European men recognize relationships with mixed-race women through a religious ceremony. Although technically interracial marriages were legal as early as the 1760s, most European men preferred to formalize relations with mixed-race partners via a form of concubinage known as a Surinamese marriage. While Surinamese marriages made the men financially responsible for their partners, they simultaneously gave the men the flexibility to take a white wife if they chose to do so. Sometimes multiracial women with property claimed they preferred concubinage, because married women were stripped of their property rights whereas concubines retained control of their estates. Although owning property was not relevant in Levij's case, it probably was a factor in Susanna Brandon's life, as she owned eleven enslaved people at the time of her death.[27]

In addition to the biases in general Surinamese society that encouraged white men not to marry women of color, the synagogues created further disincentives by demoting those who tried to legitimate their relationships. Demotion was most likely on David de Vries's mind when he delayed in marrying Levij. Shortly after de Vries wed Levij under a *chuppah* in the sweltering November heat of Paramaribo, de Vries was officially demoted to the same status as Jews of color. Although he had previously been the congregation's president, now de Vries could no longer serve in the synagogue's leadership. Moreover, when he died, he would be buried in the swampier, second-class section of the cemetery, in spite of his European origins. Although de Vries formally objected to his wife's non-white classification and to his subsequent demotion, the penalty stuck. De Vries was officially white in secular society, but in the synagogue he was nonetheless treated as non-white by virtue of his marriage. Moreover, while de Vries and Levij's children might be recognized by the secular government as white, religiously de Vries's demotion extended to his children who, according to the synagogue regulations, would be "considered mulatto until the second generation."[28] To be sure, a demoted man's descendants could eventually become white again if male heirs married white women for two generations. Still, men's loss of status was so strong a deterrent that Jewish marriages between yahidim and congreganten were extremely rare. Stories like Levij's were the norm in Paramaribo's Jewish community during the years the siblings settled there.[29]

Yet if Sarah and Isaac heard about prejudice in the Jewish community, so too did they learn something about rebellion. David de Vries's deathbed protests were a faint echo compared to the highly vocal outrage Suriname's multiracial Jewish community expressed over their mistreatment. This outrage had come to a head in 1793 when Joseph Cohen Nassy, one of the leaders of Darhe Jesarim passed away. Darhe Jesarim, literally "path of the righteous," was a fraternity or *siva* that had been set up in 1759 to provide "colored Jews" a place where they could worship without being constantly reminded that they were considered inferior. It also allowed them to be fully Jews. For in addition to being given second-class status in the white-led synagogues, the "colored Jews" were denied basic religious rights. In the regular synagogues, for example, Jews of color could not say prayers for the dead, nor could white Jews say them on their behalf. So, the colored Jews built their own *godhuis* (synagogue) on Sivaplein where they could worship in peace. At Darhe Jesarim, men of color could be yahidim, free to educate their young and themselves in the ways of the Torah.[30]

Yet despite having their own siva, the members of Darhe Jesarim had no cemetery. Thus, when Joseph Cohen Nassy died, his family found themselves once again at the mercy of the white Mahamad. Although a leader of Darhe Jesarim, Nassy was allotted only a shallow grave in the cemetery's swampiest section. When Darhe Jesarim requested a more fitting place to bury Nassy, they were bluntly told by the Mahamad, "You people have got no . . . say here and if you don't shut up we will make you shut up."[31] *You people.* As if they were not also Jews! Even the Christians present were taken aback by how horribly the members of Darhe Jesarim were being treated. The whole thing was humiliating.[32]

In the end, Nassy was buried in the swampy section, but the leaders of Darhe Jesarim filed a twenty-page complaint. Of the approximately thirty-four signers, six were women; one was Jacob's wife, and another was Simha, relative of Isaac Nassy. Like Jacob Nassy's wife, she could not sign her name except with an X. However, this did not keep her from raising her voice in protest.[33]

When Sarah and Isaac Brandon arrived in Suriname, Simha Nassy was still alive to tell the whole story. She was also old enough to remember the early glory days of the Portuguese congregation Tzedek ve-Shalom before the onerous regulations of the 1750s had denigrated people who had too many ancestors who were not solely nação. She was also strong enough to have fought back against the discriminations waged against the "colored Jews." Simha Nassy was a matriarch of Darhe Jesarim. Born around 1737, Simha Nassy was listed as aged in the 1811 census. She would die only a few months after the census was taken and before the siblings received permission to immerse themselves in the ritual bath. Simha Nassy was one of the people who had rather ingeniously argued that the Jewish community's racist practices were actually contrary to Surinamese secular law.[34]

Simha Nassy was not the only member of her family to make this argument. Nassy lived with her son Jacob Nahar, who had also signed the 1793 complaint. Like many of the key signers, they had money and education on their side. Nahar was a *kleermarker*—a tailor with two tailor's apprentices, suggesting that Nahar had his own shop. The color line that oppressed Nahar and his mother also held them up above other people with African ancestry. There was a division, for example, between Nahar and his enslaved assistants: Nahar was "colored," his assistants Black. The assistants were not the only Blacks serving the household. Nahar also had a Black *huyshoudster* (housekeeper) named Janette, with whom he had had three young children named Isak, Doris, and Willemina. *Huyshoudster* was a local euphemism for a concubine, and Janette appears to have once belonged to Nahar even though she and her children were free at the time of the census. Neither Janette nor Simha Nassy had to do the housework alone: an enslaved house-maid named Amimba lived with them.[35]

In 1793, "colored" Jews like Nassy and Nahar used the education the nação prized so highly against the white Jews. Unlike his mother, who was one of the last to sign, Nahar's name was fourth from the top, right after E. Ximenes, Jacob Jesurun, and Reuben Arias. Although Simha Nassy could not write her name, her son signed his own elegantly on the petition and later on the census form. The complaint demonstrated that some Siva members could read and write, and they understood colonial and Jewish law well enough to challenge the colony's racial hierarchies by appealing to its own rules. The elevated prose undermined the idea that the *couleurlingen joden* were second-class at anything.[36]

The 1793 complaint echoed earlier agitations for rights by members of Darhe Jesarim. In 1790, Ruben Mendes Meza and Ismael Britto had requested full community rights. In response, the white Mahamad suggested that Darhe Jesarim's leaders draw up a proposal of how to expand Darhe

Pierre Jacques Benoit, Jewish shopkeeper in Paramaribo (ca. 1831), *Voyage a Suriname . . . cent dessins pris sur nature par l'auteur* (Bruxelles, 1839), plate xvi, fig. 32. JCBL.

Jesarim from a siva (fraternity) into a separate congregation. In good faith, the leaders of Darhe Jesarim responded. They asked for a separate space with the same religious rights as other nação but with continued access to Tzedek ve-Shalom's poor relief, cemetery, and *mikveh*. Disappointment followed. Tzedek ve-Shalom was fine with a separate place for "coloured Jews" to worship but had no intention of giving them privileges even in that separate space or providing them full access to Tzedek ve-Shalom's poor relief.[37]

The white Mahamad's response to the 1793 complaint was even more brutal. The Mahamad ordered Darhe Jesarim to disband immediately. Anyone who continued to worship there or be involved in any way would be fined 75 guilders. Founders who continued their involvement would be fined 150 guilders. Either amount was a huge sum of money, given that less than 100 guilders could buy passage all the way to Amsterdam. Even more devastating than the edict itself was the response of the colonial authorities, who somewhat predictably sided with Tzedek ve-Shalom's Mahamad and white privilege. By 1794 Darhe Jesarim ceased to exist as a separate community. The couleurlingen joden were once again second-class members of the white-governed synagogues.[38]

Hence when Sarah and Isaac Brandon arrived in Paramaribo, they appealed not to Darhe Jesarim but to Tzedek ve-Shalom for their conversions. Many of the leaders of the old guard of siva were still around. The treatment of Jews of color had improved somewhat from the contentious 1790s. Joseph Nassy's gravestone appears to have sunk into the swamp, but others were buried on higher ground. When Simha Nassy died a little over two months after the census at the age of seventy-four, she was commemorated with an elegant stone in the Tzedek ve-Shalom cemetery. Yet inequities persisted in the city, even though white visitors described it as a bucolic Eden.[39]

European travelers wrote of how straight the streets were along the waterfront and how they were lined with orange, shaddock, tamarind, and lemon trees. Their branches were weighed down with fruit. Orange blossoms perfumed the air from December to May. The gravel streets and walkways reminded one visitor of England's elegant manicured neoclassical gardens, their surfaces strewn with white and purple-tinged sea shells. The depth of the gravel meant that even in the rainy season, the streets were dry. Residents could walk while keeping their shoes and skirts clean. The travelers' diaries paid little attention, though, to who had to labor daily to keep the city neat and tidy.[40]

Paramaribo's order came at a cost. Blood marred the idyllic, shell-covered streets. Advertisements for runaways highlight the daily assaults waged upon the bodies of people of color. In 1811, Benjamin de Abraham de Vries posted one such announcement, because one of the women he enslaved had escaped. De Vries promised a reward if she were returned, even as he warned that those who harbored her should "beware of the Consequences."[41] As in so many such advertisements, de Vries coldly noted he had branded her with his initials: B.A.D.V. Her name was Mariana, and Benjamin de Vries was the brother of the now deceased David de Vries. The name was an unhappy coincidence, but the brand spoke to the violent tactics whites used to keep people in their designated places.[42]

Often the very things that were designed to show the colony's order revealed its chaos. The first Dutch governor, Cornelis van Aerssen van Sommelsdijck, had planted row upon row of tall royal palms at the city's edge, a monument to the tranquil lawfulness of his reign. Yet as almost everyone knew, his control was a ruse. Van Sommelsdijck had been killed by mutinous soldiers shortly after he finished planting the regiments of palms. Moreover, for members of the militia, the palms echoed the colony's interior—a place in which Dutch order did not prevail. Paramaribo's careful urban garden was mocked by the actual gardens of the Maroons, the descendants of enslaved Africans who had escaped into the jungle and had planted crops using both local and African knowledge. As the Scottish mercenary John Gabriel Stedman noted, European soldiers often had to steal the abundant peas, rice, and cassava planted by these rebels when European provisions ran short. Yet most depictions of Surinamese life use African slaves to mark the margins of cultivated society. Artists carefully placed people of color outside the supposed pastoral bliss they helped create, as on a teacup depicting the Jewish town of Jodensavanne. For the Brandons, this Dutch-Jewish vision of a clean, orderly society with outsiders at the margins symbolized their reception within the town's Jewish community.[43]

Runaway advertisement for Mariana. *Surinaamsche Courante* (1811). University of Florida Library.

If the Portuguese synagogue seemed unwilling to help the siblings surmount Surinamese racism, Sarah and Isaac's own father was even more so. According to the 1811 census, the siblings began their stay in Suriname as free people of color. As people with at least three white grandparents, Sarah and Isaac would have been considered white if Abraham Rodrigues Brandon had married their mother. He did not. The issue of their parents' marriage was moot for the siblings while they lived in Barbados. Bajan interracial marriages were virtually impossible, but even if Brandon had married (Sarah)

Pastoral depiction of the Jewish town of Jodensavanne with people of color at the margins. Teacup (ca. 1800–1840). Jewish Historical Museum, Amsterdam.

Esther Lopez-Gill, Barbados's one-drop understanding of race meant the siblings' race would not have changed on the island anyway.[44]

Suriname was different, but their father was not. Abraham Rodrigues Brandon and (Sarah) Esther Lopez-Gill did not marry in either Surinamese congregation, even though (Sarah) Esther Lopez-Gill could easily have traveled to Suriname to convert. Isaac had his foreskin removed in order to be closer to his father. Why did Abraham Rodrigues Brandon not make an equivalent sacrifice for Sarah and Isaac? Had humiliation of demotion deterred him? After all, even if Brandon had married in Suriname, his children still would not have been white in Barbados. Moreover, unlike David de Vries, Brandon was not about to die. Abraham Rodrigues Brandon would live another twenty years after his children's conversion. He would find other ways to raise his children's status, but marrying their mother was not one of them.

So even after their hard-earned conversion, Sarah and Isaac decided not to stay in Suriname nor to marry there. Instead, the siblings journeyed back to Barbados, where they rejoined the network of their extended kin, and where Isaac could nestle into the island's synagogue life. Paramaribo had taught them more than just how to be good nação. Sarah would take this lesson forward, as she prepared for her future role as a Jewish wife and mother. Isaac, however, would also grasp hold of the path laid by the "coloured Jews" of Paramaribo, who had used legal means to rebel against injustice. It was a tradition Isaac would need to draw upon, as race was as vexed an issue in Barbados as it had been in Suriname. The question would become this: when the Barbadian Jews took sides with the island's white Anglicans, where would Isaac's father Abraham Rodrigues Brandon stand—with Isaac or against him? Before Brandon would have to face that choice, the Nidhe Israel synagogue erupted in a salacious controversy that would highlight the contested role people of color played in Barbadian Jewish life.

4

The Tumultuous Island

Bridgetown, 1812–1817

IN THE MONTHS JUST BEFORE Sarah and Isaac's conversion, rumors began to fly through the yard surrounding the Barbadian Synagogue. The yard was home to the families and servants of the congregation's four main employees—the *hazan* (spiritual leader), the beadle, the ritual slaughterer, and the bath attendant. The most devastating of these rumors involved news that Hazan Raphael Abendana suffered from a "Urethra Complaint" so similar to venereal disease the doctor found it impossible to determine which he had.[1] This complaint was most likely either gonorrhea, yaws, or "the great pox"—what today we would call syphilis.[2] The community was mortified.

On the island, venereal disease was commonly interpreted through a racial and religious lens. It was not just that African bodies were deemed more susceptible to venereal disease: some whites believed that both yaws and the pox had originated in Africa and were transmitted to Europeans through the slave trade. Venereal disease became a way to think about sexual and racial contamination. Ironically, one of the men charged with figuring out how that "contamination" had come to the synagogue complex was Abraham Rodrigues Brandon, Sarah and Isaac's father.[3]

The period of 1808 to 1812 had been years of flux in the leadership of Bridgetown's Nidhe Israel Synagogue. Ever since the death of the learned Hakham Isaac Karigal in 1777, the congregation had not had the best of luck with spiritual leaders. Barbados had gone into an economic free fall following the American Revolutionary War. Consequently, the synagogue

46

could barely afford to feed the Jewish poor, let alone attract religious elites of Karigal's caliber.

Despair rings throughout the various petitions the Barbados *Mahamad* made to London for a new hazan to lead Nidhe Israel's services between the 1790s and 1810s. Previous experience made members of the Mahamad unusually blunt. After the death of Hazan David Sarfatty de Penha in 1797, for example, they pleaded with London's Mahamad to send someone who at least had "a sufferable good Voice" and understood enough Spanish to be able to teach the children to read the Torah and prayer books in that language. Ideally the man should also be a Shochet and Bodec—that is, someone who could ritually slaughter and inspect meat.[4]

Then they were more pointed: this time could London please send someone who was married and hence less susceptible to "wicked habits" than his predecessor?[5] Apparently David Sarfatty de Penha had suffered from an attachment to strong drink. Even the schoolchildren had lost faith in him. London responded, but yet again neglected to send its finest. From 1799 to 1808, the congregation suffered through the erratic conduct of Hazan Emanuel Nunes Carvalho—even firing him once in 1805—before he finally fled north to New York in 1808.[6]

So, when Abendana arrived on the island in 1809 shortly after marrying Jessie ("Yahat") Israel at London's Bevis Marks synagogue, the community must have given a sigh of relief. Abendana was a family man. After settling into Bridgetown, Jessie Abendana gave birth to their first child, Joseph, in 1811. Unfortunately, things then went downhill. When the chaos erupted in the fall of 1812, Jessie Abendana was well into her pregnancy with their second son, Isaac. While his wife was indisposed, the Hazan appeared to have had "defiled himself" with another woman, quite possibly a woman of color who had left their employ after falling pregnant.[7] The question in the Mahamad's mind was, was it this woman who had passed along the venereal disease, or was that from yet a further indiscretion?

So it was that on Friday, September 4, 1812—a mere two days before the start of Rosh Hashana—the Mahamad found themselves at a crossroads. The Gentile doctor who examined Abendana "Leaned to the most favorable Construction" of the situation, but the synagogue governance board less generously called upon the Jewish residents of the synagogue yard to testify about the Hazan's misbehavior over the past few months. The news was not good.

Congregants repeated overheard exchanges and servants' gossip about how the Hazan had impregnated the young hired woman—a "Negress" who was "constantly following him around the yard."[8] This young woman—the alleged mother of the Hazan's unborn, illegitimate child—had subsequently been cast out of the yard by the Hazan's outraged wife.

The Hazan's indiscretions were not the only ones plaguing the community, however. Ironically, only a few months before, Hazan Abenadana had been asked to chastise other congregants for their sexual misbehavior. High on that list was Rebecca Valverde, the young wife of Raphael Gomes. Once Raphael Gomes had been a man of power. In the 1790s, he was the *Gabay* of the synagogue, and in 1799, he and Valverde wed. By 1811, however, he was dying. Valverde was not sympathetic. Instead of tending to her dying spouse, she had taken up with a Mr. Castello. When confronted by Abendana about the situation, "Mrs. Gomes came up and behaved in a most scandalous & indecent mann[er,] declared Mr. Castello had kept her nine Months & that if he left [her she] would go on the Town & much more to the same effect."[9] The synagogue board sputtered their outrage at her defiance.

The men on the board bided their time. When Mrs. Gomes's son Jacob Valverde Gomes was born in March 1811, the Mahamad huffily recalled her disobedience and refused to circumcise the child or give Mr. Gomes synagogue honors for the birth of a son that clearly wasn't his. Despite his own indiscretions, Abraham Rodrigues Brandon led the charge against Mrs. Gomes. Notably silent amid all this tension was her husband, Raphael Gomes. Then on March 31, 1811, fifteen days after Jacob was born, Raphael Gomes was dead. Mrs. Gomes continued to balk at the synagogue leaders' attempts to control her.[10]

Instead of bowing to pressure, she took her infant son Jacob north to New York, where the extended Gomes clan apparently had not heard of her scandals—or did not care. When she died two years later, her son was adopted by Isaac Gomez Jr., a prominent member of Shearith Israel, who raised the boy as his own and encouraged him to enter the jewelry trade. Sadly, Jacob, too, would die young when he drowned in a hurricane off the coast of Key West. Attempts to silence Mrs. Gomes and discredit her son were moot: she and her child simply traveled beyond the reach of the Barbadian Mahamad's wrath.[11]

If Rebecca Valverde Gomes's loud voice disrupted men's attempts to limit her sexual practices, by 1812 Abendana would find that female voices could also weigh in judgment on his own indiscretions. According to rabbinical law, witnesses should be free, mentally and morally suitable, older than thirteen, and above all men. Women—like slaves—were disqualified in most instances. It must have rankled Abendana, then, when the Mahamad not only listened to the women of the synagogue yard but also sought out their evidence.[12]

Sarah Massiah, the bath attendant, went first, inserting the gossip of the enslaved people frequenting the complex into her own testimony. Mrs. Massiah explained that it was not just that the young woman in question followed Abendana constantly around the yard, but also the other "Negroes . . . entertained no Doubt" that there had been a liaison.[13] Despite relying on testimony from non-whites, Mrs. Massiah admitted she herself had overheard no disputes or jealous spats between the Abendanas.

Mrs. Massiah also vindicated Jessie Abendana of wrongdoing: she thought the Hazan's wife did not know of or had chosen not to believe the rumors. She claimed that as far as Mrs. Abendana was concerned, the servant had been fired for losing some money Hazan Abendana had given to her to spend on the family's behalf. Mrs. Massiah's testimony would prove key in undermining Abendana, and in the Mahamad's ultimate decision to help Jessie and her children, even as the Mahamad censured Abendana himself.

After Sarah Massiah's testimony came that of the two required male witnesses. Interestingly, they too, sneaked in illegal testimony on the behalf of the enslaved and female residents of the complex. Like Mrs. Massiah, Moses Belasco had heard the "same Talk am[ong] Negroes, of such an improper Connection," and was similarly inclined to believe it.[14] Weighing heavily toward the Hazan's guilt was his own cryptic irritation in a complaint he made to Belasco that one of his female servants "would do Nothing for him."[15] Belasco took Abendana's innuendo to be sexual.

The testimony of Judah Massiah, an elderly resident of the complex, was similarly damning. Judah explained that before "he Lost his Sight he had been Eye Witness to such instances of Familiarity as left no doubt on his Mind that a connection Existed between Mr. Abendana & his hired Servant."[16] Mr. Massiah had also overheard jealous spats, and he introduced damning evidence from a second woman, Betty Massiah, who visited but did not live in the complex. Furthermore, Mr. Massiah had overheard the servant herself say she was pregnant with Abendana's child. Even if the Mahamad did not want to accept the word of a woman of color, a white woman who was a previous employee had sworn to Judah that she had been forced to leave "Mr. Abendana's Service, in consequence of his Attempting to take improper Liberties with her."[17] Altogether, the witnesses' testimony painted Abendana in a horrible light.

Despite Abendana's refusal to admit any guilt, the Mahamad removed the hazan from the yard, sending him back to London. On Mrs. Abendana, however, they took pity. Jessie Abendana was far advanced in her pregnancy, and her husband had already spent all his salary. She was given a present of $40 from the public fund. Half was offered immediately to help her through the holidays, and the other $20 would be granted upon her delivery.[18]

The Mahamad's pity did not extend, however, to the pregnant servant, about whom nothing else was said. Did she miscarry or give birth? What happened to the child? Although we will probably never know, an odd fact remained: even in one of the most Jewish spaces on the island, the testimony of one of the lowest-ranking members of Bajan Jewish society, a non-Jewish, enslaved woman of color, could undermine the authority of what should have been the highest-ranking religious voice in the Jewish community— the hazan. Over the next two decades, Jews and Protestants would find that women and the color line constantly challenged white, male, religious authority. In multiple congregations, the Brandon-Gills would be at the center of those disputes.

Yet even as Abraham Rodrigues Brandon found himself trying to quell the controversy swirling around the synagogue yard, some positive changes were happening in his family. First, there were celebrations. On January 30, 1811, Brandon's niece Jael Rodrigues Brandon married a promising young man from London, Abraham Israel Keys. For his first few years in Barbados, Keys was only a marginal figure in the synagogue, but thanks to the bad behavior of Abendana, six years after he married Jael Rodrigues Brandon, Keys would become the hazan of congregation Nidhe Israel. There, as in other congregations, he would be an essential ally to the Brandon clan.[19]

The years just before and after the siblings' trip to Suriname proved similarly crucial for their mother's family, as the multiracial Gills rose to respectability and prominence. Their mother (Sarah) Esther Lopez-Gill's large family expanded. Grandfather George Gill's old house on Hartley's Alley became home to Jemima Lopez-Gill and the siblings' uncles. (Sarah) Esther Lopez-Gill's half sister and brother and their mother Joanna lived just down the street and adjacent to the Old Church Yard.

For the Lopez-Gills, the years before and after Sarah and Isaac traveled to Suriname were filled with both joy and sorrow. By 1814, the siblings' three uncles would be deceased, but before they passed away, the men had married into the upper circles of Bridgetown's free-colored community. William and Alexander Gill also left behind a new generation of young Gills to follow in their footsteps. In addition to their cousin Jael Rodrigues Brandon, by 1813 five Gill first cousins lived in Bridgetown: George, Mary, and Sarah Ann Gill—children of William Gill and his wife Elizabeth Tate—and Edward and Alexander Bovell Gill—sons of Alexander G. Gill and his wife Ann Jordan.[20]

The match between Gill and Jordan was the most spectacular. Jordan was a young heiress and a member of the free-colored elite. Like the Brandon-Gills, Jordan owed much of her financial status to her white father, who had left her a legacy in his will. In 1799, she had inherited £1,000 and a furnished home and carriage house on Church Street. She also received a £50 annuity and four slaves.[21]

By the time of her death in 1865, Jordan had become the best-known member of the Brandon-Gill clan, though Alexander George Gill might have been hard pressed to prophesy that when he married Jordan in 1809. For despite her later courage, Jordan's early life appears to have been somewhat frivolous. One contemporary described young Jordan as a woman of "fashion and pleasure."[22] Not much distinguished her from other wealthy free women of color about Bridgetown, whom one naval surgeon disparaged as "very expensively dressed after the European fashion, parading the streets, attended by their slaves, with no small dignity."[23]

Such women were accustomed to beautiful clothes, jewelry, and a lifestyle that rivaled that of wealthy whites. According to sympathetic abolitionists, wealthy people of color in Bridgetown filled their parlors with large libraries of literary and scientific works that emphasized tasteful learning, cabinets with minerals and shells, and bell jars with rare specimens of taxidermied South American birds. The parlors and all they held were meant to symbolize their owners' inborn elevated senses. Wives dressed to display their modesty, dignity, chastity, and elevated style. In both Britain and the British West Indies, this was the era of taste, a time when the proper display of material goods spoke both to one's affiliation with London—the imperial center—and one's "natural" refinement. Taste directly informed politics and was tied to citizenship and liberty.[24]

Only Anglicans could vote or hold office. Moreover, the Anglican church had long played a crucial role in the taste making that signaled political prestige. Dress and domestic decorations spoke to a person's allegiance to the king. Likewise, devotion to the Church of England emphasized dedication to the monarch who headed it. Like any proper house, the Anglican church was, ideally, ruled by proper conduct. The elegance, refinement, and taste of church interiors encouraged that behavior.[25]

Churches like St. Michael's in Bridgetown did more than remind worshippers of the heavens to which they aspired. They embodied British values that interwove godliness, morality, and good governance. With its airy height, coral stone walls, and high classical style, the newly rebuilt St. Michael's Church was so spacious and elegant that one British visitor to Bridgetown remarked: "Its interior strikes with an air of magnificence."[26] For Anglicans it made sense that only Anglicans could vote, as their church promoted an orderly society.

In Bridgetown, part of the Anglican church's good governance required that each worshipper be delegated a proper place in the church. This meant no matter how wealthy they were, free people of color had to sit in the pews behind whites. When there was not enough room, they sat upstairs in the hotter seats with the enslaved, though more often than not the latter were not admitted at all. Wealthy women of color like Ann Jordan Gill suffered these indignities if they wished to demonstrate their attainment of imperial style.[27]

Thus, on May 20, 1809, when Ann Jordan wed Alexander George Gill, she did so at St. Michael's Church in Bridgetown. It was the same church to which Sarah and Isaac—as well as their uncle himself—had come years before to be manumitted. In order to be married there, Jordan and Gill would have first submitted to an Anglican baptism. Marrying at the island's foremost church meant Alexander George Gill and Ann Jordan had to submit to white society's rules about race, but church marriages also offered social privileges.[28]

Just like their choice of where to wed, Jordan and Gill's early married life was both conventional and revolutionary. Their children were nearly the same age as the oldest children of Raphael and Jessie Abendana: Edward George Gill was born in 1811, followed by Alexander Bovell Gill in 1813. Gill Sr. was a businessman in Bridgetown, and shortly before he died, he signed a petition to protect the interests of free men of color involved in trade and shopkeeping.[29]

Gill Sr. was similarly involved in other petitions made by free men of color leading up to a slave rebellion in 1816—for example, a request for the privilege of testifying in court. Almost no wealthy, free men of color participated in that 1816 rebellion, but it marked a turning point in their lives. By the time the rebellion hit the island, Gill Sr. had already died, yet those who were left behind—including his wife Ann Jordan Gill and his nephew Isaac Lopez Brandon—would learn from the chaos left in the rebellion's wake.[30]

The 1816 slave revolt began suddenly on the southeast part of the island. White colonists were unprepared. Robert Haynes, a white man who worked on a plantation near where the violence started, had been so convinced of his slaves' devotion that he slept with his bedroom door wide open the night the rebellion began. He also had felt comfortable enough to leave £10,000 currency unprotected in his house.[31] He wouldn't make the mistake again.

Yet despite an initial brilliance, the insurrection ended almost as quickly as it started. British troops crushed the revolt within a week, but by then more than 1,000 enslaved people had lost their lives. Others were sentenced to transportation. Property damage was estimated at £175,000—a sum with the economic power of roughly £750 million in today's money. The revolt would come to be known as Bussa's Rebellion, named for its leader, the African-born slave Bussa, who died trying to claim freedom for enslaved Barbadians.[32]

Although the rebellion failed to overthrow the island's racial hierarchy, it did encourage the Assembly to pass legislation to ameliorate the conditions of people with African ancestry. Unfortunately, most of these changes were intended to reward free people of color who had supported the rights of slaveholders rather than the enslaved themselves. Several contemporary reports applauded Afro-Barbadian militia men's role in suppressing the revolt. The largest praise was reserved for wealthy, free men of color, whom the leading whites felt were "of the most respectable of that class [and] whose conduct, with scarcely any exception, at the period of the Insurrection, had been highly meritorious."[33]

In the years following the revolt, free people of color would seek compensation for their support during the insurrection. Petitions rather than open rebellion were the new path to power. In Bridgetown, free people of partial African and Jewish ancestry often found themselves in the center of debates about civil rights and religious freedom. Men like Benjamin William Massiah and John Castello Montefiore—members of two key Sephardic families on the island—would sign and author petitions written by free men of color agitating for civil rights. Like the Jews of color in Suriname, they demanded equality with whites.[34]

As in Suriname, in Barbados women of color played a crucial part pushing for change. Mary Montefiore and Mrs. Benjamin Massiah, for example, played essential roles in Afro-Barbadian charities such as those for educating the female poor. They also led Anglican women's auxiliaries. These charities were run out of St. Mary's, a new church specifically intended for both the white and "coloured" populations in northern Bridgetown. St. Mary's was built on the grounds of the ruins of the Old Church Yard adjacent to where Christian(a), John, and Joanna Gill lived.[35]

The memory of these charitable efforts would later be emblazoned on the Bridgetown landscape, in the shape of commemorative plaques at St. Mary's Church and a public water fountain erected in John Castello Montefiore's memory after he died in a cholera epidemic. The graves of wealthy people with mixed Jewish, African, and British ancestry lie nestled under the perfumed blossoms of a plumeria tree in St. Mary's Anglican graveyard.

Yet for all their defiance, the pleas for better conditions by free people with African ancestry typically did not align with abolitionism. In 1817, more than one in five free people of color on the island owned slaves, including Ann Jordan and Alexander G. Gill. When Gill died in 1814, he left Jordan only a wooden house on leased land and a couple of enslaved people. She did better without him. By 1817, Jordan owned ten slaves: a man who worked as a carpenter, a lady's maid, a cook, two washerwomen, a house maid, three girls to help around the house, and a woman to help at the market. Like many wealthy people of color, Jordan used enslaved labor to maintain a lifestyle of privilege.[36]

Owning ten people freed Jordan from hard labor and set her apart from free people of color who owned slaves only because they had bought or inherited their own kin. Many saved to buy family members in order to free them from service to others or—if funds were available—to manumit them outright. Particularly after 1801, when the cost of manumission skyrocketed, owning kin became a common way to protect loved ones born enslaved. By 1815, the siblings joined the ranks of those who owned their family members. Once enslaved, Sarah and Isaac now became enslavers. Yet again it was their former owner Hannah Esther Lopez who played a key role in their transformation.[37]

For years Hannah Esther Lopez had lurked nearby, either emotionally supporting or draining the Brandon-Gills, depending on one's point of view. For years the siblings lived within her orbit. Lopez dwelled nearby on Swan Street, just down the road from Abraham Rodrigues Brandon's house, and around the corner from the Gill house on Hartley's Alley. Lopez's proximity was not coincidental: the siblings' ties to Lopez remained strong in ways that are difficult to understand from a modern perspective. In many ways the siblings were Lopez's closest family.

Despite convoluted kin ties to most of the Sephardic Jews on the island, all of Lopez's immediate blood relations had either died or left the island by the time the siblings returned from Suriname. Lopez was already a widow when her oldest son Isaac Lopez died in 1804. His death left her bereft of immediate family on the island. Her daughters-in-law Devora

Cohen Belinfante and Rachel Lindo had long ago died from complications in childbirth, and Belinfante's son Mathias Lopez, who shared a first name with his first cousin, had died shortly after them at the age of ten. Hannah Esther Lopez's only surviving son, Moses Lopez, lived abroad. Two decades earlier he had run a prosperous store in Bridgetown, but by 1795, he had taken Hannah Esther Lopez's remaining grandchildren off island to live in the United States.[38]

In the absence of any blood kin, Hannah Esther Lopez made a sort of family with her former slaves. Lopez's will suggests strong ties to members of the Brandon-Gill family. When Lopez died in 1815, she left the Brandon-Gills the most intimate objects from her life. (Sarah) Esther Lopez-Gill received "a Chest of Drawers, a Press that is in my Bedroom, a China Jar and all the Articles and Things that are in the Closet in the Garrett"; Isaac Brandon got "a large Desk, two small Desks and a Dutch Case"; and Sarah Brandon inherited "three Trunks, a Cedar Chest, all my Chairs and a Pitch Pine Chest."[39] These were the most personal items Lopez willed to anyone. Hannah Esther Lopez's own surviving grandchildren went completely unmentioned.

In many ways, Lopez's attention to the Brandon-Gills is surprising. Most Jewish widows on the island left their belongings to their own children, or—when they lacked close kin—to extended family or female friends of the same age. Moreover, Lopez also willed the Brandon-Gills their enslaved relatives: the children inherited their great-grandmother, Deborah, and (Sarah) Esther Lopez-Gill received "a mulatto Girl Slave named Rachel," most likely her daughter born sometime after 1801.[40] Lopez's choice to leave her former slaves their kin was odd. Slaves were valuable, and most owners willed slaves to white friends or relatives. By leaving the young Brandons their great-grandmother, Hannah Esther Lopez assured Deborah Lopez a home in her old age and freed her from the worry of being sold to new owners.[41]

In leaving personal possessions to the Brandon-Gills, Hannah Esther Lopez showed some sentiment for the siblings and their mother, but exactly how much is unclear. Did she leave Deborah Lopez to the young Brandons out of kindness or because she thought her own son and grandchildren would not be able to sell the aging woman? Likewise, one wonders whether she felt something special for her former slaves, or whether she was just lonely.

One thing we do know is that Hannah Esther Lopez's regard for the Brandon-Gills is echoed by other members of the Jewish community. When

Isaac Brandon later appeared in the synagogue board's minutes, the *parnas* not only commented on Isaac's wealth but also pointed out that "his conduct is most exemplary."[42] Female members of the congregation also favored him. Many years later when widow Rachel Lindo (née Massiah) prepared her will in 1841, she made Isaac Brandon one of her executors and spoke of him as her "esteemed friend."[43]

That friendship persisted despite Isaac's humble origins. Although Rachel Lindo was not biologically related to Isaac and Sarah, her sister-in-law had married Hannah Esther Lopez's nomadic son Moses Lopez. Lindo almost certainly knew Isaac Brandon as a child, yet their relationship survived Isaac's change in status from slave to free and from Christian to Jew. Moreover, in 1819–20, Lindo's sons Abraham Lindo and Jacob Lindo fought alongside Isaac and Abraham Rodrigues Brandon to achieve rights for Barbadian Jews. It was a fight that ended poorly for Isaac. The petition for rights sparked one of the greatest controversies within the congregation, a crusade that would ultimately end with Isaac being demoted to a second-class Jew. Lindo's regard for Isaac more than twenty years later is an important reminder of just how contentious that decision to demote him was.[44]

One person who was not part of that ill-fated decision, however, was Hannah Esther Lopez's wandering son Moses Lopez. He was too busy with troubles of his own in the far-away, cold North, in the very city where Isaac Brandon and his mother would one day land. Yet while the Brandon star was on the rise, Moses Lopez's destiny was in free fall.

5

Synagogue Seats

New York and Philadelphia, 1793–1818

ONE WOULD HAVE BEEN HARD pressed to believe it two and a half decades earlier, but by his death in 1818, Moses Lopez was teetering on the edge of poverty. Before Lopez left Barbados, Hannah Esther Lopez's son had been a prosperous merchant with a house, bustling store, country estate, and numerous enslaved people to attend to his personal whims. Yet after Moses Lopez was laid to rest in the hallowed ground in the Mikveh Israel Cemetery on Spruce Street in Philadelphia, his son Matthias Lopez was forced to swear before the Philadelphia Register's Office that his father was not worth more than $500. Most of what Moses Lopez left would have gone toward the burial. Being worth too much really *was not* the family's problem.[1]

When he died, Moses Lopez did not even own the three-story building that served as both his home and "medical repository."[2] Perhaps Lopez's potential patients had recognized that despite publicizing himself alternatively as a "Physician" and "Dentist and Bleeder," Lopez had little training.[3] The shelves of his medical room were almost empty. Most of his possessions were nostalgic reminders of Lopez's past glory: a gold-headed cane, a feather bed, two fancy chairs, a lacquered side table painted with Asian motifs, and a bundle of Hebrew books. In the end, everything added up to less than $280, including his medical supplies.[4]

Sarah and Isaac had undoubtedly grown up overhearing tales of Moses Lopez's travels north from Hannah Esther Lopez. Long before Isaac Brandon was born, Moses Lopez had been his mother's golden child. As a youth, Lopez caught the eye of Isaac Karigal, who came to the island in 1775. Karigal nurtured the young Lopez, and Lopez had dedicated a series of Kabbalistic meditations to the Palestinian sage for the counting of the Omer between Passover and Shavuot. The book was not the only sign of Lopez's friendship with the illustrious rabbi. When Karigal became ill two years later, Moses Lopez was the official witness to the rabbi's will.[5]

The relationship clearly meant something to Lopez. He cherished his copy of the small Omer book, a duplicate of the one he had given to Karigal, dragging it along on his travels. It was one of the works in that bundle of Hebrew books found in his house after his death. Judaism ran at the center of Lopez's life. Later his son Matthias Lopez would donate the small volume to the Philadelphia Library Company.[6]

Yet in addition to his religious connections, Moses Lopez was a man of the world. He had inherited his father's store just before the tropical storm of 1780 wiped out much of Bridgetown. Months later, Lopez was still paying for repairs on his house "Suffer'd by the late dreadfull Hurricane."[7] Despite the storm, his fortune grew. Then he won the hand of Rachel Lindo, one of the best matches on the island. Lindo was well connected and had inherited the queenly sum of £8,000 from her father Isaac Lindo on his death in 1780. The young couple married at the Nidhe Israel synagogue in 1782. A son was born, named Matthias for Lopez's deceased father. Then Rachel Lindo became pregnant with another child. He would be named Isaac Lopez, in honor of her father as well as her husband's mentor, the recently deceased Rabbi Karigal. The second birth, however, turned out to be a mistake.[8]

One day Rachel Lindo was a vibrant young woman of thirty. The next day, she lay dead of childbirth in the August heat. Lopez had cheerfully indicated previous life events in his store's account book, but on the dates surrounding Lindo's demise, there is no note in Lopez's register, just an appalling gap of business *not done* and the sad scratch of a pen trailing ink at the end of the summer of 1787. Lopez continued to eke out entries in the account book for another two years, his sons always on his mind. In the very last entry in the book, for example, Lopez paid Samuel Genese for a year's school fees for his elder son Matthias Lopez: 1 pound 5 shillings. The entries just before it show Lopez's mother Hannah Esther Lopez also continued to receive her son's favors, walking out of the store with fine handkerchiefs, yards of striped linen, and other sundries. Meanwhile Abraham Rodrigues Brandon was buying green silk. Moses Lopez was not the wealthiest Jew on the island, but he was far from the poorest. The yearly *finta* tax paid to the synagogue showed he owned far more than his mother.[9]

Moses Lopez's contributions mattered. The men on the synagogue board bolstered him back up after Rachel Lindo's untimely death. In 1791, Lopez was elected *Gabay*. Being treasurer was a huge responsibility. Since there was no secular welfare on the island, each congregation collected taxes and distributed funds to co-religionists who for one reason or another needed help to get by. As the holder of the synagogue funds, Lopez now listened to endless petitions from those worse off, never realizing that one day he would be on the other end of the requests. One day Lunah da Fonseca begged for "a few Suits of Cloaths [clothes] for her Son" so he could attend school and the synagogue.[10] Another day Mordecai Levy, an emissary from Shusan in Persia, pleaded for "some Soccor towards the Relief [of] their distress'd Brethren in that place."[11] Most often the *Mahamad*—including Lopez—voted, but other items were left to Lopez's discretion. Yes to the clothes, no to the Jews of faraway Shusan. The reasons were not recorded.[12]

Lopez's biggest Jewish triumph came in 1792, when five years after his wife's death his peers elected him *parnas presidente*—leader of the congregation. It was the highest office available to Lopez on the island. The next year he remained on the Mahamad. But the island's economy continued to flounder, leaving the Jewish school without a teacher. Maybe it was the yellow fever epidemic of 1793 that broke Lopez's will. The pestilential fever ravaged the Caribbean, jumping from island to island. When it reached Barbados in late 1793, 800 people died before October was over. Their skin took on a yellow cast. Blood oozed from their noses, mouths, and eyes before seizures set in. Those who did not die often wished they had.[13]

Just as the epidemic was winding down, the ill-regarded hazan David Sarfatty de Penha arrived on the island to restart the Jewish school. When Lopez and his father Mathias before him were children, the island's Jews had been able to attract a high caliber of men for the community school. Around 1700, flush with sugar money, Nidhe Israel had built a large two-story stone school building in the synagogue yard. In its heyday, the school was run by men like Karigal, Mehir Cohen Belinfante, and Abraham Gabay Yisidro, all of whom were well educated at European or Middle Eastern *yeshivot*, Jewish schools where they learned not only the Torah but also the Talmud and Jewish law. When they died, their gravestones boasted they were *hakhams*, Torah sages, not hazans like Abendana, Nunes Carvalho, or Sarfatty de Penha. By the 1790s, however, the congregation couldn't afford anything better than a hazan.[14]

Yet even as a hazan, Sarfatty de Penha was a disappointment. His alcoholism and "natural Slothfulness of disposition," the board minutes recorded, made him an unpopular educator and leader.[15] Unlike the glorious hakhams of years past who studied Talmud, Sarfatty de Penha "studied all he could to Shrink from his duty in every Sense, & would scarcely teach the Children the Hebrew & Spanish [a]ltho he Engaged so to do."[16]

For all his faults, Sarfatty de Penha initially seems to have understood that his future success depended on the good will of the Mahamad. Shortly after he arrived, he penned a manuscript for Lopez, a book of blessings for circumcision. It is unclear whether Lopez commissioned the book or Sarfatty de Penha just took the opportunity to ingratiate himself to his new boss. Either way, Sarfatty de Penha began the manuscript with an obsequious dedication. To mark the year, Sarfatty de Penha used the quote "And no prophet shall rise again in Israel like Moses," to which he appended the name "Lopez," making it an amusing variant on Deuteronomy 34:10.[17] His flattery did him little good. Lopez wasn't there to help Sarfatty de Penha when the latter drowned his reputation in drink. As the island's economy failed, those who could leave did. Among the mobile was Lopez, who along with his two young sons and his Hebrew books had left, traveling northward. Fifty years earlier, cities like Philadelphia and New York couldn't compare to the riches of the West Indies, but by the 1790s the northern cities bustled with opportunities both economically and Jewishly.

The dream of a better Jewish education awaited the Lopezes. The first record of the family in New York was Matthias and Isaac Lopez's names on the list from 1794–95 of youngsters attending Shearith Israel's newly formed Hebrew language school. The school was not a haphazard undertaking; rather, the long lists of regulations reflected parents' concerns about education. Equally crucially, they assured that there would be sufficient wood and a real schoolroom with benches, tables, and a stove. The contract with the teacher stipulated that regardless of each student's social status, the students were not to be asked to engage in "domestic or menial services under any pretense."[18] This was key, as it signaled that unlike fledgling congregational schools in London or the orphanage schools for Amsterdam's poor that trained lower-class Jews for a life of service, New York's Jewish children were to be society's leaders.[19]

Books abounded. Schoolmaster Simeon Levy proposed that he would pay strict attention to the students' morals as well their "religious duties."[20] Although coeducational, the school was meant to bind boys together; all boys under thirteen were to sit together in the southwest corner of the synagogue during services. Presumably this camaraderie spilled over into the

Sundays from 10:00 AM to 1:00 PM and weekday afternoons when they were in class.[21]

In sum, the Hebrew language school was everything Sarfatty de Penha's Barbadian school was not. Although originally under the control of Simeon Levy, by the time the Lopez boys arrived, the New York school, like the congregation, was led by the ever energetic Reverend Gershom Mendes Seixas. Gershom Mendes Seixas was held in high regard, and for good reason. Over fifty years, he had admirably guided two congregations. His main home was New York's Shearith Israel, but during the Revolutionary War, he reigned over Mikveh Israel of Philadelphia. Seixas was also a trustee or regent of the Humane Society, Columbia College, and the University of the State of New York.[22]

The contacts Matthias and Isaac Lopez made at Seixas's school were equally impressive. The first three years' rosters read like a who's who of the next generation of East Coast Jewry. It was not just the last names of Lazaus, Cohen, Hart, Henriquez, Levy, Nathan, and Zuntz. Children like Mordecai Manuel Noah, Isaac B. Seixas, and Joshua Moses would be the Jewish intellectual, religious, and financial leaders of their day. By bringing his sons to New York, Moses Lopez gave them a Jewish education unavailable on

Portrait of Reverend Gershom Mendes Seixas (1745–1816), of Congregation Shearith Israel, New York. MCNY.

Barbados and connections with the next generation's principal Jewish American families.

The Moses family epitomized the connections the Lopez boys made at the school. The patriarch of a brood of ten, Isaac Moses, sent two of his sons, Joshua and Israel, to Seixas's school. Although he lived most of his adult life in New York, Isaac Moses followed Seixas to Philadelphia during the Revolutionary War. There Moses helped establish the first Mikveh Israel synagogue, on a lot on the north side of Cherry Street, between Third and Fourth Streets. As in New York, Isaac Moses became the congregation's parnas.[23]

Moses built his empire from the ground up. After arriving in New York in 1764 from Giessen, Germany, Moses built a fortune in international trade and privateering. In 1780, his Pennsylvania property was appraised at £115,200, making him the wealthiest Jew in Philadelphia. Even after he moved back to New York, he maintained important partnerships with Philadelphians Michael Gratz, the city's most important Jewish merchant, and Stephen Girard, one of the richest Americans.[24]

When he returned to New York, Isaac Moses founded the Bank of New York and invested deeply in real estate. Yet there were few appropriate

John Wesley Jarvis, *Portrait of Isaac Moses* (early nineteenth century). Oil on canvas. MCNY.

matches for the children of affluent Jews such as himself. Of Moses's ten children, only four would marry. The oldest, his daughter Richea Moses, married her maternal uncle Aaron Levy, cementing Moses's ties to that well-to-do, devout family. This left three younger daughters: girls whom Lopez could only dream his sons might marry. Jewish New York was limited. Isaac Moses's sons Solomon and Joshua Moses found matches elsewhere.[25]

The reach of families like that of Isaac Moses was felt far beyond the upper Atlantic. As merchants, the families traded in the key ports in Europe, India, and China. As the youthful face of their family's business, Moses's sons, now young men, would venture to distant lands. Solomon Moses traveled to Madras and Calcutta in search of precious textiles that could bolster the family's fortune. If Matthias or Isaac Lopez could marry into the clan— or even form mercantile partnerships with them—the Lopezes might regain what they had left behind in Barbados.[26]

It was not to be. The Caribbean connections of New York and Philadelphia's Jewish families did mean, however, that the Lopezes' schoolmates would play a key role in the Brandons' lives. One classmate would become Isaac Lopez Brandon's business partner and marry his sister Sarah.

Before that change, however, Moses Lopez dragged his sons about the upper Atlantic coast of the newly founded United States for twenty years, living in New York, then Newport, and finally Philadelphia. Each place he moved, he seemed to get worse off. By the time he ended up in Philadelphia, Lopez was running the ill-fated medical repository. Though the term "repository" suggests pretensions of grandeur, synagogue records show Lopez struggled to make ends meet. If he had stayed in Barbados, there would have been no question of the synagogue extending a helping hand during his old age. In Philadelphia, his only hope for financial support as he grew older was a congregation filled with men who owed him nothing.[27]

Moses Lopez would learn this the hard way when, between 1813 and 1816, he wrote several letters repeatedly requesting admission to Mikveh Israel as a member. As he would later complain, each time his application was met by "Silence" for reasons the Mahamad did not bother to give.[28] On the face of things, Lopez had some right to be disgruntled, as other men were admitted into the congregation at the very meetings at which his application was ignored. Those gentlemen, however, were in good financial standing, while Lopez was not. He had become just one more impoverished, elderly outsider destined to be a burden on the community.[29]

Even the Lopez boys' former classmates did not bother to speak on Moses Lopez's behalf. Almost everyone on the Philadelphia Mahamad had connections to the small Shearith Israel class that Matthias and Isaac Lopez had attended in the 1790s. Benjamin Jonas Phillips and Hyman Marks—the *parnassim* of 1814–15—were both brothers-in-law of the Lopezes' classmates. Other men on the Mahamad were linked to the schoolroom through Joshua and Israel Moses. Joshua Moses was fourteen in 1794 and Israel Moses barely nine when the pairs of siblings met. Matthias Lopez was almost the same age as Israel Moses, just barely ten, and Isaac Lopez only seven. Although neither of the Moses boys grew up to serve on the Philadelphia Mahamad, they were related to almost everyone who did. In 1806, their older brother Solomon Moses had married Rachel Gratz. Strikingly beautiful, Rachel Gratz and her sisters were known as the three "Graces"—a play on their last name. Gratz would be the subject of a Gilbert Stuart painting, a Thomas Sully portrait, and a Romantic miniature by Edward Greene Malbone.[30]

Although today Gratz is remembered as the younger sister of philanthropist and educator Rebecca Gratz, in 1806 she was known as the daughter of Philadelphia's leading Jewish trader, Michael Gratz. Through their marriage, Solomon Moses and Rachel Gratz united two great merchant houses of the upper Atlantic coast. Solomon Moses was also the brother-in-law of three mainstays of the Philadelphia Mahamad who declined to vote on Lopez's long string of petitions.[31]

Despite these connections, there were good reasons for the board members' silence. If nothing else, Lopez's timing was extremely poor. When Lopez began to ask for admittance to the synagogue, the country was in the middle of its second great war with England, which lasted from the summer of 1812 to February 1815. The war made the coffers lean. Blockades meant trade was down, and many of the younger generation were fighting rather than earning money. For a fifty-six-year-old man of little means like Lopez to ask for admittance was tantamount to asking for the congregation to take care of him in his old age, however long that might last. Moreover, Lopez was not the only one asking. The war brought a flood of refugees. Consequently, Mikveh Israel introduced a residency requirement for membership in 1813, the year that Lopez first sought admission. Suddenly, any applicant had to have lived in the country for at least six months before applying for membership and had to be a member for two years before becoming an elector (a member with voting rights). No waiting was required, however, if the applicant was born in the United States and his father was already an elector. The new rule preemptively undercut a takeover by the refugees from the West Indies.[32]

Anonymous, Rachel Gratz
Moses. Based on miniature
by Malbone. Rosenbach
Museum.

One reason the congregation may have sought to limit West Indian influence was that Mikveh Israel was gripped with a nationalist fervor. Lopez
discovered that it was an inopportune moment for someone who was nominally British to request help from a US congregation. A generation earlier,
in the 1780s when congregation Mikveh Israel had sought to explain why
Jews deserved equality, Jewish men's willing service in the Continental Army
topped their list of their reasons. Their sons agreed. In the years following
the war of 1812, several young Philadelphian Jews would write plays lauding
American soldiers' manliness, and parodying the British soldiers as ineffec-
tual dandies who went to war with hair powdered and corsets tight.[33]

For young men of Matthias and Isaac Lopez's generation, the war was
a chance to prove themselves as a different sort of man—men who wore
their hair in a natural, republican style and all it represented. Fighting tested
Jews' patriotism, young Jewish Philadelphian Joshua Moses noted in his letters. As non-resident aliens, West Indian immigrants like the Lopezes were
excluded from the military's circle of honor.[34]

For many Philadelphians proving loyalty during wars was a family tradition. Joshua Moses's father had sold weapons to the Continental Army
during the revolution. After the war, the family returned to New York, but
later Joshua and Solomon Moses came back to Philadelphia to serve as agents
for their father's firm, Isaac Moses & Company, before striking out on their
own. They became pillars of the Philadelphia congregation. The War of 1812
was yet another opportunity to prove Jewish loyalty to the nation.[35]

One reason Philadelphia's Jews felt compelled to display their patriotism
was that Jews were often considered resident outsiders, and hence Jews' right
to vote and hold public office was far from guaranteed. Mikveh Israel's elders
had worked hard for Jewish enfranchisement in Philadelphia, but Jews' political rights still varied by state in 1812. As late as 1840, Jews had limited
rights regarding voting and holding office in New Jersey, North Carolina,
New Hampshire, Connecticut, and Rhode Island.[36]

Moreover, while Jews had struggled for the right to vote, that privilege
could easily be lost. With the help of Dutch Jews, the first Jewish settlers in
New York had fought for the right to stay in New Amsterdam, and then to
gain the privileges other colonists took for granted. By 1688 Jewish freemen
were finally able to vote in early New York. Then in 1737, Jews were singled
out and lost the right to vote in the colony's legislature. In 1777, New York
City once again gave Jews full political rights, but the state was the exception. Voting privileges were in constant flux in the early nation, and
all around them Jews saw other marginalized groups losing their rights.
Women, for example, had initially been allowed to vote in eighteenth-
century New Jersey, New York, and Massachusetts, only to have their fran-
chise eliminated by 1807. Likewise in the 1780s, free Blacks in five northern
states had the right to vote. Yet several states subsequently overturned the
privilege, including Pennsylvania in 1838. States such as New York that did
not recall enfranchisement often limited Black voting to only a handful of
people by inserting high property qualifications for free people of color into
state constitutions. Jews, like other people at the margins, must have understood that any rights they had could disappear in an instant.[37]

So when the US Army asked for volunteers, the Jews with whom the
Lopez brothers had gone to school in New York stepped up to enlist.
Matthias and Isaac Lopez's former classmate Isaac B. Seixas, later the hazan
at New York's Shearith Israel, served as a second corporal in the Richmond
Light Infantry Blues. Five other classmates also served in New York
infantries. Their relatives in Philadelphia were equally eager to volunteer.
Isaac B. Seixas's cousin David G. Seixas fought, and he survived to go

on to found the Deaf and Dumb Institute in Philadelphia. Despite their family's wealth, Benjamin and Joseph Gratz both enlisted, as did some-time Philadelphian Aaron Levy, who became the parnas of Shearith Israel as well as the captain and paymaster of the 9th Regiment. Uriah Phillips Levy, later promoted to the rank of commodore, advanced his naval career during the war.[38]

Lopez classmates who had moved to Philadelphia were also among those who enlisted, including Solomon Seixas. Even Joshua Moses, who had returned from London only a few short months before the war—he had worked there for years as a merchant—proved his mettle by becoming a major in the 2nd Battalion of the 1st Brigade of the Pennsylvania Militia. In contrast, neither Isaac nor Matthias Lopez fought. According to the logic of the time, by not serving against the British they failed to resist tyranny, thus displaying for all that they did not deserve a voice in either the new nation or the congregation. Their lack of patriotism for their adopted homeland must have reinforced their outsider status, making their father's pleas for help even more suspect.[39]

So it was that request after request made by Moses Lopez to the Philadelphia Mahamad went unanswered. Then, finally, the tide changed. In early 1815, the war ended. Moreover, Hannah Esther Lopez died back in Bridgetown, giving Moses Lopez's finances a much-needed reprieve. Hannah Esther Lopez's personal possessions and Sarah and Isaac's enslaved relatives went to the Brandons. The "Residue and Remainder" of her estate was willed to her faraway son Moses Lopez.[40] Perhaps most crucially, Moses Lopez finally inherited the £1,000 that his brother Isaac Lopez had invested in 1804 so that Hannah Esther Lopez could live off the interest "during the Term of her natural life."[41] Isaac Lopez's house, where their mother had lived, now also belatedly passed to Moses Lopez.

It was just the life raft that Moses Lopez needed. When he finally received the money, he donated a chair to Mikveh Israel and paid off his debts. After three years of waiting, he was admitted as a member of the Philadelphia congregation on September 15, 1816, a week before Rosh Hashana.[42]

His triumph would be short-lived. The donation was enough to buy him admission to membership, but Moses Lopez never played a central role in the congregation as he had in Barbados, where he was part of the Mahamad. His personal legacy in Philadelphia was so small that he is often misidentified by historians, who have tended to assume "Moses Lopez" was a Portuguese relative of Aaron Lopez, the wealthy Newport merchant, who did in fact have relatives by that name.[43]

Moses Lopez chair, Congregation Mikveh
Israel, Philadelphia. Photo by author, 2019.

Their confusion is understandable. Moses Lopez is *the* most common
male name in early Western Sephardic communities in the Americas. Were
it not for Lopez's son's more unusual first name, Matthias, and the fact that
Moses brought with him books from Barbados, it might have been impossible to disentangle him from the others. In the context of Aaron Lopez's
family, the donation had looked like typical largesse rather than the desperate bid for acceptance revealed in the congregation's minute books.

The donation, however, is a silent witness to Lopez's momentary increase
in funds and to the divide between which voices counted in early Jewish
life in Barbados and Philadelphia. Should religious training, money, or
actions determine a man's worth? For Lopez, lineage and religious devotion
trumped wealth or patriotic acts. But Philadelphia was the land of self-made
men, an ideology that infused both Jewish and Protestant congregations. It
was a city where men like Isaac Lopez Brandon could reinvent themselves,

while men who rested on the laurels of previous generations like Lopez sat on the sidelines.

Philadelphia's Franklinesque spirit of self-invention was lionized in the life story of congregant Jonas Phillips. Phillips had been one of Mikveh Israel's beloved founders; however, he had come to America with a status just above that of an enslaved person. Yet despite his humble origins, Phillips would tower over other congregants.

Phillips was born in Germany and arrived in Charleston, South Carolina, via London in 1759 as an indentured servant working for Moses Lindo, a Sephardic Jew. It is hard today to understand the lowly status indentured servants endured. Like other poor whites, apprentices and indentured servants were considered social outcasts. Their status was somewhere between colonizer or colonized, and between white and not white. Bound to their masters for a set time, indentured servants lay in a middle ground between enslaved and free. Yet Phillips served his time, moved north, and became a successful merchant. He served in the Continental Army during the Revolutionary War, proving his devotion to his new country.[44]

By the time Moses Lopez was petitioning the Philadelphia Mahamad for acceptance, Phillips and his sons were primary seat holders of the

Charles Wilson Peale attr., *Jonas Phillips* (ca. 1800). Oil on canvas. AJHS.

congregation. Having a seat meant your voice would count. In early American synagogues, the right to buy—rather than rent—a seat was the prerogative of electors. Anyone who wanted to serve on the Mahamad, or even begin or end the Torah scroll when the cycle of reading restarted on Simhat Torah and Shabbat Bereshit, had to buy a seat first.

Jonas Phillips's numerous children and grandchildren were seat holders. Although he was Ashkenazi, Phillips's children married into many of the important Sephardic families of the early republic. In 1813, his son Benjamin Phillips was a member of the Mahamad, of which he would become the parnas presidente in 1814. Jonas's younger son Zaleman Phillips likewise was one of the men who considered Lopez's fate. Other Phillipses from another branch of the family similarly served on the Mahamad, most particularly Levy Phillips, who as the Gabay controlled the congregation's funds during the years of Lopez's difficulties. Jonas Phillips epitomized the opportunity in Philadelphia to climb socially from one of the lowest ranks of society to founder of a dynasty. His grandchildren would be statesmen, playwrights, a commodore in the US Navy, and even the governor of South Carolina. Phillips was the congregation's model.[45]

His seat on the Mahamad also gave Phillips a voice in local politics. As the first parnas of Congregation Mikveh Israel in Philadelphia, Phillips addressed the Constitutional Congress in 1787, making the case against a Christian "test" for officeholders. He was key in fighting for full citizen rights for Pennsylvania's Jews. Philadelphia was a place where men made themselves rather than relying on inherited privilege. Although the congregation kept the donation, the chair given to them by Moses Lopez is a kind of emblem of Lopez's misunderstanding of what really mattered in the northern town.[46]

Lopez's donation struck to the heart of his plea for acceptance as a man who was trained not just in bleeding but in rituals like circumcision. Ritual chairs play a meaningful role in Jewish life. Other than pews, the most common seats in Western Sephardic congregations are chairs of Elijah for circumcisions, bridal couches, the *banca* where the men of the Mahamad sat, and chairs for the elected offices of Hatan Torah and Hatan Bereshit. Most surviving examples use expensive materials to showcase the high status of people leading ritual events. Conversely, the Lopez chair expressly eschews social ostentation. It centered status on rituals not money.

For anyone who has seen the elegant furniture used in London, New York, or Amsterdam's Western Sephardic synagogues, the Lopez chair is disappointing. For something that changed Lopez's fortune, the seat is deceptively simple in form. Indeed, simplicity is key to its message. Nineteenth-century Americans—Shakers, for instance—often shaped their furniture to emphasize spirituality rather than materialism. Lopez's chair emphasized spiritual values. It made the case that religious knowledge, devotion, and lineage, not money or earthly success, should play a role in determining who should have a voice in Jewish life. Some of the finest furniture made from elegant hardwoods was hand tooled by craftsmen in the upper Atlantic, but Lopez's chair rejects that ostentation.

One sign of the chair's simplicity is its awkwardness. Unlike many Jewish ritual chairs from this era, it appears to be repurposed rather than built specifically for the ceremony. The wooden back is decorated with two large, raised hands affixed with a screw. Above the hands is an inscription in Hebrew. Putting aside a few mistakes that suggest the work of a non-Jewish artisan, the phrase translates, "You shall bless the Children of Israel. Say to them [the Lord shall bless you and keep you . . .]" (Numbers 6:23). That is, it contains the introduction to the Priestly Blessing (*birkat kohanim*). Below the hands is a stylized book painted in gold and dated "RH 5577" (Rosh Hashana 1816). The oversized hands on the chair emphasize the blessing of the Kohanim, an ancient social rite dating back to the days of the Temple in Jerusalem.

The rite had weekly significance for Congregation Mikveh Israel, as Portuguese Jews tend to perform the blessing either weekly or daily. The chair acknowledges this ritual. The congregation's minutes note that the donor had the chair adapted to hold a basin and ewer for the Kohanim to wash their hands prior to the blessing of the congregation. Although at various points in the synagogue's history the chair was used as the Chair of Elijah during circumcisions, it is not clear when that tradition started or if it was the donor's intent. Either way, the chair emphasizes the routine religious devotions of Jews, but more particularly those born into Judaism rather than those like Isaac and Sarah who had had to convert.[47]

By focusing on the Kohanim, the chair pointed to the importance of male lines that could not be shared by converts. Kohanim inherit their priestly status from their fathers, but only if their mothers are also Jewish. Men like Isaac Lopez Brandon, whose father was Jewish but mother was not, could not inherit the status of a Kohen or Levite. Likewise, male Kohanim were prohibited from marrying either divorcees or converts. Women like Sarah Brandon who had converted to Judaism could never hope to give birth to sons who were Kohanim. The gift of a Kohen chair was a poignant reminder of the natural limits for converts. The chair underscores the inherent hierarchies in Judaism.

For all his bravado, Lopez's message was a bit misplaced. The ritual seat certainly would have appealed to hazan Jacob Raphael Cohen, who was—as his name suggests—a Kohen. But by 1811, Cohen was no longer the congregation's spiritual guide, as he had passed away. Instead, the Mahamad Lopez faced was made up of men who were more likely to be swayed by finances and pulling oneself up from nothing than by inherited religiosity. They included Benjamin J. Phillips (parnas), Levy Phillips (Gabay), Samuel Hays, Simon Gratz, and Benjamin Nones (*Adjuntos* [Members of the Mahamad]). Despite the fact that they used the same prayer book and same rites, the men Lopez faced as he asked for admission were different from those with whom he had grown up in Barbados.[48]

Highlighting the key role that those born into Judaism played in synagogue life was less politic in Philadelphia than Barbados. Unlike in Barbados, where conversions were rare, several members of Mikveh Israel applied to have their non-Jewish wives or partners converted so that they could remarry as Jews and so that their children would be Jewish. Thus, even men on the Mahamad had converts in their families. The Nathanses were regulars on the Philadelphia Mahamad, even though Moses Nathan wed Sarah Abrahams—a convert who had born him three children out of wedlock—and his brother Isaiah Nathan married Sophie Deacon, a gentile, in a civil ceremony before she converted in 1816. This was quite different from the Barbados congregation, which had avoided adding new members to its fold. Sarah and Isaac, after all, had had to travel to Suriname to become Jews. Philadelphia was more open-minded about what it might take to continue Jewish lines in the New World.[49]

Perhaps the greatest sign of Lopez's misplaced emphasis on unbroken lines rather than finances came just before his death, when the synagogue began to collect funds for the new congregation. Despite its reluctance to take on elderly pensioners, by the end of the War of 1812, Philadelphia's Jewish community had grown so much that its 1782 building had become too small. Thus in 1818 a subscription was started for a larger building. Money mattered because it could determine the congregation's future.[50]

Money would also tie that new building to the congregation Lopez had left behind. The small, innocent Philadelphian subscription incited a controversy in Barbados, pulling Isaac Lopez Brandon into the eye of the storm.

Sarah, however, was immune to the growing dispute. Unlike her brother, she had landed in London. As strife brewed on the faraway island, she would meet a gallant Philadelphian Jew who had once been Matthias Lopez's classmate. Their romance would spawn a new dynasty. First, however, her father would have to help her reshape her image, transforming her into a Jewish heiress. London was a place of new beginnings.

6

The Material of Race

London, 1815–1817

IT WAS SEPTEMBER 1815, AND Joshua Moses was oblivious to the controversies back at Congregation Mikveh Israel or the ones brewing on the horizon in Barbados. The thirty-five-year-old Jew was spending a series of exhausting days at the Liverpool docks examining fine cloth. His assignment was to obtain fashionable, high-quality items at the cheapest price. His reputation was at stake.

As a purveyor of fashion, Moses was his own best advertisement. With his well-tailored suits, Greco-Roman hairstyle, and stiffly starched collar that touched his ears, Moses was something of a beau-monde dandy. His clothing choices echoed that of Georgian-era style icon, Beau Brummell. A commoner whose mother had been a courtesan and his grandfather a valet, Brummell used clothes to create a new metropolitan manhood and to wheedle his way into the Prince of Wales's inner circle and polite society. Like Brummell, Joshua savored proximity to the aristocracy. After his death, Moses's children would find invitations to Napoleon Bonaparte's coronation and to a Jewish charity event sponsored by the Duke of Sussex.[1]

Yet unlike Brummell, who obtained most of his spending money through gambling, loans, and patronage, Moses had a day job as a merchant. He was only as good as the cloth he could buy for Philadelphia's market. As he hunted through the Liverpudlian warehouses, he must have had a keen sense that his future success as an American trendsetter hung in the balance.

Louis Antoine Collas, *Joshua Moses* (1804). Watercolor on ivory, 2 1/4 × 1 3/4 in. AJHS.

For while Moses was spending vast sums of money on the wharves, the banknotes were not his own. Rather, he drew from a £10,000 bank account provided by his patron, Stephen Girard. Unlike Moses, Girard was a recluse. A childhood accident had left Girard partially blind, and his damaged eye became the focal point of cruel taunts. Painters like James Lambdin, who was paid to present Girard well, made the best of things by placing Girard's unaffected side toward the viewer. Even so, with his floppy collar and limp necktie, no one would mistake Girard for a man of fashion. Shy and withdrawn, Girard sought out men like Moses to be his public persona.[2]

Like Girard, Moses earned his reputation in the trade. Moses had not always been a London man. After graduation from Shearith Israel's school

Georgian-era style icon,
Beau Brummell. John
Cook, *Beau Brummell.*
Engraving after unknown
miniaturist.

in New York, he floated back and forth between the Americas and Europe,
serving as the international liaison for his father's mercantile company, Isaac
Moses & Sons. When the War of 1812 stranded him in Philadelphia, he gal-
lantly served as a major in the Pennsylvania Militia. The military also had
its fashion lessons. With Hessian boots, tall-plumed hats, and high-collared
coats, military uniforms emphasized the same sort of over-starched mascu-
linity Brummell espoused. As soon as the war ended, Moses was back in
England hunting for the finest fabrics.[3]

His return was necessary because Girard had placed his confidence in
Moses's taste and Solomon Moses's business acumen. "Not being acquainted
with the kind of British Dry Goods which answer their Market," Girard
explained, he had turned to Solomon Moses to assemble an impressive list of
desirable items. Likewise, it was because of Joshua Moses's "long experience
and knowledge" that Girard trusted him to take that list and locate articles
that could best answer Philadelphia's Spring market.[4] Thanks to Solomon
Moses, Girard knew he needed fine white flannels, handsome light mixed
Cashmere—preferably in olive, brown, and blue—and black velveteens of
the finest quality. What Joshua Moses could not find in Liverpool, Girard expected his young Jewish protégé to scavenge up in London and Manchester.

James Reid Lambdin, *Stephen Girard* (1831). Oil on canvas. John McMaster Bach, *The Life and Times of Stephen Girard, Mariner and Merchant* (Philadelphia J. B. Lippincott Company, 1918), vol. 1. Hathitrust.

The list went on and on. Meanwhile, the boat that would take Girard's goods to the Americas was rapidly approaching the English coast.[5]

As if finding the most stylish fabrics at the best price were not enough of a challenge, Girard listed random other items (salt, copper nails, blankets) that Moses needed to obtain. Oh, and could Moses learn the price of cotton, rice, and tobacco and tips about China's market? It was a test on a mammoth scale. Ways of measuring worth today vary, but £10,000 in 1815 would have roughly the same purchasing power as £42 million today. If Moses's purchases did well, his business was made. If he floundered, Girard could find a new fashionable agent with a keen eye for cashmere and wool flannel.

For Joshua Moses, finding the right goods meant knowing his way around Liverpool's infamous docks. With roughly 100,000 inhabitants in 1810, Liverpool was twice the size of Philadelphia, and one and a half times the size of New York City. But in terms of merchandise there was no contest. Compared to the waterfront in Moses's American home ports, the Liverpool docks were enormous: wet-docks, dry-docks, graving-docks, all surrounded by warehouses with goods from around the world. Great cranes lifted cargo on and off, while passengers and sailors passed close by. In 1808 alone, 400 large ships and 300 smaller barges and sloops disembarked there.[6]

It was not just the size of the port that complicated Moses's hunt for fabric. Liverpudlians liked to say their weather was pleasantly moderate, but in truth, all through the summer of 1815 the weather was distinctly miserable. The violent volcanic eruption of Tambora in the East Indies in April had thrown vast amounts of dust and noxious gases into the atmosphere. Wind patterns were out of kilter, rainfall was up, and cold permeated the North. Moses's icon Beau Brummell might have preferred to be carried about in a sedan in wet weather (umbrellas were so tastelessly nouveau), but Moses's work was more pedantic. He would just have to make the best of it, even when water dripped down his neck or frizzed the perfectly coiffed tendrils on his forehead.[7]

In some ways, however, luck was on his side. The month leading up to the high holidays was typically exhausting for men attending Portuguese synagogues, as the special midnight *Selichot* (forgiveness) prayer service was added to the daily regimen. It was necessary either to stay up late or to get up before dawn to say the extra prayers. Trade, however, had drawn Jews with a different tradition to Liverpool. The founders of the city's Seel Street Synagogue (1807) were Ashkenazi, and they began the extra prayers only the Sunday before the Jewish New Year. While their building was less impressive than London's Bevis Marks, the local congregation saved Moses the grueling forty-eight-hour stagecoach ride back to London as well as the inevitable risk of getting stuck in the mud in the middle of nowhere. Since Moses was a perennial bachelor, he had no wife and children demanding that he return home at regular intervals. All that beckoned him to London was the empty flat he rented from the Robinsons at Christopher's Court in Tower Hamlets, near Bevis Marks and the wharves where his work lay.[8]

Another godsend was that the Jewish high holidays—which would inevitably cut into Moses's ability to attend to Girard's whims—ran late that year. Rosh Hashana did not start until the evening of Wednesday, October 4, followed by Yom Kippur and Succoth, the festival of booths. When Simhat Torah was finally over on October 27, Moses was left with a few frantic weeks before the ship left on November 17. His work bore fruit. In December, Moses wrote Girard again, this time enclosing an invoice and bill of lading for the packages, along with a detailed explanation of why he had not been able to obtain some articles on the list. He openly flattered himself that the items substituted should "pay equally" when sold in the Philadelphia market.[9]

His tasks completed, Moses sent Girard a further note in January that he had decided to remain in England. The letter appears to be all business. Moses proposed that in the upcoming months he should divide his time among London, Liverpool, Manchester, and Leeds. From a cloth merchant's perspective, Moses's choices were obvious. Inland from Liverpool, Manchester had grown exponentially in the nineteenth century, becoming crucial to the production of British cloth, thread, and cotton. Leeds was slightly farther east but similarly important for those in the textile and clothing business. Even by 1780, Leeds was the center of England's thriving woolen industry. Wool cloth was what made the new Beau Brummell style of men's wear possible, as well as the stiffly styled uniform Moses had proudly worn in the War of 1812. It was not just the way wool held dark colors; wool's ability to be stretched and molded was critical to creating the ideal physique being tailored in the new shops along Cork Street, Glasshouse Street, and Savile Row in London and parroted in American towns. Leeds's woolens were particularly exquisite, and the four cities of Liverpool, London, Manchester, and Leeds were at the heart of the new fashion Moses hoped to help Girard import.[10]

Yet the advantage of hindsight suggests another possible motive for Moses's decision to extend his stay in the British Isles. Sometime in 1815 on the very docks Moses perused for cloth, a packet ship from Bridgetown, Barbados, weighed anchor. Onboard was a trading partner who would have made Moses's father and Stephen Girard giddy with envy: Abraham Rodrigues Brandon, owner of several plantations and a key player in the sugar business. Fine cloth may have dressed wealthy bodies, but sugar was central to the coffee and tea ceremonies that allowed those with money to display their tastefulness. Sugar was also quickly becoming the mainstay of all British and American meals. The sugar trade helped fund the clothes Moses liked to buy. With a business partner like Brandon, Moses could make a fortune.[11]

Even more intriguing for Moses was Brandon's companion: seventeen-year-old Sarah Rodrigues Brandon, who had now adopted her father's full last name. She had come to London to attend school. Brandon's daughter was young, beautiful, and Jewish. With a potential dowry of £10,000, she was also a phenomenal heiress the likes of which Moses was unlikely to find in the fledgling United States. Even Moses's own mother's dowry, while extravagant, paled in comparison. Moses, it seemed, had more than one kind of business to attend to in England.

Just as Moses came to England seeking high-end fabrics that signaled class and elegance, so too Sarah Rodrigues Brandon and her father arrived with a mission to refashion her image. Jews from Barbados often made the passage back and forth to London for commerce, schooling, or marriage. After the War of 1812, many West Indian Jews rebuilt their dynasties in England. Brandon did not need to. He had already established himself as an important merchant and was on the road to becoming Barbados's richest Jew.[12]

For Jewish merchants like Brandon, children were an investment who could cement trade alliances with other Jewish merchant families. Hence, like most affluent Jews, Brandon's vision as a merchant turned toward the kind of match his children might make. Exchanging vows was as crucial a business transaction as signing a ship's manifest or captaining a vessel. So, when the War of 1812 finally ended in 1815, Brandon accompanied Sarah to England.[13]

Exclusive British schools would be key to Sarah's new identity. The quality of the Jewish school in Barbados was often hit or miss, and back on the island, even poorer Jews would sometimes petition the *Mahamad* for financial help to send their children abroad to an English school. It wasn't to be. The Mahamad might provide funds for a poor Jewish child to become an apprentice, but going abroad to school in England was something reserved for well-heeled West Indian Jews. Leading men of the Barbadian Mahamad like Eliezer Montefiore (uncle of Sir Moses Montefiore) and other members of the Barrow clan sent their children to the empire's metropole for school. With one key difference: the education that prepared Sarah for marriage would need to strip away her identity as someone whose early life had been defined by serving others.[14]

While at school, Sarah would learn how to manage servants rather than *be* a servant. In both England and the British colonies, education was a critical indicator of class during the eighteenth and nineteenth centuries. Instruction trained young men to govern themselves so that they could govern others. Upscale education likewise prepared females to take their place in polite society, including how to deal with domestics and the Jewish poor. Beyond reading, writing, and arithmetic, girls learned dancing, music, and needlework, as well as how to dress and display their piety through public acts of charity. Affluent women were expected to learn how to run a large household and to pass on household management skills to their children.[15]

For Jews in England and the British Empire, being upper class likewise required speech training. Codes of dominance were embedded in the way people spoke. Language and accent were key. Even the wealthiest Jews were tainted by association with the Jewish poor: *Punch* magazine, for example, made the accent of a ragman come out of the mouth of the upwardly mobile

Benjamin Disraeli, a convert in childhood. Speaking the right way signaled that one was meant to be part of the ruling class, deserving of deference.[16]

Language was equally important for aspiring and upper-class women. Language could make the difference in financial transactions and social activities. For non-Jews, a basic knowledge of French signified one's politeness. The goal was primarily good pronunciation and accent rather than true fluency. For high-society young Jewesses, a rudimentary knowledge of Hebrew was also crucial. Equally important, Sephardic schools taught girls how to *ladinar*, as fluency in Spanish or Portuguese was considered as crucial a part of Western Sephardic identity for women as it was for men. The eighteenth-century British prayer book owned by Bevis Marks Jewess Rachel de Crasto is illustrative: the inside cover is inscribed in Portuguese, even though the book itself is in the baroque Spanish taught in Western Sephardic schools.[17]

For a former slave and convert like Sarah Rodrigues Brandon, this education would have been almost as crucial to becoming a full member of the Jewish community as her conversion and early training in Suriname. London was the perfect place for Sarah to learn how to become part of upper-class Jewish society. An upscale education would place Sarah among the Jewish peers she would later be able to rely on to smooth her way in the Americas.

The right education would similarly distance Sarah from poorer British Jews attending the Jews' Free School in the East End. At the time, London was home to more than 15,000 Jews, roughly 2,000 of whom were *nação*. Regardless of their nationality, however, most of London's Jews were astonishingly poor. Throughout the late eighteenth and early nineteenth centuries, London drew destitute Jews from Iberia, the Netherlands, the German states, and Poland. One thing that attracted some of the poor to London's East End was the chance for their children to attend a free Jewish school.[18]

Founded in north London in 1732, the Jews' Free School served poor immigrants throughout the nineteenth century. Though it taught some Hebrew and Jewish studies, the school's main focus was training children in trades. Boys learned how to make shoes, chairs, and cabinets. Girls learned how to sew, iron, cook, and clean. Schooling tended to end by age twelve or thirteen, when boys became apprenticed in a trade and girls started their work as servants. One wealthy Jewish woman explained in an 1818 manual that while at the school, poor Jewish girls would learn their place in society through "thrift, gratitude, subservience, and industry."[19] To be admitted to the school, children had to prove their families were respectable or worthy poor. A crucial way of demonstrating worthiness was through abasement and showing oneself grateful when receiving an *obra pia* (charitable gift). The Free School trained poor Jews for their place in society, but in this instance that place was of a servile nature—a station to which Sarah hardly aspired.[20]

Wealthy Jews were certainly involved in the Free School, but rather than sending their children there, they performed piety by giving charity and attending fundraising events on the school's behalf. In March 1816, Joshua Moses was invited to one such event, a dinner on behalf of the Jew's Hospital held at Bishopsgate Street. Founded in 1806, the Jew's Hospital cared for the sick, provided a home for the poor, and taught children trades. The dinner honored the institution's patron, His Royal Highness the Duke of Sussex, the sixth son of King George III. The duke—also known as Prince Augustus Frederick—was a patron of Jews, Catholics, dissenters, and abolitionists, and was so beloved by London's Jews that his portrait would eventually be hung in the main hall of the hospital.[21]

Attending the dinner was a chance for Moses to mingle with London's Jewish high society, including the Goldsmids, Samuels, Seligs, Israels, and Warburgs. In keeping with class divisions, servants were explicitly barred from the event, with the exception of those attending the duke and others running the dinner, who apparently explicitly needed help. The elegant summons was one of the invitations that Joshua Moses cherished throughout his life. Dining with the duke signified Moses's rank among those who ruled, not those who suffered to be ruled.

By the time of Sarah's arrival in 1815, both the hospital and the free school were in the neighborhoods of Spitalfields and Whitechapel around Aldgate. Aldgate, or "old gate," was once the easternmost gateway through the old city wall. Today these East End neighborhoods are often remembered for either the nightmare years of Jack the Ripper or the rampant poverty and cholera epidemics that seized the area in the middle of the nineteenth century. But in the early 1800s when Sarah arrived, the neighborhoods were economically diverse. Fellow Barbadian Joseph Barrow Montefiore, who came to London for schooling as a boy, recalled how in his youth, rich and poor Jews in London's East End lived on adjacent streets. Joseph Montefiore was exactly the sort of peer Brandon sought for Sarah. Montefiore belonged to a wealthy family of Sephardic traders. By 1826, he was known not only for his role in the lucrative tea trade but also for being one of only a dozen Jewish brokers in the city.[22]

Jews rich and poor congregated in the East End for financial and religious reasons. The neighborhood bordered the Tower of London as well as St. Katharine's Docks along the Thames, where Moses rented an office. The East End was the historical Jewish center of London: after being readmitted to the city by Oliver Cromwell in 1656, Jews built the city's early magnificent synagogues in this neighborhood: the Portuguese Creechurch Lane Synagogue (1655), the Ashkenazi Great Synagogue at Duke's Place (1690), and the resplendent Portuguese Synagogue Qahal Kadosh Sha'ar ha-Shamayim ("Holy Congregation Gate of Heaven," 1701), commonly known as Bevis Marks, named for the street on which it was located.[23]

In the 1810s and 1820s, many members of Bevis Marks still maintained elegant houses nestled near the synagogues. Joseph Montefiore's cousin Moses Montefiore and his brother-in-law Nathan Mayer Rothschild had imposing Georgian mansions in walking distance to the west on New Court in Swithin's Lane, but the streets nearest the synagogue and northeast of it were commonly considered the most aristocratic. This is where Emanuel, a

Isaac Mendes Belisario, *Interior of the Spanish and Portuguese Synagogue, London [Bevis Marks]* (1817). Aquatint after a watercolor. Jewish Museum, London.

diamond dealer and agent for the fantastically wealthy financier Baron de Samuel, lived, as did former Barbadian Jacob Barrow, with whom Abraham Rodrigues Brandon and other members of the Barbadian Mahamad often exchanged letters.[24]

South Street likewise became the home to a generation of Barbadian men who, while perhaps not fantastically wealthy, were inarguably successful. These were men like Hananel de Crasto, Lewis Cohen, and Isaac Levi who worked on the stock exchange and who traveled between Bridgetown and London. When in London, most Barbadian Jews attended Bevis Marks and rented or owned homes in the streets near the synagogue. Prescot Street, for example, was home to the Barbadian branch of the Montefiores, the Gompertzes, and the Salomons. Leman Street in Whitechapel was where Jacob Barrow's father-in-law—Daniel Mocatta—lived. This expat community must have been a source of cheer to Sarah and her father.[25]

Another comfort was the extended Brandon clan, who also lived in a close web around the Sephardic house of worship. Joshua Brandon, one of the British Brandon patriarchs, lived on Leman Street, and Joseph Brandon's home was farther west on Alie Street. Joshua and Joseph Brandon were the brothers of Jacob Israel Brandon, the congregation's *Presidente*, who along with his wife would serve as witnesses at Sarah Rodrigues Brandon's marriage when the time came. The British Brandons were part of that large interconnected clan with key branches in Barbados, Jamaica, Amsterdam, Hamburg, and the Dutch West Indies. London's tight-knit Sephardic community was one hub of their vast network. Education connected the generations and the branches of the clan.[26]

Education also gave the Brandons and their peers a sense of superiority. If London's Jewish community was a pyramid, bottom heavy with the poor, the Brandons aimed for the pinnacle of social and financial success. In fact, the name Brandon became so closely associated with prosperous Jews that some poorer Jewish immigrants adopted it in order to give themselves greater cachet. In the late eighteenth and early nineteenth centuries, two Jewish schools signaled social prestige: Hurwitz's Academy and Garcia's school. Despite one being Ashkenazi and the other Sephardic, both shared one trait with the public schools favored by Britain's ruling class: they boarded students outside of the urban center. Like the Harrow School, Hurwitz was northwest of the city center (in Highgate), while Garcia's was south of the urban core, in Peckham.

The rural location was hardly arbitrary. As Daniel Defoe noted in his *Tour through England and Wales*, Highgate was favored by wealthy Jews who had a synagogue and *mikveh* in a private house and their own butcher in town. Highgate was home to Cromwell House, the residence of Alvares da Costa and later his daughter-in-law, the artist Catherine (Mendes) da Costa. Cromwell House was also the first Jewish-owned property in England after the Jews' expulsion in 1290. By 1700, members of the Da Costa clan had purchased three other Highgate estates: Englefield House, Moreton House, and Grove House. Even in Barbados the name Highgate signaled prestige and pastoral bliss. Barbadian widow Sarah Belinfante, for example, used the name for her ten-acre estate just southwest of Bridgetown that contained a country house from whose rooms there was a delightful view of both the surrounding fields and nearby bay.[27]

Highgate was a place where early British Jews could imitate the aristocratic obsession with country life, and educating one's children there was the Jewish version of the public school tradition treasured by non-Jews. By 1820, approximately 100 boys were being taught at the academy. Around 1810, Hurwitz's sister began leasing the adjacent house at No. 9 South Grove to run a school for Jewish girls.[28]

By 1815, when Sarah Brandon arrived in London, however, Hurwitz had competition, and pride in Sephardic identity seemed at least partially

Hurwitz's Jewish Academy in Highgate. Photo by Gareth E. Kegg, 2016.

responsible. Joseph Barrow Montefiore noted that "the pupils of the richer families objected to Hurwitz, who was a Pole and used to wear a tall Polish hat."[29] Abraham Garcia's boarding school in Camden Place, Peckham was distinctly Sephardic and considered more select. In 1826, the school was taken over by Garcia's sister, and Hannah Gomes, a Sephardic Jew, started a girls-only academy nearby. Once Garcia's school opened, many well-off Jews—including the Barrows and Montefiores—shifted their loyalty there.[30]

Although the early records from the schools have been lost along with the identity of the school Sarah attended, the earliest census records reveal Sarah's younger half-sisters living at Hannah Gomes's Ladies School in the early 1840s. Here girls learned Jewish values like *tzedakah* (charity) as well as Jewish and secular studies. During Chanukah of 1841, for example, Sarah's sisters and other schoolmates helped distribute meat and bread to seven poor families in the area. Their work was both generous and the Jewish equivalent of the showy piety required of non-Jewish gentlewomen.[31]

Like education, clothing and portraiture helped Sarah tailor herself to her new social role, so sometime around 1815–16, Sarah Rodrigues Brandon found herself back in London proper having her portrait painted. Like the Sephardic finishing school Sarah attended, the miniature prepared Sarah to become the wife of a leading Atlantic-world Jew. The portrait on ivory is the first—and only—glimpse we have of Sarah, and perhaps the most crucial evidence of how she wanted to be seen.

Just as modern suitors put on the right outfit and take a selfie to post to online dating websites, early nineteenth-century miniature portraits were a key way Jews and other Europeans and Americans entered the marriage market. Ivory miniatures were frequently commissioned for engagements and weddings, but they also functioned as a portable gift or tool in marriage negotiations. Miniatures could be sent across oceans or across town to help make a match. Portraits mattered, as they required the sitter's approval, and thus on some level, they presented the sitter as she or he wished to be understood. They were also deeply intimate: small and portable, they are meant for the eyes of the beloved. In her portrait, Sarah presents herself to her future husband as a fashionable yet modest British heiress, the appropriate bride for a wealthy New York Jew in the upper end of the textile trade. She is captivating and precious.[32]

The materials and process used to make Sarah's portrait mark her as part of London high society and call to mind how far she had traveled since being born enslaved. Sarah's portrait is small—only 2 3/4 by 2 1/4 inches—but expensive. The ivory on which it was painted was cut from an elephant's tusk, in slices less than a millimeter thick with attention to where the ivory's grain would run fine. The sheets were so thin that they were translucent, giving the miniature its luminosity. Scraping, polishing, and bleaching gave the ivory a pale warmth that was felt to mimic the skin tones of Western Europeans. When combined with watercolor, the material gave the sitter's skin and clothes an almost magical glow.[33]

This glow came at an artistic cost, however: the materials and skill required to make miniatures meant good ones could cost more than full-sized portraits in oil. Despite this cost, most Jewish portraits that remain from this era are miniatures.[34] While later in the nineteenth century they were placed within a larger black matting to be hung on walls, earlier miniatures tended to be worn on chains or jewelry, held close to the body. If the beloved died or was far away, sometimes a lock of hair was included in the case, or chopped up to create an image of someone mourning on the back of the locket. The portrait and hair were a visceral way of keeping a loved one close.[35]

This intimacy took time. Sarah's miniature would have required at least three sittings and relied on the sitter's access to leisure, a strange commodity for a woman born enslaved. Although some artists signed miniatures or used a distinctive style, Sarah's portrait is anonymous. Probably the artist was male, like most professional artists of the day. In the first sitting, as the light fell directly on Sarah's face, the portrait-maker outlined her face in pencil on drawing paper, then placed the paper below the translucent ivory so it could be copied with delicate brushings of watercolor. After outlining her face in pencil, the artist used color to create Sarah's pupils. The largeness of Sarah's eyes makes her appear even younger than she actually was, vulnerable and innocent. Her glance reclaims her body from the stranger's gaze, saving intimacy for her husband. Sarah's large eyes hold ours, her lips just barely turned up in the corners in an enigmatic smile.[36]

The artist also outlined the delicate curve of her chin and cheeks in light, neutral colors. The hues he used were no accident: watercolor miniatures on ivory are a genre dedicated to whiteness and surged in popularity just when race and skin color became increasingly aligned with elite status. When depicting a European's face, watercolors allowed the sitter's skin to appear radiant.[37] Not so in early miniatures of women of color, as most artists from this era used a hatching technique to apply darker paint to their faces. Even when used by skilled artists, this technique left the skin looking scratchy

The artist's use of hatching on face from an early New York miniature suggests he saw the sitter's skin as flawed. Detail of Anthony Meucci, *Mrs. Pierre Toussaint* (ca. 1825), with full miniature inset. Watercolor on Ivory. NYHS.

and implied the skin itself was flawed.[38] Painters who actively wanted to depict smooth, dark skin were more likely to create paintings using oil on canvas or pastels on paper than ivory miniatures. Sarah's miniature maker had two choices: light, glowing skin or racialized, scratchy skin. The artist opted for glow.

The first sitting would have taken less than an hour to ensure that Sarah would not become fatigued, as her relaxed muscles might cause the portrait to look dull and languid. With that work completed, the artist moved on to the second step, which did not require Sarah's presence at all. During this step, the portrait painter worked on the sunset-like background and posed

Detail of the face of *Portrait of Sarah Brandon Moses* (ca. 1815–16). AJHS.

a figure wearing Sarah's white dress in the light in order to paint the detail of her clothes.[39]

Although Sarah's portrait is undated, the neckline, high waist, and sleeves date the dress to about 1815, when Sarah was seventeen years old. If Sarah looks like she leapt from the pages of a Jane Austen novel, that is because she wears a neoclassical, Regency-style white gown, probably made of muslin or silk—fabrics favored for their ability to mimic the marble of classical sculpture. Below the high waist visible in the miniature, the gown would have had a long, narrow, straight skirt that, made in light material, would have draped gracefully over her lower body.[40]

Like the clothing Joshua Moses wore and sold, the neoclassical dress in Sarah's miniature positioned her as cultured, idealized her body, and emphasized her freedom. The whiteness and delicate lace of the dress would have been easily tarnished by the physical work it took to clean and run a nineteenth-century household. Wearing this dress implied that Sarah was freed from manual work.[41]

The dress also emphasized Sarah's virtue. Although when the Regency style first appeared, its exposure of the body's lines was considered indecent, by the time Sarah's portrait was made, the style was considered chaste.[42] Yet Sarah's portrait was more modest than the clothes worn in portraits of some of her North American Jewish counterparts like Eliza Myers (ca. 1808) or Sally Etting (ca. 1808), who wore lower-cut dresses with barer shoulders. Sarah's dress similarly differs from seductive depictions of Creole women by artists of the time. Sumptuary laws in the colonies sometimes forbade enslaved women from fully covering their chests. Even in places where covering one's chest was not formally forbidden for enslaved women, laws regarding how much fabric needed to be given to slaves meant that they often did not receive enough cloth to wrap themselves completely. In this context, the ability to conceal the body more signaled greater freedom not less. Sarah's portrait defies West Indian racial stereotypes and demurely covers her body.[43]

Once the painting of her clothing was completed, Sarah would have returned for her second in-person sitting, in which the artist examined and perfected every part of the miniature, starting with Sarah's hair. In the painting, Sarah's curly brown hair is pulled back in a Grecian knot, and

Depictions of multiracial women from this era often emphasize sexualized sitters. Jacques Guillaume Lucien Amans, *Creole in a Red Headdress* (ca. 1840). Oil on canvas. Historic New Orleans Collection, Williams Research Center, New Orleans, LA.

tendrils delicately frame her face. Notably, Sarah's head is bare. She lacks the stylish tignon, or turban headdress, worn by women of color in Suriname, Barbados, Haiti, and New York. Sarah's unadorned hair signals her single status in Jewish religion, but also leaves her race unmarked.[44] The neatness of Sarah's hair is equally crucial. Caricatures from this era used out-of-control hair to show that Jews could not govern their bodies and hence should not take part in politics. Likewise, loose hair, licentiousness, and Jewish practice became intertwined in drawings of multiracial Jewesses from Suriname. Sarah's neo-classically styled hair emphasizes her restraint.[45]

With the hair completed, the artist would add white to Sarah's eyes and the darkest portion of the eyelids, heightening their impact. The portrait was now done and ready to be encased under glass. Once completed, Sarah's portrait was ready to find its companion. In 1817, Sarah and her portrait did just that. Sarah became engaged to cloth merchant Joshua Moses, a man with a portrait of his own.[46]

On March 19, 1817, Sarah Rodrigues Brandon found herself underneath a *huppah*, a marriage canopy, at London's Portuguese synagogue, Bevis Marks. Standing in for Moses's parents were Jacob Israel Brandon, the congregation's Presidente, and his wife. For Sarah, there were Mr. Massiah

Use of tignon in a portrait of a multiracial woman from Suriname. Detail from Anonymous, *Portrait of Surinamese Girl* (ca. 1805), with full miniature inset. Watercolor on ivory, 6.4 cm × w 5.5 cm. RM.

Although Benoit depicts (from left to right) a Moravian, a Calvinist, a Christian, a Jew, and a Lutheran, only the Jewish woman's hair creeps down her back, emphasizing Jewish licentiousness. *Cinq femmes esclaves se rendant à leur église un jour de fête* (Five slave women going to their church on a feast day). P. J. Benoit, Voyage à Suriname (Brussels: Societe des Beaux-Arts, 1839), JCBL.

and Mrs. Lindo, important members of Bevis Marks with connections to Barbados. The official witnesses were Jacob Israel Brandon and Moses Lara, the latter one of the congregation's most important philanthropists, who eventually bequeathed £40,000 to the synagogue. He was exactly the sort of man Moses would have met a year earlier when attending the charity dinner with the duke.[47]

The £10,000 dowry Sarah brought with her to the marriage would be seed money for Moses, allowing him to take his business ventures to a new level. Perhaps it was with this in mind that Moses no longer felt compelled to stay in London as Girard's agent. Or perhaps it was the lure of family and his father's illness that called him home as well as the desire to share the birth of his first child with the people he loved. Or maybe the couple had a reason to suspect that their daughter might be born two weeks shy of nine months after their marriage? Whatever the reason, before the end of 1817 Sarah and her new husband had left London and begun the voyage home to Moses's native New York. A new life awaited her. Back in Barbados, however, the old pattern of discrimination and rejection had caught up with her brother Isaac.

7

Voices of Rebellion

Bridgetown, 1818–1824

IT HAD STARTED INNOCENTLY. In all good faith, Isaac Lopez Brandon signed the Jews' 1819 petition to the island legislature asking it to make the Bridgetown synagogue officially a vestry. That is, the petitioners wanted the synagogue elders who ruled the congregation to have the same rights and power as the men who governed the Anglican church. Brandon was not the only signer. His curling penmanship and Spanish-style *rubrica* (flourish) were placed alongside that of the most upstanding men in the congregation. Yet his signature would become the most controversial in a fight that tore the congregation apart.

At first glance, the petition seemed obviously good for Barbadian Jews. Designating the Jewish congregation a vestry comparable to the Anglican church should have laid the groundwork for Jews to vote and hold office on the island. The colonial government had only two explicit requirements for voting: owning property and belonging to a vestry, a stipulation that effectively limited the vote to white, Anglican men. Rather than forcing Jewish men to convert if they wanted to vote, the Jewish Vestry Bill provided a loophole, allowing Barbadians to be Jews *and* vestrymen. For Isaac, it also meant that even though he was not white, he too would have the explicit requirements needed to vote, as the bill allowed him to circumvent the Anglican church's exclusions.

From the perspective of the congregation's inner circle, the bill was a boon. Men of property like Isaac's father Abraham Rodrigues Brandon, as well as

Joseph Montefiore, Benjamin Elkin, Isaac Valverde, and Phineas Nunes, all heartily supported the proposal. Turning the synagogue into a vestry gave them power to ensure that all Jews paid their *finta* (religious taxes) to the synagogue. Mandatory synagogue taxes meant all Jews who could afford to do so would share the burden of caring for the ever-growing numbers of Jewish poor rather than disproportionately relying on wealthy Jews or Jews with a sense of duty. Moreover, since the Brandons, Montefiores, Elkins, Valverdes, and Nuneses owned extensive real estate, being a member of a vestry was one of the few qualifications for voting that they lacked.[1]

For Jewish men of the middling sort, though, the bill was deeply distressing. Middling men did not have sufficient property to vote in general elections anyway, and now they would lose what little money they had to mandatory synagogue taxes. These were men like Isaac Lealtad, Joshua Levi, and Moses Pinheiro—men who were either relatively new to the congregation or who had recently dragged themselves out of the swelling ranks of the synagogue's impoverished pensioners. They remembered how when they did not have enough to get by, their families were forced to beg the *Mahamad* for a pension to cover their basic needs. Any time they needed a new suit of clothes to attend the synagogue or money for an apprenticeship, they had to return with hand outstretched. The Mahamad's minutes were filled with demeaning requests and unfilled need.[2]

While the members of the Mahamad expected gratitude in return for their generosity, most of the time they got resentment. Isaac Lealtad, they explained, had been "brought up and supported from the charitable funds of the Hebrew Nation" and his "Mother, Wife, Niece, Mother-in-law and Sister-in-law, were all maintained and supported as Monthly Pensioners of the Synagogue, receiving collectively from the Year 1785 to the respective periods of their death or removal upwards of £1200."[3] Likewise, Joshua Levi, a recent immigrant, was "a man who, [even] when able to maintain his first Wife, left her to become an additional burden on the Congregation, who allowed her a Pension for above eight years!"[4] From the Mahamad's perspective, this charity signaled Lealtad's and Levi's debt to the congregation. Yet instead of gratitude, Lealtad and Levi appeared to feel only a crippling shame about their years of grubbing.

Moreover, despite having clawed their way out of poverty, Lealtad and Levi quickly realized they would never join the ranks of the Mahamad, which they quite rightly understood was run by what they disparaged as the synagogue's "hereditary Junto."[5] Key positions on the Mahamad tended to be passed from wealthy fathers to their sons, skipping past the *nouveau* middle class. As tax-paying members of the congregation, Lealtad and Levi had made the transition from *congregante* to *yahid* (voting member), but they never seemed to gain the privileges associated with that transition. After a while, they grew annoyed and stop bothering to pay the taxes they were assessed.

To make matters worse, now it appeared that wealthy men of color like Isaac Lopez Brandon would gain privileges that white Jews of a middling sort could never hope to attain. Isaac—who already paid more in synagogue taxes than most whites—stood to inherit his father Abraham Rodrigues Brandon's position on the synagogue board. If the synagogue were to become a vestry, Isaac would also be able to vote in general elections and perhaps even serve in the island legislature. It was more than middling Jews could bear.

Thus Levi, Lealtad, and other opponents tried a range of tactics to suppress the motion. They started by trying to align themselves with the gentile legislature by appealing to base antisemitism. Jews were outsiders, untrustworthy—how could they become a vestry?, they argued. This strategy failed. Unimpressed, the Anglicans expressed outrage that the opponents would think them so intolerant.

So, the opponents tried charging the petitioners with base motives. They alleged that the men in charge misused funds and lied about the short-fall caused by making contributions voluntary. In particular, the counter-petitioners bitterly resented that the Barbados Mahamad was forcing them to pay taxes when well-to-do Barbadian Jews were seemingly throwing their money away. "So far from our Synagogue *wanting* Money to meet their Expences," the discontented grumbled, the Barbadian synagogue actually had given Abraham Rodrigues Brandon $500 to "send money to America to build a Synagogue for Mr. Brandon's color'd connexions"![6] This American synagogue was none other than Mikveh Israel of Philadelphia, to which Abraham Rodrigues Brandon had sent over $200 of his own money for the building subscription.[7] Brandon's "color'd connexions" were his son Isaac, who donated $25 of his own money, and (Sarah) Esther Lopez-Gill, restyled as Mrs. Ab[m]. R. Brandon, who donated $20 from her own purse. Once again, the Anglicans saw through the ruse. The contributions had been voluntary, and men might give charity as they liked. Yet the damage was done. The opponents began to focus their ire on Isaac.

In doing so, they finally hit a nerve that made the Anglicans sit up. The Jewish vestry bill would circumvent island law by allowing Jewish men of color—men like Isaac Lopez Brandon—to vote. White privilege was at stake. Unlike the specter of Jewish corruption, this fear hit home. One of the assemblymen, a Mr. Hinds, moved that an additional clause be added to said bill "to prevent Persons descended from Negroes participating in the Privileges of said Bill."[8] The motion passed unanimously, and a clause to that effect was added. The bill returned to the synagogue for approval. Would the signatories accept the change?

Round after round of debate ensued. In addition to his father and his father's friends, Isaac had his cousin-in-law Abraham Israel Keys to back him up during each of the heated exchanges. By the time the vestry bill was written, Keys had become Nidhe Israel's hazan. Moreover, he had been in the position for seven years—almost a lifetime by Barbadian standards—as Keys had taken on the duties of religious leader after Hazan Abendana was dismissed in the wake of his "Urethra Complaint."[9]

Keys carried weight. Unlike his predecessors who had brought shame upon the Jews, Keys's talents and work were met with praise. The Mahamad was "highly Appreciating" and "Grateful" of Keys's service, and they deemed him a credit both to himself and the community.[10] The synagogue also made its gratitude felt by bestowing honors upon Keys, including the highly regarded position of *Hatan Torah* (Bridegroom of the Law) during the High Holy Days of 1820. Although some of Abraham Rodrigues Brandon's friends would later criticize Keys for being too lenient toward the rebellious opponents to the bill, Brandon clearly appreciated Keys and went out of his way to help him behind the scenes.[11]

In the end, having a powerful father and a hazan in the family was not enough. Proponents of the bill accepted the dreaded amendment, and in February 1821 they voted that "Mr. Isaac Lopez Brandon's name be taken off the list of *Yehadim*."[12] They claimed their reason was that it seemed insulting to tax Isaac as a *yahid* when he was now "debarred from the rights he heretofore possessed with all the assessed Members."[13] Rather than challenge the equation of whiteness with Jewish privilege, the Mahamad voted to make Isaac no longer a full member of the congregation. In the struggle, the synagogue had lost an important source of revenue and alienated Isaac's father Abraham Rodrigues Brandon, its biggest donor.

Ironically, all the controversy was for naught. King George IV of England overturned the Barbadian Vestry Bill in 1822. It was not until 1831 that both Jews and free men of color on the island were finally enfranchised. Meanwhile, the damage was done, and Isaac's right to vote in the congregation was not reinstated. In his willingness to risk all for what he believed, Isaac was not alone. Isaac's battle was part of a larger religious war waged by the Gill family, a battle that underscored the intertwined role of minority religions and rights on the island.[14]

Although Sarah and Isaac's uncles had signed petitions similar to the one Isaac signed asking for civil rights, it was the actions of Sarah and Isaac's aunt that would become most infamous in Barbadian history. Following her husband's death in 1814, Ann Jordan Gill turned to religion for solace, and it changed her. By 1818, a spiritual awakening caused Gill to abandon the Anglican church of her father. Yet whereas Isaac and Sarah had become Jews, Gill became a Methodist, joining the radical Bridgetown congregation run by the Reverend William Shrewsbury, a cherub-faced idealist.[15]

Although religiously at the fringes of island life, Shrewsbury's church building was physically close to Bridgetown's center and only a short block from the synagogue. The church faced James Street, one of Bridgetown's main thoroughfares. Over the next six years, Ann Jordan Gill would play a crucial role in the congregation's attempts to remake the city.

Gill quickly became central to Shrewsbury's Methodist congregation. It was a family affair. Although it is not clear who joined first, Gill's sister-in-law Christian(a) Gill—her husband's half-sister—was also an active member. The Methodist hymnal that belonged first to Christian(a)'s mother Joanna Gill, then Christian(a) Gill, and finally Ann Jordan Gill herself now resides in the Barbados National Archives. It is the only personal possession of Gill's known to survive.[16]

Despite her late start, Gill quickly rose through the congregation's ranks and became a class leader, that is, a laywoman who ran the small weekly groups during which Methodists accounted for their faith. So it was in 1820, just before Isaac was demoted, that Christian(a) Gill and Ann Jordan Gill became spiritual guides to a young white woman named Hillaria King who had a conversion experience following a particularly moving sermon by Reverend Shrewsbury. Christian(a) Gill and Ann Jordan Gill also took in King as an understudy in their "work for the benefit of the outcasts of society," as Shrewsbury himself described it.[17] Gill's central role in the congregation was enhanced when two years later King and the Reverend Shrewsbury were united in marriage.[18]

Gill's entanglement with Methodism would steer her far from the course of the respectability sought by men and women of her day. As an Anglican, she had submitted herself to the authority of the vestry and clergy. But as a Methodist, she was not obliged to follow the rule of the church elders or to behave submissively to the minister. As one Methodist theologian put it, in the Methodist church, "there are as many *rulers* as members."[19] Even the requirement of kneeling in order to receive communion was eliminated from the prayer book.[20]

Becoming a Methodist was an act of rebellion. Methodism's religious egalitarianism was taken as an affront to the class system deeply embedded in British colonial society.[21] A generation earlier, the Duchess of Buckingham had haughtily explained that Methodism's doctrines were "most repulsive and strongly tinctured with impertinence and disrespect towards their superiors, in perpetually endeavoring to level all ranks and do away with distinctions. It is monstrous to be told you have a heart as sinful as the common wretches that crawl the earth."[22] While heinous to those with power, Methodist theology offered hope to the disenfranchised by emphasizing that anyone could be saved by justification through faith. This spiritual revolution was reflected in the ideal form of the Methodist church, which was small and intimate. Unlike the race-based seating of Anglican chapels, Methodist seating plans emphasized equal access for all rather than hierarchy.[23]

Methodism also provided a place to integrate African religions and peoples, so much so that Shrewsbury noted that one critic referred to Methodist missionaries as "agents of the villainous African society."[24] Whereas the Anglican legislature had outlawed Afro-Caribbean spiritual practices involving the body, such as drumming and Obeah dances, Methodists actively used embodied religion to break down barriers. For critics, this rupture between the physical and spiritual was threatening, because Methodists envisioned a spiritual realm that rejected race-based hierarchies. Methodism offered a new power.[25]

Methodist missionaries were outspoken about courting people with African ancestry. From the Methodists' perspective, Anglicans had not only neglected the island's free-colored and enslaved communities, but it had also often prohibited them from attending church. "Hundreds of them [slaves] had never heard a single word of religious instruction in their whole lives," explained one horrified Methodist.[26] In contrast, Methodists, like Moravians, welcomed people of African ancestry, whom they addressed as Brother or Sister, a practice white Anglicans perceived as dangerous because it implied equality. Methodism also seems to have affected views on slave holding held by both Ann Jordan Gill and her sister-in-law Christian[a] Gill. Though in 1820 Gill and her sister-in-law were both still enslavers, Gill's lady's maid Lucy Ann had already been manumitted, and soon the women sold the others. By 1823, there was only one enslaved person in Gill's household. We do not know what precisely drew Ann Jordan Gill to

Methodism, but we do know that the Anglicans did not take Methodism's spiritual equality lightly.[27]

By 1823 the Anglicans on the island had had enough. On Sunday, October 19, an angry mob of white Anglicans attacked Shrewsbury's James Street Methodist Church. Enraged at how Methodists had meddled with free and enslaved people of African descent, Anglicans reduced the chapel and minister's private apartment to rubble. The next day the mob returned and threw the debris into the sea.[28]

Anglican ire against the Methodist chapel was not isolated. In 1680 the governor closed Bridgetown's Quaker meetinghouse following anti-slavery agitation. By 1760 almost no Quakers remained in Barbados. The Methodists were only one, then, of several minority religious groups Anglicans targeted for disrupting racism.[29]

Anglican mob tactics worked because, as Shrewsbury later explained, in Barbados there were not any police. Shrewsbury complained that while "some of the magistrates I knew to be enemies; I could *depend on none of them for effectual protection.*"[30] Convinced that the mob would have "killed me on the spot" if they could have gotten their hands on him, Shrewsbury chartered a vessel.[31] By three o'clock in the afternoon of October 20, the Reverend William Shrewsbury, his wife Hillaria, and their "wreck of goods" fled the island to safety. Ann Jordan Gill stepped in to fill the pastoral breach.[32]

Her work did not go unnoticed. Soon after the Shrewsburys left, a mob of 200 people surrounded Gill's house and threatened to destroy it unless she stopped preaching. She persisted. Then the magistrates stepped in and forbade her from holding religious services in her home. So she met people in groups of two or three. She was brought before the magistrates and told to renounce her evangelizing. She responded, "Sirs, I have learnt from my Bible, that in matters of conscience I ought to obey God rather than man."[33] The magistrates threatened punishment if she continued. But by January 1824, the small congregation had grown from forty to ninety people: fifteen whites, twenty-five "coloured," and fifty Blacks. Gill offered her own money to build a new chapel.[34]

Still the conflict persisted. Rumors began to spread that Gill was stockpiling weapons in her house. Anglicans burnt depictions of Gill and other Methodists in effigy. In 1825, Gill was again asked to appear before the magistrates and be tried after a complaint that she was still convening public religious meetings. The trial lingered for eight weeks, spinning into new problems. In May 1825 she was found guilty, and the case moved to the

Court of Grand Sessions—a distressing indication that her case was now considered a matter of criminal, rather than civil, justice. Ann wrote to the exiled Shrewsbury, fearful that "reports say great vengeance is denounced against me; it is thought I shall be imprisoned."[35] The trial expenses drained Gill before the air changed and the British Parliament forced local Anglicans to rethink their position. For the rest of her long life, Gill remained a Methodist leader on the island. After her death, Methodists placed "Sarah" before her name to commemorate Gill's work as a Methodist matriarch. Today the new Methodist church on James Street has several memorials to her.[36]

More than 150 years later, Gill was commemorated as one of the ten Bajan national heroes. She is the only woman to achieve that status and the only Barbadian memorialized for using religion as the primary tool in the struggle for civil rights. Isaac's attempt to use Judaism to circumvent racist barriers to the vote is a similar reminder of the larger nexus of religion and rebellion on the island. Indeed, in the decades leading up to the 1833–34 general emancipation, the island's press variously accused Methodist, Moravian, and Jewish congregations of providing people of color with a sympathetic place to congregate and a vocabulary for agitating for civil rights.[37]

While it is tempting to see the press as paranoid about a minority religion cabal, evidence suggests there actually was cross-pollination between the Methodist and Jewish congregations. Once again, the extended Brandon-Gill clan was partially to blame. Sarah and Isaac's cousin-in-law Hazan Abraham Israel Keys attended Methodist meetings on the island, and appears to have been a conduit between Ann Jordan Gill's Methodist community and the Jewish one. Keys regularly figures in Shrewsbury's Barbados journal as the synagogue's "Jewish Reader," and according to Shrewsbury, Keys was only one of many Jews who attended the Methodist congregation.[38]

Indeed, at least before the passage of the Vestry Bill, the Methodists and Jews seemed to have shared some basic beliefs. Like the Methodists, Jews initially argued on behalf of spiritual equality. When the legislature asked the Mahamad of congregation Nidhe Israel about Isaac's African ancestry, the Mahamad replied, "In a religious point of view . . . we make no distinction between Mr. [Abraham Rodrigues] Brandon's son (who is a man of colour) and any other member of our community."[39] Although the island's Jewish community would eventually be pressured into retracting this stance, its initial response reflected the theological position that all Jews had the same type of soul, regardless of race. Isaac's role in the bid for Jewish rights—for both

European and multiracial Jews—underscores the ways in which Judaism resisted the island's racial order before ultimately adapting to meet it.[40]

Isaac spent less time battling against the island's establishment than Gill, yet he lost more. Isaac mainly sought rights for himself, whereas Gill sought them for all people with African ancestors. Though she suffered more than Isaac, she also had greater support. Gill had been harassed and denigrated by Anglicans but never by members of her own Methodist community. Isaac, on the other hand, was sold out by the congregation he called home.

Yet for Isaac, the decision to demote him was also a bit too late. By the time of the vote, he had already left for the United States. He would return to Barbados for work, but his role in obtaining Jewish rights in Barbados would never get the recognition it deserved. Despite his setback, Isaac would carry the hard-earned lessons with him as he moved forward. As he traveled north to his new home in Philadelphia, "that liberal city," and later New York, Isaac figured out new ways to create networks that could not be broken when prejudice stared him in the face. His sister Sarah and her new kin would be crucial to implementing that change.

8

A Woman of Valor

New York, 1817–1819

SARAH BRANDON MOSES MUST HAVE been thrilled to finally place her feet on solid earth, when she and Joshua disembarked in New York harbor in late 1817. Even typically upbeat men like philosopher Ralph Waldo Emerson grumbled that the transatlantic passage between New York and England was "very long, crooked, rough, and eminently disagreeable."[1] Boredom, illness, discomfort, and terror were passengers' chief laments. "Sea sickness is a great drawback to travelling by water," Susannah Wells wrote in her journal when she made the voyage to London in the 1770s.[2] "Fear of having my bones broken" was also among Wells's complaints, as during rough seas, her body was thrown against the ship's walls or hit by flying furniture. Once the panic passed, storms made for a dull ride: Wells found she could not even sit up "without being lashed to the bed or trunk."[3] Yet Sarah had things worse than Wells, as her fears were larger than a few bruises or ennui.

Even putting aside the extra curse of morning sickness and concern for the baby nestled within her, Sarah's maternal turn was at best a voyage into the unknown. How would her child be received? In Barbados, Sarah's African ancestry would ensure that any of her children were treated as second-class citizens, without the right to testify in court, let alone vote. In Suriname, Sarah's legal marriage would have swung the balance and made her children white. In England, the chances of being labeled "coloured" would depend on how the children looked to others and would carry a certain stigma even if it did not affect their civil rights. What would New York's tumultuous racial landscape hold in store for the child within her womb? Moreover, would Sarah herself be fully accepted by her new kin and New York's Jewish community?

Before those questions could matter, however, Sarah and her child had to survive. About one in five young women died in childbirth in pre-industrial England, and there was no reason for Sarah to expect she would fare any better either on the boat or in the small city toward which she journeyed. Over the next ten years, Sarah would watch helpless as friends and her beloved sister-in-law died young, their children left to be raised by extended kin.[4]

After their marriage, Joshua began keeping a journal of key family events. Emblematic of his mercantile ambitions, the notes he jotted down were not in a family Bible but in the back of an account book he had started using in December 1815. By 1817, the accounts had been balanced, and his records turned to more jubilant matters: the birth of his first child, "Dear Reyna, born on Saturday Shabat Hanuca Dec. 6th 1817 about ½ past 12 oClock Meridian at my sister Richa's No. 38 Greenwich St."[5]

The location was a good omen, particularly for a child whose mother had been born without a place to call home. One door away from the southwest corner of Greenwich and Morris, 38 Greenwich Street was part of "Nob Row," also known as Millionaires' Row. After 1815, many of the city's wealthiest members settled along the block between Battery and Morris. Richa Moses had married her maternal uncle Aaron Levy, a leader in the Shearith Israel synagogue. This sort of intramarriage was not uncommon among early American Jews. After all, Richa and Joshua Moses's own parents were first cousins. The Levys clearly cared about appearances: a few short weeks after they moved into 38 Greenwich, they were wallpapering the front parlor of their fashionable home. Like her father, baby Reyna Moses would be a New Yorker, surrounded by a tight, well-decorated nest of privileged kin. For Reyna, that nest would help stave off the racism most people with African ancestry encountered in the growing city.[6]

Knowing people in New York mattered. An early guidebook emphasized all the cultural advantages of the young city—Vauxhall Garden! the theater! museums! libraries![7] Yet New York represented a sharp change from Sarah's earlier homes. She had lived in four cities in four countries before she reached the age of twenty, and New York was hardly the most racially progressive place she had resided.

The city had long been plagued by racial violence. African slaves were first imported into New Amsterdam in 1626, but by 1660 the city had become part of the North American slave trade. An official slave market opened on Wall Street between Pearl and Water in 1771, and that market helped create the largest enslaved community in the northern colonies. Many captives were from central and western Africa, and even before arriving they had undergone extraordinary suffering. Of those abducted in Africa, only about 64 percent survived the middle passage. Of those survivors, fewer than half were alive after three to four years of "seasoning" in the Americas. The living endured poor nutrition, excessive work, and downright cruelty. After reporting how a white youth taunted then "shot the Brains out" of the family's enslaved nanny for no reason other than he could, the *New-York Gazette* assured readers that the white child she held in her arms was not hurt. The murderer went unpunished.[8]

Rebellion and suppression became the norm in early New York. After a 1712 armed revolt, the legislature made it illegal for more than three enslaved people to congregate, effectively outlawing family gatherings. In 1731, further restrictions were added such that any "Negro, Mulatto, or Indian slave" caught laughing too loudly, "hollering," or gambling was liable.[9] By August 1740, even selling corn, peaches, or fruit was illegal. The suppression backfired. In 1741, free and enslaved workers conspired to burn the city and take control of what remained. For three weeks, fires erupted across the city. When they ended, thirty enslaved men were executed and another seventy enslaved people were expelled from the colony.[10]

Emancipation did not come to New York until 1799. Even then, the law passed by the New York legislature freed only children born after July 4, 1799, with the "free" children forced to work as indentured servants until adulthood. In other words, if Sarah and her brother Isaac had been born in New York, the law liberating people would not have applied to them, or their mother, grandmother, or any of their aunts and uncles. It was only on March 31, 1817—less than two weeks after Sarah married Joshua in London—that the legislature passed another bill ensuring that *all* enslaved people would be freed as of July 4, 1827. Gradual emancipation may have meant that by the 1820s New York had one of the largest communities of free people of color in the United States, but that did not end racism in the city.[11]

Many newly free New Yorkers would discover what Isaac Lopez Brandon and the Gills learned in Barbados: looming emancipation often resulted in a backlash, in which people of African ancestry found themselves at the mercy of increased legal and social discrimination. An 1821 law, for example, made voting requirements more stringent for Black New Yorkers than white ones. In passing this law, the legislature made even free Black New Yorkers unequal. The era when Sarah landed in the city was one of the most racially contentious in New York's history.[12]

Nor could Sarah depend on hiding amid a great sea of Jews. With just over 100,000 souls, New York City contained more people than *all* of the island of Barbados. Compared to London's 1.5 million inhabitants, however, the city was a huge step down. Nowhere would New York's relatively small size have been more apparent than in its fledgling Jewish community. While 15,000 Jews lived with three thriving synagogues in London's East End, New York had one congregation: Shearith Israel. As late as 1812, the congregation was made up of 350 men, women, and children, with perhaps another fifty unattached Jews spread across the city. Even after the number of Jews tripled to 950 in 1826, the city remained comparatively provincial religiously. Yet despite their small numbers, some New York Jews were quite loud when expressing their views on race.[13]

One of the most vocal of these Jews was Mordecai Manuel Noah, who had taken up residence in New York in 1817. Having returned from an unsuccessful venture as the US consul in Tunis, Noah turned to newspapers as a venue for his political activism. Under his leadership, the *National Advocate*, a New York daily owned by his uncle Naphtali Phillips, gained sharply in readership. Using a strategy he had employed earlier in Charleston, Noah appealed to readers by covering more topics aimed at women than were found in most newspapers of the time and lacing his politics with humor. Wealthy Americans were at times the target of his satires, but so was the city's burgeoning African American community. In the years following the War of 1812, the *National Advocate,* along with the *New-York Enquirer* (founded by Noah in 1826), became particularly known for their anti-Black diatribes. Given that Phillips was *parnas* of Shearith Israel from 1819 to 1821 and Noah often served on the *Mahamad* from the late 1810s through the 1820s, Sarah and Joshua must have viewed the newspapers' rather relentless denunciation of urban Blacks as unsettling at best.[14]

Still the extended Moses family was everywhere one looked on the streets around the synagogue. Could Sarah rely on her new kin for help? In London, Joshua and Sarah had been married by proxy parents, with Jacob Israel Brandon and his wife acting for Joshua's father and mother. But in New York, there was no need for substitutes. Joshua's parents Reyna Levy Moses and Isaac Moses lived at 98 Greenwich Street, one block west of the monumental Trinity Church and less than two blocks north of the fashionable No. 38, where their granddaughter was born. It was a full house.

Joshua's six unmarried sisters and brothers still lived at home. Also nearby, on Hudson and Walker Streets, were the Levy and Seixas aunts, uncles, and cousins. Likewise, more than a dozen Myers second cousins owned or rented houses scattered across the streets neighboring the small Mill Street synagogue.[15]

Yet more than Jewish kin made the Moseses' house familiar. Like Sarah's own father's house in Bridgetown and his plantations up the island's coast, the Moses clan relied on people of African ancestry to maintain their elegant interiors. Even as late as 1820, Isaac and Reyna Levy Moses's mansion at 98 Greenwich was home to two women of color, on whose labor the household most certainly ran. On some level this was not surprising. The family had been enslavers off and on for years.[16]

Nor were their slaves content. When Isaac and Reyna Levy Moses lived in Philadelphia in 1778, two of their enslaved workers, Bill and Cato, ran away to New York. Perhaps, like the majority of enslaved runaways, they were trying to visit family members. Most slaveholders in New York owned on average 2.4 slaves and prior to 1809 slaves could not marry. This meant most enslaved New Yorkers were separated from their kin. Loneliness often prompted enslaved people to flee.[17]

Whatever Bill and Cato's reason for absconding to New York, Isaac Moses was not interested in letting his workers go, and he put out an advertisement for their return. Moses described Cato as a "lusty fellow" who had been "a sailor, speaks good English, [with a] swarthy complexion."[18] Cato left with only the clothes on his back: "a short light coloured coat, black stocking breeches, and white thread stockings."[19] His clothes suggested a job at Isaac Moses & Company or a more public role in the household.

In contrast, Bill had only a "coarse shirt and trowsers [sic]" to cover his "short and hump backed" body.[20] Moses also noted that Bill "speaks bad English."[21] This was not unusual. Although many enslaved people in the city spoke multiple European languages, low fertility rates among the enslaved ensured a constant influx of newcomers into the city, and about 30 percent of the city's enslaved had come directly from Africa. Most of them spoke African languages: Kikongo, Ga, Mandinga, Soninke, Temne, Fulbe, Sere, and Akan. If Bill was African born, one wonders what his original name was. No records indicate whether the two were ever caught.[22]

Bill and Cato would not be the last people the Moses family enslaved. In 1786, Moses bought a woman named Silva for £45 from Jacob Bogardias. Silva's labor was supplemented by that of women and men whom Isaac hired as servants. The servants' pay suggests what Bill, Cato, and Silva might have received each quarter if they had been compensated for their work. Henrietta Mills, for example, received £6 for four months of work from Moses in March 1786. Presumably she did household work like Silva, as Mills could not write her name and had to sign the family's receipt book with her mark.[23]

Free workers like E. Bidwell, who could write in a decent hand, earned £88 for four months' work. A more specialized hired man, Thomas Haughton, received £9 for fifteen days of writing in his flowery handwriting. Wages varied in the Moses household according to skill and description, but Bill, Cato, and Silva received none.[24]

By 1810, the Moses family had shifted from relying on enslaved labor to hiring four free people of color. Manumission records for the family do not survive, so it is not clear if the residents at 98 Greenwich Street were some of the same people earlier enslaved by the Moses clan or were new employees.[25]

Nor is it clear what had changed Moses's mind about owning other humans. Perhaps it was the influence of key members of Shearith Israel such as Moses Judah, who was elected to the New York Manumission Society in 1799. Between 1806 and 1809, Judah served on the society's standing committee, which listened to grievances by enslaved and indentured New Yorkers. The society also helped provide legal assistance to those seeking freedom, and during the years when Judah was most active, more than fifty enslaved people were freed with the society's help. Judah worked on nine different subcommittees of the society. Or maybe Moses changed his mind about slavery because of men like Alexander Hamilton, who served as Moses's attorney and—like Judah—was a member of the New York Manumission Society. Whatever the reason, by 1820—three years after Sarah and Joshua came to New York—only two people of color remained in her in-laws' house: a woman over forty-five and a young woman, age between fourteen and twenty-five. Neither was enslaved. Possibly they were relatives of Sarah from Barbados, but given the family's history, more likely they were servants earning a wage.[26]

Regardless of how they came to the house, the women were not the only people of color in the streets around Sarah's new home. As in Bridgetown, in early New York people of Jewish and African ancestry lived in close proximity. By 1820, 10,000 black New Yorkers lived in the city, comprising roughly 10 percent of the city's entire population. Sarah may have been unusual in New York for being a Jewess with African ancestry, but her Gill relatives would have felt at home. Seven black churches arose in the city between 1796 and 1826, with most clustered in the fourth, fifth, and sixth wards. The African American church closest to the Moses family's home was the African Methodist Episcopal Zion (A.M.E. Zion) Church, located at Church and Leonard Streets.[27]

A.M.E. Zion was born from the city's deep racial divides. The white-run Methodist Episcopal Church was notably less tolerant of non-white preaching than the Barbadian Methodist congregation to which Sarah's relatives belonged. Although New York's Methodist Episcopal had officially licensed several men with African ancestry as preachers, in practice the men were rarely allowed to sermonize even to other people of color, and never to whites. So much for Methodism's spiritual egalitarianism. Frustrated, some of the most influential members decided to form their own congregation in which only people with African ancestry could be trustees. As a further safeguard, at A.M.E. Zion only people with African ancestry could vote in church elections.[28]

Yet even A.M.E. Zion was less egalitarian than the Methodist church in Bridgetown where Ann Jordan Gill preached. The issue of women's ordination would not arise at A.M.E. Zion until 1898, more than half a century after Ann Jordan Gill had led services in Bridgetown. During Sarah Brandon Moses's lifetime, only male members of A.M.E. Zion could vote or hold office. Eventually Sarah's mother would settle in New York, and she too must have viewed the nearby Methodists with surprise.[29]

Despite possible racial tensions, there were early signs of Sarah's influence on the Moses clan. According to Jewish law, a Jewish woman was supposed to take on her husband's *minhag* (customs), such that a Sephardic woman who married an Ashkenazi man followed Ashkenazi regulations after marriage. This meant that when Sarah married Joshua, they should have followed the Ashkenazi minhag dictating that children were named only after dead relatives. Yet Sarah and Joshua's newborn daughter Reyna was named in Sephardic style for Joshua's mother, who lived nearby at 86 Greenwich.[30]

The decision not to wait to honor Joshua's mother until after she died was wise, as doing so might have left Reyna Levy Moses with no namesakes at all. When little Reyna was born, only one of her paternal aunts or uncles had any children. That uncle followed Ashkenazi custom, so none of his children bore Reyna Levy Moses's name. For Joshua and Sarah's daughter, the name solidified the newborn Reyna's ties to her paternal kin: Reyna Levy Moses had herself been named for her paternal grandmother Reyna Levy of Hanover, albeit in good Ashkenazi fashion after the oldest Reyna had died.[31]

Any excitement Reyna Levy Moses felt at the arrival of her young namesake must have been undercut by a nagging fear. Joshua's father had begun a sudden decline. A tumor distended his torso, and for the next five months Isaac Moses struggled with an agonizing illness. It was a harsh end to a successful life whose riches would continue to affect Sarah and her children long after Isaac Moses's death.[32]

By the fall of 1817, the tumor sealed Isaac Moses's fate. At half past ten in the evening of April 16, 1818, Joshua recorded in the family record, his "venerable honored father departed this life" at his country estate in Mount Listen, a working farm that covered the area between 32nd and 35th Streets and Seventh Avenue to the Hudson River.[33] At the time, the real estate was worth $25,000, or an economic share of approximately $698 million in today's currency. The estate would shelter the next generations, providing both a refuge when the city was under siege and a financial safety net.[34]

Isaac Moses's legacy also meant his death was a community event. His tenure on the Mahamad led to his funeral being delayed two days to allow more congregants to attend. But even the loss of one of the community's great leaders did not stop the well-planned dedication of the renovated and enlarged Mill Street Synagogue one day later, on the Sabbath before Passover. Isaac Moses may have died, but the congregation he built up was growing.[35]

Both the first and second Mill Street buildings would have felt vaguely familiar to Sarah, as, like the synagogues in Barbados, Suriname, and London, they were built in imitation of the Esnoga (Portuguese synagogue) in Amsterdam. This meant that each synagogue had two stories and women were seated on a second-floor lattice-work or pillared gallery that ran along three sides. Below, on the first floor, was a reader's platform or *tevah* (typically placed toward the rear), an ark on the eastern wall, and benches for men facing the platform.[36]

The original Mill Street synagogue structure had been a miniature version of this design, thirty-five feet square. The second, improved Mill Street Synagogue was substantially larger: thirty-five by fifty-eight feet, and nine feet taller, running east and west rather than the original north and south. The change meant there were now 167 seats for men and 133 (later 137) for women. Sarah's new kin were among the many rapidly expanding Jewish families who took advantage of the new space. Once denied a seat in the Barbados synagogue, Sarah now had a husband and influential family members to buy her a place to view the services below.[37]

But as in Philadelphia, owning a seat at Shearith Israel meant more than just a place to sit during services. Joshua Moses had been a member of Congregation Shearith Israel since 1808, and owning a seat meant his voice could be heard and would count during votes. So in April 1818 the Moses clan paid careful attention as the new seats came up for sale. Joshua and his brothers purchased a block together (seats 36–40) downstairs. Upstairs, his brother Moses L. Moses purchased seats for Joshua's three unmarried sisters and their mother (seats 33–36), nestled between the female relations of Eleazer Samuel Lazarus and Harmon Hendricks. Brother-in-law Aaron Levy also added four more seats to his previous purchases, including one next to his wife Richea Moses Levy (seats 113–114). Was one of the new seats for Sarah?[38]

Wherever Sarah initially sat, the gallery's *mechitzah*—the boundary dividing men and women—was high. One Christian minister who visited the first building in 1812 noted that the "breast-work" in the women's gallery was "as high as their chins" giving the impression that they were sitting in a hen coop.[39] This would have been old news to Sarah: the lattice and railings in most congregations where she had lived were equally tall. Even in places where the division seemed more porous—such as Paramaribo's Tzedek ve-Shalom—the women lacked the rights men took for granted. Sarah and her mother might have found the separate yet unequal goings-on at the A.M.E. church a surprising change from Bridgetown's female-run Methodism, but regardless of where one lived in the Jewish Atlantic world, women did not have the right to vote or serve on the Mahamad. Women sat apart lest their bodies and conversations distract men from praying properly. This distance from power filtered into seating. Other than Rachel Pinto, who at seventy years of age was determined by the Mahamad to be no longer capable of arousing men's baser instincts, unmarried women were banned from the front row of the balcony where male worshippers might glimpse them through the screening and divert their concentration.[40]

Yet even as Sarah sat out of sight in the balcony, her father made sure her social status in the new congregation was visible to all. When Sarah and other parishioners looked upward, they would have seen a brass chandelier made in London and sent by her father Abraham Rodrigues Brandon. The shiny metal may have also had a more auspicious goal: Jewish tradition held that gifts like this could avert any bad decree made on *Yom haDin* (Judgment Day). In the months following the synagogue's reopening, Sarah would find she needed all the help she could get. Two months after the new seats became available, Sarah was pregnant again.[41]

Thus, 1819 was a year of both promise and terror. It began auspiciously. On March 16 at half past one in the afternoon, Sarah gave birth to a set of twins: Isaac Moses Jr. and Moses L. Moses. Unlike their sister, the boys were born at Joshua and Sarah's new home at 268 Greenwich Street. Only a few short blocks from both A.M.E. Zion and the rest of the Moses clan, 268 Greenwich Street was the former house of merchant Ephraim Hart and his son, physician Joel Hart. Like Sarah, Joel Hart's wife Louisa Levien had immigrated from London; the couple met while Hart was studying at the Royal College of Surgery. Unlike Sarah and Joshua, the Harts had married at the Ashkenazi and less prestigious Hambro Synagogue in 1810. Louisa Levien Hart and Sarah surely would have passed each other in the synagogue balcony. Louisa Levien Hart and her mother-in-law sat in seats 20 and 96, just down the row from the seats purchased by Aaron Levy.[42]

Living in the Harts' former house was something of a social coup for Sarah and Joshua. Ephraim Hart was an original member of the New York Board of Stockholders and was spectacularly wealthy. In 1810 he became a state senator. Living in the Hart house similarly connoted religious status. Born in Germany like Sarah's father-in-law, Ephraim Hart had served as the *parnas presidente* of Shearith Israel. Piety didn't always lead to abolitionist beliefs, however. Up until the year after Sarah arrived in New York City, Ephraim Hart enslaved at least one woman, Silvia, whom he finally manumitted in 1818.[43]

Religion and tradition were on Joshua and Sarah's minds. The twins' names bound them into Joshua's family and New York life. "Dear Isaac," as Joshua called him, was named in good Ashkenazi tradition for his recently departed paternal grandfather, Isaac Moses.[44] Young Moses L. Moses, though, was named in Sephardic fashion for his very much alive, oldest paternal uncle Moses Levy Moses senior. Naming the second twin for Moses L. Moses meant skipping over the more traditional (and obvious) choice of naming Sarah and Joshua's second son after his maternal grandfather, Abraham Rodrigues Brandon. Who was Moses L. Moses, and why did he matter so much to the young couple?

At first glance, Moses L. Moses may seem a weak choice for Sarah and Joshua's social aspirations. Unmarried, he still lived with his mother Reyna Levy Moses, as he had for all of his forty-six years. Unlike his married brothers, no portraits of him survive. Yet Moses L. Moses was part of a new generation of synagogue leaders: as more Jews married late or not at all, bachelors often filled Jewish congregations' time-consuming leadership roles and single women increasingly managed the care of widows, orphans, and the poor. Thus Moses L. Moses followed in his father's footsteps, both as a leading partner in the merchant house Isaac Moses & Sons and *parnas* of Congregation Shearith Israel. By 1819, when the twins were born, Moses L. Moses the elder was running the family company, advertising goods for sale from Calcutta, Madras, Canton, Britain, and the West Indies.[45]

Perhaps even more crucially, by 1819 Moses L. Moses was a member of the congregation's Mahamad. This position was crucial for Sarah and Joshua, as the twins would be the ultimate test of Sarah's acceptance within the community. Unlike the couple's first child, the twins were boys, and as such they would require the congregation's approval to be given a *brit milah*: a covenantal ceremony that would bind the infants not only to God but to the Jewish people. Would Moses L. Moses stand by the couple in their time of need?[46]

Joshua and Sarah had good reason to be hopeful. Moses L. Moses might be single, but he was a family man. If library records are anything to go by, he also filled his time with reading, as he checked out 238 books between March 1800 and January 1806 alone. His choice of material is illuminating. The works are an eclectic mix of travel narratives, romantic poetry, and stories of chivalric men and the outsiders they helped: orphans, widows, "gipsies," and adopted children.[47] Moses's predilections for sensational novels by popular female novelists suggest that like many men in the neighborhood, he probably checked out books for his sisters and mother. Women rarely had their own library accounts unless they were widowed and without sons. Although a bachelor, Moses L. Moses was the glue that held the family together at home, work, and synagogue. Sarah and Joshua's decision to bind one of the children to him proved wise, as Moses L. Moses's family-minded behavior would later prove a boon to Sarah's brother, Isaac Lopez Brandon.

In the end, Joshua and Sarah had nothing to worry about. On March 23, a week after the twins' birth, the boys were recorded in the synagogue record book. Although Joshua noted that the twins had been "named" by Dr. Phillips, Congregation Shearith Israel's record books were clearer. The twins were circumcised by a visiting *mohel* from Philadelphia, with Moses L. Moses Sr. as their godfather and Reyna Levy Moses as their godmother.[48]

The choice of mohel may have limited by how few circumcisers lived in the region, but it was fortuitous. The man performing the ceremony was Manuel Phillips, the first Jewish doctor in Philadelphia and a graduate of the University of Pennsylvania Medical School, a man whom Joshua almost certainly knew from his years in Philadelphia. Like Joshua, Phillips had served in the American military, having joined the US Navy in 1809 as an assistant surgeon. Calling on Phillips's services was not unusual, as throughout this era, Phillips regularly visited Shearith Israel and performed circumcisions. Phillips was one of the many sons of Jonas Phillips, who was particularly pious. In his spare time, he volunteered in Philadelphia with Rebecca Gratz's Orphan Society, providing medical attention to the poor. But Phillips was also a member of the Democratic Young Men, an organization that at least at times tended to be pro-slavery. Even worse, he was the brother of Naphtali Phillips.[49]

As well as the current parnas of Shearith Israel, Naphtali Phillips was the proprietor of the explicitly anti-black *National Advocate*, which his nephew Mordecai Manuel Noah ran at 211 Pearl Street. Yet despite the mohel's family connections and politics, in the end the twins were circumcised.[50]

Politics aside, having Phillips, a licensed physician, serve as the twins' mohel may have had a particular resonance for Joshua. As much as circumcision tied the twins to Jewish New York, early ceremonies also bound the youngsters to the scientific progress their father valued. Shortly after their brit milah, the twins underwent a second ritual: inoculation. Although vaccines were compulsory for infants in Bavaria, Denmark, Bohemia, Russia, and Sweden, in the United States public opposition to inoculations remained strong. Was the decision of Joshua and Sarah to vaccinate their offspring influenced by Sarah's experience with tropical diseases in the Caribbean, where the non-immunized often died in droves? Or perhaps the couple was swayed by Joshua's familiarity with London's Jew's Hospital and the popularity of vaccines in England. Whatever the reason, all of Sarah and Joshua's children were immunized.[51]

Older sister Reyna had been the first to undergo the new rite. At four months old, she was vaccinated for Kine Pox. Kine Pox—or "cowpox"— was a smallpox vaccine developed by Edward Jenner in England in the late 1790s that had made immunization safer and more reliable. Her progress was monitored closely, and Joshua noted that she "took the infection of Kine Pox apparently very finely."[52] The twins also were vaccinated with Kine Pox, this time by a Dr. Post, and they took the vaccine "apparently very favorably."[53] Yet for all their parents' foresight, the vaccine that the young twins needed most urgently would not be invented for another hundred years. In the 1790s through the 1830s, yellow fever would sweep the northeastern United States, bringing chaos in its wake. There was nothing the family could do but wait to see how the fevers would play out. Yet one thing made the waiting slightly more bearable. Sarah's mother and brother had decided to move to the North.

9

This Liberal City

Philadelphia, 1818–1833

ON JULY 6, 1820, CAPTAIN A. Latour noted in his ship's manifest that a young "Gentleman" Isaac Lopez Brandon (age twenty-two) and his mother "Mrs. Brandon" (age forty), had landed in Philadelphia.[1] They had come via the island of St. Thomas on the brig *Hannah*. The route was typical of that taken by Barbadians fleeing north, but the trip was monumental for an unusual reason: it was the first time that (Sarah) Esther's approximate birthday is recorded: 1780, give or take a year. It was approximate at best. A case in point: the age the crew wrote down for Isaac was off by six years. Regardless of their ages, the pair had fled the 1819–20 Barbadian vestry controversy. Isaac found Philadelphia's Jewish community a more congenial place to settle. The donations that the pair had given to help fund the second synagogue helped smooth their path and that of other Jews coming northward.

As the angry Barbadian opposition members had noted, the Brandons were not the only Barbadian Jews generous to the Mikveh Israel building project. What Levi, Lealtad, and other opponents may not have understood was that the Brandons' donation—and those of other Barbadian Jews— was neither completely selfless nor intended to shame the middling Jews back home. Atlantic world synagogues regularly contributed to the building funds of sister congregations with the expectation that when they were themselves in need, other congregations would return the favor. Charity also cemented alliances between individuals and other congregations. In this instance charity laid a path for migrants escaping the Caribbean by moving north.

All told, eighteen Barbadians donated sums to the Mikveh Israel synagogue fund, ranging from $4 to more than $220. Most had either trading or kinship ties to Philadelphia. The War of 1812 had disrupted Caribbean trade routes, and the subsequent economic crisis pushed many Barbadian Jews to leave the island. The migration of West Indian Jews to Philadelphia helped make the new Philadelphia synagogue necessary. One of the Barbadian donors—Moses Cohen d'Azevedo—would one day serve as the president of the Philadelphia congregation, and the Brandons would live to see one of their close relatives, Abraham Israel Keys, land the prestigious role as Philadelphia's *hazan*. Isaac Lopez Brandon was also eager to be part of that new community.[2]

Unlike Moses Lopez, who had been left out of Mikveh Israel's inner circle of influence, Isaac Lopez Brandon found Philadelphia was all a young, West Indian Jewish merchant could want. Philadelphia's Jewish community was less well established than Bridgetown's Nidhe Israel, but what the city lacked in Jewish infrastructure, it more than compensated for in terms of economic opportunities. By 1800, Philadelphia was the second largest city in the United States, with three times the population of Bridgetown. Three decades later the population had reached over 80,000. Whereas Suriname's and Barbados's Jewish communities were shrinking, Philadelphia's Jewish community was growing. In 1765 only slightly over 100 Jews had called Philadelphia home, but a decade later, the city's Jewish community had tripled. By 1781, there were nearly 1,000 Jews in Philadelphia, and Philadelphian Jews would soon outnumber even the once thriving Jewish community of Suriname.[3]

Philadelphia's growing reputation for commerce had drawn many Jews there, including those from Barbados. Its economic reputation was based on its port, into which fleets of fast-sailing clippers brought cargo from around the globe. Jews often participated in commerce, either as wealthy merchants moving ships between the Far East, the West Indies, Philadelphia, and Europe, or as petty tradesmen with small shops in town. By 1785, Jewish families had stores on the blocks near the synagogue, often clustered between Second and Third Streets near the wharves along the Delaware River. Future diplomat and newspaperman Mordecai Manuel Noah's father had an office on Water Street between Race and Arch.[4]

Trade had made many Philadelphian Jews rich. Families like that of Michael Gratz imported coffee from Brazil and rum, sugar, and cocoa from the West Indies, all of which he sold at the Gratz store on Fourth between

Market and Chestnut and later on the corner of Seventh and Market Streets. The Gratz Family shop became renowned for its magnificent array of spices. The Gratzes also entered the export game, sending local goods such as sheet iron, aluminum, and kosher food to other ports. The city's booming economy had similarly lured the family of David Franks, a son of Jacob Franks and one of the premier merchants of his day, to Philadelphia. Jacob Franks had served as the king's agent for New York and as the president of Shearith Israel. His son David Franks married a non-Jew and made (and lost) a fortune in land speculation, shipping, and the fur trade. Other early wealthy Philadelphian Jews included Benjamin Seixas, Moses Nathan, and Solomon Myers Cohen. Each worth between £30,000 (Solomon Myers Cohen) and £92,200 (Michael Gratz), these were men whom Isaac Lopez Brandon and his father Abraham Rodrigues Brandon would value both as potential distributors of Barbadian sugar and as sources for sending kosher meat to the island.[5]

Making ties to other Jewish families was crucial for the Brandons because Philadelphia, for all its economic strengths, was not immune to prejudice. On the one hand, Philadelphia—like Bridgetown—had an unusually large free African American community. Some free people of color came from the South and other northern cities, but many—like the Brandons—came from the West Indies. Others were born and bred in Philadelphia. In 1780, Philadelphia had become the first state in the new union to pass a Gradual Abolition Act that made everyone born after 1780 free. As a result, throughout the late eighteenth and early nineteenth centuries, Philadelphia was the largest and most important center of free Black life in the United States.[6]

In 1841, Black Philadelphian Joseph Willson would detail the lives of upper-class Black society in the city, noting this group's dedication to education, charity, and etiquette. This was precisely the sort of society the Brandon-Gills had aspired to in Barbados. But just as on the island, there was a great disparity within Philadelphia's Black community. Many spent most of their lives working as indentured servants, as the law indentured free children born to enslaved mothers to their mother's owners for twenty-eight years. Those who were free often struggled to make ends meet. Many Black Philadelphians were extremely poor, particularly following the War of 1812, which put one-third of the city's laborers out of work. By 1817, Black Philadelphians made up one-eighth of the city's population, but one-fifth of the people in the almshouse. Poverty also caused the crime rate to surge. Nine out of ten cases brought against Blacks in the city were for theft, yet the property taken was often worth very little. Commonly stolen items were those needed for survival such as food, clothing, or small amounts of cash. Moreover, Blacks were more likely to be convicted and punished than whites accused of the same crimes. By the end of the War of 1812, Blacks constituted 43 percent of Philadelphia's prison population.[7]

If poor Blacks were punished disproportionately, wealthier Blacks were subjected to white anger and violence. Black elites who worked to end slavery or improve the lives of poor Black workers were physically threatened. In one instance a white mob set fire to Pennsylvania Hall, the home of the Philadelphia Anti-Slavery Society. Other whites responded to assertions of Black freedom by denigrating Black Philadelphians for the way they looked and spoke. Only a year before Isaac and his mother landed in the northern city, William Thackera published a series of prints ridiculing upwardly mobile Blacks, a motif that would be taken up in the racial caricatures of Edward W. Clay and David Claypool Johnston over the next two decades.

Even whites who positioned themselves as friends often saw Black Philadelphians as outsiders. The American Colonization Society, founded in 1816, proposed to solve racial problems in the United States by forcing people with African ancestry to migrate to western Africa. By 1830, the Pennsylvania branch of the organization had become a crucial part of the anti-slavery movement in the city and nation more generally. Whereas abolitionist societies generally argued that all humankind was capable of advancement, the Pennsylvania Colonization Society (PCS) argued free Blacks could never achieve equality because they were inherently inferior. Advocates of colonization saw free Blacks as a threat to republicanism and hence argued that they should be resettled in Africa. In the meantime, white politicians openly questioned whether the right to vote of men who met property requirements applied to all men who were not enslaved, or only to white men. In 1838, the legislature made sure that the new state constitution clearly stated only white freedmen could vote.[8]

For most Philadelphians with African ancestry, the change was moot, as they did not meet the property requirements anyway. But the legislation was aimed at suppressing the roughly thousand wealthy Philadelphians of African descent. They were men like Isaac, whom Black writer Joseph Willson referred to at the time as the "higher classes of colored society."[9] As in Barbados, their homes were paragons of taste, with parlors that Willson described as "carpeted and furnished with sofas, sideboards, cardtables, mirrors" and even pianofortes.[10] Yet it was these very attempts at gentility and "racial crossing" that rankled artists like Edward W. Clay, who used the parlors as a backdrop for his caricatures of Black Philadelphians in *Life in Philadelphia* (1828–1830) and *Practical Amalgamation* (1839), the latter of which suggested ending slavery would endanger the nation. Like the anti-Black riots that rocked Philadelphia in 1834 and 1838, Clay's wrath focused on the top 10 percent of the free Black community—people who owned 70 percent of Black wealth—and more particularly the top 1 percent who owned 30 percent of Black wealth.[11]

These were men and women like Isaac Lopez Brandon and his mother (Sarah) Esther Brandon, people who had enough wealth to rely on servants of their own. Like the parlors in Clay's *Amalgamation* series that hosted interracial socializing and relationships, the Brandons' domestic spaces blurred and crossed racial lines. Clay's work echoes fears in Philadelphia newspapers about African Americans who might turn to dances, clothing, and conduct to overturn social hierarchies. After a "Coloured Fancy Ball," writers in the all-white *Pennsylvania Gazette* cried out in alarm that "if matters progress at this rate how long will it be before masters and servants change places?"[12] African American journalists rightfully chastised the anxious white Philadelphians for "exciting prejudice" and the *Gazette*'s poor journalism: the ball, they pointed out, was hardly the source of the noise and unruliness. Yet ironically, the *Gazette*'s journalists were not utterly incorrect about one thing: Philadelphia was exactly the sort of place where people who had once been enslaved could surpass their former owners in wealth. In this sense, Isaac Lopez Brandon and his mother fit right in.[13]

Yet, for all its interest in self-made men, Philadelphia's Jewish community's record on slavery was mixed. Even hazan Emmanuel Nunes Carvalho owned slaves. Although born in London, Carvalho had come to Philadelphia by way of Barbados, where from 1799 to 1806 he was the community's unpopular hazan, until he left to teach at Shearith Israel's school in New York. He was still in New York in 1810 when the census was taken, and at that time he had three enslaved people in his household. Did he bring them with him when he moved to Charleston and Philadelphia? Although the legislature had amended the Gradual Abolition Act in 1788 to allow nonresidents to bring their slaves into Pennsylvania for up to six months, visitors quickly figured out this meant one could bring slaves in indefinitely as long as they left the state at least every six months or temporarily recategorized as indentured servants.[14]

Moreover, even after slavery was abolished, at least some Jews seemed to agree with the need for the separation of races and supported efforts to disenfranchise African Americans. Most Philadelphian Jews tended to express anti-Black ideas only after they had left the city. Solomon Etting, son-in-law of merchant Barnard Gratz, was an active member of the State Colonization Society after he moved to Maryland. Similarly, as the editor of New York's *National Advocate*, Noah emphasized Blacks' inherent racial difference.[15] Noah registered outrage about Blacks who tried to "ape their masters and mistresses in everything," but particularly in clothing and conversation.[16] Noah found Black northerners' wealth and lack of fear irritating as he watched "black fashionables saunter up and down the garden, in all the pride of liberty and unconscious of want."[17] The crime here seems to be having fun while Black. For Noah, Black pleasure suggests a lack of political awareness: "They [Blacks] fear no Missouri plot; care for no political rights; happy in being permitted to dress fashionably, walk the streets, visit African Grove, and talk scandal."[18] This happiness led Noah to argue that "it is perfectly ridiculous to give them the right of suffrage—a right which they cannot value."[19]

Other Jews partook directly in Philadelphia's anti-Black backlash. In addition to belonging to congregation Mikveh Israel, Sarah and Abraham Hart owned the very stationery and booksellers store on Third Street that published Edward Williams Clay's anti-Black prints starting in 1829. Clay's *Life in Philadelphia* parodied Black English and denigrated their fashion choices. Like his later *Practical Amalgamation* series (1839), Clay's *Life in Philadelphia* presented integration of Blacks and whites not only as absurd but also dangerous to white womanhood and the American family.[20]

Both the style and content of Clay's caricatures emphasized the Black incompatibility with white American life. Clay parodied Black Philadelphians using the visual language of the minstrel shows that had recently begun to appear in Philadelphia's theaters, drawing exaggerated lips and jutting jaws to mark the figures as more like nonhuman primates than men. In contrast, Clay drew whites and domestic interiors in the style of Currier and Ives prints and *Godey's Lady's Book*. The divergent styles dramatized Black Philadelphians as interlopers. Painfully, Jews were printing this message, suggesting that some Jewish Philadelphians found multiracial families disturbing and threatening to the social order.[21]

That said, racism was not ubiquitous at Mikveh Israel. Though several members of the congregation had earlier owned slaves or relied on the labor of indentured servants, by the 1790s abolitionist arguments gained influence in the congregation. Even Benjamin Nones, who had earlier posted rewards for runaway slaves and servants, freed the people he had enslaved and became a member of the Pennsylvania Society for Promoting the Abolition

THE FRUITS OF AMALGAMATION.

Clay's prints were part of an anti-Black backlash in Philadelphia, which depicted the supposed evils of marriage between the races. Edward Clay, *Fruits of Amalgamation* from the *Practical Amalgamation* series (1839). American Antiquarian Society.

of Slavery. Since manumission was considered a transfer of property, it required a deed that was both signed and witnessed. As part of his role in encouraging other Philadelphians to free the enslaved, Nones witnessed numerous manumissions. Israel Jacobs, Mordecai M. Mordecai, Jonas Phillips, Moses Myers, Solomon Moline, and Isaac Moses either manumitted at least some people they enslaved outright instead of making them continue on as servants, or served as witnesses when the enslaved were given their complete freedom. Other members of the congregation, however, merely registered their slaves and set them free—as required by the 1780 law—but still required them to serve out a twenty-eight-year term as indentured servants.[22]

Even so, Mikveh Israel tended to be more liberal than other American synagogues regarding both non-white congregants and potential converts. First there was Lucy Marks, an elderly Black woman who died in 1838. Although not born into Judaism, she worked for the Marks family, who argued that her faithful and strict observance of Judaism should allow her to be buried in the congregation's cemetery. Despite controversy, she was eventually interred there. Even before the arrival of the Brandons there was Ana, a young woman from St. Croix in the Danish West Indies, who, along with her three sons, were converted by the congregation. Ana had married

David Nones, the son of Benjamin Nones, outside of the Jewish tradition on the island, but after she and the couple's three sons came to Philadelphia, they converted, the boys were circumcised, and the couple was remarried with Jewish rites.[23]

Mikveh Israel was also willing to convert women who had lived with male congregants out of wedlock, even though nonmarital sex was increasingly equated with prostitution in the almanacks, broadsides, pamphlets, and newspapers that made up Philadelphia's popular print. In 1794, for example, Moses Nathan requested that his housekeeper of eight years and the mother of his three children be allowed to convert. The *Mahamad* agreed. In this way, Philadelphia's Jewish congregation was as open-minded as early Christian reformers in the city, who believed that "fallen" women were completely redeemable and capable of re-entering society as teachers, caregivers for small children, and even the wives of respectable men. The acceptance of women who had borne Jewish men children outside of marriage was important for Sarah and Isaac's mother, (Sarah) Esther Lopez-Gill—who thanks to congregation Mikveh Israel appeared for the first time in the records of a Jewish congregation as "Mrs. Ab^m. R. Brandon."[24]

Mikveh Israel's relatively liberal policy regarding conversion and marriage can be gauged by other Atlantic world synagogues' negative reaction to Philadelphia's policies. The London rabbis, for example, refused to marry Sophie Deacon, who was converted in Philadelphia in 1816. Likewise, the Ashkenazi congregation in Jamaica seemed mystified that Mikveh Israel would accept a man into their congregation whom they protested should be inadmissible because of his parents' lack of marriage. Philadelphia was also more open regarding conversions than Shearith Israel in nearby New York: when a Benjamin I. Jacobs had requested that Shearith Israel convert his non-Jewish wife so that they could have a Jewish marriage in 1784, the petition was denied. Indeed, Shearith Israel's constitution explicitly forbade such conversion as early as 1763.[25]

When explaining to the congregation why the Philadelphia Mahamad was more lenient than other Atlantic world synagogues, the Mahamad noted that some other congregations' safeguards against transgression were "dangerous, and utterly uncongenial to the liberal spirit of the Constitution and Laws of this enlightened age and country."[26] This liberalism had a context. In taking a stand in favor of a "liberal spirit," Mikveh Israel echoed the words of George Washington himself, who when writing to "To the Hebrew Congregations of Philadelphia, New York, Charleston, and Richmond" in 1790 lauded US men for their "liberality of sentiment towards each other."[27]

When the Brandons made donations to the community and the new synagogue, they banked on this liberal spirit. The new synagogue they helped fund reflected their dreams. Twice the size of the original building, the new building had 356 seats, several of which would eventually be owned or rented by Barbadian families, while other West Indian families remained at the congregation's margins. The new structure reflected the community's ethos, which carefully placed one foot in the past and the other in the future. On the one hand, the new building followed the Western Sephardic tradition of placing the altar and ark at opposite ends of the synagogue. By turning the new building so it faced Cherry Street, the architect was able to place the ark at the end of the longer axis of the building—as was common in Western Sephardic congregations—and on the eastern side.

On the other hand, the new building was highly innovative and highlighted the political gains of the Philadelphia community. Congregants employed one of the finest architects in the new nation, William Strickland, who designed the synagogue in the up-and-coming Egyptian Revival style. Though the invocation of ancient Egypt—a land associated with Jewish enslavement—may seem a strange choice, Strickland's plans brought an important European design trend to the United States. Egyptomania owed a debt both to Freemasonry, which was popular among the Jews of Philadelphia, and Napoleon's recent conquest of Egypt. By using a style associated with Napoleon, Philadelphian Jews paid homage to their struggles for full equality under the law in the new republic.[28]

The new building would also have a Brandon twist. In 1824, Sarah and Isaac's cousin-in-law Abraham Israel Keys applied to become the new hazan of congregation Mikveh Israel. Abraham Rodrigues Brandon's character reference ensured that Keys was considered a worthy applicant. By autumn, Keys was appointed and made the journey to Philadelphia along with his wife Jael Brandon Keys.[29]

Abraham Israel Keys proved popular with the congregation, though member Rebecca Gratz was a bit condescending about what she deemed his "West Indian indolence." "I do not believe he [Keys] is a learned man," Gratz explained when describing Keys to her brother Benjamin, "nor indeed a very sensible one—but he is a good Hebrew scholar—an excellent Teacher, and a good man, he is moreover very popular with the congregation and reads the prayers in a manner as to make his hearers feel that he understands and is inspired with their solemnity."[30] Keys would, unfortunately, die just short of forty-eight years of age in 1828 of "bilious fever," most likely a result of the malaria that was rampant in Philadelphia.[31] By the time Keys died,

Rebecca Gratz's early skepticism had disappeared, and the synagogue made effusive eulogies for him. It built a lavish tomb for Keys and the previous hazan, Emanuel Nunes Carvalho.[32]

After Keys's death, the Brandons' cousin Jael Brandon Keys and their children would remain in Philadelphia. They continued to serve as important contacts for Sarah and Isaac, but increasingly Jael Brandon Keys found herself relying on the greater favors her once enslaved cousins and their wealthy father could provide. In 1831, their father Abraham would leave Jael Brandon Keys £100 and each of her children £50. In addition, she stood to inherit her share of what remained of the £1,000 Abraham had left his brother Moses Rodrigues Brandon. It was money she sorely needed. Although the congregation continued to pay her a widow's pension, by 1833 she was requesting special consideration for her sons. As the hazan's widow, Jael Brandon Keys had been given a seat in the new synagogue's balcony, but her sons struggled to find a place to pray during services, and the family could not afford to purchase seats. She specifically asked the *parnas* if he might appoint "such seats as they might occupy" as her son Jacob Keys had previously been "drove from place to place three times" in search of an acceptable vacant seat.[33]

The West Indians' struggle for inclusion within the strange new world of Philadelphia speaks to the larger struggle over liberty in the early American city and exactly how much was at stake in gaining an official seat in the synagogue. Money mattered more in the "liberal city" and helped the family to bypass obstacles their lineage had once created.

Moreover, with Moses Lopez now dead, the Lopez clan's influence was on the wane. After all of their father's years of struggle to become a member of Mikveh Israel, neither Matthias nor Isaac Lopez appears in the synagogue records. If where they chose to gift their father's books after his death are any sign, they were fed up with the congregation that had held their father at arm's length for so many years. Or perhaps they had other interests beyond religion.[34]

Although Matthias Lopez was still making ends meet as a grocer in 1818, his true passions were theater and publishing. In the years while his father was floundering, he moved between New York and Philadelphia, starting the short-lived *West-Chester Patriot* newspaper in the Bronx. In 1818, he edited a collection of poems by a popular American poet. By the 1820s, however, he was concentrating his time in the theater. He would go on to publish numerous plays by well-known playwrights and serve as a prompter for Philadelphia's New Theater.[35]

As part of the New York and Philadelphia theater scene, Matthias Lopez would maintain connections with former classmates, including Mordecai Manuel Noah. For in addition to being a statesman and newspaperman, Noah was a playwright. Since the age of eleven, he had been obsessed with drama, particularly the John Street Theater in New York. By 1808, he was writing his own plays, many of which focused instead on issues of manhood and nationalism and avoided openly Jewish characters.[36]

Theater also tied Lopez to other Jewish notables. Noah's younger first cousin, Jonas B. Phillips, was an important Jewish playwright by the 1820s, and Aaron J. Phillips, uncle of both Mordecai Manuel Noah and Jonas B. Phillips, was a well-known actor who played the role of the overbearing father in Noah's *She Would Be a Soldier*. In addition to performing, Phillips became the manager of Philadelphia's Arch Street Theater.[37]

After Moses Lopez's death, Matthias Lopez gave Aaron J. Phillips the Lopez account book, now housed at the New-York Historical Society. Matthias Lopez's connections to his Talmud Torah classmates continued to be a glue later in life, just not the one his father had expected. Matthias Lopez would be the end of the family line, resisting the kind of marriage that had wed Sarah to the northern Jewish communities.

A lingering reminder of Sarah and Isaac's enslaved past, Matthias Lopez was hardly the imposing figure he had cut back in 1800 in Barbados when his grandmother Hannah Esther Lopez had sent him to St. Michael's Church i n order to begin the long process of manumitting the Brandon children.[38] But by 1819, Matthias Lopez would prove the least of Sarah and Isaac's worries.

10

Feverish Love

New York, 1819–1830

WHO WOULD HAVE BELIEVED THAT the death of old Dorothy Kavanaugh, the utterly unremarkable Catholic widow who ran a small grocery at 23 Old Slip, would turn out to be so important for the lives of early American Jews? Her small shop was less than a block and a half from the offices of Isaac Moses & Sons at 63 Wall Street and around the corner from the synagogue. At first, her death seemed unexceptional; she was, as French-born doctor Felix Pascalis Ouviere explained, a "delicate weakly woman" with hardly any property.[1] But something was clearly amiss when she died in agony only two days after Catholic priest Rev. T. W. French administered her the last rites on August 27, 1819. Her death was quickly followed by those of Mr. Brown, on Front Street, and Margaret Brady, who lived with Kavanaugh in the small room behind the store, and who vomited a black substance during her final illness. By September 6, eight people were dead and an alarm was sounding in the city. Through no fault of her own, Kavanaugh had set into motion a panic that soon swept up Sarah and Joshua Moses, their young children, and the rest of the Brandon-Moses clan.[2]

Sarah had recently given birth to her twins Moses L. and Isaac Moses when the *Columbian* reported on September 6 that a committee of seven men had been appointed to look into the recent deaths. All summer, news had been circulating about yellow fever in Charleston, Baltimore, and even nearby New Haven, but when the committee reported back later the same day, the doctors were in denial. Certainly some of the essential symptoms had been present, but so were many others not typically found with yellow fever. Moreover, neither the eyes of the deceased nor their skin had the typical yellow hue. It was probably just bilious remitting fever, insisted Dr. David Hosack in a letter printed in the *Evening Post*. He was wrong. By September 8, all of the cases were listed in the paper with the verdict: yellow fever. The Board of Health quickly recommended that, despite the inconvenience, everyone living in the "suspected portion of the city" leave and that the area be thoroughly "cleansed and purified" in order to end the epidemic before it started.[3] The plan did not work. A week later, the newspapers admitted that every effort had "failed to check the spreading of this dreadful disease."[4] To make matters worse, in each case, the disease was "uniformly fatal, to all whom it . . . attacked."[5]

Even with our own experience with dreadful pandemics, it is hard to imagine how frantic Sarah must have been. Yellow fever struck down old and young, sick and healthy. Sarah had three children under the age of two. Fever turned the world of the Moses-Brandon family upside down. As Sarah and Joshua struggled to make their way in the early city, they found their lives fluctuating wildly between joy and death, with death always seeming to win in the end.

Part of the terror caused by yellow fever was that it was always lurking somewhere, so that even the hint of it caused chaos. The disease was relatively new, born out of the triangle trade. As ships carrying enslaved people and infected mosquitos traveled around the Atlantic, epidemics hit ports in the West Indies and then the American South before turning north. By 1793, the disease was ravaging Philadelphia, killing 5,000 people—one-tenth of the city's population—in a little more than three months. "So great was the general terror," one first-hand observer noted amidst the 1793 epidemic, "that for some weeks, carts, wagons, coaches, and [sedan] chairs, were almost constantly transporting families and furniture to the country in every direction."[6]

Yellow fever's symptoms were partially to blame for the panic: blood dripped from victims' noses and mouths as their skin turned a sickly yellow. Yet some victims—like the first cases in New York—hardly knew what hit them. A few started with extreme chills and fever, others with nausea and exhaustion. By the time vomiting, stupor, and the tell-tale yellowness hit, the victims understood they were doomed.[7]

All cases shared one horrifying element: the speed of the disease. As few as ten days came between a mosquito's pinpricking bite and the patient's death. Doctors were often of little use. Treatment was so rudimentary that

Sarah Simpson Wood as a child. Anonymous. Watercolor on ivory. Courtesy Ann Gegan.

it was somewhat miraculous for anyone to survive, even if ministered to by a physician. Yellow fever had become the most dreaded disease in North America, creating terror everywhere it appeared.[8]

Most New Yorkers had felt the panic before. In 1798, a summer epidemic in the city left 2,086 dead. Almost everyone in the Jewish community could later recall with horror a relative or friend who had died. Most major Jewish families lost a loved one, including members of the Hays, Myers, Hendricks, Isaacs, Israel, Judah, Levi, Lazarus, Nathan, Moss, and possibly the Moses clan. One of the Jewish victims had been Walter J. Judah, a young medical student at Columbia College, who as his tombstone noted, was "wore down by his exertions to alleviate the sufferings of his fellow citizens in that dreadful contagion" and was ultimately himself overcome.[9]

Those who survived re-lived their trauma as smaller epidemics continued to rock the city. In 1805, 50,000 people fled to the countryside to escape the miasma—the foul-smelling air that arose from rotting food, night soil (sewage), and polluted water that many felt was to blame for epidemics such as cholera and yellow fever. Although scientists would later show that mosquitos, not bad smells, were to blame, early New Yorkers were correct that their city was filthy. Traveler William Neunham Blaine, who arrived in the city during the 1822 epidemic, noted with some despair that "the streets in the lower part of town are notoriously filthy, and the stranger is not a little surprised to meet the hogs walking about in them, for the purpose of devouring the vegetable and offal that are thrown in the gutter."[10] Having come from England, Blaine was shocked by the city's lack of sewers. Each house had its own pit for collecting human waste which, when full, was dumped directly into the nearby river.[11]

While medical professionals didn't make the connection until several decades later, the lack of an adequate sewer system also meant human waste contaminated the water supply. New Yorkers were so convinced that the filth was causing their problems that when yellow fever broke out in 1819, they threatened the city's "Resident Physician" who had advised the board of health, accusing him of incompetence. According to the logic of the day, since the Resident Physician had failed to eradicate the polluted air and water in the urban center, he was to blame for yellow fever's re-emergence.[12]

More scientifically minded thinkers, however, proposed a new source for the 1819 epidemic: the Baltimore Packets, a southern shipping line. This was not utterly illogical, as the outbreak had begun near Old Slip, where the vessels embarked. Yet early investigators' attempts to map the disease's path often fell on deaf ears. More popular were the words of ministers who preached repentance, blaming the plague on sinfulness. Overall, the confusion about how the epidemic began meant preventive measures were often random. So many New Yorkers, for example, took to drinking alcohol as a prophylactic that one doctor said he did not believe that drunkenness had ever been "so common."[13]

For merchants like Joshua Moses and his brothers, the reason for the plague was less pressing than the location of the outbreak. It was not just that Old Slip was three and a half short blocks from the newly rebuilt Mill Street Synagogue. Even closer to the outbreak's center was the flagship office of Isaac Moses & Sons. Other Shearith Israel congregants, including Isaac Levy, a wholesale watchmaker, and Solomon Levy were also in jeopardy, as their stores at 1 Old Slip and 86 Coffee House Slip were in the area hit hardest. For Jewish families living near the synagogue and working by the wharves, it was only a matter of time before death knocked at their door. So, when the Board of Health recommended moving, the Moses clan fled en masse to the countryside. They were not alone. In four days, 20,000 New Yorkers beat a hasty retreat from the city.[14]

Winter brought a reprieve. With the first frost, the mosquitoes died, and New Yorkers were back. The timing was opportune, as Sarah was once again pregnant. In June 1820, she gave birth to a third son, Abraham Rodriguez Brandon Moses ("Brandon"), named for her Barbadian father. Brandon was born at Joshua and Sarah's new house, in the middle of the night on Shabbat. Sarah and Joshua had moved up in the world, abandoning Ephraim Hart's old house for an even more fashionable residence at 31 Greenwich Street, on Millionaires Row. Young Brandon was circumcised on June 24 (12 Tammuz). Perhaps the coziness of the synagogue seats had worked their magic, as this time the *mohel* was New York's own Eleazer Samuel Lazarus, grandfather of poet Emma Lazarus. Like his brothers', Brandon's rite of passage tied him to his father's kin, as his paternal uncle and aunt Aaron and Richea Levy became his godparents.[15]

Perhaps then, everything seemed normal when on August 7, 1820, the fourth US Census taker stopped by Sarah and Joshua's house. For most families in the Jewish community, the event was routine. By 1820, Jews in the United States were described as white by census takers regardless of whether they were Sephardic or Ashkenazi, unless they had obvious African ancestry. For Sarah, however, the census must have invoked a whirlpool of emotions. The 1820 census divided people by age and gender, as well as whether they were white, "colored," enslaved, or foreigners who had not been naturalized. How would Sarah and her young brood be interpreted by the census taker?

The answer was not obvious, but it would have important repercussions for her children's future rights. Although today the common perception is that the "one-drop rule" was used to define Blackness throughout US history, this definition of race was only unilaterally applied in the United States starting in the 1920s with the fourteenth census. As in early Barbados, that census decided that any multiracial person was classified according to the non-white portion of their ancestry. This definition of race was not in play, however, for the 1820 census. During Sarah's lifetime, how race was defined varied both by state and across the Americas. Moreover, how race was determined was left to the discretion of the individual census taker. Early American censuses did not define race, because as a nation, early Americans did not agree on what made someone fit into different racial categories.[16]

What was clear, however, was the result if the census taker determined that Sarah and her children were "colored." Throughout the Americas, whiteness strongly correlated with civil rights. When New Yorkers voted to gradually emancipate slaves, the Assembly suggested that the bill be amended to restrict the rights of free people of color. Assemblymen argued that free people of color should not be able to vote, nor serve as witnesses in courts of law. Similarly, they proposed interracial marriage be restricted such that if a Black and white couple chose to marry, they had to pay a £200 fee. Concerns were raised that Black spouses might influence white voters, and that multiracial children might pass for white and gain full rights.

Though ultimately the amendments were eliminated, restrictions on Black rights continued throughout the antebellum period. Property requirements for Black New Yorkers were so much higher than for whites that in 1826 only sixteen Black men could vote in the city. Even by the Civil War, only about 300 Black men were eligible out of 12,000 Black inhabitants. Education and even military service were separate. Black New Yorkers of all educational levels were underemployed. If the census taker labeled Sarah and Joshua's children "colored," that status could affect their access to jobs, education, housing, voting rights, and economic opportunities that white Jews took for granted.[17]

So it was most likely with trepidation that Sarah and her husband encountered the census taker who knocked on their door in the summer of 1820. In the end, the census taker deemed most of the household white, including Sarah and all of her children. Only one person was categorized as a "free colored female," forty-five or older. Was this Sarah's mother (Sarah) Esther Brandon, who had just arrived in Philadelphia with Isaac a month earlier and was possibly visiting her new grandchildren? If so, was the otherwise unaccounted-for free white male between sixteen and twenty-five Sarah's brother Isaac, once again categorized only slightly younger than he actually was? Or were the two unnamed household members just servants, as surely some of the many extra free white women and adolescents living in Joshua and Sarah's house were? Since all but the head of the household were unnamed, it is impossible to know.[18]

Regardless of who the unnamed woman of color was in the census, by the next year (Sarah) Esther Brandon had moved from Philadelphia to New York, setting up her own house at 78 Greenwich Street. Her daughter was once again pregnant. On October 2, 1821, in the days between Rosh Hashana and Yom Kippur, Sarah gave birth to a fourth son, Israel, who like his brothers was circumcised. Maybe the earlier nod to the Brandon clan had done its magic, as this time the godparents were none other than (Sarah) Esther and Abraham Rodrigues Brandon. (Sarah) Esther Brandon had only to walk down the street for the ceremony, but Abraham Rodrigues Brandon came all the way from Barbados, arriving a few weeks before the ceremony on the brig *Cannon* via St. Thomas.[19]

The years were close ones between (Sarah) Esther Brandon and her daughter's family. Bolstered by business success, Joshua opened his own mercantile office at 157 Pearl Street, and the family once again changed homes, this time closer to (Sarah) Esther Brandon at 50 Greenwich Street. Yet the family barely had time to get settled before yellow fever struck again. This time the epidemic was unbearably close: the first victim fell in early July at the foot of Rector Street—a mere two and a half blocks from Sarah and Joshua's new house. Brother-in-law Aaron Levy was hardly better off, as his home at 38 Greenwich was only six doors down from Sarah and Joshua. By August 8, the entire district was infected, and citizens who could, fled to nearby Greenwich Village. Alarmed that the disease seemed to be spreading at a rate of roughly forty feet a day, city officials attempted to contain the pestilence by building a fence around the hardest-hit area. However, since mosquitos could easily fly over that fence, the city officials found themselves having to expand the barricade each day.[20]

Joshua, Sarah, and their five young children escaped the plague-ridden town by going to grandmother Reyna Levy Moses's country house at Mount Listen north of Greenwich Village. The high holidays came, and no one dared return to the Mill Street Synagogue. So it was that in September a temporary synagogue was opened in Oliver Street, "the lower part of the city being deserted on account of the yellow fever," Aaron Levy reported.[21] The Jews were not alone in their concern: so great was the exodus to Greenwich Village that a map of the city published in 1822 showed where in the village the banks, custom house, post office, Merchants Exchange, and two coffee houses were located during the epidemic.[22]

Those who didn't move quickly enough perished, but so did some who fled. Early in the crisis, Naphtali Phillips—*parnas* of Shearith Israel and owner of the *National Advocate*—lost his wife Rachel Seixas Phillips, niece of the recently deceased Reverend Gershom Mendes Seixas. She died at their home on the northeast corner of Chambers and Broadway, mere blocks from the Moses clans' gilded residences, a victim of yellow fever. She was forty-nine. Two days later, Esther Gomez passed away from the fever. A fellow Barbadian, Gomez had come to New York in the 1750s to marry her first cousin when she was only fifteen years old. For the next few months, congregants continued to die, the very young and very old most likely to succumb.[23]

But by late October, the worst was once again over. On November 15, the city officially reopened all houses of public worship that had been closed to keep the pestilence from spreading. All told, 401 cases of yellow fever had been reported, with 230 dead. The family put the epidemic behind them. Aaron Levy noted in his journal that the lilac bushes were "in full bloom, a second crop."[24] Apple trees and gooseberry bushes also blossomed a second time. Amid this rebirth, the family returned to their home by the docks.

The Brandon-Moses family left behind the fever season, but grief did not let them go. After his grandson Israel's *brit milah*, Abraham Rodrigues Brandon had returned to Barbados on business, but (Sarah) Esther Brandon stayed on in New York at her house on Greenwich Street. On Saturday evening, March 29, 1823, after a long and painful illness, "Mrs. S.E. Brandon, wife of A.R. Rodrigues, Esq. of the Island of Barbados" was dead.[25]

As with her life, little about (Sarah) Esther Brandon's death is recorded. Nowhere in Barbados was her birth date written down, and Shearith Israel's records are likewise (purposefully?) vague except regarding the location of her grave. As the extended kin of M. L. Moses, the synagogue's current parnas, Sarah's mother had not had her Jewishness questioned, even though at least some must have known that she had been born to non-Jewish parents and almost certainly never officially converted. Yet God—or at least the weather—seemed to be against (Sarah) Esther Brandon's final rest. A freak March snowstorm had blanketed the city, freezing the ground and delaying the funeral entourage. Jewish law may have required that the dead be laid to rest as quickly as possible, but New York City law required that dead bodies be interred at least six feet below ground. Secular law triumphed.[26]

When the storm cleared and the ground thawed enough to dig, the simple coffin finally made its way to Shearith Israel's burial ground at Chatham Square, where (Sarah) Esther Brandon was laid to rest next to the recently deceased former slave owner Abraham Rodrigues Rivera. On Rivera's other side lay his nephew Joseph Lopez, son of slave trader Aaron Lopez. Did (Sarah) Esther Brandon's children sense the irony? At the time of her passing, Blacks had not yet attained complete emancipation in either New York or Barbados. At death, however, she finally achieved acceptance.[27]

Sarah and Isaac almost certainly were there for the burial, but the one person who does not appear to have been at the cemetery was Esther's "husband" Abraham Rodrigues Brandon. He had already taken up with a much younger woman, Sarah Simpson Wood. Like Sarah and Isaac's mother, Sarah Simpson Wood was born and bred in Barbados, but unlike (Sarah) Esther, she appears to have been born free and white. She was also Anglican.

Why then had she taken up with a Jewish man thirty-six years her senior without even the promise of marriage?

The answer may lie in the rocky hills of St. Joseph's Parish in Barbados. Set on the eastern side of the island, today St. Joseph's is known for its fantastical gardens and pristine beaches. Around 1800, however, its rocky terrain was known for landslides and inclement weather. Its residents made their fortunes elsewhere. The Woods had struggled to find social acceptance. Sarah Simpson Wood's parents, Margaret Gibson Simpson and John Wood married in 1783. Most likely, Margaret Gibson Simpson was born out of wedlock. Her father Nathaniel eventually claimed her, however, and she passed along his last name, Simpson, to several of her children. The Woods had six children who survived long enough to be baptized at the parish church, and their daughter Sarah Simpson Wood was born second to last.[28]

Like many whites who lived on the craggy hills of St. Joseph, the Woods were neither poor nor wealthy, but of a middling sort, with six fieldhands (mainly Black) and two "coloured" people working in their house. Even enslaved children were put to work: one of their house servants was a boy named George Francis who was only six years old when the slave register was tallied in 1820. Two of the enslaved workers in the field were likewise children. By the time Abraham Rodrigues Brandon took up with Sarah Simpson Wood, her father was an invalid and his son was managing his father's property. Shortly after Wood met Brandon, their first daughter Julia Brandon was born somewhere around 1823–24. Perhaps like her grandmother Margaret Gibson, Sarah Simpson Wood hoped the father of her children would eventually "make things right." It was not to be.[29]

For despite family lore regarding their nuptials and Sarah Simpson Wood's free status, the couple almost certainly never married. It was not just that neither the synagogue nor the churches on the island recorded their wedding: island records were often lost in hurricanes and are spotty at best. According to their son, they had been married in Jamaica, but no records exist from there either. More telling is that in his will, Abraham referred to her as "Sarah Simpson Wood of St. Michael's Parish" rather than as his wife or Mrs. Brandon. Sarah Brandon Moses and Isaac Lopez Brandon were "my daughter" and "my son," but Julia, Esther, Lavinia, Joseph, and Alfred were "the children of said Sarah Wood" and "my reputed children."[30] There were many ways to say children were illegitimate at the time, and reputed was one of them.

Equally telling, the Barbadian authorities considered Sarah Simpson Wood single: in 1829 she owned property, a privilege not available to married

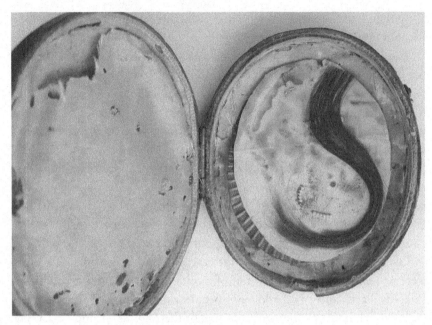

Lock of hair tucked into Sarah Simpson Wood's portrait. Portrait and hair were a visceral way of keeping a loved one close. Courtesy Ann Gegan.

women at the time. Moreover, Wood seems to have recognized the tentative nature of her status, as when she married Daniel Goody in 1833 she referred to herself as a "spinster," not a widow.[31] Abraham Rodrigues Brandon's inclination to select certain multiracial children (James, Tom, Beck, John, and William) to be freed upon his death suggests that he was probably not monogamous.[32] Regardless, Brandon's relationship with Sarah Simpson Wood was the only bond other than his liaison with (Sarah) Esther Lopez-Gill that he acknowledged in writing.[33]

It seems unlikely that Sarah Brandon Moses spent much time considering the new rival for her father's affections as she crossed the snow-driven city to pay her last respects to the mother who helped her escape enslavement. She had more pressing things on her mind. She was three months pregnant with her sixth child, Joseph Washington Moses. He was born on September 5, the eve of Rosh Hashana. Once again Sarah was lucky: the child and mother survived the birth unscathed. The godparents once again intertwined the two branches of the family: the godfather was Isaac Rodrigues Brandao and the godmother Miss Rebecca Moses, Joshua's older unmarried sister.[34]

But not everyone's childbirth stories ended so fortunately that year. The previous fall Rachel Gratz Moses, wife of Joshua's brother Solomon

Four illustrations show the progress of yellow fever. *Observations sur la fièvre jaune, faites à Cadix.* Paris: Etienne Pariset and André Mazet, 1820. National Library of Medicine.

Moses, had been pregnant with her ninth child. Unlike Sarah, Rachel Gratz Moses's pregnancies tended to end in grief, with young Harriet (1812) and Edmund (1815) dying as infants. In September 1823, as the high holidays were being observed, Rachel Gratz Moses and her infant Gertrude fell ill. On September 30, two days after the festivities of Simhat Torah, Gertrude died. This time, though, her mother was not around to mourn the loss. She had passed away a day earlier. Her niece later recounted that at the funeral, Rachel Gratz Moses lay "in her coffin with her sleeping infant beside her."[35] She was forty years old.

Rachel Gratz Moses's tragic death rocked the Gratz and Moses families. Unlike many merchant marriages, Solomon Moses and Rachel Gratz's union was a love match. After initially dismissing Moses as a "bore," Gratz had later succumbed to his pleas with an emotional fervor that matched his own.[36] Moreover, throughout their marriage Joshua had been unusually close to the couple, with Solomon Moses often serving as his business partner. After Gratz's death, the couple's six surviving children and the bereaved husband went to live in the house of Rachel's Gratz relations. The children's aunt Rebecca Gratz, known for her dedication to philanthropy and education, would raise them. The eldest of the couple's children was only twelve and the youngest just three: for some, Rebecca Gratz was the only mother they knew.[37]

The next year, Solomon and Joshua lost their own mother, Reyna Levy Moses on June 24, 1824, just before Rosh Chodesh Tamuz. Although the oldest of her ten siblings, at seventy-one Reyna Levy Moses had outlived half of them. She had also survived long enough to see her daughter Lavinia Moses marry that March. Lavinia Moses had just turned thirty-eight, so she had given her mother plenty of time to despair that she—like her older sister Rebecca and younger sister Saly Moses—might never marry. Yet just as Reyna Levy Moses's middle daughter reached middle age, Lavinia Moses attracted the attention of a radiantly attractive Jew six years her junior.[38]

If Reyna Levy Moses had been despondent that her seven still unmarried children would ever find their mates, apparently she also spent some time worrying that they would. Fortune hunters seem to have been on Moses's mind when she made her will in July 1823. She left each of her unmarried daughters $7,500—the rough equivalent of slightly over $6 million today. She clarified that it should be placed out in stock, so they could live off the interest without having to touch the principal. But there was a catch. If Lavinia Moses or any of her currently unmarried sisters married, only half would go to the woman's new husband, rather than the full amount as was the default according to state law. The other half of the $7,500 each inherited, Reyna Levy Moses safeguarded for her daughters' "own separate use and benefit free from the control and engagements" of any future husbands.[39] Maybe all the seduction novels Reyna Levy Moses's sons Moses L. Moses and David Moses had been checking out for the family from New York Library Company had made their mother think twice about leaving her daughters at the mercy of the men they might choose to marry for love.[40]

And by all accounts, that is what Lavinia Moses appears to have done. In the evening of March 24, 1824, shortly before her mother's death, she wed her brother-in-law Isaac Lopez Brandon under a chuppah. He was no fortune hunter: his father promised him a large legacy as well. Moreover, if his portrait is anything to go by, Lavinia Moses was lucky. Isaac was elegant, handsome, and debonair. His brown eyes were large and mysterious, and his curling locks fashionably swept upward to create extra height. His chin and neck were cleanshaven, with chic sideburns running down each cheek. Like Joshua and fashion icon Beau Brummel, Isaac was a man who knew his cloth. The tightly wound neckcloth held up and framed his head, with the high collar revealing the master stitching of high-end men's suits. A lacy ruffle decorated his shirt front. Mr. Darcy would be proud to be so depicted.[41]

Although he was only thirty-two when he married, Isaac appears to have made little impact on gentile New York. Some papers got the facts right, but when the wedding announcement appeared in the *New York Evening Post*, Isaac was misidentified as "Mr. Isaac L. Brandry of Barbadoes" while Lavinia Moses is correctly identified as "the daughter of the late Mr. Isaac Moses of this city."[42]

Despite the misprints, Isaac's official incorporation into one of the synagogue's leading families was a sweet reversal of his treatment in Barbados, but only one clear sign of his new status in Jewish New York. His Jewishness was so unquestioned by officials at Shearith Israel that, unlike his sister's marriage record seven years earlier, they made no mention of his conversion. He was now the son of "Abraham and Sarah" of Barbados, not Abraham and Sarah the patriarch and matriarch of us all, as was the expected formula on a convert's marriage contract.[43]

Isaac's reception was a welcome change from the treatment the Brandon men had received only three years earlier in Barbados. In February 1821, Isaac had been struck off the list of yahidim in Congregation Nidhe Israel, his fifty pounds of donated sugar thrown back in his face. Yet even before he married Lavinia Moses, Isaac secured his place at Shearith Israel. Connections to the Moses clan through his sister Sarah paved his way. As in Barbados, the New York synagogue was run by what less fortunate Jews jealously called the "hereditary junto"—a group of men from wealthy families who passed along their positions on the *Mahamad* from brother to brother and father to son.[44] In Barbados, Abraham Rodrigues Brandon's status on the Mahamad had not been enough to counteract his son's African ancestry.

This time, the status of Isaac's in-laws was enough, for front and center on the board was one of his sister Sarah's new brothers-in-law, Moses L. Moses. Perhaps Isaac had help as well from board member Cary Judah, whose father Benjamin Judah was an avid reader of abolitionist and pro-African works, as were members of the Hendricks and Gomez families whose voices carried in synagogue matters. Even the presence on the board of Mordecai Manuel Noah, arguably one of the most vocally anti-Black members of the congregation, did not change the result. Isaac's candidacy was not questioned. If anyone was so vulgar as to suggest Isaac was less a Jew or less worthy because of his ancestry, no one bothered to record it in the congregational minutes. So it was that on June 29, 1823, Isaac Lopez Brandon signed Shearith Israel's book of constitution and laws. He was now entitled to vote. What's more, the records reveal that he clearly exercised the right.[45]

It was not the last time that the Moses clan stood by Isaac. When synagogue seats came up for sale in April 1826, Isaac purchased seat number 41, next to his wife's brother-in-law, the former parnas Aaron Levy. Sarah likewise sat beside her Moses sisters-in-law, in the seat purchased by Joshua. Two years later when it was time to renew, the pattern continued, and Isaac bought his wife Lavinia Brandon her own seat next to her sisters and Sarah.[46]

The Moses clan also secured Isaac rights outside of the synagogue. He declared his intention to become a citizen in June 1826 when he appeared before Nicholas Dean, clerk of the City & County of New York. His attempt speaks to his sense of his own racial identity. The US Naturalization Act passed in March 1790 required that any alien who wanted to become a citizen had to have lived in the United States for two years and be of "good character." He also had to be a "free white person"—a criterion reaffirmed by the Naturalization Act of 1802.[47] Did Isaac understand himself as white, or just aspire to have others define him that way?

Whichever the case, in 1829 Isaac returned to court to be admitted. This time, he brought a witness: his brother-in-law Moses L. Moses, who swore to Isaac's character and fulfillment of the residency requirement. Isaac was now officially a white U.S. citizen with full voting rights. His racial assignment was no longer at the mercy of a census taker's whim.[48]

This confirmation must have been bittersweet at best, as by 1829 the world Isaac carefully built had begun to fall apart. At first, after Isaac's marriage, everything appeared glorious, with the Brandon-Moses clan rapidly expanding. In February 1825, Sarah and Joshua's son Lionel Moses was born in New York. The godparents wove together the two families: Aaron Levy and Lavinia Brandon. Another son Benjamin Frederick Moses followed in 1827, with two of Joshua's younger unmarried siblings, Hayman Levy Moses and Miss Saly Moses, becoming godparents.

Nearby at 82 Warren Street, Joshua's new business partner Isaac was also prospering. His wife Lavinia Moses Brandon gave birth to a son, Abraham Rodriguez Brandon, in September 1826. Like his sister's son, this new Abraham's middle name would bear the distinctive "z." Once the "s" in Rodrigues had been a crucial marker of the family's Portuguese origins, but in New York the tradition fell away. Like at London's Bevis Marks, at Shearith Israel congregants tended not to finesse the difference between a Spanish z and Portuguese s. More crucial were young Abraham's godparents, who helped solidify Isaac's dreams for his children's future: Moses L. Moses as godfather and Sarah Brandon Moses as the godmother.[49]

Back in Barbados, Sarah and Isaac's father Abraham Rodrigues Brandon and his new companion Sarah Simpson Wood brought forth a new brood: Julia (1823–4), Esther (1825), Lavinia (1826), Abraham (1826), Joseph (1828), and Alfred (1830). Their names honored both Abraham's family— Julia was seemingly named for Brandon's niece (Jael/Julia) who married Abraham Israel Keys—and the New York clan. Lavinia was clearly named for Isaac's young wife, and Esther, apparently for the mother of Brandon's older children.[50]

Brandon's younger children somehow escaped a fate that had plagued his firstborn: starting with Lavinia, most of the younger brood's births were recorded in the Jewish congregation's register. A mystery remains, however, why Julia and Esther Brandon were not on the books. Had something changed with regard to Sarah Simpson Wood's religious status around 1826, or were the Barbadian records—which in general are somewhat haphazard—just incomplete? Maybe given Abraham Rodrigues Brandon's ire after Isaac's expulsion, it was early 1826 before he wanted to register his children. Or maybe the death of Lavinia Brandon's twin made communal

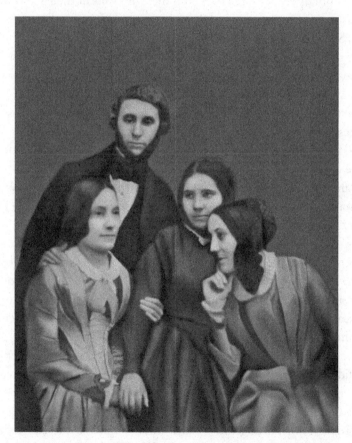

Anonymous, Brandon-Wood family portrait, ca. 1845. Daguerreotype. Courtesy Ann Gegan.

acceptance more necessary, as Brandon required the help of a minyan for the infant's burial service.[51]

Amid all the blessings, the death of Lavinia Brandon's twin when he was only a month old was a sad foreboding of premature losses to come. On February 10, 1828, Sarah Brandon Moses was in childbirth with her second set of twins, Ariel and Alfred. Alfred was named for Sarah's new half-brother, but Ariel's more explicitly Jewish name reflected the sad fact that he did not live long enough to receive an English one. By March 29, Ariel was dead.

Alfred struggled through. He was not well enough to be circumcised until more than a year later, on May 30, 1829. The godparents were new (Moses B. Seixas and Sarah H. Levy), perhaps because the family was quickly unraveling. Ariel and Alfred were Sarah's last children.

On February 20, 1828, ten days after the twins were born, Sarah was dead. No reason was given, but the timing suggests complications from the twins' births. She was laid to rest in Shearith Israel's second Beit Haim on Milligan Street, next to her mother-in-law Reyna Moses. When he followed her to the grave, Ariel's small coffin was nestled into the ground to her other side.[52]

Sarah was twenty-nine and left behind nine children, all of whom survived into adulthood. The oldest, Reyna Moses, was only ten. The youngest, Alfred Moses, was an infant. Their lack of time with their mother created gaps in the family story, riddling the next generation with questions no one could answer.

Sarah's short life had been one of constant changes and upheavals. Born in obscurity and baptized Christian while enslaved to a Sephardic family, she had not only gained her freedom but had become accepted as one of the nação—Jews of the Portuguese nation. That legacy, along with a boarding school education and impressive dowry provided by her father, allowed her to marry into the upper echelons of New York Jewish life. In Barbados and New York, her family had fought for their rights as full members of early American religious communities, and her nine surviving children benefited from the sacrifices their forefathers and foremothers had made.

Yet even in death, there was no rest for Sarah. Two years after her coffin was laid in the ground with young Ariel beside her, Eleventh Street was widened and opened through Broadway to the Bowery. The improved street gobbled up most of the synagogue's second burial ground, reducing it to a small triangle. In making these plans, the city ignored the congregation's "insuperable objections to disturbing the dead,"[53] forcing the living to relocate the graves, crowding the dead into the new, much smaller plot. What's more, the remaining lot was raised to meet the newly graded street. This necessitated the removal of all of the gravestones and their replacement, often in new locations that were tidy but bore little resemblance to where the dead actually lay.

The new configuration belied the sheer number of dead packed in the small yard. Many stones were lost or buried in the condensing process, and the tombstones chosen for display above ground were not random. The triangle houses the remains of both the congregation's poorest and most illustrious members, but today it is mainly the wealthy and influential whose stones are arrayed along the western wall. While officially the task of deciding which stones to place where was left to the synagogue, family members also played a role in the reorganization, taking part in synagogue discussions and writing petitions.

So it was that Joshua Moses found himself urgently writing the Mahamad in 1830 to ensure that "the precious remains of my Wife & Child" would be reinterred in a new cemetery, so that one day he and his wife could once again "rest side by side."[54] He was successful. Today the couple lies together with their son, Ariel, in the Twenty-First Street Burial Ground. Other kin lie nearby.

Shearith Israel's Twenty-First Street Burial Ground. Photo by author.

Before their reunion, however, there were further losses. Sarah's brother Isaac barely had time to recover from his sister's death when his own wife went into labor. On April 3, 1828, Lavinia gave birth to her second child. Seven days later, Isaac's new wife was dead. In memory of that loss, the new infant bore her mother's name, alongside that of her grandmother: Lavinia Reyna Brandon. Her mother was buried in the Beth Haim on Oliver Street next to the late Moses Gomez. Lavinia Reyna Brandon's only sibling, Abraham Rodriguez Brandon, was only a year and a half old. The first two years of Lavinia Reyna Brandon's life were filled with unending turmoil, adrift without the mother she had almost no time to know. Her father did all he could, including changing her Hebrew name from Reyna to Leah in June 1830, in hopes of tricking the angel of death.

Death was not fooled. Seven days after her name change, Lavinia Brandon also was dead. Her small coffin followed the path of her mother's to Oliver Street, where it was buried beside her. After the crushing despair of Sarah and Lavinia's deaths in the spring of 1828, Isaac and Joshua struggled to rebuild their lives and raise their surviving children without the help of wives or mothers. As business partners, the men's destinies were interwoven with each other. Their wives' unseasonable deaths were a stark warning that time was fleeting. They had their children to think about, and the legacy they would leave behind.[55]

II

When I Am Gone

New York, Barbados, London, 1830–1847

WEEKDAY MORNINGS, ISAAC LOPEZ BRANDON and Joshua Moses rattled across the cobbled streets of the city on the new horse-drawn omnibuses that raced up and down Broadway between their business office by the wharves and their grand, three-story Federal-style, marble-and-brick townhouses. The bustling young city was pushing forward, oblivious to their pain and the uncertainty that lay ahead.[1]

Joshua and his children would seem to be secure. Born into riches, Joshua had inherited real estate from his parents and had gained a fortune through his wife's dowry. Moreover, Joshua was surrounded by a nest of childless brothers and sisters who, after Sarah's death, rushed in to take care of the abundance of children Sarah had left behind. As Joshua's descendants, the children's legacy seemed secure: riches to riches to riches. In contrast Isaac, who had begun his life in poverty, would have to rely on the goodwill of his wife's kin as he sank everything into building a future for his lone surviving son. Yet in the end, it was Abraham Rodriguez Brandon the younger who inherited an empire, and Joshua and Sarah's eight sons who were left impoverished. Spiritually the reverse was true, with Sarah's brood carrying the crown and the youngest Brandon betraying Isaac's hard-won synagogue honors. For both branches, then, it was rags to riches, and riches to rags, all within two generations.

The city was only partially to blame. By 1830, New York had become a radically different place than it had been thirteen years earlier when Sarah stepped off the schooner from London, let alone when Joshua had wandered the short block between the Mill Street synagogue and his family home in the 1780s. It was not just that the unsanitary and broken cobblestones were about to be replaced by macadam, woodblocks, and even granite. Poor immigrants had started to flood the city, filling the neighborhoods around the docks. These were people like yellow fever victims Dorothy Kavanaugh and Margaret Brady, whose names epitomized the soon to be overwhelming influx of people from Ireland. Like other stylish New Yorkers, Joshua's brothers and sisters responded by moving uptown, into what is now Tribeca. Isaac and his young son moved along with them, abandoning lower Greenwich Street for a house at 82 Warren.[2]

Twenty years earlier, Warren Street still had a village-like feel, with a mismatch of wood frame and brick facades. But by the 1830s, uptown flight had transformed the neighborhood into row upon row of elegant townhouses along broad, tree-lined streets. Isaac lived in the middle of a sequence of at least ten identical facades in a home he shared with Lavinia's siblings Moses, David, Saly (Sarah), and Rebecca Moses. Residing together made sense. When Isaac went back and forth to Liverpool to meet with his father in 1829 or to Barbados in the 1830s, Abraham the younger would be raised by his Moses aunts and uncles. He became the family darling. Thirty years later in Aunt Saly and Rebecca Moses's wills, Abraham Rodriguez Brandon would be the "much beloved" and "blessed" nephew to whom they left both trinkets of their affection and substantial amounts of cash.[3]

Joshua similarly moved his brood north to be with the rest of their kin, taking up residence a few doors down from his siblings and Isaac at 74 Warren Street. It was a temporary stop. In May 1829, Joshua's sister Richea Moses Levy and her husband Aaron Levy followed the family uptown to 66 Warren, on the corner of College Place (now Broadway). Five days later, Joshua, nine children, and two women (most likely servants) moved in with them. Fashion kept pushing them onward. Moses, David, Saly, and Rebecca Moses bought a double residence at 121–123 Hudson Street in two new four-story brick buildings described in the *Commercial Advertiser* as "lately furnished and in the most expensive and elegant style."[4] Isaac and his son tagged along. It was a social coup for all. The house fronted St. John's Park, a locked, private piece of heaven modeled after garden squares in London's trend-setting West End, with keys available only to the wealthy residents in the surrounding houses. By the time the Moses clan moved there, the neighborhood was the centerpiece of upper-class New York life and was home to most of New York's top-notch families.[5]

Joshua, his nine children, and the Levys followed the rest of the Moses-Brandon clan northward to the slightly less fashionable 47 Hudson, at the corner of Staple Street. Although not quite as new, their house was advertised as "elegant and convenient" with three stories in brick and a "fine garden, under good cultivation."[6] The wide house was furnished in "modern style, with folding doors and marble mantle pieces."[7] They would soon discover the difference in address was not just about clout. When cholera swept the city in 1832, Aaron Levy's household had to take refuge at the Moses-Brandon houses at 121–123 Hudson, outside the treacherous blocks where the disease had hit.[8]

The Moses family's exodus to Warren and Hudson Streets reflected larger shifts in New York's Jewish landscape. Although Warren Street meant a longer walk to the second Shearith Israel synagogue—still at its original

Third Shearith Israel Synagogue. Esther H. Oppenheim and Delano Studios, *Shearith Israel Synagogue . . . Fifty-Six Crosby Street*. Collection of author.

location down by the wharves—most Jews who could afford it moved up-town. In 1834, the congregation also relocated northward, to 56–62 Crosby, in order to better suit its upscale congregants. New York's Jewish commu-nity had grown exponentially, and the congregation's third location, the Crosby Street Synagogue, was substantially larger than the two previous ones on Mill Street. Amid all their moves, the family maintained their ties to Jewish life, with Moses L. Moses serving on the *Mahamad* and Isaac Brandon, Joshua, Moses, and David Moses and brother-in-law Aaron Levy purchasing seats in the synagogue for the family.[9]

Meanwhile Isaac and Joshua adapted their business to meet new markets. Although Isaac lived with Moses and David Moses, who reigned supreme over the Moses family firm, he continued to work with Joshua. The pair advertised wares that reflected the international reach of their shipping networks and Joshua's expertise in cloth. Their new, larger store at 175 Pearl advertised trunks of "Real Madras Hdkfs [Handkerchiefs] in splendid new patterns" and "Suchan Pongees"—that is, the exquisite silk from the Suchan province in south China.[10]

Isaac and Joshua also expanded their Chinese wares into the entertain-ment sector: they made sure people knew they had Chinese crackers and fireworks, available in both large and small boxes, as well as quicksilver (mercury), an important component in explosives. Once the exclusive do-main of European courts and the upper class, pyrotechnics had spread to the middling sort by the early nineteenth century. One could buy cheaper Italian fireworks by the 1830s, but the more colorful and elaborate Chinese pyrotechnics remained highly sought after. By importing Chinese fireworks to New York, the Moses-Brandon firm was expanding its reputation as purveyors of the latest fashion and style.[11]

The goods were also part of a larger Moses family legacy of cosmopoli-tanism. Back in 1798, Joshua's older brother Solomon Moses had been one of the first American Jews to travel to Calcutta and Madras for business. On the long voyage, he was careful to follow his father's pre-trip advice to pay attention to the "Relegion [*sic*] of your Fathers House, and keep to every ceremony As far as you Possibly Can."[12] While on board, Solomon tried to keep Passover. The records of his travels would inspire the next generation, who decorated his travel journal with notes and drawings of houses, fire engines, and fancy block letters.[13]

The children had reason to be impressed by the house they drew that their grandfather Abraham Rodrigues Brandon was renting. The four-story New York house was accompanied by an expansive garden, with room

Drawing of Abraham Rodrigues Brandon's house at 36 Laight Street [Tribeca], New York drawn by his grandchildren in the blank pages of their uncle Solomon Moses's *Journal of Voyage to Madras and Calcutta* (1798). AJHS.

for a stable at the rear. Everything was exceptional: the rooms were generous and connected by folding doors, with marble mantels and black iron grates, and toward the rear was a separate building with a housekeeper's room and space for a library or tea room. The real coup, however, was the front, which faced the prestigious St. John's Park, and hence also came with a key to the exclusive garden where high society paraded in their best clothes.[14]

The Brandon house at 36 Laight Street brings to light the luxuriant domestic side of the well-groomed man John Wesley Jarvis had painted a few years earlier. On the first floor, one advertisement explained, were sumptuous parlors, filled with "French Imperial, Brussels and Ingrain Carpets, pier dining [tables], tea and card tables, sofas, mahogany and fancy chairs," as well as silk curtains, a bookcase, secretary, sideboard, and prints. Upstairs was no less refined, with "French canopy bedsteads, beds and bedding, [and] circle wash stands."[15] In the front room was a "very fine toned Piano, of one of the best makers," obtained by the home's original owners in Paris.[16] Musical instruments were not incidental. One of the neighborhood's claims to fame was the exquisite concerts held in nearby St. John's Chapel. As a child, Isaac worked in the background while his owner Hannah Esther Lopez and her widowed sister-in-law taught violin to middle-class island children. As part of the swanky circle of St. John's Park, Isaac quickly learned that attending and hosting musical performances was a way to showcase one's refinement.[17]

For the Brandon-Moses clan living along the park, dinner parties were another crucial forum for displaying wealth and status. Supper parties—like strolls in the exclusive park—were a venue for showing off the beautiful fabrics Isaac and Joshua imported. At least one new arrival to the houses along the square lamented that she would "need many more Cloathes [*sic*] than I have at present to hold my Scituation [*sic*] among the Polite Society."[18] And just as wearing the right fabrics and styles mattered, social dining provided an opportunity to show that one could do the right things. According to philosopher Immanuel Kant, dinner parties were opportunities to engage in the hospitality, respect, and the goodwill that made one truly human. The Laight Street residence came with all the trappings needed to host impressive gatherings: an elegant white china dinner service as well as mirrors, mantel ornaments, and lamps to make sure evening guests could see well enough to appreciate the food displayed. Wines revealed the elegance expected by the square's residents when they entertained: a later auction revealed that the cellars at 36 Laight Street contained "17 doz. Red Leoville, and a few bottles Margaux, Sautern, Chambertin, and Lunel de Fonyignan."[19] These celebrated French vineyards were much sought after in New York, as reviewers at the time noted owning bottles from them could "give the owner a high reputation for the choice of his wine."[20] Even by Moses family standards, the Brandon house was a breathtaking display of Europhilic wealth.

Although rented from non-Jews, the house also embodied for the Moses family all it meant to be Sephardic. Amid the largely Ashkenazi clan, Abraham Rodrigues Brandon Sr. and his eldest son Isaac were the lone Spanish and Portuguese Jews, and by the 1820s, being Portuguese increasingly suggested old lines and elegance in Jewish New York. Thus, while Solomon Moses's Ashkenazi daughter Becky Moses practiced signing her name in the Calcutta journal in a plain British style, Joshua and Isaac's children tried their hand at imitating the Iberian *rubricas* beneath Isaac and their grandfather Abraham's signatures, adding flourishes below their own names. World traveling, cosmopolitan elegance, and Sephardic ancestry merged together as an inheritance.[21]

Whatever domestic bliss the brothers-in-law managed to eke out in the years just after their wives' deaths and during Abraham Rodrigues Brandon Sr.'s brief presence in New York did not last. At the start of 1831, everything seemed fine. Brandon Sr. and his new brood were back in Barbados, and Isaac was expecting lucrative shipments, this time coffee and other items

Solomon Moses's journal provided a place for the family to learn Sephardic style. *Left*: Abraham Rodrigues Brandon's signature (and house number). *Right*: Isaac and Sarah's sons' imitations of Abraham Rodrigues Brandon's signature and *rubrica*. Journal of Voyage to Madras and Calcutta (1798). AJHS.

from Venezuela on the brig *Magnolia*. When the ship arrived in New York in July 1831, however, it was unlikely that Isaac was there to greet it. That March, his father had advertised in the *Barbados Mercury*, requesting that those who owed him money should settle up by the beginning of May, as he wished to "quit the Island" for good.[22] On April 7, 1831, Brandon Sr. revised his will in preparation for travel. He did not move quickly enough. By June 1, the baby of his new family—Alfred Rodrigues Brandon—was dead. Then on June 4, Brandon followed him to the grave. While the cause is unknown, the proximity of their deaths suggests one of the epidemics that often swept the island.[23]

Where exactly their graves lie is also a mystery. For a man whose legacy had been so closely tied to the Nidhe Israel synagogue, at death Abraham Rodrigues Brandon seems to have rebuffed the congregation's embrace. Although both his death and Alfred's were recorded in the community's Register of Births and Deaths, no tombstone has been found in any of the three main sections of the Nidhe Israel cemetery. Even when seventeen new graves were discovered underneath artisan shops at the edge of the synagogue complex in 2016, Brandon's grave was not among them. Perhaps he had chosen to be buried at one of his plantations along the northwest coast? If so, the location of his and young Alfred Rodrigues Brandon's gravestones have long since been lost.[24]

The lack of a tombstone for the family patriarch means that many details about Brandon's life that would typically be in evidence on a memorial stone have been obliterated by time, left to be filled in by family oral tradition and speculation by descendants and genealogists. There is no clear evidence, for example, about Brandon's precise date of birth or birthplace. The historian Eustace Maxwell Shilstone, the first to extensively study the Barbados Jewish community, gives Brandon's age at death as sixty-five, suggesting an approximate birth date of 1766. This corresponds to the approximate birth date given by Brandon himself when he traveled by ship. Yet neither Brandon's birth nor circumcision appears in either the original congregational registers that Shilstone reported he was transcribing or the synagogue records in London, where Brandon allegedly was born.[25]

Without a tombstone to provide his father's first name, Brandon's parentage is likewise ambiguous. Family tradition identifies his parents as Abraham Rodrigues Brandon and Abigail da Fonseca Brandon. Yet an 1819 court case between Abigail Brandon's brother and the executors of her husband's estate reveals that the couple had no children. All in all, Brandon's will is the clearest indication of his extended family tree: in addition to his children born by (Sarah) Esther Lopez-Gill and Sarah Simpson Wood, Brandon had a brother named Moses Rodrigues Brandon who outlived him and had fathered at least two children, Jael (wife of Abraham Israel Keys) and Jacob Rodrigues Brandon. Abraham Rodrigues Brandon also mentions a sister named Abigail who by 1831 was already deceased, but whose husband, Robert Gray, remained alive in London.[26]

Besides clarifying his kin network, Abraham's will showed the diverse interests and ethical quandaries that pulled at his life from an early age. On the one hand, like many Jewish wills of the time, it begins with religious devotion and a sense of social obligation. Abraham left legacies to the synagogues in London and Barbados and earmarked special funds for London's Portuguese Jew's Hospital, and for educating and clothing poor children by the Portuguese Jews' Orphan Society in London. The will also had good news for the residents of Bridgetown's Jewish Alms House, who received a like sum to be divided among them.

Less rosy was the news for the residents of Hopeland, Brandon's estate in St. Michael's Parish. Before it fell into Brandon's hands, the plantation had belonged to one of the wealthiest men of color on the island, Jacob Belgrave, who had sold the plantation (then only 109 acres) in 1805 to Alexander King for £15,000. Sometime before 1817, Brandon purchased the property, and officially became part of the island's planter class. Initially, the plantation was profitable, bringing in £1,771 per year, the equivalent of earning £1,480,000 a year today. By 1819, the property had increased in value to £20,000. It was this land that would have secured Brandon's right to vote in government elections, had the king not overridden the island's legislature. Undeterred by the political setback, Brandon continued to add acreage.[27]

Yet by 1831, the plantation had become a disappointment. Pressures to end slavery and a series of natural disasters brought about an economic decline on the island, and when the family finally sold the 216-acre estate in 1837 for £14,142, it did so at a loss. Land that had once been worth £138 per acre thirty years earlier was now worth less than half what Brandon had paid. It was partially this decline that led Brandon to revise his will in April 1831. He noted that he "had in a former Will given my son [Isaac Lopez Brandon] a much larger Legacy but the great depreciation which has taken place in West India property obliges me to diminish it to the present sum."[28] In death, Brandon ensured that his oldest son understood that necessity, not a decrease in affection, had changed his inheritance.

Yet for all Brandon's compassion for the son he had rescued from slavery and for the Jewish poor, he seemed to have little sympathy for the majority of the people who had given their lives to build his empire. In a single sentence, Brandon dispensed not only with his houses and plantations, but his "Slaves and all other property not specifically bequeathed."[29] The number of people affected by this sentence was substantial. As of 1817, Abraham Rodrigues Brandon owned 168 people, more than any other Jew on the island. By 1829, there were 182 people enslaved at Hopeland alone, and the figure peaked at 191 by the time of his death.[30]

The will singled out a lucky few: James and Tom Gittens were manumitted outright, and Sally Gill, who had worked as washerwoman for Abraham since at least 1817, was given "her time so she may be at liberty to work for herself."[31] While her name suggests a kin relationship to Abraham's children Isaac and Sarah, her place of origin was listed as Africa, indicating she was not born on the island. More likely, this was the "Negro Woman Slave Sally" that George Gill had given to his "beloved Daughter Sarah Gill otherwise called Esther" back in 1801.[32] Sally was not the only person formerly enslaved by the Gills to end up in Brandon's possession. When (Sarah) Esther Gill's sister-in-law Ann Jordan Gill found that slaveholding and her Methodist beliefs did not mix, Brandon bought Kitty and (her mother?) Maria, a washerwoman and house servant, and brought them to Hopeland. Like Kitty and Maria, Sally would not gain true freedom until general emancipation in 1834. By then, she was nearly seventy years old.[33]

Better off than Sally, Kitty, and Maria Gill but not as lucky as the Gittens brothers were Beck, John, and William Francis Brandon, whom Abraham Rodrigues Brandon allowed to be manumitted if someone would pay on their behalf "what appears due in my books . . . and also all expenses attending their manumission."[34] All three men had been Brandon's house servants.

Unlike Sally—but like most people manumitted in white Barbadians' wills—the men were mixed-race and born on the island. Like Sally, they were long-time residents of Hopeland, first appearing there on the 1817 census. Beck was about fifty-nine when Abraham Rodrigues Brandon died, John about thirty-four, and William about sixteen. Much of the best parts of their lives had been given over to making Brandon's life easier, but he still felt someone owed him something for their freedom. Yet even these small opportunities made Sally, Beck, John, and William Francis comparatively lucky. In July 1832, Richard William Killick and Isaac Lopez Brandon sold 160 enslaved people from Hopeland outright. They had little choice. As executors of Brandon's estate, they were fulfilling their legal obligation.[35]

Indeed, Isaac seemed to have little inclination to own enslaved people on the scale his father had. Early on, the only person he owned was his great-grandmother Deborah, who had been willed to him by Hannah Esther Lopez. Then for some reason, around 1832 he purchased Mary Ann, a twenty-one-year-old multiracial Barbadian. Maybe he felt he needed a housekeeper while on the island. Mary Ann, however, was also pregnant at the time of the sale. Was James, her baby, Isaac Lopez Brandon's son? This was once an almost impossible question to answer, but DNA testing may someday reveal the answer. Regardless of what changed his mind about owning people, Isaac never recognized James in the way that his father had once recognized him. Unlike Brandon back in 1801, though, Isaac already had a legal heir living in New York.[36]

Whatever reluctance Isaac might have had about owning slaves was not shared by his stepmother Sarah Simpson Wood. Wood not only inherited three enslaved people from Brandon after his death but also owned slaves in her own right. Slave ownership marked how her relationship with Brandon had changed her lifestyle. In 1817, before she had taken up with Brandon, Wood's father had owned six fieldhands and two domestic workers. But by 1826—three years after setting up house with Brandon—Sarah Simpson Wood owned four domestic workers all by herself: there was Jenny (29), Francis (49), Molly Ann (20), and Margaret (1). When Molly Ann and a new woman, Lucy John (43), died, Wood replaced them with a young enslaved girl named Lavinia, who at three and a half years old was only a few months older than Brandon and Wood's own daughter Lavinia. By 1832, there were six enslaved people in Wood's house on Chapel Street, which Brandon had left Wood to use while she was alive. Young Lavinia (the enslaved girl) was dead, but three women from Brandon's estate—Denniss (22), Sophia (aka Sopley [40]), and Rebecca (aka Beckey [65])—had joined Jenny, Francis, and Margaret in becoming Wood's possessions. Yet Sarah Simpson Wood and her children had little time to enjoy the house on Chapel Street or the labor of the people forced to make it run. For just two months after Brandon and his young son Alfred were laid to rest, tragedy once again swept the family, this time taking in the entire island with them.[37]

Between sunset on August 10 and sunrise on August 11, 1831, a category four hurricane ravaged the island, shredding the synagogue and laying waste most of the key structures in Bridgetown. Thousands of people lost their lives. Others were left to mourn them amid the overwhelming destruction. While Barbados had certainly not been immune to storms throughout its history, the strength of the 1831 hurricane was exceptional.[38]

The day had begun calmly with light breezes, but by 9:00 AM the weather changed, as clouds and winds started to roll in. By midnight, constant flashes of lightning and thunder shook the island. Torrents of rain flew in horizontal sheets. When the sky cleared the next morning at 10:00, roofs hung from buildings like dead skin on stubbed toes. Everywhere homes lay in ruins. Whereas earlier hurricanes had disproportionately destroyed the cottages of the poor and enslaved, now rich and poor suffered alike. The almshouses connected with the synagogue lost their roofs and their walls lay in ruins.[39]

Others were even less fortunate: Jael Pinheiro and Miss S. Lealtad, who lived near the Brandon estate in Fontabelle lost their lives. Pinheiro, a seventy-one-year-old invalid who was euphemistically described in reports as "very corpulent," was buried alive under her fallen house.[40] Despite her pitiful cries from the ruins to "take the chair off me," none of her servants "possessed the presence of mind" to assist her.[41] Or so was the opinion of a white chronicler at the time. Perhaps the twenty-odd people Jael had enslaved had enough problems of their own, or perhaps—like Brandon—the charity Pinheiro so generously displayed in her will toward the Jewish poor was not extended equally to the people held captive in her own house.[42]

Although none of the Brandons died in the hurricane, they too found their world turned upside down. All around Chapel Street, the houses were decimated. Joists from nearby Swan Street residences were found in adjoining yards, and lath from roofs was driven straight into nearby trees, shingles still attached. Just a few blocks away, St. Mary's Church was transformed into a shelter, and St. Michael's became a hospital, the pews repurposed as beds for the injured. The Brandons' Hopeland mansion was one of the few left on its foundation in the parish. The winds however had destroyed the local forest of coconut trees, hurling coconuts like cannonballs and turning the tropical garden into a desert. The once elegant neighborhood was no refuge from the wasteland of Bridgetown.[43]

In the wake of the chaos, Sarah Simpson Wood left the island for London. Two years later, she married a non-Jewish man named Daniel Goody at the Old St. Pancras Parish Chapel in central London. Their signatures suggest a difference in class that may have made up for Wood's having five children despite identifying herself as a spinster. Wood's handwriting is elegant and practiced, whereas Goody's was tentative and immature. Unlike the merchant Brandon, Goody was a builder. That said, he did offer a legitimacy Brandon had denied Wood. Whatever led the couple to marry, more children quickly followed: Alfred Brandon Goody (1835), Edwin Brandon Goody (1836), and Emily Brandon Goody (1840). The names suggest that despite what the official church register recorded, Wood intended to give her new children (and neighbors) the impression that she had been a widow, not an unwed mother. By 1841, Wood was living alone in Ratcliff (Stepney) with her younger children. Their lives would be dramatically different from that of their older Brandon half siblings. Young Alfred Goody was bound out as an apprentice by 1851. His binding was a reminder of the great divide between the halves of the family, as apprentices were viewed as social outcasts, even by the middle class.[44]

Another divide between Sarah Simpson Wood's two broods was religion. Despite their mother's (re)turn to Christianity, Wood made sure to raise her Brandon children as Jews, as she had apparently promised Abraham on his deathbed. Or perhaps this was their older brother Isaac's doing, as Abraham Rodrigues Brandon had made Isaac the guardian of his reputed younger children, Julia, Esther, Lavinia, and Joseph Brandon.[45]

By 1841, Brandon's younger daughters were enrolled in Hannah Gomes's Sephardic Ladies school for Jewish girls on Deptford Lane (now Queens Road) in Peckham, just south of London. It was a small, intimate establishment. Other than Julia, Esther, and Lavinia Brandon—ages eighteen, sixteen, and fifteen, respectively—the school was the temporary home to only four other boarders: Charlotte Levy (14), Maria Levy (12), Rachel Garcia (12), and Emma Marton (12). To meet their needs, the school had on staff Rebecca Dear (a teacher), Jane Polton (a servant), and two of the headmistress's relatives. Here, the younger Brandons received the same kind of upscale Jewish education their sister Sarah had acquired over two decades earlier.[46]

Brother Joseph Rodrigues Brandon was also away getting a highbrow education at Edmonton House, Henry Solomon's boarding school favored by wealthy British Jews. The property was as grand as Solomon's aspirations: a large Georgian house with extensive grounds, including space for playing cricket, and a carp pond. Inside was space for forty-three boarders. Subjects included not only Hebrew and English education—Solomon was considered the leading English authority on the Talmud—but also the languages and subjects required of cosmopolitan gentlemen: drama, drawing, music, French, German, Spanish, and Latin. During Purim, there was a festival, and the boys performed plays and gambled for nuts.[47]

Edmonton House was meant to be a stepping stone into upper-class life. At Edmonton, Joseph Rodrigues Brandon made connections with wealthy British Jews. Classmates included not only the Solomon children but also boys who would grow up to lead the next generation of the Raphael, Davis, Phillips, Moses, Bensasan, Lewis, Myers, Benjamin, Lyons, Marks, and Lazarus families. Solomon made sure that the education he provided was rigorous and modern. By 1826, Jews were being admitted to University College, and in 1832 Dublin's Trinity College followed suit. At Edmonton House, the expectation was that the boys would take advantage of further education, and the school prepared them for university examinations. All this came at a price: roughly £50 a year. That is, the same amount Isaac's father had once paid years ago to the Barbadian church to have his son freed would be paid every year to guarantee that Joseph Rodrigues Brandon would be recognized as Jewish.[48]

Yet before Isaac and Sarah's younger siblings got settled in their respective boarding schools, tragedy once again hit the Moses-Brandon clan, this time back in New York. On Wednesday, December 6, 1837, after a brief, severe illness Joshua Moses passed away. His young family of nine children, ages eleven to twenty-one, were left to mourn, moving from their home at 91 Chambers Street to their Aunt Richea and Uncle Aaron Levy's house at 175 Canal.[49]

Joshua clearly had not expected his death, as his last will had been written six years earlier when things looked more optimistic. He generously left not only token sums to the Hebrew Benevolent Society and the Society for the Education of Poor Israelites, but $5,000 outright to his oldest child—and only daughter—Reyna Moses, to be kept separate and away from the debts and control from any man who might marry her for her money. While thoughtful, his concern was unnecessary: Reyna Moses remained single her whole life. Moreover, she was hardly helpless. She helped restart Shearith Israel's school in 1838–40, where she taught and also served as one of the monitors who helped ensure punctual attendance. The oldest of the siblings, she was the first of those who lived to adulthood to die. Like her mother, she succumbed after a short illness before she even reached the age of thirty.[50]

Joshua used his will to thank those who had supported him and his unconventional brood. His sister Richea Moses Levy received $150. She hardly needed it, but Joshua considered it a token of his regard for her goodness to Sarah while she was ill, and their children after Sarah passed away. Aaron Levy's older, unmarried sister Sarah Levy also received a gift: $50 as a reminder of her kindness to Joshua's daughter Reyna. Nursemaid Jane McElroy likewise received $50 for her care and attention to the children, particularly to Alfred. These were affectionate gestures, but in the end Joshua's generosity outstripped his means. By placing these gifts before the main bequest, he chipped away at his sons' inheritance, leaving them poorer than the servants.[51]

Had Joshua's business been booming, the boys would have been rich. The rest of his estate, after all, was split equally among the eight boys, with brother-in-law Isaac L. Brandon, and friends David Henriques and William H. Harrison named executors. Even from the start, however, things looked bleak. Joshua's friendship was apparently misplaced. Henriques and Harrison renounced their positions, and Isaac, while presumably willing, was in Barbados. Moses L. Moses, the family's rock, became the children's official guardian, and in the end, their life raft.[52]

The boys most likely had little inkling of their father's failures. After all, Chambers Street was advertised as "one of the most fashionable, airy and pleasant streets" in the northern part of the city.[53] Their three-story brick house was warm, large, and comfortable—full of servants and beautiful mahogany furniture and bronze lamps for the parlor. Joshua had glassware and silver to grace his table. But most of his money was tied up in business, and his fashionable lifestyle had left him woefully overextended. Although he had $4,400 in the bank and slightly more invested in insurance bonds, much more was owed to him by business connections both in the city and throughout Latin American and the Caribbean. The brick house on Chambers Street may have been worth $12,500, but it was heavily mortgaged. So were the brick building and two lots Joshua owned on Third Avenue between 14th and 15th Streets.[54]

If Moses L. Moses was troubled as he did the accounts after his brother's death, his brow would have only creased further as time went on. Initially it looked like each boy's share might be a little over $3,850, less than their sister had received in her lump sum, but not utterly unrespectable. Even that sum, however, was a pipe dream, as the eight boys watched their inheritance melt away. The transnational reach of Joshua's mercantile business meant accounts weren't settled quickly. Four years after Joshua's death, Londoners James Bell and Robert Grant gave notice that Joshua's estate owed them $30,000. That meant that even if—and what an enormous *if* that was—Moses L. Moses had been able to extract all of the money owed to Joshua abroad, and he could liquidate all his brother's bonds and private possessions, the eight boys would have inherited only $828.48 total, or slightly more than $103 each.[55]

In 1846, that paltry inheritance was further diminished when the Surrogate Court decreed that Joshua owed yet another sum of $1,658.50 to another businessman. In the end, the boys got nothing. Even the Society for the Education of Poor Israelites received more from their father than they had. Their sister, Reyna Moses, was responsible for giving them a small boost; when she died in 1847, intestate, the boys inherited whatever money she had not spent.[56]

For Isaac, the ruined fortunes of Sarah's children must have felt like a dire warning about the unpredictability of mercantile life. Maybe he also felt responsible as Joshua's business partner for the boys' ruin, as he left the safe haven he had built in New York, taking up residence in Barbados. The city he left behind was a shell of his lost dreams. Other than his son, everyone he had loved in New York was already gone.

Given his horrible mistreatment by the Barbadian synagogue, however, Isaac's return to the island was somewhat mysterious. After all, unlike in New York, according to the racial policies of Barbados, Isaac was still considered a person of color who could never be reclassified as white. Moreover, shortly after King George IV had nullified the Vestry Bill, fellow Jew Benjamin Elkin had made a bid to ensure that "no Person of Colour shall be deemed eligible to be chosen a Yahid of the Kaal."[57] The motion had not passed, but it had led to more fighting in the synagogue, as Abraham Rodrigues Brandon Sr. staged a coup to make certain that no Mahamad could create rules without the backing of the majority of the congregation. Even in absentia, Isaac was a source of conflict.[58]

Yet despite the island's caste system and prejudice by some congregants, time was on Isaac's side. By Joshua's death in late 1837, island culture had shifted. The Brown Privilege Bill of 1831 had repealed all restrictions against non-whites and an "Act for the Relief of His Majesty's Subjects . . . who profess the Hebrew Religion" extended the right to vote in island elections to all men who met the requisite property requirements.[59] By 1838, whatever tangles Isaac had had with the synagogue were past, and he was once again a voting member of Congregation Nidhe IsraelWhile on the island, he

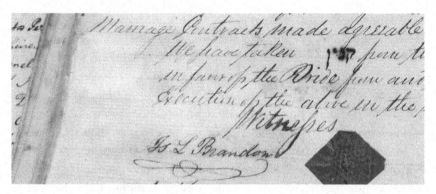

Signature of Isaac Lopez Brandon on the marriage certificate of Phillip Rubens (son of Moses Rubens) and his bride Sarah, a convert (1851). NISR.

maintained ties not only to New York but also London's Jewish community through a subscription to the newly founded newspaper *Voice of Jacob*. By 1850, Isaac was one of three members of the congregation singled out when former synagogue president E. A. Moses publicly proclaimed his gratitude for their friendship in Barbadian and London newspapers. Likewise in 1851, Isaac was central enough to the synagogue to serve as a witness for the marriage of Phillip Rubens and his bride Sarah, a convert.[60]

Isaac remained on the island through the early 1850s, engaging in public life as one of the island's leading merchants. In the 1840s, for example, he served as a committee member for the Bridgetown Water Works Company, which aimed to decrease the threat of fires and provide sanitation and comfort by piping water directly into houses rather than forcing people to gather water at wells or buy it from carts. In 1846, Isaac petitioned alongside Samuel J. Prescod, the first non-white person elected to the island legislature, to decrease taxes placed on rum, molasses, and sugar. Isaac was both a civic and a religious leader.[61]

While Isaac was away, his son Abraham Rodriguez Brandon continued to live with his Moses aunts and uncles. Yet by the age of fifteen, Brandon was already part of the family business. It was the beginning of what would be an illustrious career. Throughout his early adult life, he would continue to live with his aging Moses relatives, following them in 1847 to their new house at 181 Thompson Street, near Washington Square Park, mere blocks from the new Crosby Street synagogue. He would become the legacy Isaac had dreamed of. Isaac's life may have been winding down, but a new generation's was just beginning.[62]

12

Legacies

New York and Beyond, 1839–1860

IN 1842, AS ABRAHAM RODRIGUEZ Brandon the younger was waiting for a basket of goods to arrive from Africa on the brig *Otranto*, the Moses-Brandon clan and other fashionable Jews were rushing out to take advantage of the latest sensation in science and the arts: daguerreotypes. Invented by Louis-Jacques-Mandé Daguerre, this early form of photography traveled to New York in 1839, first via lectures and exhibitions. But by March 1840, adventuresome souls could buy their own daguerreotype apparatus at 140 Nassau Street, near City Hall.[1]

Advertisements for daguerreotype maker's kits give a sense of the complexity of the process: in addition to the camera, one needed an iodine box, mercury apparatus, plate box, spirit lamp, all the washing and finishing apparatus, and a traveling case. It was worth the trouble. Each image produced was unique, and at the time startling. In April 1840, Alexander S. Wolcott began making portraits in his rooms in the large granite building at the corner of Broadway and Chambers, nine doors down from the Moses brothers' house at 91 Chambers Street. He promised that those who could bear to sit perfectly still for the minute and three quarters it took to create the image would be blessed with an astonishingly precise duplicate of themselves. Wolcott's shop became one of the city's first thriving daguerreotype studios.[2]

Thanks to the Moses family's obsession with the new form of image making, early portraits of almost all of Joshua and Sarah's children survive.

Isaac, Brandon ("A.R.B."), Israel, Joseph, Lionel, Benjamin, and Alfred Moses all sat motionless for the requisite minutes. Other than Ariel, one of the few missing was Reyna Moses, who died suddenly just as the technology was beginning to take off.

Yet despite early artists' insistence that the form was somehow a transcription of the self, the Moses family portraits are clearly staged. Some of the Moses boys—now men—wear army uniforms. Others—like Joseph Moses—have a book in hand and a cigar in their mouth. Most of the photographers are anonymous, but some of the Moses portraits are by the famous Mathew B. Brady and Rufus Anson galleries. Today, Brady is best known for his photographs of the Civil War, but in the early 1850s, he ran a daguerreotype studio at 359 Broadway. All told, the young Moses men appear debonair and poised, unscarred by the years without their parents and the financial chaos their father had left behind.[3]

With time, the daguerreotypes became part of an aristocratic success story that the family would later perpetuate to gloss over the hardships that the brothers repeatedly faced. When Lionel Moses died in 1895, his heirs claimed that he "was reared in the house which had been the home of his ancestors for three generations, at the corner of 34th street and Ninth avenue. It was erected in the eighteenth century by Mr. Moses's great-grandfather, Moses van Giessen, from whom it was that the first John Jacob Astor got his earliest insight into the business of fur trading. Mr. Moses was educated at a private school on Chambers Street."[4] This was an interesting mishmash of fact and fiction. True, during the 1820s the family had retreated to Reyna Levy Moses's Mount Listen estate to escape yellow fever, but census reports make it clear that Lionel hadn't been raised there. Moreover, it was great-grandfather Hyman Levy who had mentored young Astor: Moses van Giessen hadn't even lived in the Americas.[5]

The posh-sounding "private school" Lionel Moses attended was also a bit of a stretch. The Moses boys had been enrolled at the same Shearith Israel school where their sister taught and served as treasurer, along with nearly a hundred other Jewish children. Some of their classmates were wealthy, but others were charity cases whose participation needed the prodding of monitors like Reyna Moses even though they received free clothes for their attendance. When the school's pupils were examined in 1839, younger brothers Frederick and Alfred Moses won awards. Lionel didn't. For Alfred—the one no one had expected to survive infancy—it was a triumph, but a small one: forty other students received awards that day. By the 1840s, the Moses line's merchant prince success story seemed more myth than reality.[6] The Moses brothers fell squarely in the middle of those around them.

To the extent they did succeed, they had their extended family to thank. Their Aunt Richea and Uncle Aaron Levy took them in after Joshua died. Uncles David and Moses L. Moses also stepped up, making sure that when the boys were old enough, they could move back into their father's former house at 91 Chambers Street. It had not been easy. Numerous court battles had gone toward ensuring that Sarah's sons would not have to sell the house to pay their father's debts.[7]

As they matured, each son forged his own path. Two of Sarah's older boys, Isaac Moses and A. R. B. Moses, followed family tradition and entered into a merchant partnership, but their brother Israel Moses went in a new direction: higher education. In 1841, two days after his twentieth birthday, Israel Moses graduated from Columbia College with a bachelor of arts degree. He was even chosen to read a work he had written, called "The Ravages of Time," at the commencement ceremony. The degree was a stepping stone to a different life.[8]

Between 1842 and 1845, Moses studied privately with Dr. Jonathan Watson, staff surgeon at New York Hospital. It was the first academic hospital in the city. Most professors were European-trained in the latest techniques, and they emphasized a medicine based on education, research, and clinical care. In keeping with this standard, Watson was not only an MD but also a published author—a model Israel Moses would follow. When it was time to recommend Moses for entrance into the program, Watson lauded his assistant as "industrious and attentive to his studies" with a "character in all other respects above reproach."[9]

Based on Watson's recommendation, Moses was admitted to the College of Physicians and Surgeons in 1845. His time there was a tremendous success: only eight months after Watson wrote his recommendation, Moses published a study on heat exhaustion in the *New York Medical and Surgical Reporter*. When his training was complete, he officially became Israel Moses, MD, Resident Physician. He was the first child of a former slave to graduate from the New York College of Physicians and Surgeons, later Columbia Medical School.[10]

Though being recognized as a Jew would not have stood in the way of Israel's medical dreams, knowledge of Sarah's past most certainly would have. The end of slavery in New York was followed by anti-Black backlash. By 1842, when Moses started working with Watson, John Doggett had started indicating who he considered non-white in his city directory. George

D. Morse, a seaman, for example, was marked "(col'd)" in 1843; the Moses brothers' names, one column over, were not. As in the 1840 census, there were only two racial categories in the 1843 directory: white and colored. Neither Doggett nor the census explained what they meant by the terms, or how they determined people were one race or the other. In Doggett's directory, the default race was white, which was left unmarked. All of the Brandon-Moses clan, along with the other members of Shearith Israel were, by default, white.[11]

The family's classification mattered. Presumably Sarah Brandon Moses's history was unknown at the time Israel Moses studied for his medical degree, as less than five years later, in 1850, another racially ambiguous student—James Parker Barnett—was expelled by the College of Physicians and Surgeons in the City of New York for having parents who were discovered to be "Creole" rather than Anglo-Saxon.[12] For Moses, not having his past uncovered helped ensure that he could go on to have a successful career as a surgeon and become known as an innovator in the field of anesthesia. Moses's path would also influence younger brother Benjamin Moses, who, while not as illustrious as Israel, bucked family tradition and became a pharmacist rather than a merchant.[13]

After graduation, being identified as white continued to be crucial for Israel Moses's career. In 1846, Moses enlisted in the US Army's 6th Infantry Regiment. Officially this was an all-white regiment, as the army still banned African Americans. Unofficially, Moses wasn't the only person with African ancestry who enlisted: about 1,000 Black Americans served in the army in the late 1840s, but Israel Moses's position as a doctor made him unique. Serving in white regiments was a tradition that would be repeated by Moses and his brother Isaac during the Civil War. To be sure, Black soldiers were able to openly volunteer in the Union Army by the early 1860s. Yet most were forced to do menial labor and were poorly treated. Israel Moses served as a white man, an officer, and a surgeon.[14]

His status was earned over the years. Israel Moses began as an assistant surgeon in the Mexican American War in January 1847. One of his first deployments was in Vera Cruz, a city on the Gulf Coast that had been founded by Spanish explorer Hernán Cortés in 1519. In the centuries that followed, Vera Cruz became Mexico's chief port to the Atlantic world. Like the Spanish Army more than 300 years earlier, the US military used the port as a launching point for the invasion of Mexico City, this time in the fall of 1847. When Vera Cruz fell, Moses was there to treat the fifty-nine wounded men, and he went on to serve in Toluca and Mexico City as well. For nearly a decade, the army would become Moses's life. After the war ended, he went on to serve at Fort Leavenworth and then at army posts in Oregon, Washington, and Texas.[15]

Throughout his early military career, Moses often found himself entangled in US imperialist efforts. Capitalism was reshaping the world, and the Moses brothers found themselves in the thick of the new market society, both beneficiaries and victims of the risky path to profit. A case in point: after briefly returning to New York to work as a surgeon at the newly formed Jews' Hospital, Moses got drawn into William Walker's invasion of Nicaragua. Walker would attempt to conquer various parts of Mexico and Central America before the Hondurans finally executed him in 1860. But Walker's invasion of Nicaragua was one of his longest campaigns, as it involved—in Moses's own words—"our immense national interests on the Pacific."[16]

Walker attacked Nicaragua as part of his obsession about creating a transcontinental passage to facilitate quicker travel west during the Gold Rush, and American settlers like Moses were crucial to Walker's attempt to take control of the region. Moses's specific job was to establish a military hospital to support the invasion, but while in Nicaragua, Moses also worked on a new smallpox vaccine and encouraged the use of lime to combat the miasma he believed was spreading cholera in the city of Granada. Disease management was crucial to Walker's strategy, as immigrants from the North often died from tropical diseases.

In retrospect, Moses's alliance with the pro-slavery Walker seems odd at best. To be sure, Moses himself expressed open disdain for locals in both Nicaragua and Mexico, seeing them as morally and physically inferior to Europeans. But did Moses really support Walker's belief that slavery was essential to American order and imperialism? Or was he—like some of Walker's other settlers who otherwise backed abolition—just willing to put up with Walker's rhetoric because it benefited himself? In the end, Moses's attempts to clean up Granada's bad smells didn't keep him from contracting cholera. Having escaped death, Moses gave up on Walker's schemes and returned to New York. Years later, he still hung on to two worthless $50 bills from the Republic of Nicaragua, signed by Walker, as a memento of the failed revolution.[17]

Of all his military postings, however, it was Moses's time in Mexico during the war of 1848 that affected the lives of his brothers and their cousin Abraham Rodriguez Brandon the most. While nominally the US Army had laid siege to Mexico City in order to force a peace, once peace was brokered,

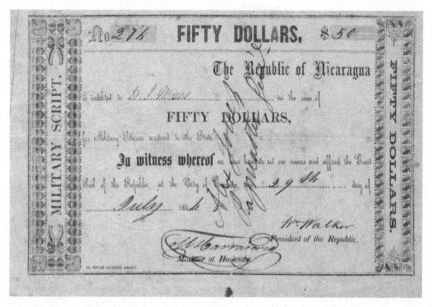

Military scrip from the Republic of Nicaragua signed by William Walker for Israel Moses (1856). AJHS.

a second battle was instigated on a commercial front. Vera Cruz became an important port for US investors, who took advantage of locally produced coffee, sugar, cotton, silver, and tobacco as well as the city's key position for bringing goods into and out of the enormous market of Mexico City. Vera Cruz also became a key transit point to the Near East, as US exports surged after the war.[18]

Some of the most prominent investors in the region were younger members of the Moses-Brandon clan. In 1849, for example, Abraham Rodriguez Brandon the younger got into the game, importing large amounts of cochineal—an important red dye made from insects—from Vera Cruz. The older Moses brothers likewise sent Lionel Moses to Vera Cruz to take care of a shipment of goods. He stayed for three years and became a US consular agent. Younger brother Alfred Moses similarly felt Mexico's lure, becoming Deputy Collector of Customs in Roma, along the Rio Grande and just across the border from Ciudad Miguel Aleman. Although Alfred Moses would go on to become a lawyer and judge and live in a variety of places across the United States, it was in Roma that he died in 1901.[19]

Lionel Moses soon found, however, that business in Mexico was a gamble. Fortunes made quickly became fortunes lost. Following a surge of prosperity, he found himself sheepishly having to petition the US government

Anonymous, *Stereoscopic portrait of Alfred Moses* (ca. 1852).
Daguerreotype. AJHS.

in 1853 for compensation for the wrongs he felt the Mexican government had committed against him, including the seizure of goods, arbitrary fines, and the dismantling of his business. In all, he had lost $100,000—nearly $3.5 million in today's money.[20]

While Lionel Moses was going from rags to riches and back again in Mexico, Sarah's middle sons Joseph and A. R. B. Moses established a branch of the family firm in Macao and Canton and advertised themselves as purveyors of Chinese goods at the store at 66 Beaver Street in New York. Canton—now called Guangzhou—lay along the Pearl River, about ninety miles north along the waterway from the port city of Macao, which sat across the river's estuary from burgeoning Hong Kong. Like Macao, Canton served as a crucial stop on the Silk Road and for the opium trade. Once again, the Moses brothers had decided to seek their fortunes in cities where great empires bumped into and wrestled with one another.[21]

Joseph Moses was sent to Canton to work on the ground, buying items to export back to New York. Despite the port's privileged trade status with the West, it was unusual for outsiders to reside in the city. The few foreign merchants in Canton all lived in the Thirteen Factories whose buildings faced the river. Named for the Portuguese word for trading post, these so-called factories did not make goods but rather contained warehouses and offices. The factories also had extensive apartments, boarding houses, and even a hotel. Fortunes were made, so prices were steep: up to $1,000–$2,000 a season for an apartment facing the river. Visitors expressed awe at the long verandas and the exquisite furnishings within. When the merchants returned home, they brought with them paintings and porcelain souvenirs depicting the glistening, white buildings. It was here that Joseph Moses set up business. Like their father before them, the Moses brothers' specialties were teas, matting, and firecrackers. Business was lucrative but risky.[22]

Joseph Moses found this out the hard way. In 1844, locals who had grown tired of the foreign influences in the city set fire to the Moses family's factory, destroying it completely, along with the offices of fellow expats and shipwrights Charles Emory and George Fraser. Rather than supporting the merchants, Chinese officials demanded that all foreigners leave Canton and retreat to Hong Kong. Prior treaties proved worthless. It was a devastating blow.[23]

Even when business boomed, the social life was cliquish in the small enclave of Canton's Thirteen Factories. Christian merchants didn't always appreciate Jews. John Heard, who ran the prestigious firm of Augustine Heard and Co. in Canton, mocked Moses's attire, noting he "sports now a ferocious whisker, dirty moustache, and a coat which a Christian would not be seen in."[24] Likewise Nathaniel Kinsman, an agent for Canton's Wetmore and Company, felt the need to apologize to his wife when the "lowly" Joseph Moses visited.[25] He similarly expressed disgust when one of the rare white women in Canton accepted Moses's attention. "It is astonishing to me," wrote Kinsman, "that Miss King permits that dissipated Jew Moses to gallant her about, there is no accounting for tastes, however, as the old woman said when she kissed the cow."[26] It is hard to square Heard and Kinsman's slovenly Moses with the debonair young man who sat for family photographs only a few years later. Yet despite some merchants' anti-Jewish sentiments, Miss King didn't seem to mind Joseph Moses's courting.

Even so, 1846 must have marked a sad year for Miss King, as Joseph Moses returned home to New York. Older brother A. R. B. Moses took his place in Canton. A. R. B. Moses shared a house in the factories built by American merchant Gideon Nye, whose American trading firm was closely allied with British interests. The firm's factories faced the Pearl riverfront in a three-storied, hipped-roof building with front and rear verandas.[27]

Even though his brother had left and he had to share a house and factory with Protestants, A. R. B. Moses found he was not the only Jew in Canton. Jews had a history in the province. Back in the Tang Dynasty, Jews

Anonymous, *Joseph Washington Moses* (ca. 1850–1865). Daguerreotype. AJHS.

had settled in Canton because of the silk trade, though later they moved to Kaifeng, where they built the first known Chinese synagogue in 1163 CE. These early residents adopted local customs, including hair styles and foot binding. By the late 1700s, Jewish merchants were back in Canton, though now they kept themselves to the foreign enclave. Some of the early returnees were Philadelphians Benjamin Etting and Horatio Etting, who had started working in Canton in the 1820s. Sons of Frances Gratz, the Etting brothers were first cousins of the extended Moses clan through Joshua's brother Solomon Moses.[28]

By 1846 when A. R. B. Moses arrived, working in Canton increasingly meant rubbing shoulders with some of the wealthiest Jewish merchant firms around the globe. The Jewish community was diverse but with a definite Sephardic-Mizrachi bent. The silk trade brought to China Sephardic traders with strong ties to India. Elias David Sassoon, scion of the prosperous and influential Baghdadi Jewish family, arrived in Canton and set up one base for the family's merchant empire. During A. R. B. Moses's residence, the Chowchow ("assorted") Factory—one of the original foreign thirteen—got its name for the diversity of its residents, whom American businessman William C. Hunter described at the time as a hodgepodge of "Malwarees, Persians, Moors, Jews, and Parsees," many from Southeast Asia.[29] Being Jewish, and three-quarters Sephardic, gave A. R. B. Moses an insider status with families who would later be nicknamed the "Rothschilds of the East."[30]

Mathew B. Brady Gallery, Abraham Rodrigues Brandon Moses (1853). Daguerreotype, 3 3/4 x 3 1/4 in. AJHS.

After Lionel Moses went bust in Mexico, he joined his older brother in Canton. Both Lionel and A. R. B. Moses learned from Joseph Moses's earlier social faux pas and used Masonic lodges to bridge the religious divides in the Thirteen Factories. Just as his grandfather Abraham Rodrigues Brandon had once risen through the ranks to become the Worshipful Master of the Hibernian Lodge in Barbados, Lionel Moses made lasting connections through the Royal Sussex Lodge in Canton.[31]

In the first half of the 1850s, the brothers continued to gain renown for their work in China. One US minister even singled out Joseph Moses for possessing "the reputation of a high-minded and honorable merchant."[32] By 1853, the family firm was respected in New York as one of the best-known purveyors of Chinese goods.[33]

Yet once again the brothers found themselves caught up in revolutions. Just as the brothers were getting ahead, the Taiping Uprising enveloped much of southern China. Even more auspicious, its leader Hong Xiuquan hailed from Canton. A religious visionary, Hong Xiuquan sparked a Chinese-inflected Christianity in which he was recognized as the younger brother of Jesus. Then he systematically began to overthrow the Qing dynasty, positioning himself as emperor of what he called the Taiping Heavenly Kingdom. The result was the bloodiest war of the century, as the emperor of the Qing dynasty ruthlessly executed all suspected rebels. Hong Xiuquan's theology added to the bloodshed. As he explained, "Our holy Father's sacred edict instructs us to behead the evildoers and sustain those who are upright."[34]

It was a terrifying time to be in Canton. British counsel at Canton John Bowring estimated that 400 to 500 people were executed every day. One British diplomat staggered back, dazed, to the Consulate after he watched sixty revolutionaries lose their heads in two and a half minutes. All told, between June and August 1855, 75,000 people were beheaded in Canton alone.[35]

In addition to the general chaos, the uprising disrupted trade. The Moses firm consequently suffered losses of around $300,000 to $400,000— somewhere between $7.3 million and $10 million in today's money. The Moses brothers' Chinese creditors were unforgiving. Yet who the Moses brothers should pay was unclear, as insurgents threatened to take the town. The Moses brothers weren't the only Americans entangled in the disputes with the enraged Chinese authorities. John Heard of Augustine Heard and Co., who had mocked Joseph Moses's lack of style, also found himself pleading for help from the US Consul. A. R. B. Moses fled the city, and in March 1855, Lionel Moses joined him back in New York.

Creditors forced A. R. B. Moses back to China in October 1855. He returned to the war zone voluntarily, but was almost immediately taken captive. Breaking free, he fled to Macao at the advice of the US Consul and safely waited for the two governments to settle the company's legal battles. In the end, the Moses Brothers firm was liquidated, and the brothers were forced to start anew in New York.[36]

The timing of the Moses brothers' business losses foreshadowed the downward spiral for foreign business more generally in Canton. While the Qing Dynasty was busy dealing with the rebels, the British used the opportunity to start the Second Opium War in 1856. By December of that year, tensions between the foreign merchants and local residents reached a new peak, and locals once again set fire to the houses on Thirteen Factories Street. This time flammable goods in the warehouses, high winds, and low tides combined to make a poisonous brew. By the time the flames died out, the entire Thirteen Factories were gone. The surviving foreign merchants and consular staff moved to Macao. The Moses brothers had gotten out just in time.[37]

When news of the fire hit, the Moses brothers were back in New York forging a new life. Lionel Moses began courting a younger, charming member of Shearith Israel, Selina Seixas. In May 1857, he won her hand.

Marrying Seixas was a social coup. Selina Seixas was the granddaughter of Gershom Mendes Seixas, the congregation's most revered and beloved rabbi. Through her father, Joshua Seixas, she was connected to almost every major Jewish family in early New York.[38]

Lionel wasn't the only one entranced by the new family member: older brother Israel Moses was also besotted with young "Lina," as he called her. When Israel Moses served as a surgeon in the Civil War, he wrote home to brothers Lionel and Brandon Moses with war news and descriptions of how enslaved people in the South had been left behind in deserted houses to tend the blooming peach orchards. But it was to Lina Moses he wrote the most, and his tone was affectionate and playful. Often he sounded more like a beau than a brother-in-law: "If you could make me a surprise visit just now, I could feast you, for I have received from Washington a box of good things. . . . I should be charmed to set it all before you—and then I could give you a stray dance on the parade to the fine music of our band."[39] In another letter he proposes "to visit you by proxy in the shape of a small note, which is to greet you first by kissing you and then all the babies . . . and ask you to sit down and make yourself comfortable on a gun chest which answers me as a sofa."[40]

Selina Seixas wrote him back, but not as often as he hoped. Sometimes he coyly suggested she write "whenever you feel amiably inclined," but elsewhere he openly chided her for not having written in two and a half months or urged her to "write soon . . . and tell me all about yourself and the babies."[41] When she did write, he was full of praise, saying how he was "charmed with your account of our [sic] little niece and nephew and I hope one of these days to play with them."[42] Her family became his family, and Israel Moses spoke wistfully of how she should "kiss little Edith and Blanche and tell them I expect them one day to grow big useful young ladies so that they can take turns and come and keep house for me when I may be as I expect to continue to be an old bachelor, and nurse me if I should be crippled with a shot."[43] Rather than discourage such dreams, Selina sent him a photo of the girls taken by Charles D. Fredricks & Co. on Broadway, to "Dr. I. Moses, U.S.A. With his nieces' love."[44] While not as effusive as Israel, Lionel's brother Alfred also went out of his way to send pictures of himself, "For my dear sister Lina. With much love from her little Brother Affy."[45] Brother Lionel went unmentioned in the gift.

Early portraits illuminate one reason the Moses brothers were obsessed with Selina Seixas. She was astonishingly beautiful. Like the Moses clan, the Seixases were early admirers of the daguerreotype process, and a wealth of photos taken of Selina Seixas Moses throughout her life have survived. Her childhood portrait is one of the oldest known daguerreotypes of an American Jew. Slightly later daguerreotypes show her with braids worn in heavy loops on each side of her head. Her gowns were made from fashionable velvets and silks, with expensive lace collars and brocade trim. Like most wealthy women of the era, she wore corsets, her waist pinched small and tight.

Yet for all her ancestral connections, Seixas had at least one skeleton in her closet. Her father was one of the era's most notorious Jewish apostates, as his life as a Christian bridged the worlds of the Boston Brahmins and rebellious, frontier Christianity. Joshua's life had started auspiciously, as the second child of Gershom Mendes Seixas's second wife Hannah Manuel. Gershom Mendes Seixas raised his son Joshua to be a future Jewish leader, educating him at the congregation's school, which offered Hebrew and secular studies. But when Joshua Seixas was only fourteen, his illustrious father died. The family struggled to make ends meet, and Joshua Seixas became an instructor at the school where he was once a student. When he was twenty, he married Henrietta Raphael, a Jew from Richmond. Seixas continued to teach Semitic languages, furthering his understanding of Hebrew and Aramaic grammar by creating a new approach based on the methods used by Latin and Greek scholars.

By the early 1830s the family had moved to Massachusetts, where Seixas tutored Harvard students. He published a book, started calling himself James, and by all appearances converted to Christianity, most likely baptized by Unitarian minister Theodore Parker in Boston. The family was appalled.

Undeterred, Seixas moved west to Ohio, where he taught Hebrew at Oberlin College and Case Western Reserve University. It was there that he met Joseph Smith Jr. and other future leaders of the Mormon church and eventually moved to Kirkland, the heart of the new religious movement. Some scholars have suggested that Seixas may have sparked Joseph Smith's interest in Kabbalah, but all agree that Seixas's lessons and books on Hebrew grammar bolstered Smith's lifelong reliance on Hebrew to validate Mormon thought and culture, including Smith's controversial prophesy about polygamy. Although Seixas left his mark on Mormonism, eventually Mormonism released its hold on him. By 1838 he had moved back to New York, where Henrietta Raphael Seixas gave birth to Selina Seixas.[46]

Joshua/James Seixas's Christian proclivities embarrassed the family, but Selina Seixas's marriage in the synagogue marked her reentrance into the inner circle of Jewish life. Standing alongside Lionel Moses, Selina Seixas would take a leading role in Shearith Israel, including serving as the secretary for the Ladies' Bikur Cholim Society, which assisted the sick and needy. The marriage must have also pleased her mother, who for at least some time lived apart from her Christianized husband. Unlike Joshua/James Seixas, Henrietta Raphael Seixas remained in the Jewish community and was buried in the congregation's cemetery. She would become "Grandma Seixas," lovingly remembered in family photographs.[47] She was the only grandmother whom Sarah Brandon Moses's grandchildren knew, Lionel Moses's parents having died long before the grandchildren were born.[48]

Seixas was an ideal match for Lionel Moses. She would bear him seven children, including Blanche, the family's genealogist and one of the girls Israel Moses had hoped would keep house for him. Like most middle-class and upper-middle-class New York Jews of this era, the family slowly moved uptown over the years, following the synagogues as the neighborhoods changed. Occasionally they branched out to new areas, renting houses in Tremont in the Bronx, Long Island, or the Park Slope and Carroll Gardens neighborhoods in Brooklyn. By the late 1880s, the large brood was back in Manhattan, living at 47 West 97th Street, half a block from Central Park. Photos from early 1888 show the family once again waylaid by a freak March storm, their brownstone hidden behind a wall of snow that fell during the blizzard. Lionel Moses was the only one of Sarah's children who married, hence most of her descendants are through him.[49]

After Lionel's death, Selina Seixas Moses ran the family import-export business with their son Brandon.[50] By then, any chance of a romance with Israel Moses was out of the question. He had passed away from consumption at the age of forty-nine, twenty-five years before his brother's death.[51] Neither Edith nor Blanche ever had a chance to tend house for their uncle. They were only eleven and twelve when he died.

Although they never married, Lionel Moses's other brothers continued the mercantile legacy established by the Moses clan. Religiously, the brothers who did not wed followed in the footsteps of their uncles and grandfathers by becoming members of the *Mahamad*. By 1870, A. R. B. Moses was vice president of Shearith Israel's relief society, and in 1878 he became the *parnas* of the congregation, just as his namesake had been parnas of Nidhe Israel in Barbados decades before.[52]

When the Moses brothers rejoined their kin in New York in the 1850s, they found their family had expanded in their absence. After they finished school, Sarah and Isaac's half siblings Joseph, Julia, Esther, and Lavinia Rodrigues Brandon lived on their own on Moorgate Street in London near

Lionel and Selina Moses's house at 47 West 97th Street. AJHS.

Bevis Marks, with Joseph Rodrigues Brandon as head of the household. But by 1849, Joseph Rodrigues Brandon had sought out greener pastures and had set up shop at 25 Merchant Exchange as a broker in New York. In August 1852, the Brandon sisters set sail from Liverpool to join him and moved into his house on East 23rd Street, near Madison Square Park. The move would change their fortunes. Although Brandon eventually migrated to San Francisco, where he started his own family, on December 23, 1852, his sister Lavinia Rodrigues Brandon married Judah "Jules" Abecasis in a ceremony led by the Reverend J. J. Lyons of New York's Congregation Shearith Israel.[53]

Abecasis was a catch. Born in Gibraltar into one of the leading Moroccan Jewish families, Abecasis had grown up in London at Congregation Bevis Marks. The family quickly become part of the synagogue's inner circle, and often donated to local Jewish institutions. Today the family's ritual Judaica, passed down through the generations, forms a part of the collection at London's Victoria and Albert Museum. Marrying an Abecasis cemented Lavinia Brandon's standing in the Sephardic world. In 1853, Abecasis opened a business with his new brother-in-law Joseph R. Brandon down near

Manhattan's wharves, while the newlyweds settled in what was then uptown on Manhattan's fashionable West 32nd Street.[54]

Isaac Lopez Brandon just missed their wedding, arriving in New York via St. Thomas in July 1853. Once back, Isaac took up residence near the synagogue, in a modern, three-story house at 181 Thompson Street with his son and his surviving in-laws, David, Rebecca, and Saly Moses. For a brief time, he was united with all his surviving siblings. He was even present to see younger brother Joseph Rodrigues Brandon wed Sarah Cecilia Florance, a Jewish heiress and distant relative of Selina Seixas, in 1854. Then gold fever set the newlyweds in motion to San Francisco. Joseph Rodrigues Brandon was not the only one to travel west: nephews Alfred and Benjamin Moses traveled on ahead, eager to claim their share of the riches. In California, Joseph Rodrigues Brandon made his fortune in the Gold Rush and established the second main surviving branch of the Brandon clan, one that continues to thrive on the West Coast today.[55]

Sarah and Isaac's younger half-sisters Esther and Julia Rodrigues Brandon stayed behind in New York with Jules and Lavinia Abecasis. Abecasis was quickly becoming the leading rubber broker in the United States. Less than a decade later, his business with his brother Moses Abecasis was worth $50,000. The family's Civil War letters suggest the Moses, Brandon, and Abecasis branches of the family remained close. News of Lavinia Abecasis's illness passed from Selina Seixas Moses to the front lines, prompting Israel Moses to note that he would "rejoice to hear of the entire recovery of Lavinia, and when you see her, give her my fondest remembrances."[56] The Brandon sisters were also close enough to be teased. "Tell Lavinia and Julia that they are shabby lazy aunts for not writing me," Israel told Selina Moses, "and I won't drive or take tea with them when I return unless they send me a long apology."[57] They might have been his aunts, but since he was born in 1831, Israel Moses was actually older than either of them.

The shabby aunts were doing quite well for themselves. The Abecasises lived in style in the mansion on West 32nd Street before moving to the even more fashionable 1427 West Broadway. By then, Esther Rodrigues Brandon had returned to London to wed Abecasis's brother Aaron Abecasis at Bevis Marks, which became their spiritual home. Although they had no children, the couple became important patrons of Jewish charities, including Yeshiva Beth Aaron in Jerusalem, which used their money to pass along Jewish values and learning to the next generation.[58]

Back in New York, Jules Abecasis was also making his mark religiously, serving as president of Congregation Shearith Israel in 1865 and 1876.

Socially, Lavinia and Jules Abecasis made the leap into the high-society world of what would later be called the Four Hundred Club: their four sons attended school with the likes of John Jacob Astor Jr. and August Belmont as well as members of the Roosevelt family. In turn, Lavinia Abecasis's sons became progenitors of the third main surviving branch of the Brandon tree.[59]

Isaac Lopez Brandon, however, did not survive to see his sister's social success. On Wednesday morning, December 12, 1855, he passed away at 91 Clinton Place, the house he and his son Abraham shared with David, Rebecca, and Saly Moses. He was sixty-three years old.[60]

The house at 91 Clinton Place symbolized how far Isaac had traveled over the course of his life. Born enslaved to a middle-class Jewish family who lived on the second floor above their store on Swan Street in Bridgetown, Isaac died a gentleman merchant, free in New York and snuggled among his son and prosperous in-laws in a mansion he could call his own. Only seven doors west of Fifth Avenue and one block from Washington Square Park, the mansion was something to behold: when his son sold the house in 1859, he advertised it as a "first-class four-story well finished dwelling house . . . with two story extension. [All] In perfect order, and well calculated for a large family."[61] It was the sort of place where Isaac's former owners only dreamed of living.

Isaac left behind a fortune. In Bridgetown, there was his house and land in Sobers Lane, another house at 25 Tudor Street near the synagogue, and land near Indian River, just south of where the Cave Hill campus of the University of the West Indies stands today. He left £50 to the Barbados General Hospital, and another £50 each to Barbados' Nidhe Israel Synagogue and New York's Shearith Israel. Joseph, Lavinia, Julia, and Esther Rodrigues Brandon all received £50 each as well as the explicit recognition that they were his brother and sisters. While by 1855 that relationship might have seemed obvious, his affirming language was a step more effusive than his father's own will, when Abraham Rodrigues Brandon called his second set of offspring "my reputed children."[62] Sisters-in-law (and housemates) Saly and Rebecca Moses received £50 and £25, respectively. Sarah's surviving sons all received £30 each. Other than a few token legacies to friends and more distant relatives, the rest went to his son Abraham Rodriguez Brandon.[63]

If Isaac had known what his son would do with his newfound financial freedom, however, he might have thought twice. On August 17, 1857, less than two years after his father's death, Abraham Rodriguez Brandon married Miriam Smith, the sister of Dr. James Owen Smith, who lived nearby at 81 Clinton Place, at the corner of Fifth Avenue. Unlike his parents and

Abraham Rodriguez
Brandon the younger
(1826–1860). Courtesy of
descendants.

cousins, Abraham Rodriguez Brandon Jr. was married at his brother-in-law's
house rather than the Shearith Israel synagogue. More to the point, the ceremony was performed by the Episcopalian minister of Trinity Church. Had
Abraham Rodriguez Brandon the younger waited to marry Smith after his
father had died, or was she only one sign of his zeal for the Trinitarian religion? Whatever the reason for his defection, Abraham kept to that path for
the rest of his life. When he died, he was not laid to rest in the Beth Olam
cemetery alongside his father or Moses relatives. Instead, he lay nestled
among his wife's kin in Trinity Cemetery in Morningside Heights. For the
first time since his father's ancestors had left Iberia, a Brandon was buried in
a Christian cemetery.[64]

Yet Abraham Rodriguez Brandon was not a dead end. He would give
rise to the fourth branch of the Brandon tree—the one that would yield
the most descendants in my later genealogical searches. For regardless of
his religious beliefs, Abraham Rodriguez Brandon's marriage was fruitful.
Miriam Smith Brandon bore him two daughters: Edith and Constance
Evelyn Rodrigues Brandon. Both were baptized, but only Constance lived
to adulthood. She went on to marry Henry William Poor, who—despite
his name—was anything but. Constance Brandon Poor's children Henry,

Menorah in the house of Constance Evelyn Rodrigues Brandon and
Henry William Poor at 1 Lexington Avenue. MCNY.

Edith, Roger, Pamela, and Constance were raised in a luxurious McKim,
Mead & White mansion at 1 Lexington Avenue and spent their summers at
an elaborate neo-Elizabethan mansion named Woodland in Tuxedo Park,
New York. Perhaps not all was forgotten about their Jewish past. Near the
elaborate wrought-iron staircase in the Lexington Avenue house stood a
large menorah on an Oriental rug.[65]

Nearly a century earlier, Constance Brandon Poor's grandfather Isaac had
converted just after the Chanukah celebration. Who would light the oil in
the menorah in the Poors' house? Their branch of the family stayed Christian,
but more than a century later, Constance Brandon Poor's descendants found
themselves wondering about the Jewish past their great-great-grandfather
Abraham Rodriguez Brandon had left behind.

Epilogue

New York, 1942–2021

WHEN BLANCHE MOSES SAT IN her apartment on West 118th Street in New York worrying over her collection of daguerreotypes and puzzling through her grandmother's ancestry, it apparently did not occur to her that Sarah Brandon Moses might have been born enslaved. But then again, Blanche Moses had not turned to genealogy to uncover family secrets or her multiracial heritage.

Although it was not nearly as popular as it is today, by the 1890s genealogy had become an important part of American self-fashioning. For Jews like Blanche Moses who could follow their families back to the colonial era, tracing family trees was a way of elevating oneself above the impoverished Eastern European Jews who had flooded the Lower East Side from the 1880s through the 1920s. Like many people connected to the first Jewish American families, Moses focused in her own writings about her heritage on her ancestors' wealth, piety, and contributions to the emerging United States.[1] Genealogy allowed Moses to underscore her family's national and religious pride. Certainly American Jews, like other ethnic groups, used ancestry to show that the nation was founded by groups other than Anglo-Saxons, but most Jewish genealogists did so with an eye toward their family's contribution to white American history. In the early publications of the American Jewish Historical Society, Jews were mentioned as slave owners, not as enslaved people.[2]

Changing notions of race between Sarah's death and the 1940s would also have made Sarah's African ancestry harder for Moses to imagine. In the late eighteenth and early nineteenth centuries, race was remarkably fluid for wealthy, racially ambiguous people such as Sarah and Isaac. What race Sarah and Isaac were assigned varied by time and place. Even toward the end of his life, Isaac was one race when he lived in New York and another in Barbados. Likewise, if Sarah and Isaac had settled in the southern United States rather than in New York, their experience might have been completely different. During their lifetimes, racial definitions varied by state within the United States, and before 1860 the census did not include any instructions for census takers explaining what the racial categories meant.[3]

In contrast, by the time Blanche Moses started working on family lore, the fourteenth census (1920) had done away with this ambiguity. As that census explained, "The term 'white' as used in the census report refers to persons understood to be *pure-blooded whites*. A person of mixed blood is classified according to the nonwhite racial strain."[4] In case this were not clear enough, the census explained that a person with *any* African ancestors, no matter how few or far back, was considered a "Negro."[5] For Blanche Moses to envision her grandmother's African ancestry, she would also have to have understood her own ties to Africa, and in doing so, she would have inferred that she and her siblings, and all her nieces and nephews, were now considered people of color by the United States government.

She never took this leap. When Moses responded to the 1920 census, she had several options for how she (and the census taker) understood her race: "W" for White, "B" for Black, "Mu" for mulatto, "Ch" for Chinese, "Jp" for Japanese, "In" for American Indian, or "Ot" for other races. Moses chose white, as she and her family had done every year of her life.[6] When the 1930 and 1940 census takers stopped by, Moses continued to designate herself as white. By the time the mammoth *Americans of Jewish Descent* first appeared in the 1960s, genealogist Malcolm Stern also did not recognize that Sarah had African ancestors. The one-drop rule had been institutionalized by the US census for decades, and perhaps it seemed obvious to Stern that someone who died white had always been designated so.

Stern's blind spot was supported by the emerging field of Jewish American history that struggled to place Jews in the ethno-racial landscape of the Americas. Although born in Philadelphia, Stern received his doctorate in American Jewish history from Hebrew Union College in Cincinnati in 1957, during the years when Jacob Rader Marcus was reworking early American Jewish history into an academic discipline. Slavery, let alone Jews of color, played a minimal role in Marcus and Stern's vision of the field. They were not alone.[7]

Most scholars who wrote about American Jewish history in the decades following World War II were Ashkenazi Jews whose ancestors had come to the country. Although nominally white according to the census, their ancestors had found upon arrival in the United States that anti-Semites did not consider them truly white. Even as the GI Bill allowed men of Stern's generation and the one that followed to enter the academy (Stern himself served as an army chaplain before getting his PhD), African Americans who had served found themselves unwelcome at white universities, making it less likely that scholars of American Jewish history would be Jews of color. Was it insecurity over their own whiteness that caused European American Jewish historians to write Jews of color out of the story of American Judaism, or just that their own genealogies led them to create histories that mirrored their families' experiences and self-understandings?[8]

Either way, I am hardly the first to notice that most interpreters of American Jewish history have seen being Jewish and black as an oxymoron. Even as recently as the early 2000s, when a large range of scholarship was dedicated to Black-Jewish relations, nearly all of these discussions were framed by a Black-Jewish binary, with Jews on one side and Blacks on the other. When Black Jewish communities were discussed, they were often presented as not quite Jewish enough. A case in point was the Black Jewish synagogues of early Harlem, a short walk north from Blanche Moses's apartment.[9]

By the second quarter of the twentieth century, Harlem was home to several Black-run synagogues. At least eight different Black religious groups linked their practices to Judaism. Yet at a 1931 talk given at a Long Island Jewish center, Rabbi Norman Salit declared that "the Negro synagogues were based on a mixture of superstition and ignorance that has nothing to do with Judaism."[10] Salit's views carried weight: in addition to being ordained by the Jewish Theological Seminary, he would later serve on its board and become president of the Synagogue Council of America. While as early as the 1940s Black anthropologists like Arthur Huff Fauset were taking the Harlem congregations seriously, the early Jewish anthropologist Ruth Schlossberg Landes dismissed the rabbis of these congregations as frauds and their congregants as "bewildered and frightened" patsies.[11]

At the heart of these attacks was the assumption that European American Judaism was the correct form of Jewishness and that white Jews had the right to *poskin* (judge) Black Jewish practice. This expectation echoes the experiences of Jews of color in early Suriname, who became annoyed with the policies of European Jews and hence founded their own congregation, only to find that such an action was ultimately not allowed. When scholars decide which synagogues count in their histories, they exercise a similar control over the past, by determining retroactively who and what is a Jew. The story of Black Jewish synagogues and the experiences of Jews of color within white-run synagogues is part of the Jewish American experience, but even today, this story is typically left out of large-scale Jewish American histories, notwithstanding a focus on Jewish Harlem. Sarah Brandon Moses and Isaac Lopez Brandon's history reveals the damage of reading Black Jews out of the American experience. By being unwilling to see Black Jewish congregations as legitimate, scholars have also failed to see the Jews of African ancestry at the heart of the oldest congregation in the United States.[12]

The subsequent silence around Sarah and Isaac's story reflects other losses in the larger story of American Judaism. The Moses-Brandons were not the only Jews with African ancestry in the synagogues they attended. In 1857, a visitor from Germany noted that there were several women of color who worshipped at Shearith Israel. In an incident that will ring true with the experience of many Jews of color today, the visitor assumed the women did not belong and asked them who they were. They explained how they had begun their lives enslaved in Suriname and had come to New York with their former owner. They were not the only Caribbean Jews of color who found upon arrival that they had to justify their existence. Two women and a child who immigrated from Jamaica in 1911 identified themselves to immigration authorities as Jewish, only to be asked to explain how it was that they were both Jewish and Black. The women disclosed that their ancestors had been enslaved by and raised as Jews, and were formally recognized as such when they were freed. In spite of the questioning to which Jews of color were subjected, Shearith Israel remained a welcome home for them. In 1895, one Black man left a third of his estate to the congregation.[13]

Even after Blanche Moses died, the congregation's ties to Western Sephardic congregations in the Caribbean meant that people with African ancestry were a normal part of synagogue life. In 1951, *hazan* Abraham Lopes Cardozo married fellow congregant Irma Fernandes Robles. Born in Suriname, Fernandes Robles was, like the Moses-Brandons, partially descended from enslaved people. As a child, she had even been photographed in a *kotomiese* and *angisa*, the dress and scarf worn as a sign of cultural pride by Afro-Surinamese women. Although in her memoirs she remarks that "this was how the native Creole Indians dressed on the market day," we know that other members of her family proudly wore this marker of ethnic identity. In a 1908 photo of her grandfather's cousin Isaac Daniel

Fernandes and his family, Fernandes's wife Klasina Elisabeth Vroom also wears a *kotomiese* and *angisa*.[14]

Today multiracial Jews make up 12 percent of American Jewry, with nearly 87,000 nonwhite, Hispanic, or multiracial Jewish households in the New York area alone.[15] Surveys done by Be'chol Lashon, an organization dedicated to Jewish diversity, indicate a larger story: as much as 20 percent of American Jews identify as ethnically diverse in some form.[16] Sarah and Isaac's story clarifies that ethnic and racial heterogeneity is not new to American Judaism. Multiracial Jews contributed to Jewish life in the United States much earlier than scholars have previously argued, but inclusion came at a heavy price for Jews of color.

Sarah and Isaac's story is a reminder of the exhausting demands that are sometimes made on Jews of color to code-switch: to adjust their behavior, speech, and dress to meet the expectations of white-run synagogues. Sarah, for example, attended school to learn not only about religion but about the social norms and expectations of the *nação*. Yet, as Isaac was to discover in the Barbadian vestry debates of 1819–20, even though he was praised for his behavior, he could not leave behind his identity as a man of color just because he was in the synagogue. Moreover, cultural expectations placed on Sarah and Isaac ultimately had an enormous cost: even their own grandchildren had no knowledge of the world they had left behind or their family's ties to civil rights movements in Barbados. Would their descendants reject that past if they had known about it?

This was the very question I found myself asking on an unusually warm September day in 2016, as I sat in the library of one of New York's elite genealogical societies waiting to meet one of the descendants of Isaac Lopez Brandon. Chance had helped our paths cross. The previous summer, I had found a letter he had written in 1991 to the archivist of the Barbados Historical Society in Bridgetown, asking for information on Isaac's father Abraham. In exchange, he recounted the history of Isaac's son after Isaac's death in 1855: conversion, marriage, and exile from the family (though later historical sleuthing would prove the exile portion of the story false). Fortunately, the archivist had saved his letter, filing it away with the other Brandon papers in a manila folder. Equally fortunately, the letter included Isaac's great-great-great-great-grandson's mailing address, and thanks to the internet, I had tracked him down. He agreed to meet.

I was nervous. On the one hand, I sincerely believed that after several years of sleuthing I had fantastic resources for him: beautiful portraits of his ancestors that he had never seen, including the charming miniatures reproduced in this book. I also had information about long-lost lines of the family, such as the names of three generations of Isaac's maternal line, whom I had lured out of the silent past.

Yet I also knew descendants often had a tricky habit of interweaving their own identities with that of their ancestors. I had made the mistake of forgetting this years earlier, when I was working on a book on the Wampanoag community of Martha's Vineyard. After a wonderful discovery in the moldering archives of the courthouse of Edgartown, I naively informed a descendant that her pilgrim foremother had had an illicit and notorious affair with a Wampanoag man before her marriage to the family patriarch. She had refused to marry the Wampanoag man and consequently was publicly whipped. It was an exceptional and fascinating case from the perspective of a distant historian. Suffice it to say, however, the descendant was not as excited as I was about the incident.

Should I expect a similar awkward silence about Isaac's being born out of wedlock and enslaved? Certainly, the location of our meeting was not a good omen. Isaac's fourth-great-grandson was generously coming into the city for the day on a train from Connecticut, and we had arranged to get together at one of his haunts: the library of the Saint Nicholas Society. For those whose ancestors are not old New York elites, this locale may not mean anything, but in some circles the location spoke volumes. The Saint Nicholas Society was formed in 1835 by Washington Irving and other high-society New Yorkers. Membership is restricted to those who were descendants of people living in New York prior to 1785, and all members must be elected after at least two members attest that the applicants are "respectable" and "of good moral character."[17]

Entering 20 West 44th Street, my anxiety only increased. As I walked up the stairs to the "Saint Nick's" library on the fifth floor, I passed the offices of the Society of Mayflower Descendants in the State of New York and the Society of Colonial Wars—the latter dedicated to "perpetuating among their descendants the memory of the brave and hardy men who assisted in establishing the Colonies of America."[18] Now all my American historian warning bells were really ringing. These organizations smell of the messy legacy of nationalism and ancestor worship that began in the nineteenth-century urban landscape. As impoverished immigrants swelled New York, genealogy became a way to make ties with some and exclude others—particularly the new arrivals. During the early years of these societies, white Protestant nativists had used family research to emphasize their racial purity and to exclude Jews like my own ancestors.[19]

Overheated and fearful, I found my anxiety settle as I relaxed into the smooth wooden chairs of St. Nick's library. It was not just the air conditioning, though that too was a relief. Isaac's descendant was charming and thrilled to hear all of the information about his ancestors. One of his sons worked as a civil rights attorney, and suddenly that seemed more poignant now that they knew about his ancestor's own struggles for equality. I showed Isaac's fourth-great-grandson an enlarged color reproduction of Isaac's portrait, and talked about hunting down (Sarah) Esther Lopez-Gill's line in faraway Barbados. I met his daughter-in-law, who would soon bear Isaac's latest descendant, and we made plans to connect again.

In the years since we first met, I have tracked down other descendants, and some have found me. Their questions begin to weigh in my mind. For example, Isaac's fourth-great-grandson and his other cousins do not understand how their branch had lost touch with the rest of the Moses clan. As one of them put it, "The Brandons' paternal memories and family ties were interred with Abraham."[20]

Family lore suggested that the Moses clan had cast aside Abraham Rodriguez Brandon the younger's family following his conversion. Yet sources from the time reveal a different story. We do not know if Isaac would have felt betrayed by his son's marriage, but we do know it did not disrupt the affection the Moses aunts felt toward Abraham Rodriguez Brandon. When Lavinia Moses Brandon's closest sister Saly Moses died four years after Isaac Lopez Brandon, she left all her money to her unmarried sister Rebecca Moses. But Saly Moses also made clear that after her sister's death it was to pass to their "much beloved" nephew, Abraham Rodriguez Brandon.

The same was true for family mementos. Most of Saly Moses's will details who will get what of the family silver, and the lion's share went to Brandon. He received nine silver table spoons, one silver porringer with cover, spoons marked "ARL" for Aaron and Richea Levy, two silver rings, two silver goblets, one sugar pot, one milk pot, eleven knives, and twelve forks. Brandon's recent marriage to a non-Jew did not deter Moses. In fact, she gave him not just one silver spice box for bringing the Sabbath to a close but two.[21]

The Moses family's love for Abraham also extended to his new family. A little more than a month after Saly Moses's will was read into the record, her beloved nephew Abraham Rodriguez Brandon was dead. He was only thirty-three. All his property, including the family silver, passed to his young Protestant wife Miriam Smith Brandon, who was left to raise their young children. Yet even then, the Moses relatives did not forget their ties. When

Israel Moses wrote his sister-in-law Selina Seixas Moses from the front lines during the Civil War just twenty-two months after Brandon's death, he expressed regret that he had not written to Miriam Brandon yet and begged Selina to "give my best love to her and kiss the little ones for me [and] tell her I should be delighted to hear from her telling of all their welfares."[22] The older generation also held Brandon's new family close. When Rebecca Moses died in 1864, not only did one-third of the bulk of her estate go to "Miriam Brandon widow of A.R. Brandon," but she specifically left her "breast pin with pearl to my darling Edith Brandon [Abraham's daughter as] it has her blessed father's hair in it."[23] Abraham Rodriguez Brandon might have been gone, but he was hardly forgotten.[24]

Questions asked by one set of descendants led me to another possible progeny. While looking closely at the details of Rebecca Moses's will, I noticed she had left money to her nephew Alfred Moses, whom Stern had marked as having died in infancy. Moreover, her executrix had tracked him down in order to deliver the legacy. He was living in Roma, in the "Empire of Mexico," or as it is known today, Texas. Moreover, while the 1900 census listed him as single, at least one family today claims him as the natural ancestor of their lineage.[25]

They may be right. In 1860, Sarah's son Alfred Moses was living in Roma not only with his older brother Joseph Moses but also with a Mexican woman, Paula Barrera, and two young children Isabel (age five) and Sarah (age two). Descendants believe that Alfred Moses was the father of Barrera's daughter Lora (Laura) Barrera, who was born in 1855. Paula Barrera was from Ciudad Mier in Tamaulipas, Mexico—a forty-five-minute drive across the Rio Grande from Roma. Whatever the nature of Alfred Moses's relationship with Barrera, it did not last. Six or seven years after Laura Barrera was born, her mother married a man named Rafael Solis, also from Mier. Ten years later, Alfred Moses was living with another Mexican woman, Bela Tamosa. At one point Laura Barrera's descendants despaired of ever finding confirmation of stories passed down about the man from New York who was Laura Barrera's alleged father, but DNA testing may finally lay their questions to rest. If Barrera turns out to be his daughter, this adds a new level of complexity to the family's racial and ethnic story.[26]

If the DNA proves Barrera was Moses's daughter, her brood will join the very small circle of Sarah's surviving progeny. Although three of Lionel and Selina Moses's seven children married, only their granddaughter Sarah Edith Moses had children of her own. Of her children only one son, Alfred C. Smith, had children, and their lineage survives. This later pruning of what was a large and flourishing branch spawned by Sarah's exhausted hours in childbirth is an important reminder of how common it was for nineteenth-century Americans to remain unmarried, and how disease often cut down whole branches in their prime.

Perhaps the most extensive part of the family, however, comes not from Sarah and Isaac's lines, but that of their half-sister Lavinia Brandon Abecasis and her brother Joseph Rodrigues Brandon. After her husband's death, Lavinia Brandon Abecasis moved back to England, and one of her sons, Abraham Rodrigues Brandon Abecasis, continued the family through his two wives, Edith Grace Levy and Florence De Castro, both of whom he married at congregation Bevis Marks. Their descendants continue to live in England to this day. One branch has even reclaimed the Brandon surname.

Lavinia Brandon Abecasis's brother also remained true to the Judaism in which Sarah Simpson Wood had pledged she would raise them. After moving to San Francisco in 1855, Joseph Rodrigues Brandon became an upstanding member of congregation Shearith Israel, which like its namesake in New York, was Orthodox, though the San Francisco congregation would later become Reform. His education at Solomon's school was apparently successful, as in addition to being a prominent lawyer and agitating for Jewish rights, he kept kosher and the Sabbath and was known for his knowledge of Hebrew texts. He also had seven children, who produced several surviving (and substantial) arms of the Brandon clan, many of whom continue to live on the West Coast today. One of those descendants also married an avid genealogist, without whom much of the Brandon family's information might still be lost.[27]

It is to all of these descendants, as well as to Jews of color in the United States, that I dedicate this book. Just as I was finishing revisions, I learned with great sadness that Isaac's fourth-great-grandson had passed away from cancer. I hope, however, that the next generations of descendants will benefit from this history of their forebears. For Jews of color who have not yet seen their own ancestors' stories written, I hope this book will be the starting point for more research. Sarah and Isaac's wealthy ascent and racial ambiguity set the siblings apart from the experiences of many multiracial Jews today, but some may still recognize the challenges they faced. I have tried to balance their story of wealth and privilege with the experiences of other people they lived among, but as more stories surface, this history will become richer.

Finally, I hope that Sarah and Isaac's story can help those Jews who identify as white understand that the diversity of Jews in their congregations is part of a long tradition. When I first began presenting Sarah and Isaac's history at the New York Public Library and American Jewish Historical Society, Jews of color in the audience spoke out about the pain of still being made to feel unwelcome in white-run synagogues, of having their Jewishness questioned just because of their skin color, of not counting for a minyan. In this book, I have tried not to shy away from occasions when organizations or individuals made Sarah and Isaac feel less than completely Jewish because that prejudice is also part of the story of American Judaism. I hope by recognizing that past we will continue to move forward toward a more equitable and inclusive future.

ACKNOWLEDGMENTS

THIS BOOK HAS BEEN A long, circuitous journey. More than a decade ago, after a sweltering day of photographing gravestones in the Nidhe Israel synagogue yard with my father, I sat down in the air-conditioned building that was once the congregation's school room to interview the illustrious Karl Watson, one of the great experts on Barbadian history and the island's Jews. At the time, I was writing the book that would become *Messianism, Secrecy, and Mysticism*, so when Karl mentioned Isaac Lopez Brandon's struggles in the synagogue's minute books, I put the story aside in my "interesting but not really relevant" category. *Messianism, Secrecy, and Mysticism* focused on the era before the American Revolutionary War, and Isaac's story was too late to really interest me. When the messianism book was done, I began working with Michael Hoberman and Hilit Surowitz Israel on *Jews in the Americas, 1776–1826*, a collection of primary sources. In part, this collection documented Jewish emancipation movements, hence I returned to the Nidhe Israel synagogue minutes. When a first set of photos of the minutes proved worthless, a Reed College Ruby-Lankford grant allowed Reed student Sam May to travel back to London to make new reproductions. Our summer's labor would result in an article in *American Jewish History* on Isaac Lopez Brandon that served as the backbone for chapter 4 in this book. I was hooked.

It would take many more years before *Jews in the Americas* was complete, but in the meantime, Isaac lurked in the background. Film producer Meighan Maloney and I plotted out how Isaac's story might make a good documentary, and while the project didn't pan out, her insights about what made the story interesting influenced my thinking. Meanwhile, as I traveled to archives across four continents looking for items to include in *Jews in the Americas*, I kept searching for signs of Isaac. In the spring of 2013, for example, when I was in the Netherlands on a Fulbright, I took the train south to The Hague to sift through the Surinamese records at the National Archives. Little by little pieces of the puzzle came together.

An early Americanist conference brought me back to London, and five years after talking with Karl, I finally found conclusive proof that Sarah, like Isaac, had been born enslaved. Ruby-Lankford grants continued to fuel my preoccupation, and two more Reed students, Laura Klinker and Jenna Routenberg, helped me dig through archives in New York and Barbados. A Joseph and Eva R. Dave Fellowship at the American Jewish Archives (AJA), a Hadassah Brandeis Institute Award, a Franklin Grant, and a Sid and Ruth Lapidus Fellowship at the American Jewish Historical Society (AJHS) all helped me fill in crucial gaps about multi-racial Jewish life in the cities where Sarah and Isaac landed.

Funding for a sabbatical in 2016–17 plus a chance to participate in the Seminar in Advanced Jewish Studies at the Oxford Centre for Hebrew and Jewish Studies gave me time to write, ongoing access to records in London and Oxford, and a rich group of colleagues interested in the history of Jewish emancipation. I am particularly grateful to Abigail Green and Simon Levis Sullam for organizing the seminar, and to Julia Phillips Cohen, Lisa Leff, David Rechter, Matt Silver, Malachi Hacohen, Julie Kalman, Jonathan Kwan, and the other members of the seminar for their collegiality and feedback. I owe a debt to Exeter College, which hosted me during that term, and Cesar Merchan-Hamann for giving me access to the Weisz Western Sephardi Collection. The essay refined during the term at Oxford helped me think about the role of fabric in Sarah and Isaac's lives. This work first appeared as "The Material of Race: Clothing, Anti-Semitism, and Manhood in the Caribbean during the Era of Emancipation," in *Jews, Liberalism, Anti-Semitism: A Global History*, edited by Abigail Green and Simon Levis Sullam.

Another godsend was my time as the Leon Levy Foundation Professor of Material Culture at Bard Graduate Center (BGC) in the spring of 2018. This gave me not only more time to write, but extended access to records in New York and Philadelphia and time to meet with Nancy Toff, who would become my editor. I am grateful to the Leon Levy Foundation and the David Berg Foundation, which provided funding for my position at BGC, as well as Peter Miller and all the BGC faculty, staff, and students who made my stay so fruitful. The third chapter from the book written while I was at BGC, *The Art of the Jewish Family: A History of Women in Early New York in Five Objects*, focuses on Sarah's portrait, and I am grateful to Bard Graduate Center for allowing a revised version of some of that material to appear in this volume.

No book is written in a vacuum, and I am beholden to the members of my various writing groups including Julia Phillips Cohen, Naomi Caffee, Nicole Reisnour, Mónica López Lerma, Gail Sherman, Sarah Wagner-McCoy, Julia Lieberman, Hilit Surowitz-Israel, Michael Hoberman, Gail Sherman, and Walter Englert, all of whom gave me detailed feedback and encouragement. I am also deeply grateful to those who helped shape the manuscript for publication, most important my incredible editor at Oxford University Press, Nancy Toff, and my agent Amaryah Orenstein. Jeremy Toynbee, Isabelle Prince, Patterson Lamb, and Sarah Payne all helped midwife the manuscript, and I am grateful for their help. Thank you also to Shari Rabin and the anonymous reviewer #2 for their suggestions for how to make this a better book, and to Lewis Gordon, Judith Weisenfeld, and Jonathan Sarna for reading the manuscript and encouraging others to do so as well.

Large sections of this book are about Congregations Shearith Israel and Mikveh Israel, and I am grateful to the friendship and support shown to me by members of both congregations during my residency in New York and over the years, particularly Seth Haberman, Zachary Edinger, Jennifer Ash, Lisa Rohde, Rabbi Shalom Morris, Rabbi Meir Soloveichik, Barbara Reiss, Rabbi Albert E. Gabbai, Lou Kessler, Ida Pomerantz, and Gail Lindo. I am indebted to Seth Haberman and Rabbi Morris, now of Bevis Marks, for originally bringing me to Shearith Israel to speak about Sarah Brandon Moses. Zachary Edinger, thank you so much for providing me access to the congregational archives and for the cemetery visits.

This book begins with Blanche and the collections she gave to the American Jewish Historical Society (AJHS). Without this historical society, this book simply would not exist. I owe a special thank-you to librarian emerita Susan Malbin, to Jennifer Rodewald of the digital media lab at the Center for Jewish History for the incredible close-ups of Sarah Rodrigues Brandon Moses's miniatures, and to Tanya Elder and Melanie Meyers for responding to all my pleas for acquisition information and images. Annie

Polland, Shirly Bahar, Lila Corwin Berman, Riv-Ellen Prell, and Rachel Lithgow all have my deepest appreciation for what they have done and continue to do for the organization and for the mentorship and comradery they have shown me throughout this project.

In addition to the work completed at AJHS, I am grateful to the American Jewish Archives; the Metropolitan Museum of Art; the Victoria and Albert Museum; the American Philosophical Society; the Barbados Department of Archives; the Jewish Museum; the Library of Congress; the London Metropolitan Archives; Congregation Bevis Marks; the National Archives of the Netherlands; the National Museum of American Jewish History; the New York City Municipal Archives; the North Carolina Museum of Art; the New-York Historical Society; New York Public Library; the Winterthur Museum, Garden, and Library; and Yeshiva University. I also owe a special thank-you to the descendants who answered my questions and responded to requests for photos and family memorabilia.

Last but not least, I owe so much to my family, particularly my husband and son, who enthusiastically followed me around the Atlantic world to many of the places where Sarah lived, including Barbados, London, and New York.

FAMILY TREES

People referenced in the book have double lines around their names, and people with known African ancestry appear in shaded boxes.

The family trees in the appendices are intended to help readers understand the relationships between the historical figures mentioned in this book rather than to be an exhaustive account of each family. In some instances, people's birth or death dates are unknown, either because early records were lost or because multiple family members had the same name and it was impossible given the surviving records to distinguish definitively the birth and death dates. Records were missing for a variety of reasons including natural disasters such as hurricanes, but also because of racialized policies that reserved baptism, circumcision, marriage, and even death records for people deemed white or Jewish.

Family trees were created from obituaries in historical newspapers as well as the following sources.

Account Book of Moses Lopez, 1779–1789. Barbadian Wills and Deeds, Barbados Department of Archives and American Jewish Archives. *Barbados Church Records, 1637–1887.* Brian P. T. Blake, "Introduction to the Brandon Family." Congregation Mikveh Israel (Philadelphia, PA) Manuscript Collection no. 552, AJA. Congregation Shearith Israel Records, 1759–1932, AJA. David De Sola Pool, *Portraits Etched in Stone; Early Jewish Settlers, 1682–1831.* Edward S. Daniels, "Extracts from Various Records." Eleazer Samuel Lazarus, *Circumcision Register, 1819–1843.* Findagrave.com. *Goody*

Family Tree. Jewish Atlantic World Database. *London, England, Church of England Marriages and Banns, 1754–1932.* Leon H. Elmaleh and Joseph Bunford Samuel, *The Jewish Cemetery.* Lionel D. Barnett, *Abstracts of the Ketubot or Marriage-Contracts of the Congregation from Earliest Times until 1837.* Malcolm H. Stern, *First American Jewish Families: 600 Genealogies, 1654–1977.* Meyers Family Papers, Ms. Coll. 480, AJA. Miriam Rodrigues-Pereira and Chloe Loewe, *The Burial Register (1733–1918) of the Novo (New) Cemetery of the Spanish & Portuguese Jews' Congregation, London.* Nidhe Israel Synagogue Records, LMA. Papers of the Moses Family of New York, undated, 1767–1941, 1971. Records of Congregation Bevis Marks, LMA. Richard D. Barnett, ed., *The Circumcision Register of Isaac and Abraham de Paiba (1715–1775).* "SchumanGeganBruendermanSchirrmacherRittmeye r's Family Tree."

Brandon Family Tree

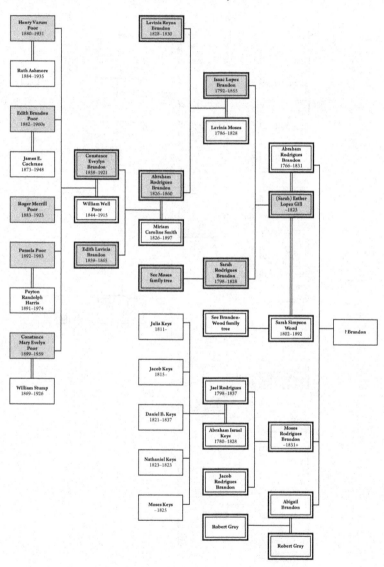

Gill Family Tree

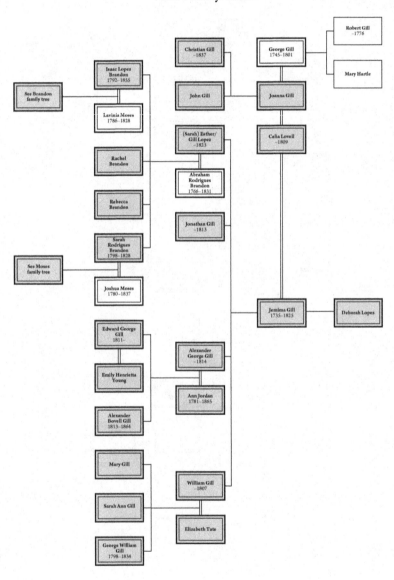

Lopez Family Tree

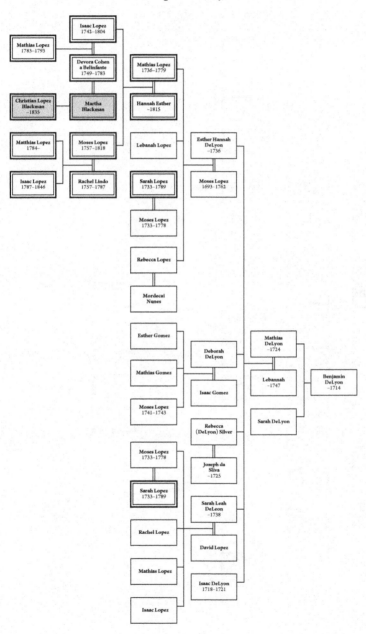

Moses Family Tree

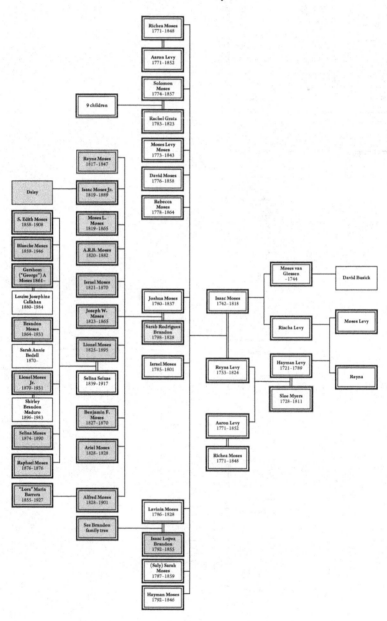

Seixas Family Tree

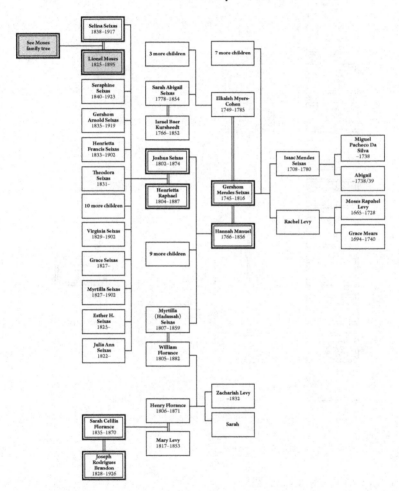

Brandon-Wood Family Tree

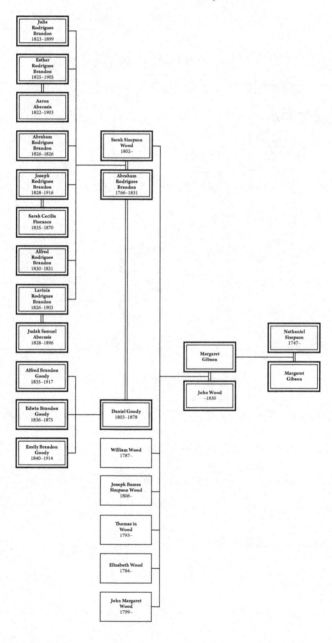

NOTES

Abbreviations

ACLS   American Council of Learned Societies

ACS   American Colonization Society (1816–1964)

AJA   American Jewish Archives

AJHQ   *American Jewish Historical Quarterly*, Coverage: 1961–
                1978 (Vol. 51, No. 1-Vol. 67, No. 4). Johns Hopkins
                University Press.

AJHS   American Jewish Historical Society

A.M.E. Zion   African Methodist Episcopal Zion Church, founded in
                New York, NY, 1821.

ANTT   *Arquivo Nacional da Torre do Tombo* [National Archive of
                Torre do Tombo]

ASC   Archives and Special Collections, Augustus C. Long
                Health Sciences Library of Columbia University

BCR   Barbados Church Records, 1637–1887. (database)

BDA   Barbados Department of Archives

BMHS   Barbados Museum and Historical Society

CMIP   Congregation Mikveh Israel (Philadelphia, PA)
                Manuscript Collection no. 552, American Jewish
                Archives

CSIR	Congregation Shearith Israel Records, 1759–1932, American Jewish Archives
DCNYPL	Digital Collections of New York Public Library
GKS	Inventaris van het digitaal duplicaat van het archief van de Gouvernmentssecretarie der Kolonie Suriname, (1684) 1722–1828, Ingekomen rekesten van ingezetenen van de Joodse natie met daarop genomen beschikkingen, benevens de op de rekesten ingewonnen berichten enz, 1780–1784 Juli, Nationaal Archief (National Archive), Den Haag, Netherlands
JBMHS	*Journal of the Barbados Museum and Historical Society* [1934–present], published by the Barbados Museum and Historical Society
JCBL	John Carter Brown Library, Brown University
JMNY	The Jewish Museum, New York
KKSI	Kahal Kadosh Shearith Israel, New York
LB	Levy Books, St. Michael's Vestry Books 1792–1801, Barbados Department of Archives
LCP	Library Company of Pennsylvania
LMA	London Metropolitan Archives
MBMNI	Minute Books of the Mahamad of Nidhe Israel, 1790–1826, Nidhe Israel Synagogue Records, 4521/D/01/01/002, 4521/D/01/01/003, 4521/D/01/01/004, 4521/D/01/01/008, London Metropolitan Archives
MCNY	Museum of the City of New York
Met	Metropolitan Museum of Art, New York
NA	Nationaal Archief (National Archive), Den Haag, Netherlands.
NARA	National Archives and Records Administration, National Archives Building
NISR	Nidhe Israel Synagogue Records, London Metropolitan Archives
NPIGS	Inventaris van het digitaal duplicaat van het archief van de Nederlandse Portugees-Israëlitische Gemeente in Suriname, 1678–1909, Nationaal Archief (National Archive), Den Haag, Netherlands
NYHS	New-York Historical Society
PAJHS	*Publications of the American Jewish Historical Society*, Coverage: 1893–1961 (No. 1-Vol. 50, No. 4)

PMFNY   Papers of the Moses Family of New York, undated, 1767–1941, 1971, P-1, American Jewish Historical Society
PRO   Public Record Office, United Kingdom
RM   Rijksmuseum, Amsterdam, Netherlands, https://www.rijksmuseum.nl/
RML   Rosenbach Museum and Library, Philadelphia, PA
SGP   Stephen Girard Papers (1789–1829), Ms. Coll. 257, American Jewish Archives
SPJS   Spanish and Portuguese Jews' Synagogue, Bevis Marks, LMA 4521, London Metropolitan Archives
TNA   The National Archives, United Kingdom.

Preface

1. Blanche Moses Correspondence, PMFNY, Box 2, Folder 9.
2. Ibid.
3. Gregory Rodriguez, "Roots of Genealogy Craze," *USAToday*, 12 May 2014.
4. Blanche Moses Correspondence, PMFNY, Box 2, Folder 9.
5. Genealogy researched by Blanche Moses of the Moses, Levy, and Seixas families, 1895–1941. PMFNY, Box 2, Folder 6.
6. Malcolm H. Stern, *First American Jewish Families: 600 Genealogies, 1654–1977* (Cincinnati: American Jewish Archives, 1978), 27.
7. Will of George Gill (1801), RB 4 53.133, BDA; will of Hannah Esther Lopez (1815), RL 1/6, BDA; Sarah Brandon, 28 June 1798, *Barbados Church Records, 1637–1887* (database); *FamilySearch*, https://www.familysearch.org/search/collection/1923399; Joshua Moses, New York Ward 1, New York, Census of the United States, 1820, Ancestry.com; *Soundex Index to Petitions for Naturalizations Filed in Federal, State, and Local Courts in New York City, 1792–1906 (M1674)*, NARA.
8. Aviva Ben-Ur and Jessica Vance Roitman, "Adultery Here and There: Crossing Sexual Boundaries in the Dutch Jewish Atlantic," in *Dutch Atlantic Connections, 1680–1800: Linking Empires, Bridging Borders*, ed. Gert Oostindie and Jessica V. Roitman (Leiden: Brill, 2014), 205; Aviva Ben-Ur, *Jewish Autonomy in a Slave Society: Suriname in the Atlantic World, 1651–1825* (Philadelphia: University of Pennsylvania Press, 2020), 155.

Chapter 1

1. Marriage Register of Joshua Moses and Sarah Rodrigues Brandon (17 March 1817), SPGS, LMA/4521/A/02/03/009.
2. Sarah Brandon, record of baptism, 28 June 1798, BCR.
3. MBMNI, II; LB, 1793, Part 1.
4. Karl Watson, "Shifting Identities: Religion, Race, and Creolization among the Sephardi Jews of Barbados, 1654–1900," in *The Jews in the Caribbean*,

ed. Jane S. Gerber (Portland, OR: Littman Library, 2014), 198; Laura
Arnold Leibman and Sam May, "Making Jews: Race, Gender and Identity
in Barbados in the Age of Emancipation," *American Jewish History* 99, no.
1 (2015): 4; Eli Faber, *Jews, Slaves and the Slave-Trade: Setting the Record
Straight* (New York: New York University Press, 1998), Plate 11, between
pp. 86 and 87; MBMNI, II.27; MBMNI, III.29–30.

5.   Will of Abraham Rodrigues Brandon (1831), RB 4 66/178, BDA. Also
     New York, Wills and Probate Records, 1659–1999, Ancestry.com.

6.   MBMNI, VIII.106.

7.   Ibid.

8.   Sarah Brandon, record of baptism, 28 June 1798, BCR.

9.   Isaac Brandon, arrival on "Steinn Mertin" 1 July 1853, *1853 Arrival,
     New York, New York*; Ancestry.com. "Died," *Evening Post*, 13 December
     1855; Isaac L. Brandon, naturalization 22 Apr 1829, *Index to Petitions for
     Naturalization Filed in New York City, 1792–1989*, Provo: Ancestry.com;
     Jerome Handler, *The Unappropriated People: Freedmen in the Slave Society
     of Barbados* (Baltimore: Johns Hopkins University Press, 1974), 161;
     Nicholas Beasley, "Domestic Rituals: Marriage and Baptism in the British
     Plantation Colonies, 1650–1780," *Anglican and Episcopal History* 76, no. 3
     (2007): 329.

10. Sarah Brandon, record of baptism, 28 June 1798, BCR; Conveyance of
     Sarah, Rebecca, and Isaac Lopez (1800), deed Hannah Esther Lopez
     to Abraham Rodrigues Brandon, 20 August 1800, R/1 Deeds 1801, vol.
     212.459, BDA; Janette Elice Gayle, "Ann Gill: Free Woman of Color at the
     Nexus of Politics and Religion in Nineteenth-Century Barbados" (master's
     thesis, University of California–Los Angeles, 2004), 24.

11. Elizabeth Abbott, *Sugar: A Bittersweet History* (London: Duckworth
     Overlook, 2009), 89–90; Richard Bulliet et al., *The Earth and Its Peoples: A
     Global History* (Boston: Cengage Learning, 2014), 485.

12. Abbott, *Sugar,* 39; Jennifer L. Anderson, *Mahogany* (Cambridge,
     MA: Harvard University Press, 2012), 236–237; Derek St. Romaine,
     Barbados in Bloom (Edgehill, Barbados: Miller Publishing, 2005), 61, 125;
     Hilary Beckles, "City the Limit: The Enslaved Community in Bridgetown
     1800–1834," in *Beyond the Bridge: Lectures Commemorating Bridgetown's
     375th Anniversary*, ed. Woodville K. Marshall and Pedro L. V. Welch (St.
     Michael, Barbados: Barbados Museum, 2005), 113; Melanie Newton,
     *Children of Africa in the Colonies: Free People of Color in Barbados in the Age
     of Emancipation* (Baton Rouge: Louisiana State University Press, 2008), 29.

13. Abbott, *Sugar,* 39.

14. Hilary Beckles, *A History of Barbados: From Amerindian Settlement to
     Caribbean Single Market*, 2nd ed. (Cambridge: Cambridge University
     Press, 2006), 32–33; Jennifer Lewis, email message to author, 19
     February 2018; Marcellina Ulunma Okehie-Offoha, *Ethnic & Cultural
     Diversity in Nigeria* (Trenton, NJ: Africa World Press, 1996), 5–6,
     38, 63, 125; Junius P. Rodriquez, *The Historical Encyclopedia of World*

Slavery (Oxford: ABC-CLIO, 1997), 1: 69; Rene J. Herrera and Ralph Garcia-Bertrand, *Ancestral DNA, Human Origins, and Migrations* (London: Academic Press, 2018), 395.

15. Kenneth Morgan, "The Trans-Atlantic Trade from the Bight of Biafra," in *Igbo in the Atlantic World*, ed. Toyin Falola (Bloomington: Indiana University Press, 2016), 82; Felicity Nussbaum, *The Global Eighteenth Century* (Baltimore, MD: Johns Hopkins University Press, 2003), 61.

16. Abbott, *Sugar*, 84, 88–89.

17. Newton, *Children of Africa in the Colonies*, 33–34.

18. Beckles, *Natural Rebels*, 143–144.

19. Findlay and Holdsworth, *The History of the Wesleyan Methodist Missionary Society*, II, 195; will of Robert Gill (25 Sept. 1776), RB6 44.47, BDA; Keith Stanford, "The Roots of a Great School: Combermere's First 200 Years." *JBMHS* 41 (1993): 18.

20. Handler, *Unappropriated People*, 201; will of George Gill (1801), RB 4 53.133, BDA.

21. Pedro L. V. Welch and Richard A. Goodridge, *"Red" and Black over White: Free Coloured Women in Pre-Emancipation Barbados* (Bridgetown: Carib Research, 2000), 17, 20, 26, 36, 41–48; Hilary Beckles, *Natural Rebels: A Social History of Enslaved Black Women in Barbados* (New Brunswick, NJ: Rutgers University Press, 1989), 126–127; Newton, *Children of Africa*, 48–49; will of George Gill (1801); will of Hannah Esther Lopez (1815), RL 1/6, BDA; Conveyance of Sarah, Rebecca, and Isaac Lopez (1800), deed Hannah Esther Lopez to Abraham Rodrigues Brandon, 20 Aug. 1800; "Jemima's Bill of Sale," deed between Hannah Esther Lopez and George Gill, entered 15 October 1801, written 17 August 1801, Deeds (1801), vol. 218, R/1, BDA.

22. Saidiya Hartman, "Venus in Two Acts," *Small Axe* 12, no. 2 (2008): 1; Mia L. Bagneris, *Colouring the Caribbean: Race and the Art of Agostino Brunias* (Manchester: Manchester University Press, 2018), 114, 136–138, 145.

23. Will of George Gill (1801).

24. Will of Hannah Esther Lopez (1815), RL 1/6, BDA; will of George Gill (1801).

25. Jane S. Gerber, *Jews of Spain: A History of the Sephardic Experience* (New York: Simon and Schuster, 1994), vii; António José Saraiva et al., *The Marrano Factory: The Portuguese Inquisition and Its New Christians, 1536–1765* (Leiden: Brill, 2001), 6; Angel Alcalá, *Judíos, Sefarditas, Conversos: la Expulsión de 1492 y sus Consecuencias* (Spain: Ambito, 1995), 125–133; Elijah Capsali, *Chronique de l'expulsion: Seder Eliahou zouta*, trans. Sultan Sultan-Bohbot (Paris: Editions du Cerf, 1994), 96–98; Ronnie Perelis, *Narratives from the Sephardic Atlantic: Blood and Faith* (Bloomington: Indiana University Press, 2016), 4.

26. François Soyer, *The Persecution of the Jews and Muslims of Portugal: King Manuel I and the End of Religious Tolerance (1496-7)* (Leiden: Brill, 2007), 8, 92–93, 210; Saraiva et al., *The Marrano Factory*, x, 127.

27. Processo de João Rodrigues Brandão (1725-01-25 to 1727-12-05), PT/TT/ TSO-IC/025/08281, ANTT ; Processo de Gaspar Rodrigues Brandão (1724-11-29 to 1727-11-19), PT/TT/TSO-IC/025/09247, ANTT; Processo de Luísa Mendes, PT/TT/TSO-IC/025/00790, ANTT; Lionel D. Barnett, *Abstracts of the Ketubot or Marriage-Contracts of the Congregation from Earliest Times until 1837* (London: Board of Elders of the Congregation, 1949), 97; David Gibbins, "The Portuguese Jewish Ancestry of Rebecca de Daniel Brandon (1783–1820)," http://davidgibbins.com; Arlindo N. M. Correia, "Os 'judeus' de Tondela," http://arlindo-correia.com/161207.html ; Almeida: *História da Igreja em Portugal*, Vol. IV (Coimbra: De Almeida, 1923), Appendix IX; Richard D. Barnett, *The Circumcision Register of Isaac and Abraham de Paiba (1715–1775)* (London: Jewish Historical Society of England, 1991), 48, 99; will of Joshua Rodrigues or Joshua Rodriguez Brandao, Merchant of Mile End, Essex (1784), PROB 11/1124/317, TNA; will of Abraham Rodrigues Brandao, Merchant of Bevis Marks, City of London (1769), PROB 11/950/396, TNA.
28. Studemund-Halévy, *Biographisches Lexikon Der Hamburger Sefarden* (Hamburg: Christians, 2000); Amsterdam—Burials of the Portuguese Israelite Congregation (Database), https://web.archive.org/web/20080706133856/http://akevoth.org/beithhaim/login.asp; E. M. Shilstone, *Monumental Inscriptions in the Jewish Synagogue at Bridgetown, Barbados: with Historical Notes from 1630* (Roberts Stationery, Barbados: Macmillan, 1988), 1, 28, 39, 50, 51; will of Lebaneh Delyon, Barbados (1747), De Lyon Family Wills, AJA, SC-2775; will of Abraham Brandon, Barbados (1756), Brandon Family Wills, AJA, SC-1337; will of Moses Brandon, Barbados (1718), Brandon Family Wills, AJA, SC-1337; will of Jacob Brandon, Jamaica (1710), Brandon Family Wills, AJA, SC-1337.
29. Stuart B. Schwartz, ed., *Tropical Babylons: Sugar and the Making of the Atlantic World, 1450–1680* (Chapel Hill: University of North Carolina Press, 2011), 262. Cândido Pinheiro de Lima, *Branca Dias* (Fortaleza: Fundação Ana Lima, 2009); Malyn Newitt, *A History of Portuguese Overseas Expansion 1400–1668* (New York: Routledge, 2004), 168; Dean Phillip Bell, *Jews in the Early Modern World* (Lanham, MD: Rowman & Littlefield, 2008), 65; Pedro Welch, "Jews in a Caribbean Colonial Society: Resistance and Accommodation in Bridgetown, Barbados, 1675–1834," *JBMHS* 44 (1998): 54–55; Y. Schreuder, "A True Global Community: Sephardic Jews, the Sugar Trade, and Barbados in the Seventeenth Century," *JBMHS* 50 (2004): 166–94.
30. Faber, *Jews, Slaves, and the Slave Trade,* 47; Account Book of Moses Lopez, 1779–1789, NYHS Library, Mss. Collection; Karl Watson, "The Sephardic Jews of Bridgetown," in *Beyond the Bridge: Lectures Commemorating Bridgetown's 375th Anniversary*, ed. Woodville K. Marshall and Pedro L. V. Welch (St. Michael, Barbados: Barbados Museum, 2005), 40, 46.

31. Maria J. Fuentes, *Dispossessed Lives: Enslaved Women, Violence, and the Archive* (Philadelphia: University of Pennsylvania Press, 2016), 19, 23–24.

32. Pedro Welch, "Celebrating Bridgetown: The First 100 Years," in *Beyond the Bridge: Lectures Commemorating Bridgetown's 375th Anniversary*, ed. Woodville Marshall and Pedro Welch (Bridgetown, Barbados: BMHS, 2005), 6.

33. Mordehay Arbell, *The Jewish Nation of the Caribbean: The Spanish-Portuguese Jewish Settlements in the Caribbean and the Guianas* (New York: Gefen, 2002), 199; N. Darnell Davis, "Notes on the History of the Jews in Barbados," *PAJHS* 18 (1909): 144.

34. Barry L. Stiefel, *Jewish Sanctuary in the Atlantic World: A Social and Architectural History* (Columbia: University of South Carolina Press, 2014), 44, 211, 223–224; Karl Watson, "1806 Plat of the Nidhe Israel Synagogue in Bridgetown," *JBMHS* 61 (2015): 82–85; Laura Arnold Leibman, *Messianism, Secrecy, and Mysticism: A New Interpretation of Early American Jewish Life* (London: Vallentine Mitchell, 2012), 43–45, 63–69, 199.

35. Malcom H. Stern, "Portuguese Sephardim in the Americas," in *Sephardim in the Americas: Studies in Culture and History*, ed. Martin A. Cohen and Abraham J. Peck (Tuscaloosa: University of Alabama Press, 2003), 114, 144; "At a Meeting on the MM^d and Adjunto on Sunday 10th Kisleb 5553 Corresponding 25th November 1792," MBMNI, II.

36. Will of Raphael Hayyim Isaac Carigal (1777), RB6 25, BDA.

37. R. J. Morris, *Men, Women and Property in England: A Social and Economic History of Family Strategies amongst the Leeds Middle Class* (Cambridge: Cambridge University Press, 2005), 377; Account Book of Moses Lopez, 1779–1789, NYHS Library, Mss. collection; will of Isaac Lopez (1804), RB6 54.122, BDA; Watson, "The Sephardic Jews of Bridgetown," 51—52; At an Election of the Parnassim [29 September 1791], MBMNI, II; "At a Meeting of the Mahamad and Adjunto on Monday 17th Nissan 5552 Corresponding to 9th April 1792," MBMNI, II; will of Raphael Hayyim Isaac Carigal (1777); Israel Joel, Abraham Isaacs, and Jonas N. Phillips, "Items Relating to Congregation Shearith Israel, New York," *PAJHS* 27 (1920): 54–55.

38. Will of Hannah Esther Lopez (1815); will of Abraham Rodrigues Brandon (1831); Conveyance of Sarah, Rebecca, and Isaac Lopez (1800); "Jemima's Bill of Sale"; Manumission of Sarah and Isaac Lopez (1801/2), deed Hannah Esther Lopez to Abraham Rodrigues Brandon, 5 Aug. 1802, R/ 1 Deeds 1801, vol. 219.9, BDA; Shilstone, *Monumental Inscriptions*, 124, 163, 170.

39. LB, 1793, Part 1; Suzanne Bost, *Mulattas and Mestizas: Representing Mixed Identities in the Americas, 1850–2000* (Athens: University of Georgia Press, 2010), 97; Karl Watson, *Civilised Island, Barbados: A Social History, 1750–1816* (Ellerton, Barbados: Caribbean Graphic Production, 1979), 31; "MBMNI, II.5; A. F. Wedd, ed. *Fate of the Fenwicks* (London: Methuen, 1927), 163.

40.   Account Book of Moses Lopez; E. Jennifer Monaghan, *Learning to Read and Write in Colonial America* (Amherst: University of Massachusetts Press, 2007), 231, 434.

41.   Welch and Goodridge, *"Red" & Black over White*, 76; will of Isaac Lopez (1804); LB, 1793, Part 1.

42.   Faber, *Jews, Slaves, and the Slave Trade*, 81–102; Stanley Mirvis, "Sephardic Family Life in the Eighteenth-Century British West Indies" (PhD diss., New York University, 2013); Newton, *The Children of Africa*, 40, 44; Fuentes, *Dispossessed Lives*, 73; Pedro Welch, *Slave Society in the City: Bridgetown, Barbados, 1680–1834* (Kingston, Jamaica: I. Randle, 2003), 94–96.

43.   Edith Bruder, *The Black Jews of Africa: History, Religion, Identity* (Oxford: Oxford University Press, 2008), 100–101.

44.   Nicholas Beasley, "Domestic Rituals: Marriage and Baptism in the British Plantation Colonies, 1650–1780," *Anglican and Episcopal History* 76, no. 3 (2007): 329, 337.

Chapter 2

1.   Will of George Gill (1801), RB 4 53.133, BDA.

2.   Will of Isaac Lopez (1804), RB 6 54.122, BDA.

3.   Ibid.

4.   Will of George Gill (1801); Will of Emmanuel Baruch Lousada (1795), Louzada Family Wills, 1695–1797, AJA; Stanley Mirvis, "Sephardic Family Life in the Eighteenth-Century British West Indies" (PhD diss., New York University, 2013), 102–103.

5.   Will of George Gill (1801).

6.   6 Jan. 1796, Wills & Deeds (1796), BDA, RL1/6: 39; Joanne McRee Sanders, *Barbados Records: Baptisms, 1637–1800* (Baltimore: Genealogical Publishing, 1984), 230

7.   Burial of George Gill, 19 Nov. 1801, Parish of St. Michael, BCR, 1637–1887; Will of George Gill (1801).

8.   Will of George Gill (1801).

9.   Ibid.

10.   Ibid.

11.   Melanie Newton, *The Children of Africa in the Colonies: Free People of Color in Barbados in the Age of Emancipation* (Baton Rouge: Louisiana State University Press, 2008), 49; Jerome Handler, *The Unappropriated People: Freedmen in the Slave Society of Barbados* (Baltimore: Johns Hopkins University Press, 1974), 147, 151.

12.   Newton, *Children of Africa*, 66.

13.   Ibid.

14.   Will of George Gill (1801); Hilary Beckles, *Natural Rebels: A Social History of Enslaved Black Women in Barbados* (Brunswick, NJ: Rutgers University Press, 1989), 33, 145. "Jemima's Bill of Sale;," Deed between Hannah Esther

Lopez and George Gill. Entered 15 Oct. 1801, written 17 August 1801, *Deeds* (1801), vol. 218, BDA, R/1; Will of Isaac Lopez (1804).

15. Baptism of Jemima Gill, 20 Oct. 1805, Parish of St. Michael, BCR 1637–1887.

16. Will of George Gill (1801). Burial of Jemima Gill, 21 Sept. 1825, Parish of St. Michael, BCR, 1637–1887.

17. Will of George Gill (1801).

18. Henry Fraser, *Historic Houses of Barbados* (Bridgetown: Barbados National Trust, 1986), 13; Louis P. Nelson, "The Architectures of Black Identity: Buildings, Slavery, and Freedom in the Caribbean and the American South," *Winterthur Portfolio* 45, no. 2/3 (2011): 183, 188.

19. Pedro L. V Welch and Richard A. Goodridge, *"Red" and Black over White: Free Coloured Women in Pre-Emancipation Barbados* (Bridgetown: Carib Research, 2000), 51, 73, 74, 76.

20. Will of George Gill (1801).

21. *Fate of the Fenwicks*, edited by A. F. Wedd (London: Methuen & Co., 1927), 168, 172.

22. Henry Fraser, "Historic Bridgetown: Development and Architecture," in *Beyond the Bridge: Lectures Commemorating Bridgetown's 375th Anniversary*, ed. Woodville K. Marshall and Pedro L. V. Welch (St. Michael: Barbados Museum, 2005), 86.

23. *Acts: Barbados, No. 225*. CO 30/17, fos. 48–50, TNA.

24. Conveyance of Sarah, Rebecca, and Isaac Lopez (1800), deed of Hannah Esther Lopez to Abraham Rodrigues Brandon, 20 Aug 1800, R/1 Deeds 1801, vol. 212.459, BDA.

25. Manumission of Sarah and Isaac Lopez (1801/2), deed of Hannah Esther Lopez to Abraham Rodrigues Brandon, 5 Aug 1802, R/1 Deeds 1801, vol. 219.9, BDA.

26. Ibid.

Chapter 3

1. Cohen d'Azevedo Receipt Book 1811–1816, 3–8, AJHS; MBMNI II.4, 9–10, III46; Elizabeth A. Austin's Inventory Filed 5th June 1818, BDA; Appraisement of the Estate of Katherine Bab Barrow Deceas'd Reced & filed 11 July 1809, BDA; Susannah Ostrehan's Inventory Recd & filed 30 Nov. 1809, BDA.;

2. Conversion and Circumcision of Isaac Lopez Brandon, 24 December 1812, trans. Aviva Ben-Ur, NA 1.05.11.18: 5, 56, NPIGS.

3. Laura Arnold Leibman, *Messianism, Secrecy and Mysticism: A New Interpretation of Early American Jewish Life* (London: Vallentine Mitchell, 2012), 32–33, 45.

4. Salomon Levy Maduro, *Sefer Brit Itschak* (Amsterdam: n.p., 1767/68), appendix, Jewish Atlantic World Database, Reed College Digital Collections, 2013, https://rdc.reed.edu/c/jewishatl/.

5. Wieke Vink, *Creole Jews Negotiating Community in Colonial Suriname* (Leiden: Brill, 2010), 141; Maduro, *Sefer Brit Yitzhak*, 16–17, appendix.
6. Vink, *Creole Jews*, 178; Temminck Groll, *De Architektuur van Suriname 1667–1930* (Zutphen: De Walburg Pers, 1973), 357–363.
7. Groll, *De Architektuur van Suriname*, 357–363.
8. Susan Vincent, *The Anatomy of Fashion: Dressing the Body from the Renaissance to Today* (New York: Bloomsbury Academic, 2010), 24–25. See also the miniature of Jacob Judah Lyons (Loeb Jewish Portrait Database [2018] http://loebjewishportraits.com/.), the silhouette of Mozes Meijer de Hart (Rijksmuseum, https://www.rijksmuseum.nl/ RP-F-2012-58), and Portraits of Surinamese Girls, ca. 105c. 1805–1810 (Rijksmuseum, https://www.rijksmuseum.nl/ SK-A-2641, SK-A-2635); J. P. Benoit, *Voyage a Surinam: description des possessions Néerlandaises dans la Guyane* (Amsterdam: Emmering, 1967).
9. Jonathan Schorsch, *Swimming the Christian Atlantic: Judeoconversos, Afroiberians and Amerindians in the Seventeenth Century* (Leiden: Brill, 2009), 467–468.
10. Yosef Kaplan, *An Alternative Path to Modernity: The Sephardi Diaspora in Western Europe* (Leiden: Brill, 2000), 64–65; Todd M. Endelman, *The Jews of Britain, 1656 to 2000* (Berkeley: University of California Press, 2002), 41–42.
11. Vink, *Creole Jews*, 245–247.
12. Jacob Barrow to the London Mahamad, April 31, 1797, MBMNI, II.33–34.
13. *Surinaamsche Courant*, 16 Feb. 1811; Robert Cohen, *Jews in Another Environment: Surinam in the Second Half of the Eighteenth Century* (Leiden: E. J. Brill, 1991), 99.
14. David Cohen Nassy, *Historical Essay on the Colony of Surinam, 1788* (Cincinnati: American Jewish Archives, 1974), 213–218; Michael Hoberman, Laura Arnold Leibman, and Hilit Surowitz-Israel, *Jews in the Americas, 1776–1826* (London: Taylor and Francis, 2017), 355–369.
15. R. N. Ferro, *Suasso's kookrecepten een Portugees-joods kookboek uit de 18e eeuw* (Amsterdam: Amphora, 2006), 18–19; Jacob Van der Wijk, Justus van de Kamp, and Jan van Wijk, *Koosjer Nederlands: Joodse woorden in de Nederlandse taal* (Amsterdam: Contact, 2006).
16. Population [census] returns number 201–490 collected as required by the governor's proclamation of 17 October 1811, CO 278/23: 389, TNA; Vink, *Creole Jews*, 229; a list of 1,351 "free black and coloured" heads of families with the total number of their families and of their slaves, together with the first batch of population [census] returns number 1–200 collected as required by the governor's proclamation of 17 October 1811, CO 278/ 22, TNA.
17. Advertisement, *Surinamese Courant*, 19 Jan. 1811; Groll, *De Architektuur van Suriname*, 362–363; Population [census] returns number 491–690 collected

as required by the governor's proclamation of 17 October 1811, CO 278/ 24: 576, TNA; Vink, *Creole Jews*, 41.

18. Population [census] returns number 491–690, CO 278/24: 576, TNA.

19. Denie, "Adjuba van Jona van Ketie van Princes van Dinisie," *Surinaamse Genealogie, Familiegeschiedenis en Stambomen* (blog), July 2, 2013, https:// deniekasan.wordpress.com/2013/07/03/adjuba-van-jona-van-ketie-van-princes-van-dinisie/; a list of 1,351 "free black and coloured" heads of families, CO 278/22: 140, TNA.

20. Population [census] returns number 491–690, CO 278/24: 576, TNA. Laura Arnold Leibman, *Art of the Jewish Family A History of Women in Early New York in Five Objects* (New York: Bard Graduate Center, 2020), 40–41; John Sang-Ajang, *Overlijdensadvertenties en onbeheerde boedels: overledenen in Suriname, 1 januari 1800 tot en met 31 december 1828* (Paramaribo: Stichting voor Surinaamse Genealogie, 2010), 63.

21. Sang-Ajang, *Overlijdensadvertenties en onbeheerde boedels*, 62.

22. Ibid.

23. Aviva Ben-Ur and Jessica Roitman, "Adultery Here and There: Crossing Sexual Boundaries in the Dutch Jewish Atlantic." In *Dutch Atlantic Connections, 1680–1800: Linking Empires, Bridging Borders*, ed. Gert Oostindie and Jessica V. Roitman (Leiden: Brill, 2014), 205; Aviva Ben-Ur, *Jewish Autonomy in a Slave Society: Suriname in the Atlantic World, 1651–1825* (Philadelphia: University of Pennsylvania Press, 2020), 155.

24. Rosemarijn Hoefte and Jean Jacques Vrij, "Free Black and Colored Women in Early-Nineteenth-Century Paramaribo, Suriname," in *Beyond Bondage: Free Women of Color in the Americas*, ed. David Barry Gaspar and Darlene Clark Hine (Urbana: University of Illinois Press, 2004), 157; Population [census] returns number 601–800 collected as required by the governor's proclamation of 17 October 1811, CO 278/20: 605, TNA.

25. Aviva Ben-Ur and Rachel Frankel, *Remnant Stones: The Jewish Cemeteries of Suriname: Epitaphs* (Cincinnati: Hebrew Union College, 2009), 513, 515.

26. Ibid..

27. Hoefte and Vrij, "Free Black and Colored Women in Early-Nineteenth-Century Paramaribo," 156; Vink, *Creole Jews*, 284–286; Population [census] returns number 491–690, CO 278/24: 576, TNA.

28. Vink, *Creole Jews*, 284–285, t; Aviva Ben-Ur, "Peripheral Inclusion: Communal Belonging in Suriname's Sephardic Community," in *Religion, Gender, and Culture in the Pre-modern World*, ed. Alexandra Cuffel and Brian M. Britt (New York: Palgrave Macmillan, 2007), 191.

29. Vink, *Creole Jews*, 202; Ben-Ur, *Jewish Autonomy in a Slave Society*, 127.

30. Vink, *Creole Jews*, 209–211, 275–277.

31. "Response of the Portuguese Regents to the Memorandum of the Coloured Jews," translation by Vink, NA 1.05.10.01:528, 512, GKS; Vink, *Creole Jews*, 210.

32. Vink, *Creole Jews*, 210.

33. "Memorandum of the Coloured Jews to Governor De Frederici" (1793), NA 1.05.10.01:528, 413–414, GKS.
34. Vink, *Creole Jews*, 212.
35. Hoefte and Vrij, "Free Black and Colored Women in Suriname," 155; a list of 1,351 "free black and coloured" heads of families, CO 278/22: 67, TNA .
36. "Memorandum of the Coloured Jews to Governor De Frederici" (1793), NA 1.05.10.01:528, 396–414, GKS; Vink, *Creole Jews*, 282.
37. Vink, *Creole Jews*, 279–280.
38. Vink, *Creole Jews*, 60–61, 280–281; Ben-Ur, *Jewish Autonomy in a Slave Society*, 181.
39. A list of 1,351 "free black and coloured" heads of families, CO 278/22, TNA; Ben-Ur and Frankel, *Remnant Stones*, 312.
40. John Gabriel Stedman, *Narrative of a Five Years' Expedition Against the Revolted Negroes of Surinam, in Guiana, on the Wild Coast of South America* (London: J. Johnson, 1806), 285; Nassy, *Historical Essay on the Colony of Surinam*, 132.
41. Runaway Advertisement, *Surinaamsche Courante*, 1811.
42. Ibid.
43. T. R. van Andel, A. van der Velden, and M. Reijers, "The 'Botanical Gardens of the Dispossessed' Revisited: Richness and Significance of Old World Crops Grown by Suriname Maroons," *Genetic Resources and Crop Evolution* 63 (2016): 697, https://doi.org/10.1007/s10722-015-0277-8; Stedman, *Narrative of a Five Years' Expedition*, 122–123.
44. A list of 1,351 "free black and coloured" heads of families, CO 278/22, TNA.

Chapter 4

1. MBMNI, III.40–43.
2. Katherine Paugh, *The Politics of Reproduction: Race, Medicine, and Fertility in the Age of Abolition* (Oxford: Oxford University Press, 2017), 15, 107–108.
3. Ibid., 12–13, 108, 118.
4. Jacob Barrow to the London Mahamad, April 31, 1797, MBMNI, II.33–34.
5. Ibid.
6. Edwin Wolf and Maxwell Whiteman, *The History of the Jews of Philadelphia: From Colonial Times to the Age of Jackson* (Philadelphia: Jewish Publication Society of America, 1975), 249, 454.
7. MBMNI, III: .40; Lionel D. Barnett, *Abstracts of the Ketubot or Marriage-Contracts of the Congregation from Earliest Times until 1837* (London: Board of Elders of the Congregation, 1949), 2, 117.
8. MBMNI, III:. 40–42.
9. : Ibid., III.30, 37, 46; Samuel, "Marriages," 166.
10. MBMNI, III: .30; Shilstone, *Monumental Inscriptions*, 175; David De Sola Pool, *Portraits Etched in Stone; Early Jewish Settlers, 1682–1831* (New York: Columbia University Press, 1953), 333.
11. De Sola Pool, *Portraits Etched in Stone*, 333.

12. Moshe Meiselman, *Jewish Woman in Jewish Law* (New York: Ktav Publishing House, 1978), 75.

13. MBMNI, II 42—possibly Joseph and Rebecca, two "colored" people owned by Sarah Massiah who would later be baptized at St. Michael's Cathedral; Faber, *Jews, Slaves, and the Slave Trade*, 227; 14 Jan. 1824, Barbados Church Records, 303.

14. MBMNI, III: 42.

15. Ibid., III: 43.

16. Ibid. It is unclear how Judah (?–1816) and Sarah Massiah were related. Shilstone, *Monumental Inscriptions*, 175.

17. MBMNI, III:.43.

18. MBMNI, III:.40–41.

19. Edgar Samuel, "Marriages at the Nidhe Yisrael Synagogue, Bridgetown, Barbados." *JHS* 45 (2013): 168; MBMNI, II.44, 80, 136, 147–150, VIII.2, 32, 44, 68, 70, 85, 102–104, 128, 132, 139–140.

20. Will of George Gill (1801), Baptism, Marriages, Burials 1794–1815, St. Michael's Parish, Barbados, BCR, 366, 462; Will of William Gill (1807), RB6 57.18, BDA.

21. Janette Elice Gayle, "Ann Gill: Free Woman of Color at the Nexus of Politics and Religion in Nineteenth-Century Barbados" (master's thesis, University of California–Los Angeles, 2004), 23.

22. Rev. Hurd's eulogy, in Gayle, "Ann Gill," 30.

23. Gayle, "Ann Gill," 30. John Augustine Waller, *A Voyage in the West Indies: containing various observations made during a residence in Barbadoes, and several of the Leeward Islands: with some notices and illustrations relative to the city of Paramaribo, in Surinam* (London: Richard Phillips and Co., 1820), 139.

24. James A. Thome and J. Horace Kimball, *Emancipation in the West Indies; a six months' tour in Antigua, Barbadoes, and Jamaica, in 1837* (New York: American Anti-Slavery Society, 1838), 73–75; Catherine E. Kelly, *Republic of Taste: Art, Politics, and Everyday Life in Early America* (Philadelphia: University of Pennsylvania Press), 1, 4–5.

25. Louis P. Nelson, *The Beauty of Holiness: Anglicanism and Architecture in Colonial South Carolina* (Chapel Hill: University of North Carolina Press, 2009), 347.

26. Waller, *Voyage in the West Indies*, 6; G. A. Bremner, *Architecture and Urbanism in the British Empire* (New York: Oxford University Press, 2016), 23–24.

27. Noel Titus, *The Development of Methodism in Barbados, 1823–1883* (New York: Peter Lang, 1994), 85.

28. Marriage of Ann Jordan and Alexander George Gill, 20 May 1809, St, Michael's Parish, BCR; Nicholas Beasley, "Domestic Rituals: Marriage and Baptism in the British Plantation Colonies, 1650–1780," *Anglican and Episcopal History* 76, no. 3 (2007): 329, 337.

29. Gayle, "Ann Gill," 27–28.

30. Ibid.
31. Hilary Beckles, "Creolisation in Action: The Slave Labour Élite and Anti-Slavery in Barbados," *Caribbean Quarterly* 44, no. 1/2 (1998): 123, 125.
32. Beckles, "Creolisation in Action," 123–124; Glenford D. Howe and Don D. Marshall, *The Empowering Impulse: The Nationalist Tradition of Barbados* (Barbados: Canoe Press, 2001), 3, 6; Measuring Worth—Relative Worth Comparators and Data Sets, 2017, https://measuringworth.com/.
33. Melanie Newton, *The Children of Africa in the Colonies: Free People of Color in Barbados in the Age of Emancipation* (Baton Rouge: Louisiana State University Press, 2008), 72–73.
34. "Petition to the House of Assembly," 19 Feb. 1811, in Minutes of the House of Assembly, 19 February 1811, BDA; "Loyal Address," 21 October 1823, in the Minutes of the Barbados Council, 21 October 1823, BDA, .
35. Newton, *Children of Africa*, 105; Sehon S. Goodridge and Anthony de V. Phillips, *Facing the Challenge of Emancipation: A Study of the Ministry of William Hart Coleridge, First Bishop of Barbados, 1824–1842* (St. Michael: BMHS, 2014), 17.
36. Newton, *Children of Africa*, 49; Paugh, *Politics of Reproduction*, 216–217.
37. Newton, *Children of Africa*, 49–51; Will of Hannah Esther Lopez (1815), BDA.
38. E.M. Shilstone, *Monumental Inscriptions in the Jewish Synagogue at Bridgetown, Barbados: with Historical Notes from 1630* (Roberts Stationery, Barbados: Macmillan, 1988), 163, 169–170; Account Book of Moses Lopez; Israel Joel, Abraham Isaacs and Jonas N. Phillips, "Items Relating to Congregation Shearith Israel," *PAJHS* 27 (1920): 55.
39. Will of Hannah Esther Lopez (1815).
40. Ibid. See wills of Barbados families at AJA, such as Will of Judith Pixotto (1791) 19/377, BDA, copy at AJA, SC-9780.
41. Welch and Goodridge, *"Red" and Black over White*, 48–49, 77.
42. MBMNI, VIII: .34.
43. Will of Rachel Lindo (1847), RB 4 72.428, BDA.
44. Rachel Lindo Lopez (1757–1787); Shilstone, *Monumental Inscriptions*; Account Book of Moses Lopez, 1779–1789; Michael Hoberman, Laura Arnold Leibman, andHilit Surowitz-Israel, *Jews in the Americas, 1776–1826* (London: Taylor and Francis, 2017), 115–116, 235, 237, 242, 334–350; Laura Arnold Leibman and Sam May, "Making Jews: Race, Gender and Identity in Barbados in the Age of Emancipation" *American Jewish History* 99, no. 1 (2015): 1–26.

Chapter 5

1. Account Book of Moses Lopez, NYHS Library, Mss. Collection; Leon H. Elmaleh and Joseph Bunford Samuel, *The Jewish Cemetery, Ninth and Spruce Streets, Philadelphia* (Philadelphia: Congregation Mikveh Israel, 1962), 21; John Adams Paxton, William Kneass, and J. H. Young,

The Philadelphia Directory and Register, for 1818: Containing the Names, Professions, and Residence, of All the Heads of Families and Persons in Business of the City and Suburbs, Hamiltonville, and Camden, N.J.: With Other Useful Information. Early American Imprints, Second Series; No. 45218 (Philadelphia: Kneass, Young & Co., 1818), 6, 11, 219; Moses Lopez Probate Records (1818), *Register of Wills*, Philadelphia, Pennsylvania.

2. Moses Lopez Probate Records (1818).

3. *The Philadelphia Directory and Register, for 1818: Containing the Names, Professions, and Residence, of All the Heads of Families and Persons in Business of the City and Suburbs, Hamiltonville, and Camden, N.J.: With Other Useful Information* Early American Imprints. Second Series; No. 45218 (Philadelphia: Kneass, Young & Co., 1818), 6, 11, 219.

4. Moses Lopez Probate Records (1818), 142.

5. Moses Lopez Jr., Prayer Book (1775), LCP in HSP28, Historical Society of Pennsylvania; Will of Raphael Haim Isaac Carrigal (1777), BDA.

6. Moses Lopez, Prayer Book (1775).

7. June 22, 1781, Account Book of Moses Lopez, 1779–1789, NYHS.

8. Will of Isaac Lindo (10 Nov. 1780), RB 6/23.346, BDA; Edgar Samuel, "Marriages at the Nidhe Yisrael Synagogue, Bridgetown, Barbados," *JHS* 45 (2013): 163; Account Book of Moses Lopez.

9. E.M. Shilstone, *Monumental Inscriptions in the Jewish Synagogue at Bridgetown, Barbados: with Historical Notes from 1630* (Roberts Stationery, Barbados: Macmillan, 1988), 170; Miriam Rodrigues-Pereira and Chloe Loewe, *The Burial Register (1733–1918) of the Novo (New) Cemetery of the Spanish & Portuguese Jews' Congregation, London: with some later entries* [SPJS, Part V] (London: Spanish and Portuguese Jews' Congregation, 1997), 99, MBMNI, I.7.

10. MBMNI, II: .3.

11. Ibid, II: .5.

12. Ibid, II: 3, 5.

13. MBMNI, II.7, 19; David Geggus, "Yellow Fever in the 1790s: The British Army in Occupied Saint Domingue," *Medical History* 23, no. 1 (1979): 39.

14. Shilstone, *Monumental Inscriptions*, 101, 142; Jewish Atlantic World Database, Reed College Digital Collections, 2013, https://rdc.reed.edu/c/jewishatl/; MBMNI III.40–41, 86, IV.136, 146.

15. MBMNI II: .34.

16. Ibid.

17. Title page of Moses Lopez, *B'rakhot ha-Mila: u-minhag ye-seder ha-milah ke-fi ha-nahug be-zot ha-kehilah be-i Barbados* (1794), Jewish Theological Seminary, MS 8267.

18. Israel Joel, Abraham Isaacs and Jonas N. Phillips, "Items Relating to Congregation Shearith Israel," *PAJHS* 27 (1920): 51–53.

19. Gerry Black, *JFS: A History of the Jews' Free School, London, since 1732* (London: Tymsder, 1998), 28; Tirtsah Levie Bernfeld, *Poverty and Welfare*

among the Portuguese Jews in Early Modern Amsterdam (Liverpool, UK: Littman Library of Jewish Civilization, 2012), 85, 92, 102. For information on Ashkenazi poor-relief schools in Amsterdam, see Karina Sonnenberg-Stern, *Emancipation and Poverty: The Ashkenazi Jews of Amsterdam, 1796–1850* (Oxford: Saint Antony's College, 2000), 131.

20. Joel, Isaacs, and Phillips, "Items Relating to Congregation Shearith Israel," 51.

21. Ibid., 51–53.

22. Ibid.; Letter from Mr. Jacob Barrow to the London Mahamad April 31, 1797, MBMNI II.33–34; Moshe D. Sherman, *Orthodox Judaism in America: A Biographical Dictionary and Sourcebook* (Westport, CT: Greenwood Press, 1996), 195.

23. Joel, Isaacs, and Phillips, "Items Relating to Congregation Shearith Israel," 54–55, 89.

24. ACLS, *American National Biography* (Oxford: Oxford University Press, 1999), 396; David De Sola Pool, *Portraits Etched in Stone; Early Jewish Settlers, 1682–1831* (New York: Columbia University Press, 1953), 384; Edwin Wolf and Maxwell Whiteman, *The History of the Jews of Philadelphia: From Colonial Times to the Age of Jackson* (Philadelphia: Jewish Publication Society of America, 1975), 99; Robert P. Swierenga, *The Forerunners: Dutch Jewry in the North American Diaspora* (Detroit: Wayne State University Press, 1994), 50; "Banking in Philadelphia," *Moody's Magazine* 17 (1914): 63.

25. Malcolm H. Stern, *First American Jewish Families: 600 Genealogies, 1654–1977* (Cincinnati: American Jewish Archives, 1978), 159, 209.

26. Stephen Girard Papers (1789–1829), AJA, Ms. Coll. 257 (SGP); Solomon Moses, "Journal of Voyage to Madras and Calcutta," PMFNY, Box 1, Folder 5; Jonathan Goldstein, *The Jews of China* (Armonk, NY: M. E. Sharpe, 1999), I: xii.

27. Paxton, Kneass, and Young, *The Philadelphia Directory*, 43, 259; Edward Whitely, *The Philadelphia Directory and Register, for 1822* (Philadelphia: M'Carty & Davis, 1822), 320.

28. Correspondence 1813/14/15 of CMIP, 94/226, 94/227, Box 1; Minute Books 1816/17/18, of CMIP, 93/334, 93/336, Box 6 .

29. Correspondence 1813/14/15 of CMIP, 94/219, 94/218, 94/224, 94/226, 94/227, Box 1; Minute Books 1816/17/18, of CMIP, 93/308, 93/336, 93/347–48, Box 6.

30. Stern, *First American Jewish Families*, 140, 185, 243, 263; Minute Books 1814–1815 of CMIP, 93/308–93/332, Box 6; Gilbert Stuart, "Rachel Gratz [Moses]" (1806), Rosenbach Museum and Library (RML), 2008–2010 Delancey Pl., Philadelphia, PA 19103. Solomon Moses (1806), RML; Ruth Hannah London, *Miniatures of Early American Jews* (Springfield, MA: Pond-Ekberg, 1953), 38, 39, 40, 41, 65, 123; Ruth Hannah London, *Portraits of Jews by Gilbert Stuart and Other Early American Artists* (Rutland, VT: C. E. Tuttle, 1969), 45, 53, 54, 66, 69, 71, Ports. 155, 169.

31. Stern, *First American Jewish Families*, 87, 209; Minute Books 1816/17/18, of CMIP, 93/334, 93/336, Box 6.

32. Wolf and Whiteman, *The History of the Jews of Philadelphia*, 230.

33. Mordecai Manuel Noah, *She Would Be a Soldier, Or, The Plains of Chippewa—an Historical Drama in Three Acts: Performed for the First Time on the 21st of June, 1819* (New York: Longworth's Dramatic Repository, 1819), 35.

34. Letter from Joshua Moses to John Myers (Baltimore, Md.), 28 June 1814 and 29 July 1814, Meyers Family Papers, Ms. Coll. 480, AJA. Emphasis in the original.

35. Wolf and Whiteman, *History of the Jews of Philadelphia*, 289, 347, 362–364, 409, 496–497.

36. Stanley F. Chyet, "The Political Rights of the Jews in the United States, 1776–1840," in *Critical Studies in American Jewish History*, ed. Jacob Rader Marcus (Cincinnati: American Jewish Archives, 1971), 19, 46, 67; Wolf and Whiteman, *History of the Jews of Philadelphia*, 147–150.

37. Marc Lee Raphael, *The Columbia History of Jews and Judaism in America* (New York: Columbia University Press, 2008), 25, 36. Max J. Kohler, "Civil Status of the Jews in Colonial New York," *Publications of the American Jewish Historical Society* 6, no. 6 (1897): 98; Thomas G. West, *Vindicating the Founders: Race, Sex, Class, and Justice in the Origins of America* (Lanham, MD: Rowman & Littlefield, 2000), 76–78; Eric Ledell Smith, "The End of Black Voting Rights in Pennsylvania: African Americans and the Pennsylvania Constitutional Convention of 1837–1838," *Pennsylvania History: A Journal of Mid-Atlantic Studies* 65, no. 3 (1998): 279.

38. Samuel Abrahams, David Hart, Jacob Hart, Israel Moses, and Judah Zunts, *New York War of 1812 Payroll. U.S. War of 1812 Service Records, 1812–1815* [database on-line], Ancestry.com, 2013. Also see *For God and Country: A Record of the Patriotic Service of Shearith Israel* (New York: Congregation Shearith Israel, 2019), 23; "Items Relating to the Moses and Levy Families, New York," *PAJHS* 27 (1920): 337.

39. "Guide to the Papers of the Seixas Family, Undated, 1746–1911, 1926, 1939 *P-60," Text, *Center for Jewish History*, accessed 10 February 2017, http://digifindingaids.cjh.org/?pID=109167; "Nathan-Kraus Family Collection," accessed 10 February 2017, http://collections.americanjewisharchives.org/ms/ms0107/ms0107.html; Wolf and Whiteman, *The History of the Jews of Philadelphia*, 289; F. Furstenberg, "Beyond Freedom and Slavery: Autonomy, Virtue, and Resistance in Early American Political Discourse," *Journal of American History* 89, no. 4 (2003): 1326.

40. Will of Hannah Ester Lopez (1815).

41. Will of Isaac Lopez (1804).

42. Will of Hannah Ester Lopez (1815); Minute Books 1781–1851 of CMIP, 93/305, 93/308, 93/334, 93/336, 93/337, 93/347–48, 93/373, Box 6; Correspondence 1813/14/15 of CMIP, 94/226, 94/227, Box 1; Minute Book Resolutions 1810–1883, of CMIP, 102/05, 102/09, Box 1; Charter of the

Congregation Granted 31st May 1824 of CMIP, Box 3; and the Offerings
Book 1824–1856, of CMIP, Box 5.

43. Andrew Gluck, "The Chair in Front of the Tebah," *Mikveh Israel Record*,
April 20–21, 2012, 3.

44. Cecily Jones, *Engendering Whiteness: White Women and Colonialism
in Barbados and North Carolina, 1627–1865* (Manchester: Manchester
University Press, 2007), 18, 32; Wolf and Whiteman, *History of the Jews of
Philadelphia*, 84, 96, 173, 176, 186, 346.

45. Stern, *First American Jewish Families*, 243; Correspondence 1813/14/15 of
CMIP, 94/219, 94/218, 94/224, 94/226, 94/227, Box 1; Minute Books 1816/
17/18, of CMIP, 93/308, 93/336, 93/347–48, Box 6.

46. Joseph R. Rosenbloom, *A Biographical Dictionary of Early American
Jews: Colonial Times through 1800* (Lexington: University of Kentucky
Press, 1960), 141; Wolf and Whiteman, *History of the Jews of
Philadelphia*, 62–63.

47. Tilley et al., *Handbook of Material Culture* (London: SAGE, 2006), 241;
David Jaffee, "Sideboards, Side Chairs, and Globes: Changing Modes
of Furnishing Provincial Culture in the Early Republic, 1790–1820," in
*Furnishing the Eighteenth Century: What Furniture Can Tell Us about the
European and American Past*, ed. Dena Goodman and Kathryn Norberg
(New York: Routledge, 2007), 79; Gluck, "The Chair in Front of the
Tebah," 3.

48. Malcolm Stern, "Two Jewish Functionaries in Colonial Pennsylvania,"
AJHQ 57, no. 1 (1967): 34–35.

49. Wolf and Whiteman, *History of the Jews of Philadelphia*, 234–236; Minute
Book and Correspondence 1782–1890 of CMIP, 94/308, 94/274, 94/30, 94/
309, 94/366, and 94/367, Box 3.

50. Minute Books 1816/17/18, of CMIP, 93/351–352, Box 6.

Chapter 6

1. Joshua Moses, "Papers and Estate Inventory," Series IV: Joshua Moses,
PMFNY, Box 1, Folder 10; Mollie Gillen, *Royal Duke: Augustus Frederick,
Duke of Sussex (1773–1843)* (London: Sidgwick and Jackson, 1978), 32,
178, 185; John Van der Kiste, *George III's Children* (New York: History
Press, 2013).

2. James J. Raciti, *Stephen Girard: America's Colonial Olympian, 1750–1831*
(Santa Fe, NM: Sunstone Press, 2015), 37.

3. Israel Joel, Abraham Isaacs and Jonas N. Phillips, "Items Relating to
Congregation Shearith Israel," *PAJHS* 27 (1920): 51–53; Edwin Wolf and
Maxwell Whiteman, *The History of the Jews of Philadelphia: From Colonial
Times to the Age of Jackson* (Philadelphia: Jewish Publication Society of
America, 1975), 289.

4. Letter from Stephen Girard to Joshua Moses (London), August 26, 1815,
Joshua Moses 1815–1816 Folder, SGP in AJA.

5. Ibid.

6. John Corry, Thomas Troughton, and George Perry, *The History of Liverpool: From the Earliest Authenticated Period down to the Present Time* (Liverpool: William Robinson, 1810), 81–82; Richard L. Forstall, *Population of States and Counties of the United States: 1790–1990* (Washington, DC: US Department of Commerce, 1996), 137, 211; Thomas Kaye, *The Stranger in Liverpool: or, an Historical and Descriptive View of the Town of Liverpool and Its Environs* (Liverpool: T. Kaye, 1820), 64–65, 72.

7. William K. Klingaman and Nicholas P. Klingaman, *The Year without Summer: 1816 and the Volcano That Darkened the World and Changed History* (New York: St. Martin's Press, 2013); Ian Kelly, *Beau Brummell: The Ultimate Man of Style* (New York: Free Press, 2006), 109.

8. Edwin Pratt, *A History of Inland Transport and Communication in England* (London: K. Paul, Trench, Trübner & Co., 1912), 54. Joshua Moses, Occupant (1817), St. Mary, Whitechapel, Tower Hamlets, *London, England, Land Tax Records, 1692–1932* [database on-line], Ancestry. com 2011.

9. Michael J. Radwin, "Jewish Calendar, Hebrew Date Converter, Holidays," accessed March 24, 2020, https://www.hebcal.com/; Letter from Joshua Moses to Stephen Girard (Philadelphia), November 16, 1815, Joshua Moses 1815–1816 Folder, SGP in AJA; Letter from Joshua Moses to Stephen Girard (Philadelphia), December 26, 1815, Joshua Moses 1815–1816 Folder, SGP in AJA.

10. Letter from Joshua Moses to Stephen Girard (Philadelphia), December 26, 1815, Joshua Moses 1815–1816 Folder, SGP in AJA; Richard Tames, *Documents of the Industrial Revolution 1750–1850: Select Economic and Social Documents for Sixth Forms* (London: Routledge, 2015), 159; W. B. Crump, Joseph Rogerson, and Benjamin Gott, *The Leeds Woolen Industry 1780–1820* (Leeds: Thoresby Society, 1931), 51–58; James Sherwood, *Savile Row: The Master Tailors of British Bespoke* (Farnborough: Thames & Hudson, 2017), 20–21; José Blanco, ed., *Clothing and Fashion: American Fashion from Head to Toe* (Santa Barbara, CA: ABC-CLIO, 2018), 114; Ian Kelly, *Beau Brummell: The Ultimate Man of Style* (New York: Free Press, 2006), 111.

11. Elizabeth Abbott, *Sugar: A Bittersweet History* (London: Duckworth Overlook, 2009), 56, 60, 68.

12. MBMNI; II.29–31, 40–41, 44–46, 51, 92, 94, IV.123; Karl Watson, "Shifting Identities: Religion, Race, and Creolization among the Sephardi Jews of Barbados, 1654—1900," in *The Jews in the Caribbean*, ed. Jane S. Gerber (Portland: Littman Library, 2014), 212, 220–221.

13. Hannah Ruth London, *Miniatures and Silhouettes of Early American Jews* (Rutland, VT: C. E. Tuttle, 1970), 34; Lucien Wolf, "Recollections of a Veteran," *Jewish Chronicle*, 15 Sep. 1893, 12.

14. MBMNI, II: 25, 34; "Shangare Limmud School of Barbadoes," *The Occident* 3, no. 5 (1845).

15. Mark Rothery and Henry French, *Making Men: The Formation of Elite Male Identities in England, c. 1660–1900* (Houndmills, UK: Palgrave

Macmillan, 2012), 15; Katherine Glover, *Elite Women and Polite Society in Eighteenth-Century Scotland* (Woodbridge: Boydell, 2011), 27–28, 32.

16. Adam Kirsch, *Benjamin Disraeli* (New York: Nextbook, 2008), 131; Todd M. Endelman, *Broadening Jewish History: Towards a Social History of Ordinary Jews* (Oxford: Littman Library, 2014), 78, 106–108, 205;: Wolf, "Recollections of a Veteran," 12; Gerry Black, *JFS: A History of the Jews' Free School, London, since 1732* (London: Tymsder, 1998), 17.

17. Glover, *Elite Women and Polite Society,* 27, 32; MBMNI, II: 34. See also J. Mocatta, *An Address to the Congregation of Portuguese Jews: Delivered at a Meeting of Their Elders, on the Examination of the Report, Presented by the Committee on the Ecclesiastical State* (London: 1803), 10, 24.

18. Todd M. Endelman, *The Jews of Georgian England, 1714–1830: Tradition and Change in a Liberal Society* (Philadelphia: Jewish Publication Society of America, 1979), 119, 170, 172, 173.

19. Mordechai Rozin, *The Rich and the Poor: Jewish Philanthropy and Social Control in Nineteenth-Century London* (Brighton: Sussex Academic Press, 1999), 69.

20. Black, *JFS,* 28; Rozin, *The Rich and the Poor,* 68–71; Laura Arnold Leibman, *The Art of the Jewish Family: A History of Women in Early New York in Five Objects* (New York: Bard Graduate Center, 2020), 32.

21. Joshua Moses, "Papers and Estate Inventory," PMFNY, Box 1, Folder 10; Black, *JFS,* 27.

22. Herbert Fry, *London in . . . .: illustrated with bird's eye views of the principal streets* (London: David Bogue, 1886), 176; Wolf, "Recollections of a Veteran," 12; Lucien Wolf, *Essays in Jewish History* (London: Jewish Historical Society of England, 1934), 25; Julian Land and James Greener, "The Lineage of the Montefiore Family and Major Connected Families," unpublished manuscript, last modified 2016, supplied by authors.

23. Joshua Moses, Tenant (1814, 1816), Precinct of St. Katherine by the Tower, Tower Hamlets, *London, England, Land Tax Records, 1692–1932.*

24. Abigail Green, *Moses Montefiore* (Cambridge, MA: Harvard University Press, 2012), 34; Wolf, "Recollections of a Veteran," 12; Bruce Hunt, *Bruce's Lists of London Street Name Changes* (Linton: Bruce Hunt, 2013), 1028; William D. Rubinstein, Michael Jolles, and Hilary L. Rubinstein, *The Palgrave Dictionary of Anglo-Jewish History* (Houndmills, UK: Palgrave Macmillan, 2011), 850.

25. MBMNI, III.29–30, 45, VIII;70, 123, 125. Wilfred S. Samuel, "Tentative List of Jewish Underwriting Members of Lloyd's (from Some Time Prior to 1800 until the Year 1901)," *Miscellanies (Jewish Historical Society of England)* 5 (1948): 176–192.

26. Wolf, *Essays in Jewish History,* 217.

27. Emma Tanya Harris, "Anglo-Jewry's Experience of Secondary Education from the 1830s until 1920" (PhD diss., University of London, 2007), 106; Caroline Knight, *London's Country Houses* (Chichester, UK: Phillimore, 2009); Phillip Norman, "Cromwell House;: Historical Notes." In *Survey*

of London Monograph 12, Cromwell House, Highgate, 15–35. London, 1926. *British History Online* http://www.british-history.ac.uk/survey-london/ bk12/pp15-35; Michael Hoberman, Laura Arnold Leibman, and Hilit Surowitz-Israel, *Jews in the Americas, 1776–1826* (London: Taylor and Francis, 2017), 109.

28. Harris, "Anglo-Jewry's Experience of Secondary Education," 106.
29. Ibid.
30. Malcolm Brown, "The Jews of Gravesend before 1915," *Jewish Historical Studies* 35 (1996): 123.
31. Ibid., 121–123. Household of Hannah Gomes, Camberwell, Surrey, England, *Census Returns of England and Wales, 1841*, PRO (Provo: Ancestry.com).
32. Paul Caffrey, "Jewels Above All Prize: Portrait Miniatures on Enamel and Ivory," in *Ireland: Crossroads of Art and Design, 1690–1840*, ed. William Laffan, Christopher Monkhouse, and Leslie Fitzpatrick (New Haven, CT: Yale University Press, 2015), 161; Carrie Rebora Barratt and Lori Zabar, *American Portrait Miniatures in the Metropolitan Museum of Art* (New York: Metropolitan Museum of Art, 2010), 38; Stephen Lloyd, *Portrait Miniatures from Scottish Private Collections* (Edinburgh: National Galleries of Scotland, 2006), 9; Robin Jaffee Frank, *Love and Loss: American Portrait and Mourning Miniatures* (New Haven, CT: Yale University Press, 2000), 190; Helen Sheumaker, *Love Entwined: The Curious History of Hairwork in America* (Philadelphia: University of Pennsylvania Press, 2007), 15, 230; Jeff Broadwater, *James Madison: A Son of Virginia & a Founder of the Nation* (Chapel Hill: University of North Carolina Press, 2012), 114; Hanneke Grootenboer, *Treasuring the Gaze: Intimate Vision in Late Eighteenth-Century Eye Miniatures* (Chicago: University of Chicago Press, 2012), 11, 22–23, 42–46.
33. Nathaniel Whittock, *The Miniature Painter's Manual: Containing Progressive Lessons on the Art of Drawing and Painting Likenesses from Life on Card-Board, Vellum and Ivory: With Concise Remarks on the Delineation of Character and Caricature* (London: Sherwood, Gilbert and Piper, 1844), 30–32.
34. Elena Arias Riera, "The Collection of Miniatures in the Museo del Prado," Museo Nacional del Prado, 2019, https://www.museodelprado. es;en/learn/research/studies-and-restorations/resource/the-collection-of-miniatures-in-the-museo-del/e8b31ab8-746e-46d7-a031-329d808a4b4e; "Making a Miniature," The Gibbes Museum of Art, 2016, http://www. gibbesmuseum.org/miniatures;/about/making-a-miniature/; "Portrait Miniatures: Materials & Techniques"; "Portrait Miniatures," 21 March 2013, Cleveland Museum of Art; Carrie Rebora Barratt and Lori Zabar, *American Portrait Miniatures; in the Metropolitan Museum of Art* (New York: Metropolitan Museum of Art, 2010), 75; "Paintings," Loeb Jewish Portrait Database, 2018, http://loebjewishportraits.com/paintings/; London, *Miniatures and Silhouettes*.

35. See the portrait of Sarah Simpson Wood in this book, but also the Portraits of Sarah Moses Levy and Chapman Levy (South Carolina, ca. 1798) now in the collection of the College of Charleston.

36. Whittock, *The Miniature Painter's Manual*, 8, 33, 35, 40; Riera, "The Collection of Miniatures."

37. Riera, "The Collection of Miniatures"; Sander Gilman, *Making the Body Beautiful: A Cultural History of Aesthetic Surgery* (Princeton, NJ: Princeton University Press, 1999), 89; Barratt and Zabar, *American Portrait Miniatures*, 32; Catherine E. Kelly, *Republic of Taste: Art, Politics, and Everyday Life in Early America* (Philadelphia: University of Pennsylvania Press, 2016), 105; Dale T. Johnson, *American Portrait Miniatures in the Manney Collection* (New York: Metropolitan Museum of Art, 1990), 21–22.

38. For examples of the Indian miniatures, see the "Twelve miniatures depicting Mughal rulers of India" (c. 1850) at the Victoria and Albert Museum, Cromwell Road, London, SW7 2RL England, https://collections. vam.ac.uk/search/?q=twelve%20miniatures%20india&page=1&id_ category=THES49045; Natasha Eaton, "The Art of Colonial Despotism: Portraits, Politics, and Empire in South India, 1750–1795," *Cultural Critique* 70, no. 1 (2008): 88; Whittock, *The Miniature Painter's Manual*, 52–53.

39. Whittock, *The Miniature Painter's Manual*, 41, 44, 54.

40. C. Willett Cunnington, *English Women's Clothing in the Nineteenth Century: A Comprehensive Guide with 1,117 Illustrations* (New York: Dover, 1990), 34, 38–54; Penelope Byrde, *Nineteenth-Century Fashion* (London: Batsford, 1992), 23; London, *Miniatures and Silhouettes*, 34; Brown, "The Jews of Gravesend," 121–123; *Census Returns of England and Wales, 1841* PRO (Provo: Ancestry.com).

41. "Items Relating to the Moses and Levy Families, New York" *PAJHS*, 27 (1920): 23–24.

42. Cunnington, *English Women's Clothing*, 28; Aileen Ribeiro, *The Art of Dress: Fashion in England and France 1750–1820* (New Haven, CT: Yale University Press, 1995), 118.

43. Thomas Sully, *Sally Etting* (1808), JMNY; Anna Claypoole Peale, *Sally Etting* (ca. 1815–1818), RML; Gilbert Stuart, *Eliza Myers* (ca. 1808), Chrysler Museum of Art; Robert DuPlessis, "Sartorial Sorting in the Colonial Caribbean and North America," in *The Right to Dress: Sumptuary Laws in a Global Perspective, 1200–1800*, ed. Giorgio Riello and Ulinka Rublack (New York: Cambridge University Press, 2019), 355–357, 365, 351; Tony Martin, *Caribbean History: From Pre-Colonial Origins to the Present* (Boston: Pearson, 2012), 84–86; Kelly Mohs Gage, "Forced Crossing: The Dress of African Slave Women in Rio de Janeiro, Brazil, 1861," *Dress* 39, no. 2 (2013): 112, 120, 124. See also Anonymous, *Portrait of a Young Woman* (late eighteenth century), Pastel, Saint Louis Art Museum.

44. Roulhac Toledano, Mary Louise Christovich, and Robin Derbes, *New Orleans Architecture: Faubourg Tremé and the Bayou Road* (Gretna, LA: Pelican, 2003), 97; Melissa Blanco Borelli, *She Is Cuba: A Genealogy of the Mulata Body* (New York: Oxford University Press, 2016), 34–35; Hannah Farnham Sawyer Lee, *Memoir of Pierre Toussaint, born a Slave in St. Domingo* (Boston: Crosby, Nichols and Co., 1854), 2, 16, 22, 32–35, 38, 82, 121; Thomas J. Shelley, "Black and Catholic in Nineteenth-Century New York: The Case of Pierre Toussaint," *Records of the American Catholic Historical Society of Philadelphia* 102, no. 4 (1991): 6–7; Hoberman, Leibman, and Surowitz-Israel, *Jews in the Americas*, 110–111.

45. Sander L. Gilman, "Zwetschkenbaum's Competence: Madness and the Discourse of the Jews," *Modern Austrian Literature* 26, no. 2 (1993): 4; Richard Brilliant, ed., *Facing the New World: Jewish Portraits in Colonial and Federal America* (New York: Jewish Museum, 1997), 66–67; Wieke Vink, *Creole Jews Negotiating Community in Colonial Suriname* (Leiden: Brill, 2010), 165.

46. Whittock, *The Miniature Painter's Manual*, 56–57.

47. Joshua Moses, "Family Record Book, 1817-1820," PMFNY, Box 1, Folder 11; Marriage Register of Joshua Moses and Sarah Rodrigues Brandon;,, "The Jessurun Family," *Jewish Quarterly Review* 1 (1888): 440–441.

Chapter 7

1. Laura Arnold Leibman and Sam May, "Making Jews: Race, Gender and Identity in Barbados in the Age of Emancipation" *American Jewish History* 99, no. 1 (2015): 7–8, 12, 15; MBMNI, VIII.1–45

2. MBMNI, II, III, VIII.1–30, 41–42, 44, 55–56, 59–60; Leibman and May, "Making Jews," 9–10.

3. MBMNI, VIII.41.

4. MBMNI, VII.41.

5. MBMNI, VIII.7; Leibman and May, "Making Jews," 10.

6. MBMNI, VIII.77.

7. Financial Records 1817–1858 of CMIP, Box 5.

8. MBMNI, VIII.47–48.

9. MBMNI, VIII.32, 85.

10. 20 May 1817, MBMNI, III.80.

11. MBMNI, VIII: .102; Correspondence 1823–1824 of CMIP, Box 1.

12. MBMNI, VIII.126.

13. MBMNI, VIII.126.

14. F. A. Hoyos, *Barbados Comes of Age: From Early Strivings to Happy Fulfilment* (London: Macmillan Caribbean, 1987), 23. For more on this debate or on the "Brown Privilege Bill," see Leibman and May, "Making Jews," 1–26; Arnold S. Sio, "Race, Colour, and Miscegenation: The Free Coloured of Jamaica and Barbados," *Caribbean Studies* 16, no. 1 (1976): 8–12.

15. Vere Langford Oliver, *The Monumental Inscriptions in the Churches and Churchyards of the Island of Barbados, British West Indies* (London: M. Hughes & Clarke, 1914), 137; St. James Parish Church; John Shrewsbury, *Memorials of the Rev. William J. Shrewsbury* (London: Hamilton, Adams, & Co., 1869), 90, 92.

16. Gayle, "Ann Gill," 38, 45, 77; William James Shrewsbury, *The Family Memorial and Pastoral Remembrancer; being a short memoir of Mrs. Hillaria Shrewsbury* (London: J. Mason, 1839), 9.

17. Shrewsbury, *The Family Memorial*, 9.

18. Shrewsbury, *Memorials*, 129–131.

19. Emphasis in the original; *The Methodist Magazine* (1812): 344.

20. Bufford W. Coe, *John Wesley and Marriage* (Bethlehem, PA: Lehigh University Press, 1996); Cohen, *Sephardim in the Americas*, 97.

21. Gayle, "Ann Gill," 31–33.

22. Titus, *The Development of Methodism*, 19.

23. Gayle, "Ann Gill," 31; Kenneth Cracknell and Susan J. White, *An Introduction to World Methodism* (Cambridge: Cambridge University Press, 2005), 195.

24. Shrewsbury, *Memorials*, 148.

25. Titus, *Development of Methodism*, 5–6; Randy Browne, "The 'Bad Business' of Obeah: Power, Authority, and the Politics of Slave Culture in the British Caribbean," *William and Mary Quarterly* 68, no. 3 (2011): 456, 459; John H. Wigger, "Taking Heaven by Storm: Enthusiasm and Early American Methodism, 1770–1820," *Journal of the Early Republic* 14, no. 2 (1994): 186.

26. Shrewsbury, *Memorials*, 93.

27. Office of Registry of Colonial Slaves and Slave Compensation Commission: T 71, 524: 251, 406, TNA.

28. Gayle, "Ann Gill," 48; Shrewsbury, *Memorials*, 147.

29. Larry Gragg, *Quaker Community on Barbados* (Columbia: University of Missouri Press, 2009), 129–134, 142–144, 149.

30. Shrewsbury, *Memorials*, 137. Emphasis in the original.

31. Ibid., 144.

32. Ibid.

33. Ibid., 158.

34. Ibid., 90, 157–160, 172–175.

35. Gayle, "Ann Gill," 56–58.

36. Shrewsbury, *Memorials*, 176–177, 184–185; Gayle, "Ann Gill," 59–60.

37. Hilary Beckles, *For Love of Country: National Heroes of Barbados* (St. Michael, Barbados: Foundation Publishing, 2001).

38. Shrewsbury, *Memorials*, 100–104.

39. MBMNI, VIII:.33.

40. Moses Hayyim Luzzatto, *Way of God* [Derekh ha-Shem], trans. Aryeh Kaplan (Jerusalem: Feldheim, 1981), 139–143.

Chapter 8

1. Ralph Waldo Emerson, *Journals of Ralph Waldo Emerson, 1820–1872 [1876]*, edited by Edward Waldo Emerson and Waldo Emerson Forbes (Cambridge: Riverside Press, 1909), 201.

2. Louisa Susannah Wells, *The Journal of a Voyage from Charlestown, S.C., to London Undertaken During the American Revolution by a Daughter of an Eminent American Loyalist (Louisa Susannah Wells) in the year 1778 and Written from Memory only in 1779* (New York: New-York Historical Society, 1906), 49.

3. Ibid., 52.

4. Irvine Loudon, *Death in Childbirth: An International Study of Maternal Care and Maternal Mortality, 1800–1950* (Oxford: Clarendon Press, 1992), 162; Malcolm H. Stern, *First American Jewish Families: 600 Genealogies, 1654–1977* (Cincinnati: American Jewish Archives, 1978), 159, 217.

5. Joshua Moses, "Family Record Book, 1817–1820," PMFNY, Box 1, Folder 11: 6.

6. Howard B. Rock and Deborah Dash Moore, *Cityscapes: A History of New York in Images* (New York: Columbia University Press, 2001), 52; Stern, *First American Jewish Families*, 159, 217; "The Diary of Aaron Levy" in "Items Relating to the Moses and Levy Families, New York," *PAJHS*, 27 (1920): 336.

7. Edmund M. Blunt, *Blunt's Stranger's Guide to the City of New-York: Comprising a Description of Public Buildings, Dwelling Houses* (New York: E. M. Blunt, 1817), ix.

8. Leslie M. Harris, *In the Shadow of Slavery: African Americans in New York City, 1626–1863* (Chicago: University of Chicago Press, 2003), 14–15, 28–29; Helena Woodard, *Slave Sites on Display: Reflecting Slavery's Legacy through Contemporary "Flash" Moments* (Jackson: University Press of Mississippi, 2019), 50; Ira Berlin and Leslie M. Harris, eds., *Slavery in New York* (New York: New Press, 2005), 62, 66.

9. Berlin and Harris, *Slavery in New York*, 76.

10. Ibid., 29, 37, 43, 76; Harris, *In the Shadow of Slavery*, 43, 45–46.

11. Edgar J. McManus, *A History of Negro Slavery in New York* (Syracuse, NY: Syracuse University Press. 2001), 178; New York (State), Laws of the State of New York, 136; Harris, *In the Shadow of Slavery*, 3.

12. Harris, *In the Shadow of Slavery*, 5.

13. Blunt, *Blunt's Stranger's Guide*, 44; GB Historical GIS, A Vision of Britain through Time, http://www.visionofbritain.org.uk/unit/10097836/cube/TOT_POP, accessed 5 January 2020; Todd M. Endelman, *The Jews of Georgian England, 1714–1830: Tradition and Change in a Liberal Society* (Philadelphia: Jewish Publication Society of America, 1979), 119, 141, 172.

14. Jonathan D. Sarna, *Jacksonian Jew: The Two Worlds of Mordecai Noah* (New York: Holmes & Meier, 1981), 35; Harris, *In the Shadow of Slavery*,

112–113; Minutes of the Trustees, Microfilm, MF-1e, Reel 2, Microdex 1, CSIR; Letters to Rev. Peixotto Announcing Election of Naphtali Phillips as *Parnas*, 1819–1821, Papers of Jacques Judah Lyons (1813–1877), AJHS.

15. Stern, *First American Jewish Families*, 159, 217; *Longworth's American Almanac, New York Register, and City 1817/18* (New-York: David Longworth, 1817), 281, 324, 377.

16. Moses L. Moses, New York Ward 9, New York, New York, Census of the United States, 1820, Ancestry.com.

17. Berlin and Harris, *Slavery in New York*, 67.

18. Advertisement, *Pennsylvania Packet*, September 22, 1778, 3.

19. Ibid.

20. Ibid.

21. Ibid.

22. Berlin and Harris, *Slavery in New York*, 68–69.

23. Isaac Moses Receipt Book, 1785–1787, PMFNY, Box 1, Folders 3: 39, 45.

24. Ibid., 64, 83.

25. Isaac Moses, New York Ward 1, New York, New York, Census of the United States, 1810, Ancestry.com.

26. Jerald Nadler, "In Honor of the 350th Anniversary of the Congregation Shearith Israel," *Congressional Record*, 150, No. 126 (2004): E1831; Morris U. Schappes and Joshua Bloch, *A Documentary History of the Jews in the United States, 1654–1875* (New York: Citadel Press, 1952), 118; Joseph Leon Blau and Salo Wittmayer Baron, *The Jews of the United States, 1790–1840: A Documentary History* (New York: Columbia University Press, 1963), 270; Marc Angel, *Remnant of Israel: A Portrait of America's First Jewish Congregation: Shearith Israel* (New York: Riverside Book Company, 2004), 107, 180;: Julius Goebeland and Joseph Smith, eds., *The Law Practice of Alexander Hamilton: Documents and Commentary*, Volume V (New York: Columbia University Press, 1964), 319; Alexander Hamilton, *Papers of Alexander Hamilton*, ed. Harold C. Syrett (New York: Columbia University Press, 1963), 26, 597, 600, 655, 681; Leslie M. Harris, "The Greatest City in the World? Slavery in New York in the Age of Hamilton," in *Historians on Hamilton: How a Blockbuster Musical Is Restaging America's Past*, ed. Renee Christine Romano and Claire Bond Potter (New Brunswick: Rutgers University Press, 2018), 84; Moses L. Moses, New York Ward 9, New York, New York, Census of the United States, 1820, Ancestry.com.

27. Harris, *In the Shadow of Slavery*, 83, 117; John Jamison Moore, *History of the A.M.E. Zion Church in America: Founded in 1796, in the City of New York* (Charlotte, NC: A.M.E. Zion Historical Society, 2004), 28.

28. Moore, *History of the A.M.E. Zion Church*, 15, 22.

29. Martha Jones, "'Make Us a Power': African American Methodists Debate the 'Woman Question,' 1870–1900," in *Women and Religion in the African Diaspora: Knowledge, Power, and Performance*, ed. Marie R. Griffith and

Barbara Dianne Savage (Baltimore: Johns Hopkins University Press, 2006), 145; Moore, *History of the A.M.E. Zion Church*, 16, 22, 30.

30. In 1818/19 she lived at 86 Greenwich Street; *Longworth's New York Register, and City Directory* (New-York: Thomas Longworth, 1818), 240; *Longworth's American Almanac* (1817), 320.

31. David De Sola Pool, *Portraits Etched in Stone: Early Jewish Settlers, 1682–1831* (New York: Columbia University Press, 1953), 382; Malcolm H. Stern, *First American Jewish Families: 600 Genealogies, 1654–1977* (Cincinnati: American Jewish Archives, 1978), 159.

32. Joshua Moses, "Family Record Book, 1817–1820," PMFNY, Box 1, Folder 11: 6.

33. Ibid.

34. De Sola Pool, *Portraits Etched in Stone*, 391; Measuring Worth—Relative Worth Comparators and Data Sets, 2017, https://measuringworth.com/.

35. David De Sola Pool, *An Old Faith in the New World: Portrait of Shearith Israel, 1654–1954* (New York: Columbia University Press, 1955), 50.

36. Laura Arnold Leibman, *Messianism, Secrecy and Mysticism: A New Interpretation of Early American Jewish Life* (London: Vallentine Mitchell, 2012), 63.

37. Henry Stolzman, Daniel Stolzman, and Tami Hausman, *Synagogue Architecture in America: Faith, Spirit & Identity* (Mulgrave, Victoria, Australia: Images Publishing, 2004), 36; De Sola Pool, *An Old Faith in the New World*, 49.

38. Register Book for the Electors of the Trustees of the Kaal Kadosh Shearith Israel, MF-1e, Reel 6, Microdex 1, CSIR, 7; Minutes of the Trustees, Microfilm, MF-1e, Reel 2, Microdex 1, CSIR, 338–342, 414–420.

39. Karla Goldman, *Beyond the Synagogue Gallery: Finding a Place for Women in American Judaism* (Cambridge, MA: Harvard University Press, 2000), 41.

40. Ibid., 51.

41. David De Sola Pool, *The Mill Street Synagogue (1730–1817) of the Congregation Shearith Israel (founded in the City of New York in 1655)* (New York: n.p., 1930), 49.

42. Joshua Moses, "Family Record Book, 1817–1820," PMFNY, Box 1, Folder 11: 6; Stern, *First American Jewish Families*, 209; Longworth's New York Register (1818), 269; Leo Herskowitz, "Some Aspects of the New York Jewish Merchant and Community, 1654–1820," *AJHQ* 66, no. 1 (1976): 34; *Longworth's American Almanac* (1817), 232; Rob Wills, *Alias Blind Larry: The Mostly True Memoir of James Laurence, the Singing Convict* (Melbourne: Australian Scholarly Publishing, 2015), 26; Minutes of the Trustees, Microfilm, MF-1e, Reel 2, Microdex 1, CSIR, 417, 419.

43. Leo Herskowitz, "History, Herstory, Ourstory: Twelve Jewish Jurors," *Jewish Currents*, 20 Oct. 2013, https://jewishcurrents.org/history-herstory-story-twelve-jewish-jurors/; Ira Rosenswaike, "An Estimate and Analysis of the Jewish Population of the United States in 1790," in *American Jewish History: The Colonial and Early National Periods, 1654–1840*, ed. Jeffrey S.

Gurock (New York: Routledge, 1998), 373; Maurice U. Schappes, "Four Documents concerning Jews and Slavery (1762; 1806–09; 1814; 1860)," in *Strangers & Neighbors: Relations between Blacks & Jews in the United States*, ed. Maurianne Adams (Amherst: University of Massachusetts Press, 1999), 145.

44. Moses, "Family Record Book, 1817–1820," PMFNY, Box 1, Folder 11: 6.
45. Moses L. Moses, New York Ward 9, New York, New York, Fourth Census of the United States; Advertisements, *Columbian*, 16 Sep. 1818, 3; Advertisements, *New-York Gazette & General Advertiser*, 23 Apr. 1819, 3.
46. Minutes of the Trustees, Microfilm, MF-1e, Reel 2, Microdex 1, CSIR.
47. Borrowing activity of Moses L. Moses, "City Readers," Digital Historic Collections at the New York Society Library," *New York Society Library*. https://cityreaders.nysoclib.org/.
48. Joshua Moses, "Family Record Book, 1817–1820," PMFNY, Box 1, Folder 11: 6; Registers of Births, Deaths, Marriages, Vol. 1 1759-S, Microfilm, MF-1e, Reel 3, CSIR, 71.
49. Michael Hoberman, Laura Arnold Leibman, and Hilit Surowitz-Israel, *Jews in the Americas, 1776–1826* (London: Taylor and Francis, 2017), 172; Edwin Wolf and Maxwell Whiteman, *The History of the Jews of Philadelphia: From Colonial Times to the Age of Jackson* (Philadelphia: Jewish Publication Society of America, 1975), 219, 276—277, 325–326, 440–441; Registers of Births, Deaths, Marriages, Vol. 1 1759-S, Microfilm, MF-1e, Reel 3, CSIR, 71–72; Eugene Fitch Ware, *Lyon Campaign in Missouri: Being a History of the First Iowa Infantry and of the Causes which Led up to its Organization, and how it earned the Thanks of Congress, which it Got: Together with a Birdseye View of the Conditions in Iowa Preceding the Great Civil War of 1861* (Topeka, KS: Crane & Co., 1907), 239.
50. *Longworth's New York Register* (1818), 315; "Naphtali Phillips," *PAJHS* 21 (1913): 173.
51. Joshua Moses, "Family Record Book, 1817–1820," PMFNY, Box 1, Folder 11: 6; Jonathan B. Tucker, *Scourge: The Once and Future Threat of Smallpox* (New York: Grove Press, 2002), 31.
52. Joshua Moses, "Family Record Book, 1817–1820," PMFNY, Box 1, Folder 11: 6; Edward Jenner, *An Inquiry into the Causes and Effects of the Variolae Vaccinae* (London: Sampson Low, 1798), 54.
53. Joshua Moses, "Family Record Book, 1817–1820," PMFNY, Box 1, Folder 11: 6.

Chapter 9

1. *Passenger Lists of Vessels Arriving at Philadelphia, Pennsylvania, Records of the United States Customs Service, 1745–1997*, Ancestry.com.
2. Financial Records 1817–1858 of CMIP, Box 5; Edward S. Daniels, "Extracts from Various Records of the Early Settlement of the Jews in the Island of Barbados, W. I.," *PAJHS* 26 (1918): 254; Samuel Morais, *The Jews of*

Philadelphia: Their History from the Earliest Times to the Present Times (Philadelphia: Levytype Company, 1894), 59.

3. David Marley, *Historic Cities of the Americas: An Illustrated Encyclopedia* (Santa Barbara, CA: ABC-CLIO, 2005), 27; Census of the United States, 1810, Ancestry.com; Census of the United States, 1820; Edwin Wolf and Maxwell Whiteman, *The History of the Jews of Philadelphia: From Colonial Times to the Age of Jackson* (Philadelphia: Jewish Publication Society of America, 1975), 114, 339.

4. Morais, *The Jews of Philadelphia*, 444.

5. Wolf and Whiteman, *History of the Jews of Philadelphia*, 338–339; Morais, *The Jews of Philadelphia*, 444; Joseph R. Rosenbloom, *A Biographical Dictionary of Early American Jews: Colonial Times through 1800* (Lexington: University of Kentucky Press, 1960), 38–39.

6. W. E. B. DuBois, *The Philadelphia Negro: A Social Study* (New York: Schocken Books, 1967), 17, 25; Gary B. Nash, *The Unknown American Revolution: The Unruly Birth of Democracy and the Struggle to Create America* (New York: Penguin, 2006), 325; Marley, *Historic Cities of the Americas*, 27; Gary B. Nash, *Forging Freedom: The Formation of Philadelphia's Black Community, 1720–1840* (Cambridge, MA: Harvard University Press, 1988), 2.

7. Julie Winch, *The Elite of Our People: Joseph Willson's Sketches of Black Upper-Class Life in Antebellum Philadelphia* (University Park: Pennsylvania State University Press, 2000), 23–24, 87, 99, 103; Nash, *The Unknown American Revolution*, 325; Nash, *Forging Freedom*, 214; G. S. Rowe, "Black Offenders, Criminal Courts, and Philadelphia Society in the Late Eighteenth Century," *Journal of Social History* 22, no. 4 (1989): 692, 694–695, 703; P. Franklin, "The Philadelphia Race Riot of 1918," in African Americans in Pennsylvania: Shifting Historical Perspectives, ed. Joe Trotter (University Park: Pennsylvania State University Press, 2010), 323.

8. Erica Armstrong Dunbar, *A Fragile Freedom: African American Women and Emancipation in the Antebellum City*, Society and the Sexes in the Modern World (New Haven, CT: Yale University Press, 2008), 87, 449; Winch, *Philadelphia's Black Elite*, 46, 135–137; Gary Nash, "Race and Citizenship in the Early Republic," in *Antislavery and Abolition in Philadelphia: Emancipation and the Long Struggle for Racial Justice in the City of Brotherly Love*, ed. Richard Newman and James Mueller (Baton Rouge: Louisiana State University Press, 2011), 115; Beverly C. Tomek, *Colonization and Its Discontents: Emancipation, Emigration, and Antislavery in Antebellum Pennsylvania* (New York: New York University Press, 2011), 43; Allan E. Yarema, *The American Colonization Society: An Avenue to Freedom?* (Oxford, UK: University Press of America, 2006), 71; Frederick Douglass, *The Frederick Douglass Papers* (New Haven, CT: Yale University Press, 2018), 244.

9. Winch, *The Elite of Our People*, 1.

10. Ibid., 98.

11. Ibid., 24.
12. "From the Pennsylvania Gazette. High Life below the Stairs," *Freedom's Journal*, 14 Mar. 1828, 3; Emma Jones Lapsansky, " 'Since They Got Those Separate Churches': Afro-Americans and Racism in Jacksonian Philadelphia," *American Quarterly* 32, no. 1 (1980): 67.
13. "From the Pennsylvania Gazette. High Life below the Stairs," 3.
14. Eman¹ N. Carvalho, York Ward 8, New York, New York, 32:709, Census of the United States, 1810, Ancestry.com; Marc Howard Ross, *Slavery in the North: Forgetting History and Recovering Memory* (Philadelphia: University of Pennsylvania Press, 2018); Dunbar, *Fragile Freedom*, 29, 41; John Hare, *The Supreme Court of Pennsylvania: Life and Law in the Commonwealth, 1684–2017* (University Park: Pennsylvania State University Press, 2018)).
15. Wolf and Whiteman, *History of the Jews of Philadelphia*, 192.
16. *National Advocate*, 24 Sep. 1821, quoted in David N. Gellman and David Quigley, *Jim Crow New York: A Documentary History of Race and Citizenship, 1777–1877* (New York: New York University Press, 2004), 88–89.
17. Ibid.
18. Ibid.
19. Ibid., 88.
20. Dunbar, *A Fragile Freedom*, 172; DeSilver's Philadelphia *Directory and Stranger's Guide, 1829* (Philadelphia: Robert DeSilver, 1829), 82.
21. Lemire, *"Miscegenation": Making Race in America* (Philadelphia: University of Pennsylvania Press, 2002), 7; Dale Cockrell, *Demons of Disorder: Early Blackface Minstrels and Their World* (New York: Cambridge University Press, 1997), 47, 71.
22. Wolf and Whiteman, *History of the Jews of Philadelphia*, 190–191; Manumission Books, A, B, C & D, AmS .05, AmS .051, AmS .052, AmS .053, AmS .054, Pennsylvania Abolition Society Papers, Collection 0490, Historical Society of Pennsylvania, Philadelphia, PA; Kate E. R. Pickard, *The Kidnapped and the Ransomed: The Narrative of Peter and Vina Still after Forty Years of Slavery* (Lincoln: University of Nebraska Press, 1995), 20–21.
23. Morais, *The Jews of Philadelphia*, 203; Wolf and Whiteman, *Jews of Philadelphia*, 236–237; Pickard, *The Kidnapped and the Ransomed*, 22–24.
24. Minute Book and Correspondence 1782–1936 of CMIP, 24/62, 24/63, Box 3; Wolf and Whiteman, *History of the Jews of Philadelphia*, 127; Clare A. Lyons, *Sex among the Rabble: An Intimate History of Gender and Power in the Age of Revolution, Philadelphia, 1730–1830* (Chapel Hill: University of North Carolina Press, 2012), 116, 312, 328–329.
25. Wolf and Whiteman, *History of the Jews of Philadelphia*, 127, 237; "From the 2nd Volume of the Minute Books of the Congrn: Shearith Israel in New York," *PAJHS*, no. 21 (1913): 143.
26. Board of Managers Minute Books 1824–1879 of CMIP, 100/10, Box 8, Folder 1.

27. Board of Managers Minute Books 1824–1879 of CMIP, 100/10, 24/70, 24/ 96;, Box 8, Folder 1; George Washington, "To the Hebrew Congregations of Philadelphia, New York, Charleston, and Richmond" (13 December 1790). *Founders Online* https://founders.archives.gov/documents/ Washington/05-07-02-0036.

28. Wolf and Whiteman, *History of the Jews of Philadelphia*, 146–164, 252–253, 264–366; David Brownlee, *Frederick Weinbrenner, Architect of Karlsruhe* (Philadelphia: University of Pennsylvania Press, 1986), 92; Rachel Wischnitzer, "The Egyptian Revival in Synagogue Architecture," *PAJHS* 41, no. 1 (1951): 61–75.

29. Wolf and Whiteman, *History of the Jews of Philadelphia*, 253–254.

30. Letter from Rebecca Gratz to her brother Benjamin, 25 Feb. 1825, in David Philipson, *Letters of Rebecca Gratz* (Philadelphia: Jewish Publication Society of America, 1929), 74–76; Wolf and Whiteman, *The History of the Jews of Philadelphia*, 254.

31. Alan Corré and Malcolm Stern, "The Record Book of the Revered Jacob Raphael Cohen," *AJHQ* 59, no. 1 (1969): 60, 69.

32. Minute Book Resolutions 1810–1883 of CMIP, 102/65, Box 1; Wolf and Whiteman, *The History of the Jews of Philadelphia*, 249.

33. Corré and Stern, "The Record Book," 60, 69; Will of Abraham Rodrigues Brandon (1831), 22 Sept. 1833, *New York, Wills and Probate Records, 1659–1999*. Ancestry.com; Letter to Parnas Mr. L. Philips, Correspondence 1831–1857 of CMIP, 94/446, Box 2; Financial Records 1817–1858 of CMIP, 96/ 642, Box 5.

34. Today, Moses Lopez's books are in the collections at the Library Company in Philadelphia, Jewish Theological Society, and New-York Historical Society. Matthias donated at least one book directly to the Library Company and gave the book now at NYHS to Phillips. The more obvious recipient for the ritual books would have been Congregation Mikveh Israel.

35. Morais, *The Jews of Philadelphia*, 446.

36. Daniel J. Kleinfeld, "Mordecai Manuel Noah," in *The Selected Writings of Mordecai Noah*, ed. Daniel J. Kleinfeld and Michael Joseph Schuldiner (Westport, CT: Greenwood Press, 1999), 5. One of Jonas's other grandsons, Commodore Uriah Phillips Levy, would eventually purchase and restore Jefferson's Monticello. Marc Leepson, *Saving Monticello: The Levy Family's Epic Quest to Rescue the House That Jefferson Built* (New York: Free Press, 2001), 52.

37. Heather S. Nathans, *Hideous Characters and Beautiful Pagans: Performing Jewish Identity on the Antebellum American Stage* (Ann Arbor: University of Michigan Press, 2017), 105–107.

38. Conveyance of Sarah, Rebecca, and Isaac Lopez (1800), Deed Hannah Esther Lopez to Abraham Rodrigues Brandon, 20 Aug 1800, R/1 Deeds 1801, vol. 212.459, BDA.

Chapter 10

1. Felix Pascalis Ouviere, *A Statement of the Occurrences during a Malignant Yellow Fever, in the City of New York, in the Summer and Autumnal Months of 1819 and of the Check given to Its Progress, by the Measures Adopted by the Board of Health* (New York: William A. Mercein, 1819), 25.

2. *Longworth's American Almanac, New York Register, and City Directory* (New-York: Jonas Olmstead, 1819), 229, 289; Pascalis Ouviere, *A Statement of the Occurrences*, 25–26.

3. "The Board of Health," *Commercial Advertiser*, 8 Sep. 1819, 2; "Postscript," *Columbian*, 6 Sep. 1819, 3; "Additional Letter from Doctor Hosack to the Recorder. New-York, Sept. 6, 1819," *Evening Post*, 6 Sep. 1819, 2.

4. *American*, 15 Sep. 1819, 2.

5. Ibid.

6. Jane Margaret Smith, *Ship of Death: The Tragedy of the "Emigrant"* (Carindale, Australia: Independent Ink, 2019), 207; Thomas A. Apel, *Feverish Bodies, Enlightened Minds: Science and the Yellow Fever Controversy in the Early American Republic* (Stanford, CA: Stanford University Press, 2016), 1–2.

7. Smith, *Ship of Death*, 206; J. H. Powell, *Bring out Your Dead: The Great Plague of Yellow Fever in Philadelphia in 1793* (Mansfield Centre, CT: Martino, 2016), 48.

8. Smith, *Ship of Death*, 206; Powell, *Bring out Your Dead*, 125; Molly Caldwell Crosby, *The American Plague* (New York: Berkley Books, 2014), 12.

9. David De Sola Pool, *Portraits Etched in Stone; Early Jewish Settlers, 1682–1831* (New York: Columbia University Press, 1953), 269–270; C. E. Heaton, "Yellow Fever in New York City," *Bulletin of the Medical Library Association* 34, no. 2 (1946): 74; Samuel Oppenheim, "Jews Who Died of Yellow Fever in the Epidemic in New York in 1798," *PAJHS*, no. 25 (1917): 123; Joseph R. Rosenbloom, *A Biographical Dictionary of Early American Jews: Colonial Times through 1800* (Lexington: University of Kentucky Press, 1960), 123.

10. William Newnham Blane, *An Excursion through the United States and Canada during the Years 1822–23* (London: Baldwin, Cradock, and Joy, 1824), 12.

11. Heaton, "Yellow Fever in New York City," 77; Wietske Smeele, "Grounding Miasma, or Anticipating the Germ Theory of Disease in Victorian Cholera Satire," *Journal of the Midwest Modern Language Association* 49, no. 2 (2016): 17; Blane, *An Excursion through the United States and Canada*, 11–12.

12. David Soll, *Empire of Water: An Environmental and Political History of the New York City Water Supply* (Ithaca, NY: Cornell University Press, 2013), 3; Peter Solomon Townsend, *An Account of the Yellow Fever: As It Prevailed in the City of New York, in the Summer and Autumn of 1822* (New York: O. Halsted, 1823), 231.

13. Heaton, "Yellow Fever in New York City," 78.

14. *Longworth's American Almanac* (1819), 246, 247; John, "Nineteenth-Century Public Health in New York and New Orleans: A Comparison," *Louisiana History: The Journal of the Louisiana Historical Association* 15, no. 4 (1974): 330.

15. Malcolm H. Stern, *First American Jewish Families: 600 Genealogies, 1654–1977* (Cincinnati: American Jewish Archives, 1978), 150, 209; Joshua Moses, "Family Record Book, 1817–1820," PMFNY, Box 1, Folder 11: 6; *Longworth's American Almanac, New York Register, and City Directory* (New-York: Thomas Longworth, 1820), 234, 321; Eleazer Samuel Lazarus, *Circumcision Register, 1819–1843*, AJA, n.p.; Registers of Births, Deaths, Marriages, Vol. 1 1759-S, Microfilm, MF-1e, Reel 3, CSIR, 74.

16. Christine B. Hickman, "The Devil and the One Drop Rule: Racial Categories, African Americans, and the U.S. Census," *Michigan Law Review* 95, no. 5 (1997): 1178, 1187; Jane Riblett Wilkie, "The United States Population by Race and Urban-Rural Residence 1790–1860: Reference Tables," *Demography* 13, no. 1 (1976): 141.

17. Leslie M. Harris, *In the Shadow of Slavery: African Americans in New York City, 1626–1863* (Chicago: University of Chicago Press, 2003), 58, 59, 119, 121.

18. Joshua Moses, New York Ward 1, New York, New York, Census of the United States, 1820, Ancestry.com.

19. Stern, *First American Jewish Families*, 209; Registers of Births, Deaths, Marriages, Vol. 1 1759-S, Microfilm, MF-1e, Reel 3, CSIR, 79, 81; Abram R. Brandon, arrival in New York, 18 Aug 1821, *New York, Passenger and Immigration Lists, 1820–1850* [database on-line] (Ancestry.com Operations Inc, 2003).

20. *Longworth's American Almanac* 1822), 330; "The Diary of Aaron Levy" in "Items Relating to the Moses and Levy Families, New York" *PAJHS*, 27 (1920): 340; Duffy, "Nineteenth-Century Public Health in New York and New Orleans," 330; "The Life History of the Mosquito," *Monthly Bulletin of the Department of Health in the City of New York* 2, no. 7 (1912): 162; J. D. Plunkett, "Cotton as a Fomite of Yellow Fever," *The Sanitarian* 8, no. 83 (1880): 78.

21. "The Diary of Aaron Levy," 340.

22. James DeForest Stout, *Plan of Greenwich from Actual Survey, 1822*, M7.5.45, negative no. 80058d, NYHS.

23. Registers of Births, Deaths, Marriages, Vol. 1 1759-S, Microfilm, MF-1e, Reel 3, CSIR, 84; De Sola Pool, *Portraits Etched in Stone*, 413.

24. "The Diary of Aaron Levy," 339.

25. "Mortuary Notice," *National Advocate*, 5 Apr. 1823, 2.

26. Registers of Births, Deaths, Marriages, Vol. 1 1759-S, Microfilm, MF-1e, Reel 3, CSIR, 89; "The Diary of Aaron Levy," 340; Edmund M. Blunt, *Blunt's Stranger's Guide to the City of New-York: Comprising a Description of Public Buildings, Dwelling Houses* (New York: E. M. Blunt, 1817), 245.

27. Registers of Births, Deaths, Marriages, Vol. 1 1759-S, Microfilm, MF-1e, Reel 3, CSIR, 43, 89; Eli Faber, *Jews, Slaves and the*

Slave-trade: Setting the Record Straight (New York University Press, 1998), 134–135; Jonathan Schorsch, *Jews and Blacks in the Early Modern World* (New York: Cambridge University Press, 2004), 261.

28. Marriage of Margaret Gibson and John Wood (5 Feb. 1783) and Marriage of Nathaniel Simpson and Margaret Gibson (10 Aug. 1769), St. Joseph Parish, ;BCR; Baptisms of Elizabeth Wood (18 Jun. 1784), William Wood (7 Apr. 1787), Thomasin Wood (27 Oct. 1793), John Margaret Wood (6 Oct. 1799), Sarah Simpson Wood (7 Nov. 1802), Joseph Barnes Simpson Wood (16 Feb. 1806), St. Joseph Parish, BCR.

29. *Former British Colonial Dependencies Slave Registers*, 1817, 1820, 1826, 1829, 1830 [database on-line] (Ancestry.com, 2007;); Julia R. Brandon, District 20c, St. Mary Paddington, Paddington, London, *Census Returns of England and Wales, 1881*, PRO (Provo: Ancestry.com)

30. Will of Abraham Rodrigues Brandon (1831), RB 4 66/178, BDA.

31. Parish Chapel, St. Pancras, Camden, England, 68; *Church of England Parish Registers* (Provo: Ancestry.com).

32. Will of Abraham Rodrigues Brandon (1831).

33. *Former British Colonial Dependencies Slave Registers*, 1829 [database on-line] (Ancestry.com, 2007); Cheryl King, "According to the Law: Women's Property Rights in Bridgetown, Barbados, 1800–1834(1)," *Journal of Caribbean History* 36, no. 2 (2002): 268–269.

34. Stern, *First American Jewish Families*, 209; Lazarus, *Circumcision Register, 1819–1843*.

35. Sarah Ann Hays Mordecai, *Recollections of My Aunt, Rebecca Gratz* (Philadelphia, 1893), 16; Stern, *First American Jewish Families*, 209.

36. Laura Arnold Leibman, *The Art of the Jewish Family: A History of Women in Early New York in Five Objects* (New York: Bard Graduate Center, 2020), 77.

37. Mordecai, *Recollections of My Aunt*, 16–17.

38. Stern, *First American Jewish Families*, 159, 209.

39. Will of Reyna Moses (1824), *New York, Wills and Probate Records, 1659–1999* [database on-line] (Ancestry.com, 2015), x.

40. Will of Reyna Moses (1824), *New York, Wills and Probate Records, 1659–1999* [database on-line] (Ancestry.com, 2015); Measuring Worth;—Relative Worth Comparators and Data Sets, 2017. https://measuringworth.com/; Borrowing activity of Moses L. Moses and David Moses, "City Readers: Digital Historic Collections at the New York Society Library," *New York Society Library*, https://cityreaders.nysoclib.org/.

41. "Married," *Evening* Post, 25 Mar. 1824, 2; Will of Abraham Rodrigues Brandon (1831).

42. *Evening Post*, Mar. 25, 1824, 2.

43. Registers of Births, Deaths, Marriages, Vol. 1 1759-S, Microfilm, MF-1e, Reel 3, CSIR.

44. MBMNI, VIII. 7, 126.

45. Borrowing activity of Benjamin Judah, Isaac M. Gomez, Uriah Hendricks, "City Readers"; Minutes of the Trustees, Microfilm, MF-1e, Reel 2, Microdex 1, CSIR, 70–72; Register Book for the Electors of the Trustees, of the Kaal Kadosh Shearith Israel, MF-1e, Reel 6, Microdex 1, CSIR. Congregational By-Laws, Commencing 24th Sivan 5330, Microfilm, MF-1e, Reel 3, CSIR 35, 36, 39, 43.

46. Minutes of the Trustees, Microfilm, MF-1e, Reel 2, Microdex 1, CSIR, 191–193, 225–227.

47. United States, "An Act to Establish an Uniform Rule of Naturalization," 1 Stat. 103; 2 Stat. 153; Declaration of Isaac L. Brandon, 27 Jun 1826, Court of Common Pleas for the City and County of New York (005-008), Common Pleas City and County of NY (1-801), *Index to Petitions for Naturalization filed in New York City, 1792–1989* (Provo: Ancestry.com).

48. *Index to Petitions for Naturalization*, 22 April 1829.

49. Registers of Births, Deaths, Marriages, Vol. 1 1759-S, Microfilm, MF-1e, Reel 3, CSIR, 125, 129, 150.

50. *Goody Family Tree*, http://www.cvgoody.co.uk/home.htm; Register of Births 1779–1905, NISR, LMA/4521/D/01/03/002; Register Births, Marriages, Deaths—1779–1835, NISR, LMA/4521/D/01/03/001; Stern, *First American Jewish Families*, 27.

51. Register of Births 1779–1905, NISR. LMA/4521/D/01/03/002; Register Births, Marriages, Deaths—1779–1835, NISR. LMA/4521/D/01/03/001.

52. Registers of Births, Deaths, Marriages, Vol. 1 1759-S, Microfilm, MF-1e, Reel 3, CSIR.

53. De Sola Pool, *Portraits Etched in Stone*, 128. Emphasis in original.

54. Ibid., 128, 137.

55. Registers of Births, Deaths, Marriages, Vol. 1 1759-S, Microfilm, MF-1e, Reel 3, CSIR, 147.

Chapter 11

1. Roger P. Roess and Gene Sansone, *The Wheels That Drove New York: A History of the New York City Transit System* (London: Springer Science & Business Media, 2012), 4; Gerald Koeppel, *City on a Grid: How New York Became New York* (New York: Hachette Books, 2015), 182.

2. Koeppel, *City on a Grid*, 182; Felix Pascalis Ouviere, *A Statement of the Occurrences during a Malignant Yellow Fever, in the City of New York, in the Summer and Autumnal Months of 1819 and of the Check given to Its Progress, by the Measures Adopted by the Board of Health* (New York: William A. Mercein, 1819), 25: *Longworth's American Almanac, New York Register, and City Directory* (New-York: Thomas Longworth, 1828), 98, 138, 357; *Maps of the City of New York by William Perris Civil Engineer and Surveyor*, 3rd ed. (1857), Plate 8, *New York Public Library Digital Collections*, https://digitalcollections.nypl.org/items/5e66b3e9-07d4-d471-e040-e00a180654d7, accessed 16 Feb. 2020.

3. Charles Lockwood, *Manhattan Moves Uptown: An Illustrated History* (New York: Barnes, 1995), 42; Oliver E. Allen, *Tribeca: A Pictorial History* (New York: Tribeca Trib, 2010), 13; *Longworth's American Almanac, New York Register, and City Directory* (New-York: Thomas Longworth, 1830); Moses L. Moses, New York Ward 5, New York, New York, Census of the United States, 1830, Ancestry.com; "Items Relating to the Moses and Levy Families," New York." *PAJHS*, 27 (1920): 343; Will of Sarah Moses (1860), *New York, Wills and Probate Records, 1659–1999* [database on-line] (Ancestry.com, 2015); Will of Rebecca Moses (1864), *New York, Wills and Probate Records, 1659–1999* [database on-line] (Ancestry. com, 2015).

4. Advertisement, *Commercial Advertiser*, 5 Oct. 1830, 4.

5. *Longworth's American Almanac, New York Register, and City Directory* (New-York: Thomas Longworth, 1827), 98, 357; *Longworth's American Almanac, New York Register, and City Directory* (New-York: Thomas Longworth, 1828), 138, 434; *Longworth's American Almanac, New York Register, and City Directory* (New-York: Thomas Longworth, 1829), 107, 352, 415; *Maps of the City of New York*, Plate 8; "Items Relating to the Moses and Levy Families," 343; Lockwood, *Manhattan Moves Uptown*, 7, 45; Allen, *Tribeca*, 11.

6. Advertisement, *Albany Argus*, 14 Jun. 1816, 3.

7. Ibid.

8. *Longworth's American Almanac* (1830), 499, 430; Advertisement, *Commercial Advertiser*, 14 May 1830, 4; Advertisement, *Evening Post*, 26 Dec. 1831, 3; Advertisement, *Evening Post*, 10 Jan. 1832, 3; "Items Relating to the Moses and Levy Families," 343.

9. David De Sola Pool, *An Old Faith in the New World; Portrait of Shearith Israel, 1654–1954* (New York: Columbia University Press, 1955), 53; Minutes of the Trustees, Microfilm, MF-1e, Reel 2, Microdex 1, CSIR, 286–289, 305–349.

10. Advertisement, *Evening Post*, 11 Jan. 1828, 3; *Longworth's American Almanac* (1827), 98, 357; *Longworth's American Almanac* (1828); Helen Ainslie Smith, *The Great Cities of the Modern World* (New York: Routledge and Sons, 1887), 313–314.

11. Advertisement, *Evening Post*, 8 Dec. 1828, 3; Advertisement, *Evening Post*, 11 Aug. 1828, 3; Advertisement, *Evening Post*, 19 Jun. 1829: 3; Simon Werrett, *Fireworks: Pyrotechnic Arts and Sciences in European History* (Chicago: University of Chicago Press, 2010), 169, 181, 183.

12. Michael Hoberman, Laura Arnold Leibman, and Hilit Surowitz-Israel, *Jews in the Americas, 1776–1826* (London: Taylor and Francis, 2017), 40–42.

13. Jonathan Goldstein, *The Jews of China* (Armonk, NY: M. E. Sharpe, 1999), xii; Toni Pitock, "Commerce and Connection: Jewish Merchants, Philadelphia, and the Atlantic World, 1736–1822" (PhD diss., University of Delaware, 2016), 464; Solomon Moses, Journal of Voyage to Madras and Calcutta, PMFNY, Box 1, Folder 5.

14. "Activity in Real Estate. Augustin Daly Buys a Homestead on Riverside-Sales near the Appraisers' Stores," *New York Herald*, 8 Nov. 1889, 9; *New-York American for the Country*, 21 Jul. 1837, 3; Advertisement, *New York Herald*, 2 Dec. 1866, 3.

15. Advertisement, *Commercial Advertiser*, 29 Sept. 1834, 3.

16. Advertisement, *American*, 11 Jan. 1828, 2.

17. Allen, *Tribeca*, 11.

18. Ibid.

19. Advertisement, *Evening Post*, 9 Jan. 1828, 3; Advertisement, *Commercial Advertiser*, 29 Sept. 1834, 3; Georg Cavallar, *Kant's Embedded Cosmopolitanism* (Berlin: De Gruyter, 2015), 138.

20. Advertisement, *Evening Post*, 25 May 1829, 1; *The Wine-Drinker's Manual* (London: Marsh and Miller, 1830), 53.

21. Solomon Moses, Journal of Voyage to Madras and Calcutta, PMFNY, Box 1, Folder 5.

22. Advertisement, *Barbados Mercury, and Bridge-Town Gazette*, 22 Mar. 1831, 2; "Shipping News," *American*, 7 Jul. 1831, 2.

23. Will of Abraham Rodrigues Brandon (4 July 1831), RB 4 66/178, BDA; Register Births, Marriages, Deaths, 1779–1835, NISR, LMA/4521/D/01/03/001.

24. E. M. Shilstone, "The Cemetery," in *Monumental Inscriptions in the Jewish Synagogue at Bridgetown, Barbados: With Historical Notes from 1630* (Roberts Stationery, Barbados: Macmillan, 1988).

25. Shilstone, *Monumental Inscriptions*, 177; Register Births, Marriages, Deaths, 1779–1835, NISR, LMA/4521/D/01/03/001; Register of Deaths, 1660–1925, NISR, LMA/4521/D/01/03/006.

26. "SchumanGeganBruendermanSchirrmacherRittmeyer's Family Tree," Geneanet, https://gw.geneanet.org/schumangegan; Parliament of Great Britain, House of Lords, *The English Reports* (Edinburgh: W. Green & Son, 1900), 36: 876–877; Will of Abraham Rodrigues Brandon (1831), 117–118.

27. Robert Morris, "Progenitors and Coloured Elite Families: Case Studies of the Belgraves, Collymores, and Cummins," *JBMHS* 47, no. 1 (2001): 60; Kathleen M. Butler, *The Economics of Emancipation: Jamaica & Barbados, 1823–1843* (Chapel Hill: University of North Carolina Press, 1995), 88; MeasuringWorth.com.

28. Will of Abraham Rodrigues Brandon (1831), 112; Butler, *The Economics of Emancipation*, 78, 83, 109, 158, 161; *Account of the fatal hurricane, by which Barbados suffered in August 1831: to which is prefixed a succinct narrative of the convulsions of the elements, which at several times have visited and injured the West Indian Islands* (Bridge-town: Samuel Hyde, 1831), 16–29.

29. Will of Abraham Rodrigues Brandon (1831), 112.

30. Eli Faber, *Jews, Slaves and the Slave-trade: Setting the Record Straight* (New York University Press, 1998), 226–227; "Hopeland Plantation [Barbados | St Michael]," Legacies of British Slave-ownership database, http://wwwdepts-live.ucl.ac.uk/lbs/estate/view/762, accessed 3 March 2020.

31. Will of Abraham Rodrigues Brandon (1831), 118; Karl Watson, "Shifting Identities: Religion, Race, and Creolization among the Sephardi Jews of Barbados, 1654–1900," in *The Jews in the Caribbean*, ed. Jane S. Gerber (Portland: Littman Library, 2014), 221.

32. *Former British Colonial Dependencies Slave Registers*, 1817 [database on-line] (Ancestry.com, 2007), Part 1: 55; Will of George Gill (1801), RB 4 53.133, BDA.

33. *Former British Colonial Dependencies Slave Registers, 1832*, [database on-line] (Ancestry.com, 2007), Part 2: 243; Watson, "Shifting Identities," 221.

34. Will of Abraham Rodrigues Brandon (1831), 118.

35. *Former British Colonial Dependencies Slave Registers, 1817* [database on-line] (Ancestry.com, 2007), Part 1: 56; "Hopeland," Hughes/Queree Papers, Plantations, H-LAK 171-220–St. Michael, BDA; Will of Abraham Rodrigues Brandon (1831), 119.

36. *Former British Colonial Dependencies Slave Registers, 1834*, Parts 1–3: 54; Burial of Thomas Pollard (23 Apr. 1832), St. George Parish, Church of England, Burials 1801–1840, BCR; Laura Arnold Leibman, "Using Technology and DNA Genealogy to Solve Historical Mysteries," *Heritage* (Winter 2015): 21.

37. Watson, "Shifting Identities," 221; *Former British Colonial Dependencies Slave Registers, 1817*, Part 2: 801; 1826, Parts 2–5: 231; 1829, Part 3: 283; Will of Abraham Rodrigues Brandon (1831), 115.

38. Shilstone, *Monumental Inscriptions*, xix; *Account of the fatal hurricane*, Preface, 65.

39. *Account of the fatal hurricane*, 30, 33–34, 38.

40. Ibid., 65.

41. Ibid., 65–66.

42. *Former British Colonial Dependencies Slave Registers*, 1829, Parts 1, 2, 4, 5: 116.

43. *Account of the fatal hurricane*, 53, 102, 144.

44. Marriage of Sarah Simpson Wood and Daniel Goody (10 Oct. 1833), Parish Chapel, St. Pancras, Camden, England; *London, England, Church of England Marriages and Banns, 1754–1932* [database on-line], Ancestry. com; Alfred B. Goody, District 10, Ratcliff, Stepney St. Dustan, Middlesex, *1861 England Census* [database on-line] (Provo: Ancestry.com, 2005;); Daniel Goody, *Goody Family Tree*;, http://www.cvgoody.co.uk/home. htm; Sarah, Alfred, Edwin, and Emily Goody, District 10, Ratcliff, Stepney St. Dustan, Middlesex, *Census Returns of England and Wales, 1841*, PRO (Provo: Ancestry.com); Alfred B. Goody, Servants of W.T. Walmsley, Marple 1b, Cheshire, *Census Returns of England and Wales, 1851*;, PRO (Provo: Ancestry.com); Cecily Jones, *Engendering Whiteness: White Women and Colonialism in Barbados and North Carolina, 1627–1865* (Manchester: Manchester University Press, 2007), 18, 32.

45. Annie Gegan, instant message to Laura Arnold Leibman, 24 Jan. 2020; Will of Abraham Rodrigues Brandon (1831), 119.

46. Esther Brandon, District 13, Peckham, St. Giles Camberwell, Surrey, *Census Returns of England and Wales, 1841,* PRO (Provo: Ancestry.com).

47. Israel Finestein, *Anglo-Jewry in Changing Times: Studies in Diversity 1840–1914* (London: Mitchell, 1999), 40; Jeffrey Baum, *A Light unto My Path: The Story of H.N. Solomon of Edmonton* (Edmonton, UK: Edmonton Hundred Historical Society, 1981), 10–11, 22.

48. Joseph Brandon, District 2, Edmonton, Middlesex, *Census Returns of England and Wales, 1841,* PRO (Provo: Ancestry.com); Baum, *A Light unto My Path,* 22; Cecil Roth, "The Jews in the English Universities," *Miscellanies (Jewish Historical Society of England)* 4 (1942): 107–108; Herbert Fry, *Our Schools and Colleges. Containing the principal particulars respecting endowed Grammar Schools . . . as also information respecting Colleges and Universities* (London: R. Hardwicke, 1868), 98; Manumission of Sarah and Isaac Lopez (1801/2), Deed Hannah Esther Lopez to Abraham Rodrigues Brandon, 5 Aug 1802, R/1 Deeds 1801, vol. 219.9, BDA.

49. "Mortuary Notice," *Evening Post,* 8 Dec. 1837, 3; *New York City Directory, 1837/38* (New-York: Thomas Longworth, 1837), 382, 450, DCNYPL; Aaron Levy, New York Ward 5, New York, New York, Census of the United States, 1840, Ancestry.com.

50. Congregation Shearith Israel, "Association for the Moral & Religious Instruction of Children of the Jewish Faith Meeting Minutes, 1838–1846," Sunday November 24, 1839, Sunday October 14, 1838, and Sunday March 1, 1840, Sisterhood Records, CSIA; Will of Joshua Moses (1838), 158, *New York, Wills and Probate Records, 1659–1999,* Ancestry.com; "Mortuary Notice [of Reyna Moses]," *Spectator,* 8 Sep. 1847, 3.

51. Will of Joshua Moses (3 Jan. 1838), 158–159.

52. Ibid.; Joshua Moses, Papers and Estate Inventory, PMFNY, Box 1, Folder 10; Petition Papers for Joshua Moses (22 Jan. 1838), 1671, *New York, Wills and Probate Records, 1659–1999,* Ancestry.com.

53. Advertisement, *Mercantile Advertiser,* 18 Sep. 1819, 3.

54. Advertisement, *Commercial Advertiser,* 13 Dec. 1833, 4; Advertisement, *American,* 25 Oct. 1833, 3; Moses, Papers and Estate Inventory, 13–15.

55. Petition Papers for Joshua Moses (19 Mar. 1842), 2060, *New York, Wills and Probate Records, 1659–1999,* Ancestry.com.

56. Real Estate Proceedings for the Estate of Joshua Moses (Case 16), 72, Records of Wills and Probates, 1659–1999, Ancestry.com.

57. MBMNI, IV.122.

58. MBMNI, IV.122–135.

59. Aviva Ben-Ur, *Jewish Autonomy in a Slave Society: Suriname in the Atlantic World, 1651–1825* (Philadelphia: University of Pennsylvania Press, 2020), 223.

60. Melanie Newton, *The Children of Africa in the Colonies: Free People of Color in Barbados in the Age of Emancipation* (Baton Rouge: Louisiana State University Press, 2008), 121; MBMNI, VI.1; "List of Annual Subscribers," *The Voice of Jacob,* 29 Sept. 1843: 8; "List of Subscribers," *The Voice of Jacob,*

26 Sept. 1845: 12; "Testimonial to E. A. Moses, Esq.," *Jewish Chronicle*, 8 Feb. 1850, 139–140; Ketubot Marriage Contract Book, 1786–1851.

61. News Article, *Barbados Globe*, 25 Oct. 1846, 4; *Barbados Globe*, 17 Sep. 1846, 2; Tim J. Watts, "Brown Privilege Bill (1831)," in *Encyclopedia of Blacks in European History and Culture*, ed. Eric Martone (Westport, CT: Greenwood Press, 2008), 97.

62. News Article, *[New York] Herald*, 28 Dec. 1842, 5; *Doggett's New York City Directory for 1847 & 1848* (New-York: John Doggett, 1847), 60, 296.

Chapter 12

1. "Foreign: Seven Days Later from Europe," *Christian Intelligencer*, 1 Jun. 1839, 3; "Custom-House Notice," *Herald*, 16 Jan. 1843, 5; "A Lecture," *Commercial Advertiser*, 9 Oct. 1839, 2; "The Daguerreotype Apparatus," *Evening Post*, 3 Mar. 1840, 1.

2. "The Daguerreotype Apparatus," *Evening Post*, 6 Mar. 1840, 4; "Mr. Woolcott; Granite; Building; Corner; Broadway; Chambers; Improved; Face," *Evening Post*, 20 Apr. 1840, 2.

3. Robert Wilson, *Mathew Brady: Portraits of a Nation* (New York: Bloomsbury, 2013), 38.

4. "Recent Deaths," *Jewish Messenger*, 1 Mar. 1895, 2.

5. N. Taylor Phillips, "The Levy and Seixas Families of Newport and New York," PAJHS, no. 4 (1896): 210.

6. July 14, 1839, Nov. 7, 1841, Dec. 21, 1839, Nov. 24, 1839;, Oct. 27, 1839, July 7, 1839, in Congregation Shearith Israel, "Association for the Moral & Religious Instruction of Children of the Jewish Faith Meeting Minutes, 1838–1846," Sisterhood Records. CSIA.

7. *Doggett's New-York City Directory for 1845 & 1846* (New-York: John Doggett, 1845), 218, 262; *Doggett's New-York City Directory for 1846 & 1847* (New-York: John Doggett, 1846), 284.

8. Advertisement for Isaac Moses & Brother, *New York Journal of Commerce*, 29 Jul. 1843, 1; "Commencement; Columbia College; Tuesday; St. George Chapel; Notified; Persons; Columns," *Commercial Advertiser*, 15 Oct. 1841, 2.

9. John Watson, Letter of Recommendation, 14 Feb. 1845, for Israel Moses, College of Physicians and Surgeons Student Records ca. 1828–1857, 1873–1902, ASC; Israel Moses, "Exhaustion by Heat and the Effects of Cold Drinks When Heated," *New York Medical and Surgical Reporter*, 1, no. 1 (1845): 11–15; William Logie Russell, *The New York Hospital* (New York: Arno Press, 1973), 36, 3; I. Michael Leitman, "The Evolution of Surgery at the New York Hospital," *Bulletin of the New York Academy of Medicine* 67, no. 5 (1991): 475; John Watson, "An Inquiry into the Pathology and Treatment of Secondary Abscesses, and Other Consecutive Disorders Resulting from Injuries and Surgical Operations," *American Journal of the Medical Sciences* 21, no. 41 (1837): 37–76; John Watson, "Observations on the Nature and Treatment of Telangiectasis, or that Morbid State of the Blood-Vessels which Gives Rise to Naevus and

Aneurism from Anastomosis," *American Journal of the Medical Sciences* 24, no. 47 (1839): 24–49.

10. College of Physicians and Surgeons Student Records, c. 1828–1857, 1873–1902, ASC; Moses, "Exhaustion by Heat and the Effects of Cold Drinks When Heated."

11. *New-York City and Co-Partnership Directory, 1843 & 1844* (New-York: John Doggett, 1843), 246.

12. Bob Vietrogoski, "The Case of Mr. J. P. Barnet (Col. Student): An Unusual Instance of Racial Discrimination in 19th-Century Medical Education" (2011), 1–3, ASC.

13. Arthur H. Aufses Jr. and Barbara Niss, *This House of Noble Deeds: The Mount Sinai Hospital, 1852–2002* (New York: New York University Press, 2002), 2, 161; *Doggett's New-York City Directory for 1847 & 1848* (New-York: John Doggett, 1847), 296.

14. Israel Moses, 6th Infantry, 1844–1848, U.S. Returns from Regular Army Infantry Regiments, 1821–1916, Ancestry.com; Jonathan Sutherland, *African Americans at War: An Encyclopedia* (Santa Barbara, CA: ABC-CLIO, 2004), 434–440; Christine McEvilly, Guide to the Papers of the Moses Family of New York, undated, 1767–1941, 1971, P-1, *Center for Jewish History,* https://digifindingaids.cjh.org/?pID=364719.

15. Charles K. Gardner, *A Dictionary of all Officers: who have been commissioned, or have been appointed and served, in the army of the United States, since the inauguration of their first president, in 1789, to the first January, 1853* (New York: D. Van Nostrand, 1860), 331, 513, 620; Karl Jack Bauer and Robert Johansen, *The Mexican War 1846–1848* (Lincoln: University of Nebraska Press, 1992), 232; Marley, *Historic Cities of the Americas,* 2: 301, 316; Israel Moses, Map, Correspondence, and Military Records", PMFNY, Box 2, Folder 3.

16. Israel Moses, "ART. II. Military Surgery and Operations following the Battle of Rivas, Nicaragua, April, 1856," *American Journal of the Medical Sciences* 65, no. 1 (1857): 26; Michael Zakim and Gary J. Kornblith, "Introduction," in *Capitalism Takes Command: The Social Transformation of Nineteenth-Century America,* ed. Michael Zakim and Gary J. Kornblith (Chicago: University of Chicago Press, 2012), 1–12.;

17. William Walker, *The War in Nicaragua* (New York: S. H. Goetzel & Company, 1860), 25, 159, 258–259; Michel Gobat, *Empire by Invitation: William Walker and Manifest Destiny in Central America* (Cambridge, MA: Harvard University Press, 2018), 123, 206, 237–238; Marco Cabrera Geserick, *The Legacy of the Filibuster War: National Identity and Collective Memory in Central America* (London: Lexington Books, 2019), xv–xvi; Mark Allan Goldberg, *Conquering Sickness: Race, Health, and Colonization in the Texas Borderlands* (Lincoln: University of Nebraska Press, 2017), 146–147; Moses, "ART. II," 33.

18. Heather Fowler-Salamini and Mary Vaughan, eds., *Women of the Mexican Countryside, 1850–1990: Creating Spaces, Shaping Transitions*

(Tucson: University of Arizona Press, 1994), 54–55; Richard J. Salvucci, "The Origins and Progress of U.S.–Mexican Trade, 1825–1884: 'Hoc Opus, Hic Labor Est,'" *Hispanic American Historical Review* 71, no. 4 (1991): 704, 708, 711.

19. "Importations at New York: Foreign," *Shipping and Commercial List and New-York Price Current*, 21 Mar. 1849; "Trade Items," *American Stationer*, 1 Apr. 1897, 519; Richard Edwards, *New York's Great Industries: Exchange and Commercial Review* (New York: Historical, 1884), 206; "Report from the Secretary of State," *Congressional Edition*, 591 (1851): 37; *Selections from the Collected Papers of the Lower Rio Grande Valley Historical Society* (Harlington, TX: Lon C. Hill Memorial Library, 1979); "Recent Deaths," *American Lawyer* 9, no. 3 (1901): 134.

20. United States, *Treaties and other International Acts of the United States of America* (Washington, DC: United States. Dept. of State, 1931), 6: 435; "Report from the Secretary of State," *Congressional Edition*, 591 (1851): 37; United States Senate, *Executive Documents*, 1858–59, 83; Measuring Worth–Relative Worth Comparators and Data Sets. 2017. https://measuringworth.com/.

21. *Doggett's New-York City Directory for 1847 & 1848*, 296; United States Senate, *Executive Documents*, 1858–59, 702, 727–728, 730, 733–734; John D. Wong, *Global Trade in the Nineteenth Century: The House of Houqua and the Canton System* (Cambridge: Cambridge University Press, 2016), 25, 87; Paul Arthur Van Dyke, *The Canton Trade: Life and Enterprise on the China Coast, 1700–1845* (Hong Kong: Hong Kong University Press, 2005), 1, 36, 95–96, 113, 122–124.

22. Johnathan Farris, *Enclave to Urbanity: Canton, Foreigners, and Architecture from the Late Eighteenth to the Early Twentieth Centuries* (Hong Kong: Hong Kong University Press, 2017), 16; Paul Arthur Van Dyke and Maria Kar-wing Mok, *Images of the Canton Factories 1760–1822: Reading History in Art* (Hong Kong: Hong Kong University Press, 2015), 73–74, 86–87; "List of Foreign Residents in Canton," *Chinese Repository*, Aug. 1846: 426–430; Edwards, *New York's Great Industries*, 206.

23. Jacques M. Downs, *Golden Ghetto—the American Commercial Community at Canton and the Shaping of American China Policy, 1784–1844* (Hong Kong: Hong Kong University Press, 2015), 311.

24. Letter, John Heard (Canton) to "Capt. Graves," 5 May 1844, quoted in Goldstein, Jonathan Goldstein, *The Jews of China* (Armonk, NY: M. E. Sharpe, 1999), xvi; Paul Arthur Van Dyke, "Ambiguous Faces of the Canton Trade: Moors, Greeks, Armenians, Parsees, Jews, and Southeast Asians," in *The Private Side of the Canton Trade, 1700–1840: Beyond the Companies*, ed. Paul Arthur Van Dyke and Susan E. Schopp (Hong Kong: Hong Kong University Press, 2018), 21.

25. Letter, Nathaniel Kinsman to Rebecca Kinsman, 4 Dec. 1844, quoted in Goldstein, *The Jews of China*, xvi.

26. Letter, Nathaniel Kinsman to Rebecca Kinsman, 17 Dec. 1844, quoted in Goldstein, *The Jews of China*, xvi.

27. Joseph Moses, Arrival in New York from Canton, 3 Oct. 1846, *New York, U.S., Arriving Passenger and Immigration Lists, 1820–1850*, Ancestry. com; "List of Foreign Residents in Canton," *Chinese Repository*, August 1846: 426–430; Farris, *Enclave to Urbanity*, 13, 28–29.

28. "Trade Items," *The American Stationer*, 1 Apr. 1897, 519; Dana Leo-Paul, "The Mizrahim: Anglicized Orientals with Transnational Networks and 'Ethics Capital,'" in *Entrepreneurship and Religion*, ed. Leo-Paul Dana (Cheltenham, UK: Edward Elgar, 2010), 66–67; Jonathan Goldstein, *Jewish Identities in East and Southeast Asia: Singapore, Manila, Taipei, Harbin, Shanghai, Rangoon, and Surabaya* (Boston: De Gruyter Oldenbourg, 2015), 136; Goldstein, *Jews of China*, xii; Malcolm H. Stern, *First American Jewish Families: 600 Genealogies, 1654–1977* (Cincinnati: American Jewish Archives, 1978), 67, 87, 209; Van Dyke, "Ambiguous Faces of the Canton Trade," 35.

29. William C. Hunter, *Bits of Old China* (Taiwan: K. Paul, Trench, & Company, 1885), 35; Van Dyke, "Ambiguous Faces of the Canton Trade," 35, 37; Farris, *Enclave to Urbanity*, 10; Christian Henriot, *New Frontiers: Imperialism's New Communities in East Asia, 1842–1953* (Manchester: Manchester University Press, 2000), 39–40.

30. Joan S. Rowland, *The Jewish Communities of India: Identity in a Colonial Era* (New Brunswick, NJ: Transaction, 1998), 16.

31. Watson, "Shifting Identities," 210; Lionel Moses, Letter on Masonic Business, Odd Fellows Membership Certificates and Resolution on Death, PMFNY, Box 2, Folder 4.

32. United States Senate, *Executive Documents*, 1858–59, 728.

33. Edwards, *New York's Great Industries*, 206.

34. Richard Allen Landes, *Heaven on Earth: The Varieties of the Millennial Experience* (New York: Oxford University Press, 2011), 207; Christopher Munn, *Anglo-China: Chinese People and British Rule in Hong Kong, 1841–1880* (London: Taylor & Francis, 2013), 236; Stephen R. Platt, *Autumn in the Heavenly Kingdom: China, the West, and the Epic Story of the Taiping Civil War* (New York: Alfred A. Knopf, 2012), xxii, 18; Dorothy Perkins, *Encyclopedia of China: History and Culture* (London: Taylor & Francis, 2013), 194.

35. Steve A. Tsang, *Modern History of Hong Kong: 1841–1997* (London: Bloomsbury, 2003), 54; Munn, *Anglo-China*, 236.

36. United States Senate, *Executive Documents*, 1858–59, 725, 727, 733; "Obituary," *New York Herald*, 16 Dec. 1889, 10; Jules Davids, *American Diplomatic and Public Papers: The United States and China* (Wilmington: Scholarly Press, 1973), 352; "Arrivals," *Herald*, 1 Jul. 1853, 9; Letter on Masonic Business.

37. Farris, *Enclave to Urbanity*, 64–65.

38. "Trade Items," *The American Stationer*, 1 Apr. 1897, 519; Stern, *First American Jewish Families*, 264.

39. Letter from Israel Moses to Selina Seixas Moses (March 15, 1862;), Letter from Israel Moses to Lionel and Brandon Moses (April 19, 1862;), in Israel Moses, Map, Correspondence, and Military Records, PMFNY, Box 2, Folder 3.
40. Letter from Israel Moses to Selina Seixas Moses (February 2, 1862;) in Israel Moses, Map, Correspondence, and Military Records, PMFNY, Box 2, Folder 3.
41. Letter from Israel Moses to Selina Seixas Moses (February 2, 1862;), Letter from Israel Moses to Selina Seixas Moses (March 15, 1862;), Letter from Israel Moses to Selina Seixas Moses (November 7, 1861;) in Israel Moses, Map, Correspondence, and Military Records, PMFNY, Box 2, Folder 3.
42. Letter from Israel Moses to Selina Seixas Moses (March 15, 1862,) in Israel Moses, Map, Correspondence, and Military Records, PMFNY, Box 2, Folder 3.
43. Letter from Israel Moses to Selina Seixas Moses (November 7, 1861,) in Israel Moses, Map, Correspondence, and Military Records, PMFNY, Box 2, Folder 3.
44. Photograph 19, verso, Photographs, PMFNY, Box 3, Folder 3.
45. Photograph 46, verso, Photographs, PMFNY, Box 3, Folder 3.
46. Shalom Goldman, "Joshua/James Seixas (1802–1874): Jewish Apostasy and Christian Hebraism in Early Nineteenth-Century America," *Jewish History* 7, no. 1 (1993): 66–67, 71, 73, 77, 82. Shalom Goldman, *God's Sacred Tongue: Hebrew and the American Imagination* (Chapel Hill: University of North Carolina Press, 2004), 177, 193–194.
47. Photographs 33, verso, & 39, Photographs, PMFNY, Box 3, Folder 3.
48. David De Sola Pool, *An Old Faith in the New World; Portrait of Shearith Israel, 1654–1954* (New York: Columbia University Press, 1955), 143; *The New York Charities Directory* (New York: Charity Organization Society in the City of New York, 1890), 42; Goldman, "Joshua/James Seixas," 83.
49. Stern, *First American Jewish Families*, 209; *Trow's New York City Directory for the Year Ending in 1860*, ed. H. Wilson (New York: Trow, 1859), 578; *Trow's New York City Directory for the Year Ending in 1861*, ed. H. Wilson (New York: Trow, 1860), 618; *Trow's New York City Directory for the Year Ending in 1866*, ed. H. Wilson (New York: Trow, 1865), 698; *Trow's New York City Directory for the Year Ending in 1871*, ed. H. Wilson (New York: Trow, 1870), 868; *Trow's New York City Directory for the Year Ending in 1876*, ed. H. Wilson (New York: Trow, 1875), 954; *Trow's New York City Directory for the Year Ending in 1881*, ed. H. Wilson (New York: Trow, 1880), 1114; *Trow's New York City Directory for the Year Ending in 1886*, (New York: Trow, 1885), 1366; *Trow's New York City Directory for the Year Ending in 1889* (New York: Trow, 1888), 1422.
50. "Trade Items," *American Stationer*, 1 Apr. 1897, 519.
51. "Mortuary Notice," *Evening Post*, 6 Oct. 1870, 3.

52. "Hebrew Relief Society," *Manual of the Corporation of the City of New York* (1970): 596; *Trow's New York City Directory*, vol. 92 (New York: Trow, 1879), 18.

53. Joseph R. Brandon, 6., St. Stephen Coleman Street, Middlesex, *Census Returns of England and Wales, 1851*, PRO (Provo: Ancestry.com); *Trow's New York City Directory for the Year Ending 1851–52* (New York: Trow, 1888), 71; Steamship *Pacific*, 9 Aug. 1852, *New York, Passenger and Immigration Lists, 1820–1850* [database on-line] (Ancestry.com Operations Inc, 2003); News article, *Shipping and Commercial List and New-York Price Current*, 31 Dec. 1851, 4; "Marriages (1849–1852)," *New York Evening Post, U.S. Newspaper Extractions from the Northeast.*

54. Judah Samuel Abecasis, 8a, All Hallows London Wall, Middlesex, *Census Returns of England and Wales, 1851*; Daniel J. Schroeter, *The Sultan's Jew: Morocco and the Sephardi World* (Palo Alto, CA: Stanford University Press, 2002), 71; *Jews' Infant School, 127 Houndsditch . . . Address on the opening of the School . . . 14 Sept. 1841, with a list of Subscribers, etc.* (London: J. Wertheimer & Company, 1841), 8; A. G. Grimwade, "Anglo-Jewish Silver," *Transactions (Jewish Historical Society of England)* 18 (1953): 117–118; "Letter Paper," *Shipping and Commercial List and New-York Price Current*, 15 Dec. 1852, 3; *New York City Directory, 1853/54* (New-York: John F. Trow, 1853), 21, 84, DCNYPL.

55. *Steinn Mertin* (1 Jul. 1853), *New York, Passenger and Immigration Lists, 1820–1850;* [database on-line] (Ancestry.com Operations Inc, 2003); "For sale or to let the three story basement house," *[New York] Herald*, 5 Mar. 1854, 8; Steamship *Peytona* (2 Sept. 1854) and Bark *Francis* (8 March 1855), *Hawaii, Passenger Lists, 1843–1898* [database on-line] (Provo: Ancestry.com, 2016;); "J.R. Brandon & Co.," *Shipping and Commercial List and New-York Price Current*, 31 Mar. 1855, 3.

56. Letter from Israel Moses to Selina Seixas Moses (February 2, 1862,) in Israel Moses, Map, Correspondence, and Military Records, PMFNY, Box 2, Folder 3; Lavinia Abecasis, New York City Ward 21, E.D. 1, New York, "New York State Census, 1855," database with images, *FamilySearch*, http://FamilySearch.org, 4 March 2020; *Finance and Industry: The New York Stock Exchange: Banks, Bankers, Business Houses, and Moneyed Institutions* (New York: Historical Pub. Co., 1866), 131; J. S. Abecasis (1866, New York), *U.S. IRS Tax Assessment Lists, 1862–1918* [database on-line] (Ancestry.com, 2008).

57. Letter from Israel Moses to Selina Seixas Moses (November 7, 1861),, in Israel Moses, Map, Correspondence, and Military Records, PMFNY, Box 2, Folder 3

58. *New York City Directory, 1855/56* (New-York: John F. Trow, 1853), 22, 100, DCNYPL; "Jules S. Abecasis Buried," *New York Tribune*, 7 July 1896, 4; Esther and Aaron Abecasis, District 10, Christchurch, St. Marylebone, Middlesex, *1861 England Census;* Moses Gaster, *History of the Ancient Synagogue of the Spanish and Portuguese Jews* (London: 1901),

195; *Ascamot: or, Laws and Regulations of the Congregation of Spanish and Portuguese Jews, entitled [Sha' ar ha-shamayim] London, and Congregational Trusts* (London: Wertheimer, Lea, 1906), 47.

59. Robert Macoy, *How to See New York and Its Environs, 1776–1876: A Complete Guide and Hand-book of Useful Information, Collected from the Latest Reliable Sources* (New York: R. Macoy, 1875), 88; Ward McAllister, "The Only Four Hundred," *New York Times*, 16 Feb. 1892; Advertisement, *Harper's New Monthly Magazine* 37, no. 220 (1868): 581.

60. "By the Pilot Line Things in New York New York, December 13th. 1855," *Public Ledger*, 14 Dec. 1855, 3; *New York City Directory, 1854/55* (New-York: John F. Trow, 1853), 535, DCNYPL.

61. "For Sale–The First Class Four Story," *Evening Post*, 23 Sep. 1859, 3.

62. Will of Abraham Rodrigues Brandon (1831).

63. Will of Isaac Lopez Brandon (10 Oct. 1856), *New York, Wills and Probate Records, 1659–1999*, Ancestry.com.

64. "A Gentleman and His Wife Can Obtain," *New York Herald*, 7 Sep. 1863, 3; Marriage of Abraham R. Brandon and Miriam Smith (17 Aug. 1857), *New York, Episcopal Diocese of New York Church Records, 1767–1970* [database on-line], Ancestry.com, 2017.

65. Baptism of Constance Evelyn R. Brandon (6 May 1869), *New York, Episcopal Diocese of New York Church Records, 1767–1970*; Photographs related to Henry William Poor, MCNY. I am grateful to Brian T. P. Blake for noting the menorah in his family history.

Epilogue

1. Blanche Moses, Genealogy researched by Blanche of the Moses, Levy, and Seixas, 1895–1941, PMFNY, Box 2, Folder 6.

2. François Weil, *Family Trees* (Cambridge, MA: Harvard University Press, 2013), 112, 136; Morris Jastrow, "Notes on the Jews of Philadelphia, from Published Annals," *Publications of the American Jewish Historical Society*, no. 1 (1893): 56, 57, http://www.jstor.org/stable/43058507.

3. Jane Riblett Wilkie, "The United States Population by Race and Urban-Rural Residence 1790–1860: Reference Tables," *Demography* 13, no. 1 (1976): 141; Christine B. Hickman, "The Devil and the One Drop Rule: Racial Categories, African Americans, and the U.S. Census." *Michigan Law Review* 95, no. 5 (1997): 1178.

4. Bureau of the Census, Fourteenth Census of the United States (1923), emphasis added.

5. Hickman, "The Devil and the One Drop Rule," 1187; Jennifer Lee and Frank D. Bean, *The Diversity Paradox: Immigration and the Color Line in Twenty-First-Century America* (New York: Russell Sage Foundation, 2010), 121.

6. Blanche Moses, Manhattan Assembly District 13, New York, New York, Census of the United States, 1920, Ancestry.com .

7. Malcolm H. Stern, "Two Studies in the Assimilation of Early American Jewry" (PhD diss., Hebrew Union College, 1957); Jonathan Schorsch, "American Jewish Historians, Colonial Jews and Blacks, and the Limits of 'Wissenschaft': A Critical Review," *Jewish Social Studies* 6, no. 2 (2000): 104, 108–111.

8. Karen Brodkin, *How Jews Became White Folks and What That Says about Race in America* (New Brunswick, NJ: Rutgers University Press, 1998), 2, 25–26, 44.

9. Lewis R. Gordon, "Rarely Kosher: Studying Jews of Color in North America," *American Jewish History* 100, no. 1 (2016): 110; Bruce D. Haynes, *The Soul of Judaism: Jews of African Descent in America* (New York: New York University Press, 2018), 78; Roberta S. Gold, "The Black Jews of Harlem: Representation, Identity, and Race, 1920–1939," *American Quarterly* 55, no. 2 (2003): 183–84; Maurianne Adams and John H. Bracey, eds., *Strangers & Neighbors: Relations between Blacks & Jews in the United States* (Amherst: University of Massachusetts Press, 1999); Eric J. Sundquist, *Strangers in the Land: Blacks, Jews, Post-Holocaust America* (Cambridge, MA: Harvard University Press, 2005).

10. Gold, "The Black Jews of Harlem," 194; James E. Landing, *Black Judaism: Story of an American Movement* (Durham, NC: Carolina Academic Press, 2001), 181.

11. Gold, "The Black Jews of Harlem," 195.

12. Jonathan D. Sarna, *American Judaism: A History* (New Haven, CT: Yale University Press, 2019); Hasia R. Diner, *The Jews of the United States, 1654 to 2000* (Berkeley: University of California Press, 2004); Jeffrey S. Gurock, *When Harlem Was Jewish, 1870–1930* (New York: Columbia University Press, 1979). Gurock has corrected this in his more recent *The Jews of Harlem: The Rise, Decline, and Revival of a Jewish Community* (New York: New York University Press, 2016), though they still receive little space; Haynes, *The Soul of Judaism*, 67–82; Tudor Parfitt, *Black Jews in Africa and the Americas* (Cambridge, MA: Harvard University Press, 2013), 76; Marla Brettschneider, *The Jewish Phenomenon in Sub-Saharan Africa: The Politics of Contradictory Discourses* (Lewiston, NY: Edwin Mellen Press, 2015); Noah Tamarkin, *Genetic Afterlives: Black Jewish Indigeneity in South Africa* (Durham, NC: Duke University Press, 2020), 6, 70.

13. Landing, *Black Judaism*, 119–120.

14. Irma Miriam Lopes Cardozo, *As I Lived It* (New York: Irma Miriam Lopes, 2010), 102.

15. UJA-Federation of New York, *Special Study on Nonwhite, Hispanic, and Multiracial Jewish Households*, Berman Jewish Databank, June 2014, https://www.ujafedny.org/api/v2/assets/789938/, accessed 25 March 2015.

16. Marc Dollinger, *Black Power, Jewish Politics: Reinventing the Alliance in the 1960s* (Waltham, MA: Brandeis University Press, 2018), 189.

17. *Charter, Constitution and By-laws of the Saint Nicholas Society of the City of New York* (New York: Printed by Order of the Society, 1904), 23–24.
18. "The Society of Colonial Wars," https://www.colonialwarsny.org/, accessed 25 March 2020.
19. Weil, *Family Trees*, 112.
20. Brian P. T. Blake, "Introduction to the Brandon Family" (unpublished manuscript, 2016), 1, In collection of Laura Arnold Leibman.
21. Will of Sarah Moses (1860), *New York, Wills and Probate Records, 1659–1999* [database on-line] (Ancestry.com, 2015).
22. Letter from Israel Moses to Selina Seixas Moses, 7 November1861, "Map, Correspondence, and Military Records," Moses Family Papers, PMFNY in AJHS.
23. Will of Rebecca Moses (1864), 382, *New York, Wills and Probate Records, 165–1999* [database on-line] (Ancestry.com, 2015).
24. Will of Abraham Rodriguez Brandon (1860), 418, *New York, Wills and Probate Records, 1659–1999* [database on-line] (Ancestry.com, 2015); Malcolm H. Stern, *First American Jewish Families: 600 Genealogies, 1654– 1977* (Cincinnati: American Jewish Archives, 1978), 27.
25. Probate Proceedings for the Estate of Rebecca Moses, 6396, *New York, Wills and Probate Records, 1659–1999* [database on-line] (Ancestry.com, 2015); Stern, *First American Jewish Families*, 209.
26. Alfred Moses and Paula Barrera (Roma, Texas), Eighth Census of the United States; Bertha C. Ramirez, email to Laura Leibman, 28 February 2020; Alfred Moses (Roma, Starr, Texas), all in Ninth Census of the United States, 1870, Ancestry.com.
27. Annie Gegan, instant message to Laura Arnold Leibman, 24 January 2020; Ava Fran Kahn, *Jewish Voices of the California Gold Rush: A Documentary History, 1849–1880* (Detroit: Wayne State University Press, 2002), 451.

BIBLIOGRAPHY

PERIODICALS

Albany Argus (Albany, NY), 1813–1856
American (New York, NY), 1819–1834
The American Lawyer (New York, NY), 1893–1908
The American Stationer (New York, NY), 1873–1916
Barbados Globe (Bridgetown, Barbados), 1837–1926
Barbados Mercury, and Bridge-Town Gazette (Bridgetown, Barbados), 1762–1848
The Chinese Repository (Canton, China), 1832–1851
Columbian (New York, NY), 1850–1919
Christian Intelligencer (New York, NY), 1830–1920
Commercial Advertiser (New York, NY), 1797–1904
Evening Post (New York, NY), 1801–1934
Freedom's Journal (New York, NY), 1827–1829
Harper's New Monthly Magazine (New York, NY), 1850–present
The Jewish Chronicle (London, England), 1841–present
Manual of the Corporation of the City of New York (New York, NY), 1841–1870
Mercantile Advertiser (New York, NY), 1798–1833
The Methodist Magazine (London, England), 1798–1821
Moody's Magazine (New York, NY), 1906–1917
The National Advocate (New York, NY), 1812–1829
New-York American for the Country (New York, NY), 1821–1845
New-York Gazette & General Advertiser, 1795–1820
New York Herald (New York, NY), 1835–1924
New York Journal of Commerce (New York, NY), 1827–present
New York Times (New York, NY), 1851–present

New York Tribune (New York, NY), 1841–1966
The Occident and American Jewish Advocate (Philadelphia, PA), 1843–1869
Pennsylvania Packet (Philadelphia, PA), 1771–1840
Public Ledger (Philadelphia, PA), 1836–1942
Shipping and Commercial List and New-York Price Current (New York, NY), 1815–1926
Spectator (New York, NY), 1804–1867
Surinaamsche Courant (Paramaribo, Suriname), 1804–1842

PRIMARY SOURCES

1853 Arrival: New York, New York. Microfilm Serial: *M237, 1820–1897*; Microfilm Roll: *Roll 128.*
1861 England Census [database online]. Provo: Ancestry.com, 2005.
Account Book of Moses Lopez, 1779–1789, NYHS Library, Mss. Collection.
Account of the fatal hurricane, by which Barbados suffered in August 1831: to which is prefixed a succinct narrative of the convulsions of the elements, which at several times have visited and injured the West Indian Islands. Bridge-town: Samuel Hyde, 1831.
Acts: Barbados, No. 225. CO 30/17, fos. 48–50, TNA.
A list of 1,351 "free black and coloured" heads of families with the total number of their families and of their slaves, together with the first batch of population [census] returns number 1–200 collected as required by the governor's proclamation of 17 October 1811. Kew, Surrey, England: CO 278/22.
Amsterdam—Burials of the Portuguese Israelite Congregation (Database), https://web.archive.org/web/20080706133856/http://akevoth.org/beithhaim/login.asp.
Appraisement of the Estate of Katherine Bab Barrow Deceas'd Reced & filed 11 July 1809, BDA.
Ascamot: or, Laws and Regulations of the Congregation of Spanish and Portuguese Jews, entitled [Sha' ar ha-shamayim] London, and Congregational Trusts. London: Wertheimer, Lea, 1906.
Barbados Church Records, 1637–1887 (database). *FamilySearch*, https://www.familysearch.org/search/collection/1923399.
Benoit, J. P. *Voyage a Surinam: description des possessions Néerlandaises dans la Guyane.* Amsterdam: Emmering, 1967.
Blane, William Newnham. *An Excursion Through the United States and Canada During the Years 1822–23.* London: Baldwin, Cradock, and Joy, 1824.
Blunt, Edmund M. *Blunt's Stranger's Guide to the City of New-York: Comprising a Description of Public Buildings, Dwelling Houses.* New York: E. M. Blunt, 1817.
Census Returns of England and Wales, 1841. PRO. Provo: Ancestry.com.
Census Returns of England and Wales, 1851. PRO. Provo: Ancestry.com.
Census Returns of England and Wales, 1881. .
Census of the United States, 1790, 1810, 1820, 1830, 1840, 1860, 1870, 1920.PRO. Provo: Ancestry.com.

Charter, Constitution and By-laws of the Saint Nicholas Society of the City of New York. New York: Printed by Order of the Society, 1904.

Church of England Parish Registers. Parish Chapel, St. Pancras, Camden, England. Provo: Ancestry.com.

"City Readers: Digital Historic Collections at the New York Society Library." *New York Society Library.* https://cityreaders.nysoclib.org/.

Cohen d'Azevedo Receipt book 1811–1816, AJHS.

College of Physicians and Surgeons Student Records c. 1828–1857, 1873–1902. Columbia University Health Sciences Library, Archives and Special Collections, New York, NY.

Congregation Mikveh Israel (Philadelphia, PA). Manuscript Collection no. 552, American Jewish Archives.

Congregation Shearith Israel Records, 1759–1932, American Jewish Archives.

Conversion and Circumcision of Isaac Lopez Brandon, 24 December 1812. Trans. Aviva Ben-.Ur, 1.05.11.18:5, 56 Inventaris van het digitaal duplicaat van het archief van de Nederlandse Portugees-Israëlitische Gemeente in Suriname, 1678-1909 (NPIGS). 1812 apr. 11 - 1817 mrt. 30. NA.

Conveyance of Sarah, Rebecca, and Isaac Lopez (1800). Deed Hannah Esther Lopez to Abraham Rodrigues Brandon. 20 Aug 1800. R/1 Deeds 1801, vol. 212.459. BDA.

Corry, John, Thomas Troughton, and George Perry. *The History of Liverpool: From the Earliest Authenticated Period down to the Present Time.* Liverpool: William Robinson, 1810.

DeSilver's Philadelphia Directory and Stranger's Guide, 1829. Philadelphia: Robert DeSilver, 1829.

Doggett's New-York City Directory for 1845 & 1846. New-York: John Doggett, 1845. DCNYPL.

Doggett's New-York City Directory for 1846 & 1847. New-York: John Doggett, 1846. DCNYPL.

Doggett's New-York City Directory for 1847 & 1848. New-York: John Doggett, 1847. DCNYPL.

Doggett's New-York City Directory for 1851 & 1852. New-York: John Doggett, 1851. DCNYPL.

Elizabeth A. Austin's Inventory Filed 5th June 1818, BDA.

Financial Records 1817–1858 of CMIP, Box 5.

Former British Colonial Dependencies Slave Registers, 1813–1834 [database on-line]. Ancestry.com, 2007.

Hawaii, Passenger Lists, 1843–1898 [database on-line]. Provo: Ancestry.com, 2016.

"Hopeland Plantation [Barbados | St Michael]." Legacies of British Slave-ownership database. http://wwwdepts-live.ucl.ac.uk/lbs/estate/view/762. Accessed 3 March 2020.

Hughes/Queree Papers, Plantations, BDA.

Index to Petitions for Naturalization filed in New York City, 1792–1989 Provo: Ancestry.com.

"Jemima's Bill of Sale." Deed between Hannah Esther Lopez and George Gill. Entered 15 Oct. 1801, written 17 Aug. 1801. *Deeds* (1801), vol. 218, BDA, R/1.

Jewish Atlantic World Database. Reed College Digital Collections, 2013. https:// rdc.reed.edu/c/jewishatl/.

Jews' Infant School, 127 Houndsditch . . . Address on the opening of the School . . . 14 Sept. 1841, with a list of Subscribers, etc. London: J. Wertheimer & Company, 1841.

Lazarus, Eleazer Samuel. *Circumcision Register, 1819–1843.* AJA.

Levy Books. St. Michael's Vestry Books 1792–1801, Part 1. BDA.

Levy Maduro, Salomon. *Sefer Brit Itschak.* Amsterdam: n.p., 1767/68.

Loeb Jewish Portrait Database. 2018. http://loebjewishportraits.com/.

London, England, Church of England Marriages and Banns, 1754–1932 [database online]. Ancestry.com, 2010.

London, England, Land Tax Records, 1692–1932 [database on-line]. Ancestry. com, 2011.

Longworth's American Almanac, New York Register, and City Directory. New-York: David Longworth, 1817, 1818, 1819, 1820, 1827, 1828, 1829, 1830. DCNYPL.

Lopez, Moses. B'rakhot ha-Mila: *u-minhag ve-seder ha-milah ke-fi ha-nahug be-zot ha-ḳehilah be-i Barbados* (1794). Jewish Theological Seminary, MS 8267.

Lopez, Moses. Prayer Book (1775, Library Company of Philadelphia, LCP in HSP28.

Lopez, Moses. Probate Records (1818). *Register of Wills.* Philadelphia, Pennsylvania. Administration Files, 133–50, 152–98. Ancestry.com.

"Loyal Address." 21 October 1823, in the Minutes of the Barbados Council 21 October 1823, BDA.

Manumission Books, A, B, C & D, AmS .05, AmS .051, AmS .052, AmS .053, AmS .054, Pennsylvania Abolition Society Papers, Collection 0490, Historical Society of Pennsylvania, Philadelphia, PA.

Manumission of Sarah and Isaac Lopez (1801/2). Deed Hannah Esther Lopez to Abraham Rodrigues Brandon. 5 Aug. 1802. R/1 Deeds 1801, vol. 219.9. BDA.

Maps of the City of New York by William Perris Civil Engineer and Surveyor, 3rd ed. (1857). *New York Public Library Digital Collections.* https://digitalcollections. nypl.org/items/5e66b3e9-07d4-d471-e040-e00a180654d7.

Marriage of Sarah Simpson Wood and Daniel Goody (10 Oct. Pancras, Camden, England. *London, England, Church of England Marriages and Banns, 1754–1932* [database on-line]. Ancestry.com.

Marriage Register of Joshua Moses and Sarah Rodrigues Brandon (17 March 1817), Records of Congregation Bevis Marks, LMA/4521/A/02/03/009. LMA. 1833), Parish Chapel, St.

"Memorandum of the Coloured Jews to Governor De Frederici" (1793), NA 1.05.10.01:528, 396-414, GKS.

Mercein's City Directory, New York Register and Almanac. New York: William A. Mercein, 1820.

Meyers Family Papers, Ms. Coll. 480, AJA.

Mocatta, J. *An Address to the Congregation of Portuguese Jews: Delivered at a Meeting of Their Elders, on the Examination of the Report, Presented by the Committee on the Ecclesiastical State.* London: 1803.

Moses, Joshua. Family Record Book, 1817–1820. MFPNY.

Moses, Joshua. Papers and Estate Inventory, 1803, 1816, 1837, 1838. MFPNY.

New York. *Episcopal Diocese of New York Church Records, 1767–1970* 2017.

New York. *Passenger and Immigration Lists, 1820–1850* Ancestry.com Operations Inc, 2003.

New York. *War of 1812 Payroll Abstracts for New York State Militia, 1812–1815* [database on-line]. Ancestry.com, 2013.

"New York State Census, 1855." *FamilySearch.* http://FamilySearch.org.

New York (State). *Laws of the State of New York.* Albany, NY: 1777.

The New York Charities Directory. New York: Charity Organization Society in the City of New York, 1890.

New-York City and Co-Partnership Directory, 1843 & 1844. New-York: John Doggett, 1843. DCNYPL.

New York City Directory, 1837/38. New-York: Thomas Longworth, 1837. DCNYPL

New York City Directory, 1851/52. New-York: Doggett & Rode, 1851. DCNYPL.

Nidhe Israel Synagogue Records. London Metropolitan Archives. LMA/4521/D/01/03/001, LMA/4521/D/01/03/002, LMA/4521/D/01/03/003, LMA 4521/D/01/01/004, LMA/4521/D/01/03/006, LMA 4521/D/01/01/008.

Noah, Mordecai Manuel. *She Would Be a Soldier, Or, The Plains of Chippewa an Historical Drama in Three Acts: Performed for the First Time on the 21st of June, 1819.* New York: Longworth's Dramatic Repository, 1819.

Office of Registry of Colonial Slaves and Slave Compensation Commission. T 71, 524: 251, 406, TNA.

Papers of Jacques Judah Lyons (1813–1877). AJHS.

Papers of the Moses Family of New York, undated 1767–1941, 1971. P-1. AJHS.

Pascalis Ouviere, Felix. *A Statement of the Occurrences during a Malignant Yellow Fever, in the City of New York, in the Summer and Autumnal Months of 1819 and of the Check given to Its Progress, by the Measures Adopted by the Board of Health.* New York: William A. Mercein, 1819.

Passenger Lists of Vessels Arriving at Philadelphia, Pennsylvania. Records of the United States Customs Service, 1745–1997. Ancestry.com.

Paxton, John Adams, William Kneass, and J. H. Young. *The Philadelphia Directory and Register, for 1818: Containing the Names, Professions, and Residence, of All the Heads of Families and Persons in Business of the City and Suburbs, Hamiltonville, and Camden, N.J.: With Other Useful Information.* Early American Imprints. Second Series; No. 45218. Philadelphia: Kneass, Young & Co., 1818.

Petition to the House of Assembly, 19 February 1811. In Minutes of the House of Assembly 19 February 1811, BDA.

Petition Papers for Joshua Moses (22 Jan. 1838). *New York, Wills and Probate Records, 1659–1999.* Ancestry.com.

Petition Papers for Joshua Moses (19 Mar. 1842). *New York, Wills and Probate Records, 1659–1999.* Ancestry.com.

Population [census] returns number 201–490 collected as required by the
governor's proclamation of 17 October 1811. Kew, Surrey, England: CO 278/23.

Population [census] returns number 491–690 collected as required by the
governor's proclamation of 17 October 1811. Kew, Surrey, England: CO 278/24.

Population [census] returns number 601–800 collected as required by the
governor's proclamation of 17 October 1811. Kew, Surrey, England: CO 278/20.

Probate Proceedings for the Estate of Rebecca Moses. *New York, Wills and Probate
Records, 1659–1999.* [database on-line]. Ancestry.com, 2015.

Processo de Gaspar Rodrigues Brandão (1724–11–29 to 1727–11–19). *Arquivo
Nacional da Torre do Tombo.* PT/TT/TSO-IC/025/09247.

Processo de João Rodrigues Brandão (1725–01–25 to 1727–12–05). *Arquivo
Nacional da Torre do Tombo.* PT/TT/TSO-IC/025/08281.

Processo de Luísa Mendes (1706–10–02 to 1708–12–06). *Arquivo Nacional da Torre
do Tombo.* PT/TT/TSO-IC/025/00790.

Real Estate Proceedings for the Estate of Joshua Moses (Case 16). Records of Wills
and Probates, 1659–1999. Ancestry.com.

"Response of the Portuguese Regents to the Memorandum of the Coloured Jews."
NA 1.05.10.01:528, 512, GKS..

Shrewsbury, John. *Memorials of the Rev. William J. Shrewsbury.*
London: Hamilton, Adams, & Co., 1869.

Shrewsbury, William James. *The Family Memorial and Pastoral Remembrancer;
being a short memoir of Mrs. Hillaria Shrewsbury.* London: J. Mason, 1839.

Sisterhood Records. CSIA.

*Soundex Index to Petitions for Naturalizations Filed in Federal, State, and Local
Courts in New York City, 1792–1906 (M1674).* NARA.

Stedman, John Gabriel. *Narrative of a Five Years' Expedition Against the Revolted
Negroes of Surinam, in Guiana, on the Wild Coast of South America.* London: J.
Johnson, 1806.

Stephen Girard Papers (1789–1829), Ms. Coll. 257. AJA.

Stout, James DeForest. *Plan of Greenwich from Actual Survey, 1822.* M7.5.45,
negative no. 80058d, NYHS.

Susannah Ostrehan's Inventory Recd & filed 30 Nov. 1809, BDA.

Thome, James A., and J. Horace Kimball. *Emancipation in the West Indies; a six
months' tour in Antigua, Barbadoes, and Jamaica, in 1837.* New York: American
Anti-Slavery Society, 1838.

Townsend, Peter Solomon. *An Account of the Yellow Fever: As It Prevailed in
the City of New York, in the Summer and Autumn of 1822.* New York: O.
Halsted, 1823.

Trow's New York City Directory. New York: Trow, 1853, 1854, 1855, 1859, 1860, 1865,
1870, 1875, 1879, 1880, 1885, 1888.

United States. "An Act to Establish an Uniform Rule of Naturalization, and to
Repeal the Acts Heretofore Passed on the Subject." Early American Imprints.
Second Series; No. 3199. Washington[?]: Duane, Printer, 1802.

United States. *Treaties and Other International Acts of the United States of America.*
Washington, DC: United States Department of State, 1931.

United States Senate. *Executive Documents, 1858–59*. Washington, DC: William Harris, 1859.

U.S. IRS Tax Assessment Lists, 1862–1918 [database on-line]. Ancestry.com, 2008.

U.S. War of 1812 Service Records, 1812–1815 [database on-line]. Ancestry.com, 1999.

U.S. Newspaper Extractions from the Northeast, 1704–1930 [database on-line]. Ancestry.com, 2014.

Walker, William. *The War in Nicaragua*. New York: S. H. Goetzel & Company, 1860.

Waller, John Augustine. *A Voyage in the West Indies: containing various observations made during a residence in Barbadoes, and several of the Leeward Islands: with some notices and illustrations relative to the city of Paramaribo, in Surinam*. London: Richard Phillips and Co., 1820.

Washington, George. "To the Hebrew Congregations of Philadelphia, New York, Charleston, and Richmond" (13 December 1790). *Founders Online*. https:// founders.archives.gov/documents/Washington/05-07-02-0036.

Watson, John. "An Inquiry into the Pathology and Treatment of Secondary Abscesses, and Other Consecutive Disorders Resulting from Injuries and Surgical Operations." *American Journal of the Medical Sciences*, 21, no. 41 (1837): 37–76.

Watson, John. "Observations on the Nature and Treatment of Telangiectasis, Or that Morbid State of the Blood-Vessels which Gives Rise to Naevus and Aneurism from Anastomosis." *American Journal of the Medical Sciences*, 24, no. 47 (1839): 24–49.

Whitely, Edward. *The Philadelphia Directory and Register, for 1822*. Philadelphia: M'Carty & Davis, 1822.

Will of Abraham Brandon, Barbados (1756), AJA.

Will of Abraham Rodrigues Brandao, Merchant of Bevis Marks. City of London (1769). TNA. PROB 11/950/396.

Will of Abraham Rodrigues Brandon (4 July 1831), RB 4 66/178, BDA. Also *New York, Wills and Probate Records, 1659–1999*. Ancestry.com.

Will of Abraham Rodriguez Brandon (1860). *New York, Wills and Probate Records, 1659–1999*. [database on-line]. Ancestry.com, 2015.

Will of Emmanuel Baruch Lousada (1795). Louzada Family Wills, 1695–1797. AJA.

Will of George Gill (1801), RB 4 53.133, BDA.

Will of Hannah Ester Lopez (1815), RL 1/6, BDA.

Will of Isaac Lindo (1780), RB 6/23.346, BDA.

Will of Isaac Lopez (1804), RB 6 54.122, BDA.

Will of Isaac Lopez Brandon (10 Oct. 1856), *New York, Wills and Probate Records, 1659–1999*. Ancestry.com.

Will of Jacob Brandon, Jamaica (1710), AJA.

Will of Joshua Moses (3 Jan. 1838), *New York, Wills and Probate Records, 1659–1999*. Ancestry.com.

Will of Joshua Rodrigues or Joshua Rodriguez Brandao, Merchant of Mile End, Essex (1784). TNA. PROB 11/1124/317.

Will of Judith Pixotto (1791), 19/377, BDA. Copy at AJA.

Will of Lebaneh Delyon, Barbados (1747), AJA.
Will of Moses Brandon, Barbados (1718), AJA.
Will of Rachel Lindo (1847), RB 4 72.428, BDA.
Will of [Rabbi] Raphael Hayyim Isaac Carigal (27 May 1777), BDA.
Will of Rebecca Moses (1 Jul. 1864), *New York, Wills and Probate Records, 1659–1999*
    [database on-line]. Ancestry.com, 2015.
Will of Reyna Moses (1824). *New York, Wills and Probate Records, 1659–1999*
    [database on-line]. Ancestry.com, 2015.
Will of Robert Gill (25 Sept. 1776), BDA.
Will of Sarah Moses (7 Mar. 1860), *New York, Wills and Probate Records, 1659–1999*
    [database on-line]. Ancestry.com, 2015.
Wills & Deeds (1796), BDA, RL1/6.

SECONDARY SOURCES

Abbott, Elizabeth. *Sugar: A Bittersweet History*. London: Duckworth
    Overlook, 2009.
Adams, Maurianne, and John H. Bracey, eds. *Strangers & Neighbors: Relations
    between Blacks & Jews in the United States*. Amherst: University of
    Massachusetts Press, 1999.
Alcalá, Angel. *Judíos, Sefarditas, Conversos: la Expulsión de 1492 y sus Consecuencias*.
    Valladolid, Spain: Ambito, 1995.
Allen, Oliver E. *Tribeca: A Pictorial History*. New York: Tribeca Trib, 2010.
Almeida, F. *História da Igreja em Portugal*, Vol. IV (Oporto). Coimbra: De
    Almeida, 1923.
Anderson, Jennifer L. *Mahogany*. Cambridge, MA: Harvard University
    Press, 2012.
Angel, Marc. *Remnant of Israel: A Portrait of America's First Jewish
    Congregation: Shearith Israel*. New York: Riverside Book Company, 2004.
Apel, Thomas A. *Feverish Bodies, Enlightened Minds: Science and the Yellow Fever
    Controversy in the Early American Republic*. Stanford, CA: Stanford University
    Press, 2016.
Arbell, Mordehay. *The Jewish Nation of the Caribbean: The Spanish-Portuguese
    Jewish Settlements in the Caribbean and the Guianas*. New York: Gefen, 2002.
Aufses, Arthur H., Jr., and Barbara Niss. *This House of Noble Deeds: The Mount
    Sinai Hospital, 1852–2002*. New York: New York University Press, 2002.
Bagneris, Mia L. *Colouring the Caribbean: Race and the Art of Agostino Brunias*.
    Manchester: Manchester University Press, 2018.
Barnett, Lionel D. *Abstracts of the Ketubot or Marriage-Contracts of the
    Congregation from Earliest Times until 1837*. London: Board of Elders of the
    Congregation, 1949.
Barnett, Richard D., ed. *The Circumcision Register of Isaac and Abraham de Paiba
    (1715–1775)*. London: Jewish Historical Society of England, 1991.
Barratt, Carrie Rebora, and Lori Zabar. *American Portrait Miniatures in the
    Metropolitan Museum of Art*. New York: Metropolitan Museum of Art, 2010.

Bauer, Karl Jack, and Robert Johansen. *The Mexican War 1846–1848*.
Lincoln: University of Nebraska Press, 1992.

Baum, Jeffrey. *A Light unto My Path: The Story of H. N. Solomon of Edmonton*.
Edmonton, UK: Edmonton Hundred Historical Society, 1981.

Beasley, Nicholas. "Domestic Rituals: Marriage and Baptism in the British
Plantation Colonies, 1650–1780." *Anglican and Episcopal History* 76, no. 3
(2007): 327–357.

Beckles, Hilary. "City the Limit: The Enslaved Community in Bridgetown
1800–1834." In *Beyond the Bridge: Lectures Commemorating Bridgetown's 375th
Anniversary*. Edited by Woodville K. Marshall and Pedro L. V. Welch, 112–131.
St. Michael: Barbados Museum, 2005.

Beckles, Hilary. "Creolisation in Action: The Slave Labour Élite and Anti-Slavery
in Barbados." *Caribbean Quarterly* 44, no. 1/2 (1998): 108–128.

Beckles, Hilary. *For Love of Country: The National Heroes of Barbados*. St. Michael,
Barbados: Foundation Publishing, 2001.

Beckles, Hilary. *A History of Barbados: From Amerindian Settlement to Caribbean
Single Market*. 2nd ed. Cambridge: Cambridge University Press, 2006.

Beckles, Hilary. *Natural Rebels: A Social History of Enslaved Black Women in
Barbados*. Brunswick, NJ: Rutgers University Press, 1989.

Bell, Dean Phillip. *Jews in the Early Modern World*. Lanham, MD: Rowman &
Littlefield, 2008.

Ben-Ur, Aviva. *Jewish Autonomy in a Slave Society: Suriname in the Atlantic World,
1651–1825*. Philadelphia: University of Pennsylvania Press, 2020.

Ben-Ur, Aviva. "Peripheral Inclusion: Communal Belonging in Suriname's
Sephardic Community." In *Religion, Gender, and Culture in the Pre-
modern World*. Edited by Alexandra Cuffel and Brian M. Britt, 185–210.
New York: Palgrave Macmillan, 2007.

Ben-Ur, Aviva, and Rachel Frankel. *Remnant Stones: The Jewish Cemeteries of
Suriname: Epitaphs*. Cincinnati: Hebrew Union College, 2009.

Ben-Ur, Aviva, and Jessica Vance Roitman. "Adultery Here and There: Crossing
Sexual Boundaries in the Dutch Jewish Atlantic." In *Dutch Atlantic
Connections, 1680–1800: Linking Empires, Bridging Borders*. Edited by Gert
Oostindie and Jessica V. Roitman, 185–223. Leiden: Brill, 2014.

Berlin, Ira, and Leslie M. Harris, eds. *Slavery in New York*. New York: New
Press, 2005.

Bindman, David. *Ape to Apollo: Aesthetics and the Idea of Race in the 18th Century*.
Ithaca, NY: Cornell University Press, 2002.

Black, Gerry. *JFS: A History of the Jews' Free School, London, since 1732*.
London: Tymsder, 1998.

Blake, Brian P. T. "Introduction to the Brandon Family." Unpublished
manuscript, 2016.

Blanco, José F., ed. *Clothing and Fashion: American Fashion from Head to Toe*.
Santa Barbara, CA: ABC-CLIO, 2018.

Blau, Joseph Leon, and Salo Wittmayer Baron. *The Jews of the United States, 1790–
1840: A Documentary History*. New York: Columbia University Press, 1963.

Borelli, Melissa Blanco. *She Is Cuba: A Genealogy of the Mulata Body.*
New York: Oxford University Press, 2016.

Bost, Suzanne. *Mulattas and Mestizas: Representing Mixed Identities in the Americas, 1850–2000.* Athens: University of Georgia Press, 2010.

Bremner, G. A. *Architecture and Urbanism in the British Empire.*
New York: Oxford University Press, 2016.

Brettschneider, Marla. *The Jewish Phenomenon in Sub-Saharan Africa: The Politics of Contradictory Discourses.* Lewiston, NY: Edwin Mellen Press, 2015.

Brilliant, Richard, ed. *Facing the New World: Jewish Portraits in Colonial and Federal America.* New York: Jewish Museum, 1997.

Broadwater, Jeff. *James Madison: A Son of Virginia & a Founder of the Nation.*
Chapel Hill: University of North Carolina Press, 2012.

Brodkin, Karen. *How Jews Became White Folks and What That Says about Race in America.* New Brunswick, NJ: Rutgers University Press, 1998.

Brown, Malcolm. "The Jews of Gravesend before 1915." *Jewish Historical Studies* 35 (1996): 119–139.

Browne, Randy. "The 'Bad Business' of Obeah: Power, Authority, and the Politics of Slave Culture in the British Caribbean." *William and Mary Quarterly* 68, no. 3 (2011): 451–480.

Brownlee, David. *Frederich Weinbrenner, Architect of Karlsruhe.*
Philadelphia: University of Pennsylvania Press, 1986.

Bruder, Edith. *The Black Jews of Africa: History, Religion, Identity.* Oxford: Oxford University Press, 2008.

Butler, Kathleen Mary. *The Economics of Emancipation: Jamaica & Barbados, 1823–1843.* Chapel Hill: University of North Carolina Press, 1995.

Byrde, Penelope. *Nineteenth-Century Fashion.* London: Batsford, 1992.

Caffrey, Paul. "Jewels above All Prize: Portrait Miniatures on Enamel and Ivory." In *Ireland: Crossroads of Art and Design, 1690–1840.* Edited by William Laffan, Christopher Monkhouse, and Leslie Fitzpatrick, 161–166. New Haven, CT: Yale University Press, 2015.

Capsali, Elijah. *Chronique de l'expulsion: Seder Eliahou zouta.* Translated by Sultan Sultan-Bohbot. Paris: Editions du Cerf, 1994.

Cardozo, Irma Miriam Lopes. *As I Lived It.* New York: Irma Miriam Lopes, 2010.

Cavallar, Georg. *Kant's Embedded Cosmopolitanism.* Berlin: De Gruyter, 2015.

"The Cemetery." Barbados Synagogue Historic District. https:// synagoguehistoricdistrict.com/cemetery. Accessed 3 March 2020.

Chyet, Stanley F. "The Political Rights of the Jews in the United States, 1776–1840." In *Critical Studies in American Jewish History.* Edited by Jacob Rader Marcus, 14–71. Cincinnati: American Jewish Archives, 1971.

Cockrell, Dale. *Demons of Disorder: Early Blackface Minstrels and Their World.*
New York: Cambridge University Press, 1997.

Coe, Bufford W. *John Wesley and Marriage.* Bethlehem, PA: Lehigh University Press, 1996.

Cohen, Martin A. *Sephardim in the Americas: Studies in Culture and History.*
Tuscaloosa: University of Alabama Press, 1993.

Cohen, Robert. *Jews in Another Environment: Surinam in the Second Half of the Eighteenth Century*. Leiden: E. J. Brill, 1991.

Corré, Alan, and Malcolm Stern. "The Record Book of the Revered Jacob Raphael Cohen." *AJHQ* 59, no. 1 (1969): 23–82.

Correia, Arlindo N. M. "Os 'judeus' de Tondela." http://arlindo-correia.com/161207.html.

Cracknell, Kenneth, and Susan J. White. *An Introduction to World Methodism*. Cambridge: Cambridge University Press, 2005.

Crosby, Molly Caldwell. *The American Plague*. New York: Berkley Books, 2014.

Crump, W. B., Joseph Rogerson, and Benjamin Gott. *The Leeds Woolen Industry 1780–1820*. Leeds: Thoresby Society, 1931.

Cunnington, C. Willett. *English Women's Clothing in the Nineteenth Century: A Comprehensive Guide with 1,117 Illustrations*. New York: Dover, 1990.

Daniels, Edward S., "Extracts from Various Records of the Early Settlement of the Jews in the Island of Barbados, W. I." *PAJHS* 26 (1918): 250–256.

Davids, Jules. *American Diplomatic and Public Papers: The United States and China*. Wilmington, DE: Scholarly Press, 1973.

Davis, N. Darnell. "Notes on the History of the Jews in Barbados." *PAJHS* 18 (1909): 129–148.

DeLorme, Eleanor P., and Bernard Chevallier. *Joséphine and the Arts of the Empire*. Los Angeles: Getty Museum, 2005.

Denie. "Adjuba van Jona van Ketie van Princes van Dinisie." *Surinaamse Genealogie, Familiegeschiedenis en Stambomen* (blog), July 2, 2013. https://deniekasan.wordpress.com/2013/07/03/adjuba-van-jona-van-ketie-van-princes-van-dinisie/.

De Sola Pool, David. *The Mill Street Synagogue (1730–1817) of the Congregation Shearith Israel (founded in the City of New York in 1655)*. New York: n.p., 1930.

De Sola Pool, David. *An Old Faith in the New World: Portrait of Shearith Israel, 1654–1954*. New York: Columbia University Press, 1955.

De Sola Pool, David. *Portraits Etched in Stone; Early Jewish Settlers, 1682–1831*. New York: Columbia University Press, 1953.

"The Diary of Aaron Levy." In "Items Relating to the Moses and Levy Families, New York." *PAJHS* 27 (1920): 335–345.

Diner, Hasia R. *The Jews of the United States, 1654 to 2000*. Berkeley: University of California Press, 2004.

Dollinger, Marc. *Black Power, Jewish Politics: Reinventing the Alliance in the 1960s*. Waltham, MA: Brandeis University Press, 2018.

Douglass, Frederick. *The Frederick Douglass Papers*. New Haven, CT: Yale University Press, 2018.

Downs, Jacques M. 2015. *Golden Ghetto—The American Commercial Community at Canton and the Shaping of American China Policy, 1784–1844*. Hong Kong: Hong Kong University Press, 2015.

Du Bois, W. E. B. *The Philadelphia Negro: A Social Study*. New York: Schocken Books, 1967.

Duffy, John. "Nineteenth-Century Public Health in New York and New Orleans: A Comparison." *Louisiana History: The Journal of the Louisiana Historical Association* 15, no. 4 (1974): 325–337, www.jstor.org/stable/4231424.

Dunbar, Erica Armstrong. *A Fragile Freedom: African American Women and Emancipation in the Antebellum City*. Society and the Sexes in the Modern World. New Haven, CT: Yale University Press, 2008.

DuPlessis, Robert. "Sartorial Sorting in the Colonial Caribbean and North America." In *The Right to Dress: Sumptuary Laws in a Global Perspective, 1200–1800*. Edited by Giorgio Riello and Ulinka Rublack, 346–374. New York: Cambridge University Press, 2019.

Eaton, Natasha. "The Art of Colonial Despotism: Portraits, Politics, and Empire in South India, 1750–1795." *Cultural Critique* 70, no. 1 (2008): 63–93.

Edwards, Richard. *New York's Great Industries: Exchange and Commercial Review*. New York: Historical, 1884.

Elmaleh, Leon H., and Joseph Bunford Samuel. *The Jewish Cemetery, Ninth and Spruce Streets, Philadelphia*. Philadelphia: Congregation Mikveh Israel, 1962.

Emerson, Ralph Waldo, *Journals of Ralph Waldo Emerson, 1820–1872 [1876]*. Edited by Edward Waldo Emerson and Waldo Emerson Forbes. Cambridge: Riverside Press, 1909.

Endelman, Todd M. *Broadening Jewish History: Towards a Social History of Ordinary Jews*. Oxford: Littman Library, 2014.

Endelman, Todd M. *The Jews of Britain, 1656 to 2000*. Berkeley: University of California Press, 2002.

Endelman, Todd M. *The Jews of Georgian England, 1714–1830: Tradition and Change in a Liberal Society*. Philadelphia: Jewish Publication Society of America, 1979.

Faber, Eli. *Jews, Slaves and the Slave-Trade: Setting the Record Straight*. New York University Press, 1998.

Farris, Johnathan. *Enclave to Urbanity: Canton, Foreigners, and Architecture from the Late Eighteenth to the Early Twentieth Centuries*. Hong Kong: Hong Kong University Press, 2017.

The Fate of the Fenwicks. Edited by A. F. Wedd. London: Methuen & Co., 1927.

Fields, Karen E., and Barbara J. Fields. *Racecraft: The Soul of Inequality in American Life*. London: Verso, 2016.

Finance and Industry: The New York Stock Exchange: Banks, Bankers, Business Houses, and Moneyed Institutions. New York: Historical Publishing Company, 1866.

Findlay, George Gillanders, and William West Holdsworth. *The History of the Wesleyan Methodist Missionary Society*. London: Epworth Press, 1921.

Finestein, Israel. *Anglo-Jewry in Changing Times: Studies in Diversity, 1840–1914*. London: Mitchell, 1999.

For God and Country: A Record of the Patriotic Service of Shearith Israel. New York: Congregation Shearith Israel, 2019.

Forstall, Richard L. *Population of States and Counties of the United States: 1790–1990*. Washington, DC: US Department of Commerce, 1996.

Fowler-Salamini, Heather, and Mary K. Vaughan, eds. *Women of the Mexican Countryside, 1850–1990: Creating Spaces, Shaping Transitions*. Tucson: University of Arizona Press, 1994.

Frank, Robin Jaffee. *Love and Loss: American Portrait and Mourning Miniatures*. New Haven: Yale University Press, 2000.

Franklin, P. "The Philadelphia Race Riot of 1918." In *African Americans in Pennsylvania: Shifting Historical Perspectives*. Edited by Joe Trotter, 316–329. University Park: Pennsylvania State University Press, 2010.

Fraser, Henry. "Historic Bridgetown: Development and Architecture." In *Beyond the Bridge: Lectures Commemorating Bridgetown's 375th Anniversary*. Edited by Woodville K. Marshall and Pedro L. V. Welch, 82–93. St. Michael: Barbados Museum, 2005.

Fraser, Henry. *Historic Houses of Barbados*. Bridgetown: Barbados National Trust, 1986.

Friedman, Saul S. *Jews and the American Slave Trade*. New Brunswick, NJ: Transaction, 1998.

"From the 2nd Volume of the Minute Books of the Congrn: Shearith Israel in New York." *PAJHS*, no. 21 (1913): 83–171.

Fry, Herbert. *London in . . . illustrated with bird's eye views of the principal streets*. London: David Bogue, 1886.

Fry, Herbert. *Our Schools and Colleges. Containing the principal particulars respecting endowed Grammar Schools . . . as also information respecting Colleges and Universities*. London: R. Hardwicke, 1868.

Fuentes, Marisa J. *Dispossessed Lives: Enslaved Women, Violence, and the Archive*. Philadelphia: University of Pennsylvania Press, 2016.

Furstenberg, F. "Beyond Freedom and Slavery: Autonomy, Virtue, and Resistance in Early American Political Discourse." *Journal of American History* 89, no. 4 (2003): 1295–1330.

Gage, Kelly Mohs. "Forced Crossing: The Dress of African Slave Women in Rio de Janeiro, Brazil, 1861." *Dress* 39, no. 2 (2013): 111–133.

Gardner, Charles K. *A Dictionary of all Officers: who have been commissioned, or have been appointed and served, in the army of the United States, since the inauguration of their first president, in 1789, to the first January, 1853*. New York: D. Van Nostrand, 1860.

Garraty, John Arthur, and Mark Christopher Carnes, eds. *American National Biography*. Oxford: Oxford University Press, 1999.

Gaster, Moses. *History of the Ancient Synagogue of the Spanish and Portuguese Jews*. London: 1901.

Gayle, Janette Elice. 2004. "Ann Gill: Free Woman of Color at the Nexus of Politics and Religion in Nineteenth-Century Barbados." Master's thesis, University of California–Los Angeles, 2004.

GB Historical GIS. *A Vision of Britain through Time*. http://www.visionofbritain.org.uk/unit/10097836/cube/TOT_POP. Accessed 5 January 2020.

Geggus, David. "Yellow Fever in the 1790s: The British Army in Occupied Saint Domingue." *Medical History* 23, no. 1 (1979): 38–58.

Gellman, David N., and David Quigley. *Jim Crow New York: A Documentary History of Race and Citizenship, 1777–1877*. New York: New York University Press, 2004.

Gerber, Jane S. *Jews of Spain: A History of the Sephardic Experience.* New York: Simon and Schuster, 1994.

Geserick, Marco Cabrera. *The Legacy of the Filibuster War: National Identity and Collective Memory in Central America.* London: Lexington Books, 2019.

Gibbins, David. "The Portuguese Jewish Ancestry of Rebecca de Daniel Brandon (1783–1820)." http://davidgibbins.com.

Gillen, Mollie. *Royal Duke: Augustus Frederick, Duke of Sussex (1773–1843).* London: Sidgwick and Jackson, 1978.

Gilman, Sander L. *Making the Body Beautiful: A Cultural History of Aesthetic Surgery.* Princeton, NJ: Princeton University Press, 1999.

Gilman, Sander L. "Zwetschkenbaum's Competence: Madness and the Discourse of the Jews." *Modern Austrian Literature* 26, no. 2 (1993): 1–34.

Glover, Katharine. *Elite Women and Polite Society in Eighteenth-Century Scotland.* Woodbridge: Boydell, 2011.

Gluck, Andrew. "The Chair in Front of the Tebah." *Mikveh Israel Record,* 20–21 April (2012): 3.

Gobat, Michel. *Empire by Invitation: William Walker and Manifest Destiny in Central America.* Cambridge, MA: Harvard University Press, 2018.

Goebeland, Julius, and Joseph Smith, eds. *The Law Practice of Alexander Hamilton: Documents and Commentary,* vol. 5. New York: Columbia University Press, 1964.

Gold, Roberta S. "The Black Jews of Harlem: Representation, Identity, and Race, 1920–1939." *American Quarterly* 55, no. 2 (2003): 179–225.

Goldberg, Mark Allan. *Conquering Sickness: Race, Health, and Colonization in the Texas Borderlands.* Lincoln: University of Nebraska Press, 2017.

Goldman, Karla. *Beyond the Synagogue Gallery: Finding a Place for Women in American Judaism.* Cambridge, MA: Harvard University Press, 2000.

Goldman, Shalom. *God's Sacred Tongue: Hebrew and the American Imagination.* Chapel Hill: University of North Carolina Press, 2004.

Goldman, Shalom. "Joshua/James Seixas (1802–1874): Jewish Apostasy and Christian Hebraism in Early Nineteenth-Century America." *Jewish History* 7, no. 1 (1993): 65–88.

Goldstein, Jonathan. *Jewish Identities in East and Southeast Asia: Singapore, Manila, Taipei, Harbin, Shanghai, Rangoon, and Surabaya.* Boston: De Gruyter Oldenbourg, 2015.

Goldstein, Jonathan. *The Jews of China.* Armonk, NY: M. E. Sharpe, 1999.

Goodridge, Sehon S., and Anthony de V. Phillips. *Facing the Challenge of Emancipation: A Study of the Ministry of William Hart Coleridge, First Bishop of Barbados, 1824–1842.* St. Michael: BMHS, 2014.

Goody Family Tree. http://www.cvgoody.co.uk/home.htm.

Gordon, Lewis R. "Rarely Kosher: Studying Jews of Color in North America." *American Jewish History* 100, no. 1 (2016): 105–116.

Grootenboer, Hanneke. *Treasuring the Gaze: Intimate Vision in Late Eighteenth-Century Eye Miniatures*. Chicago: University of Chicago Press, 2012.

Gragg, Larry. *Quaker Community on Barbados*. Columbia: University of Missouri Press, 2009.

Green, Abigail. *Moses Montefiore*. Cambridge, MA: Harvard University Press, 2012.

Grimwade, A. G. "Anglo-Jewish Silver." *Transactions (Jewish Historical Society of England)* 18 (1953): 113–125.

Groll, Temminck. *De Architektuur van Suriname 1667–1930*. Zutphen: De Walburg Pers, 1973.

"Guide to the Papers of the Seixas Family, Undated, 1746–1911, 1926, 1939 *P-60." *Center for Jewish History*. http://digifindingaids.cjh.org/?pID=109167. Accessed February 10, 2017.

Gurock, Jeffrey S. *The Jews of Harlem: The Rise, Decline, and Revival of a Jewish Community*. New York: New York University Press, 2016.

Gurock, Jeffrey S. *When Harlem Was Jewish, 1870–1930*. New York: Columbia University Press, 1979.

Hamilton, Alexander. *Papers of Alexander Hamilton*. Edited by Harold C. Syrett. New York: Columbia University Press, 1963.

Handler, Jerome. *The Unappropriated People: Freedmen in the Slave Society of Barbados*. Baltimore: Johns Hopkins University Press, 1974.

Hare, John. *The Supreme Court of Pennsylvania: Life and Law in the Commonwealth, 1684–2017*. University Park: Pennsylvania State University Press, 2018.

Harris, Emma Tanya. "Anglo-Jewry's Experience of Secondary Education from the 1830s until 1920." PhD diss., University of London, 2007.

Harris, Leslie J., Lee E. Teitelbaum, and June Carbone. *Family Law*. New York: Aspen, 2005.

Harris, Leslie M. "The Greatest City in the World? Slavery in New York in the Age of Hamilton." In *Historians on Hamilton: How a Blockbuster Musical Is Restaging America's Past*. Edited by Renee Christine Romano and Claire Bond Potter, 71–93. New Brunswick: Rutgers University Press, 2018.

Harris, Leslie M. *In the Shadow of Slavery: African Americans in New York City, 1626–1863*. Chicago: University of Chicago Press, 2003.

Hartman, Saidiya. "Venus in Two Acts." *Small Axe* 12, no. 2 (2008): 1–14.

Haynes, Bruce D. *The Soul of Judaism: Jews of African Descent in America*. New York: New York University Press, 2018.

Heaton, C. E. "Yellow Fever in New York City." *Bulletin of the Medical Library Association* 34, no. 2 (1946): 67–78.

Hebrew Calendar. https://www.hebcal.com. 1999.

Henriot, Christian. *New Frontiers: Imperialism's New Communities in East Asia, 1842–1953*. Manchester: Manchester University Press, 2000.

Herrera, Rene J., and Ralph Garcia-Bertrand. *Ancestral DNA, Human Origins, and Migrations*. London: Academic Press, 2018.

Herskowitz, Leo. "History, Herstory, Ourstory: Twelve Jewish Jurors." *Jewish Currents*, October 20,2013. https://jewishcurrents.org/history-herstory-story-twelve-jewish-jurors/.

Herskowitz, Leo. "Some Aspects of the New York Jewish Merchant and Community, 1654–1820." *AJHQ* 66, no. 1 (1976): 10–34.

Hickman, Christine B. "The Devil and the One Drop Rule: Racial Categories, African Americans, and the U.S. Census." *Michigan Law Review* 95, no. 5 (1997): 1161–1265.

Hoberman, Michael, Laura Arnold Leibman, and Hilit Surowitz-Israel. *Jews in the Americas, 1776–1826*. London: Taylor and Francis, 2017.

Hoefte, Rosemarijn, and Jean Jacques Vrij. "Free Black and Colored Women in Early-Nineteenth-Century Paramaribo, Suriname." In *Beyond Bondage: Free Women of Color in the Americas*. Edited by David Barry Gaspar and Darlene Clark Hine, 145–168. Urbana: University of Illinois Press, 2004.

Hollander, Anne. *Sex and Suits*. New York: Knopf, 1994.

Howe, Glenford D., and Don D. Marshall, *The Empowering Impulse: The Nationalist Tradition of Barbados*. Barbados: Canoe Press, 2001.

Hoyos, F. A. *Barbados Comes of Age: From Early Strivings to Happy Fulfilment*. London: Macmillan Caribbean, 1987.

Hunt, Bruce. *Bruce's Lists of London Street Name Changes*. Linton: Bruce Hunt, 2013.

Hunter, William C. *Bits of Old China*. Taiwan: K. Paul, Trench, & Company, 1885.

Jaffee, David. "Sideboards, Side Chairs, and Globes: Changing Modes of Furnishing Provincial Culture in the Early Republic, 1790–1820." In *Furnishing the Eighteenth Century: What Furniture Can Tell Us about the European and American Past*. Edited by Dena Goodman and Kathryn Norberg, 79–95. New York: Routledge, 2007.

Jaher, Frederic Cople. *The Jews and the Nation: Revolution, Emancipation, State Formation, and the Liberal Paradigm in America and France*. Princeton, NJ: Princeton University Press, 2003.

Jastrow, Morris. "Notes on the Jews of Philadelphia, From Published Annals." *Publications of the American Jewish Historical Society*, no. 1 (1893): 49–61.

Jenner, Edward. *An Inquiry into the Causes and Effects of the Variolae Vaccinae*. London: Sampson Low, 1798.

"The Jessurun Family." *Jewish Quarterly Review* 1 (1888): 439–441.

Joel, Israel, Abraham Isaacs, and Jonas N. Phillips. "Items Relating to Congregation Shearith Israel, New York." *PAJHS* 27 (1920): 1–125.

Johnson, Dale T. *American Portrait Miniatures in the Manney Collection*. New York: Metropolitan Museum of Art, 1990.

Jones, Cecily. *Engendering Whiteness: White Women and Colonialism in Barbados and North Carolina, 1627–1865*. Manchester: Manchester University Press, 2007.

Jones, Martha. "'Make Us a Power': African American Methodists Debate the 'Woman Question,' 1870–1900." In *Women and Religion in the African Diaspora: Knowledge, Power, and Performance*. Edited by Marie R. Griffith and Barbara Dianne Savage, 128–154. Baltimore: Johns Hopkins University Press, 2006.

"Judah Samuel Abecasis." Dutch Jewry. Akevoth. https://www.dutchjewry.org/genealogy/belinfante/176.shtml. Accessed March 6, 2020.

Kahn, Ava Fran. *Jewish Voices of the California Gold Rush: A Documentary History, 1849–1880*. Detroit: Wayne State University Press, 2002.

Kaplan, Yosef. *An Alternative Path to Modernity: The Sephardi Diaspora in Western Europe*. Leiden: Brill, 2000.

Katzew, Ilona. *Casta Painting: Images of Race in Eighteenth-Century Mexico*. New Haven, CT: Yale University Press, 2004.

Kaye, Thomas. *The Stranger in Liverpool: Or, an Historical and Descriptive View of the Town of Liverpool and Its Environs*. Liverpool: T. Kaye, 1820.

Kelly, Catherine E. *Republic of Taste: Art, Politics, and Everyday Life in Early America*. Philadelphia: University of Pennsylvania Press, 2016.

Kelly, Ian. *Beau Brummell: The Ultimate Man of Style*. New York: Free Press, 2006.

King, Cheryl. "According to the Law: Women's Property Rights in Bridgetown, Barbados, 1800–1834(1)." *Journal of Caribbean History* 36, no. 2 (2002): 267–284.

Kirsch, Adam. *Benjamin Disraeli*. New York: Nextbook, 2008.

Kleinfeld, Daniel J. "Mordecai Manuel Noah." In *The Selected Writings of Mordecai Noah*. Edited by Daniel J. Kleinfeld and Michael Joseph Schuldiner. Westport, CT: Greenwood Press, 1999.

Klingaman, William K., and Nicholas P. Klingaman. *The Year without Summer: 1816 and the Volcano That Darkened the World and Changed History*. New York: St. Martin's Press, 2013.

Knight, Caroline. *London's Country Houses*. Chichester, UK: Phillimore, 2009.

Koeppel, Gerard. *City on a Grid: How New York Became New York*. New York: Hachette Books, 2015.

Koeppel, Gerard. *Water for Gotham: A History*. Princeton, NJ: Princeton University Press, 2000.

Kohler, Max J. "Civil Status of the Jews in Colonial New York." *Publications of the American Jewish Historical Society* 6, no. 6 (1897): 81–106.

Land, Julian, and James Greener. "The Lineage of the Montefiore Family and Major Connected Families." Unpublished manuscript, last modified 2016. Supplied by the authors.

Landes, Richard Allen. *Heaven on Earth: The Varieties of the Millennial Experience*. New York: Oxford University Press, 2011.

Landing, James E. *Black Judaism: Story of an American Movement*. Durham, NC: Carolina Academic Press, 2001.

Lapsansky, Emma Jones. "'Since They Got Those Separate Churches': Afro-Americans and Racism in Jacksonian Philadelphia." *American Quarterly* 32, no. 1 (1980): 54–78.

Lee, Hannah Farnham Sawyer. *Memoir of Pierre Toussaint, born a Slave in St. Domingo*. Boston: Crosby, Nichols and Co., 1854.

Lee, Jennifer, and Frank D. Bean. *The Diversity Paradox: Immigration and the Color Line in Twenty-First-Century America*. New York: Russell Sage Foundation, 2010.

Leepson, Marc. *Saving Monticello: The Levy Family's Epic Quest to Rescue the House That Jefferson Built*. New York: Free Press, 2001.

Leibman, Laura Arnold. *The Art of the Jewish Family: A History of Women in Early New York in Five Objects*. New York: Bard Graduate Center, 2020.

Leibman, Laura Arnold. "The Material of Race: Clothing, Anti-Semitism, and Manhood in the Caribbean During the Era of Emancipation." In *Jews, Liberalism, Anti-Semitism: Towards a New History*. Edited by Abigail Green and Simon Levis Sullam, 97–130. Basingstoke, UK: Palgrave Macmillan, 2020.

Leibman, Laura Arnold. *Messianism, Secrecy and Mysticism: A New Interpretation of Early American Jewish Life*. London: Vallentine Mitchell, 2012.

Leibman, Laura Arnold. "Using Technology and DNA Genealogy to Solve Historical Mysteries." *Heritage* (Winter 2015): 19–21.

Leibman, Laura Arnold, and Sam May. "Making Jews: Race, Gender and Identity in Barbados in the Age of Emancipation." *American Jewish History* 99, no. 1 (2015): 1–26.

Leitman, Michael. "The Evolution of Surgery at the New York Hospital." *Bulletin of the New York Academy of Medicine* 67, no. 5 (1991): 475–500.

Lemire, Elise. *"Miscegenation": Making Race in America*. Philadelphia: University of Pennsylvania Press, 2002.

Leo-Paul, Dana. "The Mizrahim: Anglicized Orientals with Transnational Networks and 'Ethics Capital'." In *Entrepreneurship and Religion*. Edited by Leo-Paul Dana, 61–112. Cheltenham, UK: Edward Elgar Publishing, 2010.

Levie Bernfeld, Tirtsah. *Poverty and Welfare among the Portuguese Jews in Early Modern Amsterdam*. Liverpool, UK: Littman Library of Jewish Civilization, 2012.

Libo, Kenneth, and Abigail Kursheedt Hoffman. *The Seixas-Kursheedts and the Rise of Early American Jewry*. New York: Bloch, 2001.

"The Life History of the Mosquito." *Monthly Bulletin of the Department of Health in the City of New York* 2, no. 7 (1912): 162.

Lima, Cândido Pinheiro de. *Branca Dias*. Fortaleza: Fundação Ana Lima, 2009.

Lloyd, Stephen. *Portrait Miniatures from Scottish Private Collections*. Edinburgh: National Galleries of Scotland, 2006.

Lockwood, Charles. *Manhattan Moves Uptown: An Illustrated History*. New York: Barnes, 1995.

London, Hannah Ruth. *Miniatures of Early American Jews*. Springfield, MA: Pond-Ekberg, 1953.

London, Hannah Ruth. *Miniatures and Silhouettes of Early American Jews*. Rutland, VT: C. E. Tuttle, 1970.

London, Hannah Ruth. *Portraits of Jews by Gilbert Stuart and Other Early American Artists*. Rutland, VT: C. E. Tuttle, 1969.

Loudon, Irvine. *Death in Childbirth: An International Study of Maternal Care and Maternal Mortality, 1800–1950*. Oxford: Clarendon Press, 1992.

Luzzatto, Moses Hayyim. *Way of God* [Derekh ha-Shem], trans. Aryeh Kaplan. Jerusalem: Feldheim, 1981.

Lyons, Clare A. *Sex among the Rabble: An Intimate History of Gender and Power in the Age of Revolution, Philadelphia, 1730–1830.* Chapel Hill: University of North Carolina Press, 2012.

Macoy, Robert. *How to See New York and Its Environs, 1776–1876: A Complete Guide and Hand-book of Useful Information, Collected from the Latest Reliable Sources.* New York: R. Macoy, 1875.

"Making a Miniature." Gibbes Museum of Art. 2016. http://www.gibbesmuseum. org/miniatures/.

Marley, David. *Historic Cities of the Americas: An Illustrated Encyclopedia.* Santa Barbara, CA: ABC-CLIO, 2005.

Mars, Florence. *Witness in Philadelphia.* Baton Rouge: Louisiana State University Press, 1989.

Martin, Tony. *Caribbean History: From Pre-colonial Origins to the Present.* Boston: Pearson, 2012.

Marshall, Woodville, and Pedro Welch. "Introduction." *Beyond the Bridge: Lectures Commemorating Bridgetown's 375th Anniversary.* Edited by Woodville Marshall and Pedro Welch, 1–2. Bridgetown: BMHS, 2005.

McEvilly, Christine. "Guide to the Papers of the Moses Family of New York, undated, 1767–1941, 1971, P-1." *Center for Jewish History.* https:// digifindingaids.cjh.org/?pID=364719.

McManus, Edgar J. *A History of Negro Slavery in New York.* Syracuse, NY: Syracuse University Press. 2001.

Measuring Worth—Relative Worth Comparators and Data Sets. 2017. https:// measuringworth.com/.

Meiselman, Moshe. *Jewish Woman in Jewish Law.* New York: Ktav Publishing House, 1978.

Mirvis, Stanley. "Sephardic Family Life in the Eighteenth-Century British West Indies." PhD diss., New York University, 2013.

Monaghan, E. Jennifer. *Learning to Read and Write in Colonial America.* Amherst: University of Massachusetts Press, 2007.

Moore, John Jamison. *History of the A.M.E. Zion Church in America: Founded in 1796, in the City of New York.* Charlotte, NC: A.M.E. Zion Historical Society, 2004.

Morais, Samuel, *The Jews of Philadelphia: Their History from the Earliest Times to the Present Times.* Philadelphia: Levytype, 1894.

Mordecai, Sarah Ann Hays. *Recollections of My Aunt, Rebecca Gratz.* Philadelphia, 1893.

Morgan, Kenneth. "The Trans-Atlantic Trade from the Bight of Biafra." In *Igbo in the Atlantic World.* Edited by Toyin Falola, 82–98. Bloomington: Indiana University Press, 2016.

Morris, R. J. *Men, Women and Property in England, 1780–1870: A Social and Economic History of Family Strategies amongst the Leeds Middle Class.* Cambridge: Cambridge University Press, 2005.

Morris, Robert. "Progenitors and Coloured Elite Families: Case Studies of the Belgraves, Collymores, and Cummins." *JBMHS* 47, no. 1 (2001): 52–65.

Munn, Christopher. *Anglo-China: Chinese People and British Rule in Hong Kong, 1841–1880*. London: Taylor & Francis, 2013.

Nadler, Jerald. "In Honor of the 350th Anniversary of the Congregation Shearith Israel." *Congressional Record* 150, no. 126 (2004).

"Naphtali Phillips." *PAJHS* 21 (1913): 172–174.

Nash, Gary B. *Forging Freedom: The Formation of Philadelphia's Black Community, 1720–1840*. Cambridge, MA: Harvard University Press, 1988.

Nash, Gary B. "Race and Citizenship in the Early Republic." In *Antislavery and Abolition in Philadelphia: Emancipation and the Long Struggle for Racial Justice in the City of Brotherly Love*. Edited by Richard Newman and James Mueller. Baton Rouge: Louisiana State University Press, 2011.

Nash, Gary B. *The Unknown American Revolution: The Unruly Birth of Democracy and the Struggle to Create America*. New York: Penguin, 2006.

Nassy, David Cohen. *Historical Essay on the Colony of Surinam, 1788*. Cincinnati: American Jewish Archives, 1974.

Nathan-Kraus Family Collection. http://collections.americanjewisharchives.org/ms/ms0107/ms0107.html.

Nathans, Heather S. *Hideous Characters and Beautiful Pagans: Performing Jewish Identity on the Antebellum American Stage*. Ann Arbor: University of Michigan Press, 2017.

National Heroes of Barbados: National Heroes Day 28 April [1998]. St. Michael, Barbados, Barbados Government Information Service, 1998.

Nelson, Louis P. "The Architectures of Black Identity: Buildings, Slavery, and Freedom in the Caribbean and the American South." *Winterthur Portfolio* 45, no. 2/3 (2011): 177–194.

Nelson, Louis P. *The Beauty of Holiness: Anglicanism and Architecture in Colonial South Carolina*. Chapel Hill: University of North Carolina Press, 2009.

Newitt, Malyn. *A History of Portuguese Overseas Expansion 1400–1668*. New York: Routledge, 2004.

Newton, Melanie. *The Children of Africa in the Colonies: Free People of Color in Barbados in the Age of Emancipation*. Baton Rouge: Louisiana State University Press, 2008.

Nichols, Bill. *Movies and Methods: An Anthology*. Berkeley: University of California Press, 1985.

Norman, Philip. "Cromwell House: Historical Notes." In *Survey of London Monograph 12, Cromwell House, Highgate*, 15–35. London, 1926. *British History Online*, http://www.british-history.ac.uk/survey-london/bk12/pp15-35.

Nussbaum, Felicity. *The Global Eighteenth Century*. Baltimore: Johns Hopkins University Press, 2003.

Okehie-Offoha, Marcellina Ulunma. *Ethnic & Cultural Diversity in Nigeria*. Trenton, NJ: Africa World Press, 1996.

Oliver, Vere Langford. *The Monumental Inscriptions in the Churches and Churchyards of the Island of Barbados, British West Indies*. London: M. Hughes & Clarke, 1914.

Oppenheim, Samuel. "Jews Who Died of Yellow Fever in the Epidemic in New York in 1798." *PAJHS*, no. 25 (1917): 123.

Parfitt, Tudor. *Black Jews in Africa and the Americas*. Cambridge, MA: Harvard University Press, 2013.

Parliament of Great Britain, House of Lords. *The English Reports*. Edinburgh: W. Green & Son, 1900.

Paugh, Katherine. *The Politics of Reproduction: Race, Medicine, and Fertility in the Age of Abolition*. Oxford: Oxford University Press, 2017.

Perelis, Ronnie. *Narratives from the Sephardic Atlantic: Blood and Faith*. Bloomington: Indiana University Press, 2016.

Perkins, Dorothy. *Encyclopedia of China: History and Culture*. London: Taylor & Francis, 2013.

Philipson, David. *Letters of Rebecca Gratz*. Philadelphia: Jewish Publication Society of America, 1929.

Pickard, Kate E. R. *The Kidnapped and the Ransomed: The Narrative of Peter and Vina Still after Forty Years of Slavery*. Lincoln: University of Nebraska Press, 1995.

Pitock, Toni. "Commerce and Connection: Jewish Merchants, Philadelphia, and the Atlantic World, 173—1822." PhD diss., University of Delaware, 2016.

Platt, Stephen R. *Autumn in the Heavenly Kingdom: China, the West, and the Epic Story of the Taiping Civil War*. New York: Alfred A. Knopf, 2012.

Plunkett, J. D. "Cotton as a Fomite of Yellow Fever." *The Sanitarian* 8, no. 83 (1880): 78.

"Portrait Miniatures." Cleveland Museum of Art, March 21, 2013.

"Portrait Miniatures: Materials & Techniques." Victoria and Albert Museum. London, 2016.

Powell, J. H. *Bring out Your Dead: The Great Plague of Yellow Fever in Philadelphia in 1793*. Mansfield Centre, CT: Martino Publishing, 2016.

Pratt, Edwin A. *A History of Inland Transport and Communication in England*. London: K. Paul, Trench, Trübner & Co., 1912.

Raciti, James J. *Stephen Girard: America's Colonial Olympian, 1750–1831*. Sante Fe: Sunstone Press, 2015.

Radwin, Michael J. Jewish Calendar, Hebrew Date Converter, Holidays. https://www.hebcal.com/.

Raphael, Marc Lee. *The Columbia History of Jews and Judaism in America*. New York: Columbia University Press, 2008.

"Recent Deaths." *American Lawyer* 9, no. 3 (1901): 134.

Reiman, Tonya. *The Power of Body Language: How to Succeed in Every Business and Social Encounter*. New York: Pocket Books, 2007.

"Report from the Secretary of State." *Congressional Edition*, 591 (1851): 37.

Ribeiro, Aileen. *The Art of Dress: Fashion in England and France 1750–1820*. New Haven, CT: Yale University Press, 1995.

Riera, Elena Arias. "The Collection of Miniatures in the Museo del Prado." Museo Nacional del Prado. 2019. https://www.museodelprado.es.

Rock, Howard B., and Deborah Dash Moore. *Cityscapes: A History of New York in Images*. New York: Columbia University Press, 2001.

Rodrigues-Pereira, Miriam, and Chloe Loewe. *The Burial Register (1733–1918) of the Novo (New) Cemetery of the Spanish & Portuguese Jews' Congregation, London: with some later entries* [SPJS, Part V]. London: Spanish and Portuguese Jews' Congregation, 1997.

Rodriguez, Gregory. "Roots of Genealogy Craze." *USA Today*, May 12, 2014.

Rodriquez, Junius P. *The Historical Encyclopedia of World Slavery*. Oxford: ABC-CLIO, 1997.

Roess, Roger P., and Gene Sansone. *The Wheels That Drove New York: A History of the New York City Transit System*. New York: Springer Science & Business Media, 2012.

Rosenbloom, Joseph R. *A Biographical Dictionary of Early American Jews: Colonial Times through 1800*. Lexington: University of Kentucky Press, 1960.

Rosenswaike, Ira. "An Estimate and Analysis of the Jewish Population of the United States in 1790." In *American Jewish History: The Colonial and Early National Periods, 1654–1840*. Edited by Jeffrey S. Gurock, 347–392. New York: Routledge, 1998.

Ross, Marc Howard. *Slavery in the North: Forgetting History and Recovering Memory*. Philadelphia: University of Pennsylvania Press, 2018.

Roth, Cecil. "The Jews in the English Universities." *Miscellanies (Jewish Historical Society of England)* 4 (1942): 102–115.

Rothery, Mark, and Henry French. *Making Men: The Formation of Elite Male Identities in England, c. 1660–1900*. Houndmills, UK: Palgrave Macmillan, 2012.

Rowe, G. S. "Black Offenders, Criminal Courts, and Philadelphia Society in the Late Eighteenth Century." *Journal of Social History* 22, no. 4 (1989): 685–712.

Rowland, Joan S. *The Jewish Communities of India: Identity in a Colonial Era*. New Brunswick, NJ: Transaction Publishers, 1998.

Rozin, Mordechai. *The Rich and the Poor: Jewish Philanthropy and Social Control in Nineteenth-Century London*. Brighton: Sussex Academic Press, 1999.

Rubens, Alfred. "Francis Town of Bond Street (1738–1826) and His Family: With Further Notes on Early Anglo-Jewish Artists." *Transactions (Jewish Historical Society of England)* 18 (1953): 89–111, http://www.jstor.org/stable/29777924.

Rubinstein, William D., Michael Jolles, and Hilary L. Rubinstein. *The Palgrave Dictionary of Anglo-Jewish History*. Houndmills, UK: Palgrave Macmillan, 2011.

Russell, William Logie. *The New York Hospital*. New York: Arno Press, 1973.

Edgehill, Barbados: Salvucci, Richard J. "The Origins and Progress of U.S.-Mexican Trade, 1825–1884: 'Hoc Opus, Hic Labor Est.'" *Hispanic American Historical Review* 71, no. 4 (1991): 697–735.

Samuel, Edgar. "Costa [née Mendes], Catherine [Rachel] da (1679–1756), miniature painter." *Oxford Dictionary of National Biography*. 23 Sep. 2004. https://www.oxforddnb.com/view/10.1093/ref:odnb/9780198614128.001.0001/odnb-9780198614128-e-72024.

Samuel, Edgar. "Marriages at the Nidhe Yisrael Synagogue, Bridgetown, Barbados." *JHS* 45 (2013): 163–171.

Samuel, Wilfred S. "Tentative List of Jewish Underwriting Members of Lloyd's (from Some Time Prior to 1800 until the Year 1901)." *Miscellanies (Jewish Historical Society of England)* 5 (1948): 176–192.

Sanders, Joanne McRee. *Barbados Records: Baptisms, 1637–1800.*
Baltimore: Genealogical Publishing, 1984.

Sang-Ajang, John. *Overlijdens Advertenties en Onbeheerde Boedels: Overledenen in Suriname 1 januari 1800 tot en met 31 december 1828.* Paramaribo: Stichting voor Surinaamse Genealogie, 2010.

Saraiva, António José, H. P. Salomon, and I. S. D. Sassoon. *The Marrano Factory: The Portuguese Inquisition and Its New Christians, 1536–1765.* Leiden: Brill, 2001.

Sarna, Jonathan D. *American Judaism: A History.* New Haven, CT: Yale University Press, 2019.

Sarna, Jonathan D. *Jacksonian Jew: The Two Worlds of Mordecai Noah.* New York: Holmes & Meier, 1981.

Schappes, Maurice U. "Four Documents concerning Jews and Slavery (1762; 1806–09; 1814; 1860)." In *Strangers & Neighbors: Relations between Blacks & Jews in the United States.* Edited by Maurianne Adams, 137–146. Amherst, MA: University of Massachusetts Press, 1999.

Schappes, Morris U., and Joshua Bloch. *A Documentary History of the Jews in the United States, 1654–1875.* New York: Citadel Press, 1952.

Schorsch, Jonathan. "American Jewish Historians, Colonial Jews and Blacks, and the Limits of 'Wissenschaft': A Critical Review." *Jewish Social Studies* 6, no. 2 (2000): 102–132.

Schorsch, Jonathan. *Jews and Blacks in the Early Modern World.* New York: Cambridge University Press, 2004.

Schorsch, Jonathan. *Swimming the Christian Atlantic: Judeoconversos, Afroiberians and Amerindians in the Seventeenth Century.* Leiden: Brill, 2009.

Schreuder, Y. "A True Global Community: Sephardic Jews, the Sugar Trade, and Barbados in the Seventeenth Century." *JBMHS* 50 (2004): 166–194.

Schroeter, Daniel J. *The Sultan's Jew: Morocco and the Sephardi World.* Palo Alto, CA: Stanford University Press, 2002.

"SchumanGeganBruendermanSchirrmacherRittmeyer's Family Tree." Geneanet. https://gw.geneanet.org/schumangegan.

Schwartz, Stuart B., ed. *Tropical Babylons: Sugar and the Making of the Atlantic World, 1450–1680.* Chapel Hill: University of North Carolina Press, 2011.

Selections from the Collected Papers of the Lower Rio Grande Valley Historical Society 1949–1979. Harlington, TX: Lon C. Hill Memorial Library, 1979.

Shelley, Thomas J. "Black and Catholic in Nineteenth-Century New York: The Case of Pierre Toussaint." *Records of the American Catholic Historical Society of Philadelphia* 102, no. 4 (1991): 1–17.

Sherman, Moshe D. *Orthodox Judaism in America: A Biographical Dictionary and Sourcebook.* Westport, CT: Greenwood Press, 1996.

Sherwood, James. *Savile Row. The Master Tailors of British Bespoke.* Farnborough: Thames & Hudson, 2017.

Sheumaker, Helen. *Love Entwined: The Curious History of Hairwork in America.* Philadelphia: University of Pennsylvania Press, 2007.

Shilstone, E. M. *Monumental Inscriptions in the Jewish Synagogue at Bridgetown, Barbados: with Historical Notes from 1630.* Roberts Stationery, Barbados: Macmillan, 1988.

Sio, Arnold S. "Race, Colour, and Miscegenation: The Free Coloured of Jamaica and Barbados." *Caribbean Studies* 16, no. 1 (1976): 8–12.

Smeele, Wietske. "Grounding Miasma, or Anticipating the Germ Theory of Disease in Victorian Cholera Satire." *Journal of the Midwest Modern Language Association* 49, no. 2 (2016): 15–27.

Smith, Eric Ledell. "The End of Black Voting Rights in Pennsylvania: African Americans and the Pennsylvania Constitutional Convention of 1837–1838." *Pennsylvania History: A Journal of Mid-Atlantic Studies* 65, no. 3 (1998): 279–299.

Smith, Helen Ainslie. *The Great Cities of the Modern World.* New York: Routledge and Sons, 1887.

Smith, Jane Margaret. *Ship of Death: The Tragedy of the "Emigrant."* Carindale, Australia: Independent Ink, 2019.

Society of Colonial Wars. https://www.colonialwarsny.org/.

Soll, David. *Empire of Water: An Environmental and Political History of the New York City Water Supply.* Ithaca, NY: Cornell University Press, 2013.

Sonnenberg-Stern, Karina. *Emancipation and Poverty: The Ashkenazi Jews of Amsterdam, 1796–1850.* Oxford: Saint Antony's College, 2000.

Soyer, François. *The Persecution of the Jews and Muslims of Portugal: King Manuel I and the End of Religious Tolerance (1496–7).* Leiden: Brill, 2007.

Stanford, Keith. "The Roots of a Great School: Combermere's First 200 Years." *JBMHS* 41 (1993): 16–31.

Stern, Malcolm H. *First American Jewish Families: 600 Genealogies, 1654–1977.* Cincinnati: American Jewish Archives, 1978.

Stern, Malcolm H. "Portuguese Sephardim in the Americas." In *Sephardim in the Americas: Studies in Culture and History.* Edited by Martin A. Cohen and Abraham J. Peck, 141–178. Tuscaloosa: University of Alabama Press, 2003.

Stern, Malcolm H. "Two Jewish Functionaries in Colonial Pennsylvania." *AJHQ* 57, no. 1 (1967): 24–51.

Stern, Malcolm H. "Two Studies in the Assimilation of Early American Jewry." PhD diss., Hebrew Union College, 1957.

Stiefel, Barry L. *Jewish Sanctuary in the Atlantic World: A Social and Architectural History.* Columbia: University of South Carolina Press, 2014.

Stolzman, Henry, Daniel Stolzman, and Tami Hausman. *Synagogue Architecture in America: Faith, Spirit & Identity.* Victoria: Images Publishing, 2004.

St. Romaine, Derek. *Barbados in Bloom.* Miller Publishing, 2005

Van Andel, T.R., A. van der Velden, and M. Reijers, "The 'Botanical Gardens of the Dispossessed' Revisited: Richness and Significance of Old World Crops Grown by Suriname Maroons." *Genetic Resources and Crop Evolution* 63 (2016): 697. https://doi.org/10.1007/s10722-015-0277-8.

Van der Kiste, John. *George III's Children.* New York: History Press, 2013.

Van der Wijk, Jacob, Justus van de Kamp, and Jan van Wijk. *Koosjer Nederlands: Joodse woorden in de Nederlandse taal.* Amsterdam: Contact, 2006.

Van Dyke, Paul Arthur. "Ambiguous Faces of the Canton Trade: Moors, Greeks, Armenians, Parsees, Jews, and Southeast Asians." In *The Private Side of the*

Canton Trade, 1700–1840: Beyond the Companies. Edited by Paul Arthur Van Dyke and Susan E. Schopp, 21–44. Hong Kong: Hong Kong University Press, 2018.

Van Dyke, Paul Arthur. *The Canton Trade: Life and Enterprise on the China Coast, 1700–1845.* Hong Kong: Hong Kong University Press, 2005.

Van Dyke, Paul Arthur, and Maria Kar-wing Mok. *Images of the Canton Factories 1760–1822: Reading History in Art.* Hong Kong: Hong Kong University Press, 2015.

Vietrogoski, Bob. "The Case of Mr. J. P. Barnet (Col. Student): An Unusual Instance of Racial Discrimination in 19th-Century Medical Education." 2011. ASC.

Vink, Wieke. *Creole Jews Negotiating Community in Colonial Suriname.* Leiden: Brill, 2010.

Ware, Eugene Fitch. *Lyon Campaign in Missouri: Being a History of the First Iowa Infantry and of the Causes which Led up to its Organization, and how it earned the Thanks of Congress, which it Got: Together with a Birdseye View of the Conditions in Iowa Preceding the Great Civil War of 1861.* Topeka, KS: Crane & Co., 1907.

Watson, Karl. *The Civilised Island, Barbados: A Social History, 1750–1816.* Ellerton, Barbados: Caribbean Graphic Production, 1979.

. "1806 Plat of the Nidhe Israel Synagogue in Bridgetown." *JBMHS* 61 (2015): 82–85.

Watson, Karl. "The Sephardic Jews of Bridgetown." In *Beyond the Bridge: Lectures Commemorating Bridgetown's 375th Anniversary.* Edited by Woodville K. Marshall and Pedro L. V. Welch. St. Michael, Barbados: Barbados Museum, 2005.

Watson, Karl. "Shifting Identities: Religion, Race, and Creolization among the Sephardi Jews of Barbados, 1654–1900." In *The Jews in the Caribbean.* Edited by Jane S. Gerber, 195–222. Portland: Littman Library, 2014.

Watts, Tim J. "Brown Privilege Bill (1831)." In *Encyclopedia of Blacks in European History and Culture.* Edited by Eric Martone, 95s–97. Westport, CT: Greenwood Press, 2008.

Wegenstein, Bernadette. *The Cosmetic Gaze Body Modification and the Construction of Beauty.* Cambridge, MA: MIT Press, 2012.

Weil, François. *Family Trees: A History of Genealogy in America.* Cambridge, MA: Harvard University Press, 2013.

Welch, Pedro. "Celebrating Bridgetown: The First 100 Years." In *Beyond the Bridge: Lectures Commemorating Bridgetown's 375th Anniversary.* Edited by Woodville Marshall and Pedro Welch, 3–36. Bridgetown: BMHS, 2005.

Welch, Pedro. "Jews in a Caribbean Colonial Society: Resistance and Accommodation in Bridgetown, Barbados, 1675–1834." *JBMHS* 44 (1998): 54–64.

Welch, Pedro. *Slave Society in the City: Bridgetown, Barbados, 1680–1834.* Kingston, Jamaica: I. Randle, 2003.

Welch, Pedro L. V., and Richard A. Goodridge. *"Red" and Black over White: Free Coloured Women in Pre-Emancipation Barbados*. Bridgetown: Carib Research, 2000.

Wells, Louisa Susannah. *The Journal of a Voyage from Charlestown, S.C., to London Undertaken During the American Revolution by a Daughter of an Eminent American Loyalist (Louisa Susannah Wells) in the year 1778 and Written from Memory only in 1779*. New York: New-York Historical Society, 1906.

Werrett, Simon. *Fireworks: Pyrotechnic Arts and Sciences in European History*. Chicago: University of Chicago Press, 2010.

West, Thomas G. *Vindicating the Founders: Race, Sex, Class, and Justice in the Origins of America*. Lanham, MD: Rowman & Littlefield, 2000.

Wilkie, Jane Riblett. "The United States Population by Race and Urban-Rural Residence 1790–1860: Reference Tables." *Demography* 13, no. 1 (1976): 139–148.

Whiting, Keith. *Adventure Guide Barbados*. Edison, NJ: Hunter Publishing, 2007.

Whittock, Nathaniel. *The Miniature Painter's Manual: Containing Progressive Lessons on the Art of Drawing and Painting Likenesses from Life on Card-Board, Vellum and Ivory: With Concise Remarks on the Delineation of Character and Caricature*. London: Sherwood, Gilbert and Piper, 1844.

Wigger, John H. "Taking Heaven by Storm: Enthusiasm and Early American Methodism, 1770–1820." *Journal of the Early Republic* 14, no. 2 (1994): 167–194.

Wills, Rob. *Alias Blind Larry: The Mostly True Memoir of James Laurence, the Singing Convict*. Melbourne: Australian Scholarly Publishing, 2015.

Wilson, Robert. *Mathew Brady: Portraits of a Nation*. New York: Bloomsbury, 2013.

Winch, Julie. *The Elite of Our People: Joseph Willson's Sketches of Black Upper-Class Life in Antebellum Philadelphia*. University Park: Pennsylvania State University Press, 2000.

Winch, Julie. *Philadelphia's Black Elite: Activism, Accommodation, and the Struggle for Autonomy, 1787–1848*. Philadelphia: Temple University Press, 1988.

The Wine-drinker's Manual. London: Marsh and Miller, 1830.

Wischnitzer, Rachel. "The Egyptian Revival in Synagogue Architecture." *PAJHS* 41, no. 1 (1951): 61–75.

Wolf, Edwin, and Maxwell Whiteman. *The History of the Jews of Philadelphia: From Colonial Times to the Age of Jackson*. Philadelphia: Jewish Publication Society of America, 1975.

Wolf, Lucien. *Essays in Jewish History*. London: Jewish Historical Society of England, 1934.

Wolf, Lucien. "Recollections of a Veteran." *Jewish Chronicle*, 15 Sep. 1893: 12.

Wong, John D. *Global Trade in the Nineteenth Century: The House of Houqua and the Canton System*. Cambridge: Cambridge University Press, 2016.

Woodard, Helena. *Slave Sites on Display: Reflecting Slavery's Legacy through Contemporary "Flash" Moments*. Jackson: University Press of Mississippi, 2019.

Yarema, Allan E. *The American Colonization Society: An Avenue to Freedom?* Oxford: University Press of America, 2006.

Zakim, Michael, and Gary J. Kornblith. "Introduction." In *Capitalism Takes Command: The Social Transformation of Nineteenth-Century America*. Edited by Michael Zakim and Gary J. Kornblith, 1–12. Chicago: University of Chicago Press, 2012.

Zieseniss, Charles-Otto, and Katell Le Bourhis. *The Age of Napoleon: Costume from Revolution to Empire, 1789–1815*. New York: H. N. Abrams, 1989.

INDEX

For the benefit of digital users, indexed terms that span two pages (e.g., 52–53) may, on occasion, appear on only one of those pages.